The God and the Bureaucrat

Why is Roman law so boring? In this book, Zachary Herz argues that the bureaucratic, positivistic world of Roman law is not a distraction from the violent autocracy of the Roman empire, but an imagined escape. Lawyers, bureaucrats, and even emperors used legal writing to think about worlds that were safer or fairer than the one in which they lived. This archive of political imagination slowly became a law-code, and now guides readers through a legal system about which its authors could only dream. From Augustus to Justinian, this book shows how law symbolized order in chaotic times, and how that symbol eventually took on a life of its own. From the enlightened judgments of Hadrian to the great jurists and child rulers of Severan Rome, Herz reveals what Romans were really talking about when they talked about law.

Zachary Herz is an Assistant Professor of Classics at the University of Colorado-Boulder. His research employs legal theory and methodology to better understand the distinctive role of law in Roman political and ethical discourse. This is his first book.

See the Studies in Legal History series website at
http://studiesinlegalhistory.org/

Studies in Legal History

Other Books in the Series:

Kevin Arlyck, *The Nation at Sea: The Federal Courts and American Sovereignty, 1789–1825*
Alastair McClure, *Trials of Sovereignty: Mercy, Violence, and the Making of Criminal Law in British India, 1857–1922*
James Q. Whitman, *From Masters of Slaves to Lords of Lands: The Transformation of Ownership in the Western World*
Marie-Amélie George, *Family Matters: Queer Households and the Half-Century Struggle for Legal Recognition*
Simon Devereaux, *Execution, State and Society in England, 1660–1900*
Giuliana Perrone, *Nothing More than Freedom: The Failure of Abolition in American Law*
Christian G. Fritz, *Monitoring American Federalism: The History of State Legislative Resistance*
Ada Maria Kuskowski, *Vernacular Law: Writing and the Reinvention of Customary Law in Medieval France*

(Continued after the Index)

The God and the Bureaucrat

Roman Law, Imperial Sovereignty, and Other Stories

ZACHARY HERZ
University of Colorado, Boulder

CAMBRIDGE
UNIVERSITY PRESS

CAMBRIDGE
UNIVERSITY PRESS

Shaftesbury Road, Cambridge CB2 8EA, United Kingdom

One Liberty Plaza, 20th Floor, New York, NY 10006, USA

477 Williamstown Road, Port Melbourne, VIC 3207, Australia

314–321, 3rd Floor, Plot 3, Splendor Forum, Jasola District Centre, New Delhi – 110025, India

103 Penang Road, #05–06/07, Visioncrest Commercial, Singapore 238467

Cambridge University Press is part of Cambridge University Press & Assessment, a department of the University of Cambridge.

We share the University's mission to contribute to society through the pursuit of education, learning and research at the highest international levels of excellence.

www.cambridge.org
Information on this title: www.cambridge.org/9781009629935

DOI: 10.1017/9781009629928

When citing thiswork, please include a reference to the DOI 10.1017/9781009629928

First published 2025

A catalogue record for this publication is available from the British Library

ISBN 978-1-009-62995-9 Hardback
ISBN 978-1-009-62993-5 Paperback

Matri, Muri, Jeffrey

What pleases the emperor has the force of a law, inasmuch as the *populus* grants all of their *imperium* and *potestas* to him, and confers it upon him, by means of a kingly law which has been passed regarding his powers.

Ulpian, Institutes

Contents

Figures

Acknowledgments

The God and the Bureaucrat has been an obsession of mine for over a decade. Accordingly, almost everyone who has put up with me in the last ten years belongs in my acknowledgements – I have had to make some cuts for reasons of space. The people and institutions below have been enormously important to me, and if I seem to be name-dropping I apologize, but *the names are the point of the bit.*

This book grew out of a dissertation written at Columbia University, under the supervision of Francesco de Angelis, W.V. Harris, Katja Maria Vogt, and James Zetzel. It is difficult to describe that process of supervision without becoming maudlin, but anything I know of how to write or reason can be traced back to one of the four.

That said, none of them are lawyers and one of the biggest hurdles I faced in making my dissertation a book was learning how lawyers like to talk about the past. My J.D. helped, and in getting it I worked with wonderful mentors like William N. Eskridge, Jr., Vicki Schultz, Reva Siegel, and James Q. Whitman. But I really learned how to do legal history in the summer of 2021, as part of the American Society for Legal History's Hurst Summer Institute. This is a Hurst book, for anyone who knows what that means; its approach to law as a mode of social ordering was transformed by that seminar and the conversations that followed it. Lauren Benton and Sally Gordon have been invaluable resources on everything from historiography to book production, and I should also mention the colleagues and friends I met through the seminar: Lauren Catterson, Hardeep Dhillon, Naama Maor, Ángela Pérez-Villa, Sarath Pillai, Jake Richards, Geneva Smith, Lila Teeters, Lauren MacIvor Thompson, and Kent Weber (Jonathan Connolly is excluded on a technicality, because I've known him since kindergarten). The Hurst also introduced me to Cambridge's *Studies in Legal History* series, which you may recognize from the cover of this book. Working with the series has been a privilege and has allowed me to benefit from the feedback and encouragement of a really fabulous editor: Tom McSweeney. This book would look very different without Tom's involvement – for one thing it probably wouldn't exist – and given how closed the universe of Roman law can often be, publishing in a non-Classical series with a non-Classicist editor has been invaluable in helping me see broader connections and audiences.

From here on, things get granular. When possible, I've run arguments by subject-matter experts, which has meant pestering some of the kindest and most brilliant people working on the Roman world. This book reflects the guidance of, in a by no means exhaustive list: Cynthia Bannon, Shadi Bartsch, Sarah E. Bond, Ari Bryen, Andy Cain, Serena Connolly, Elsemieke Daalder, Jackie Elliott, Mary-Evelyn Farrior, Harriet Fertik, Nicole Giannella, Caitlin Gillespie, Joseph Howley, Kat Huemoeller, Isabel Köster, Noel Lenski, Mark Letteney, Michèle Lowrie, Ted Mason, Lindsey Mazurek, Tom McGinn, Kristina Milnor, Carole Newlands, Carlos Noreña, Nandini Pandey, Michael Peachin, Paul J. du Plessis, Sailakshmi Ramgopal, Anise K. Strong, Chiara Sulprizio, Kaius Tuori, Caroline Wazer, Matthijs Wibier, and Liv Mariah Yarrow.

Four Romanists merit special mention. Clifford Ando, Leanne Bablitz, Bruce W. Frier, and Andrew Riggsby all read and commented on a draft of this book for a workshop held in Boulder, CO. The workshop transformed what you're holding and improved it greatly – it was also interrupted by a glamorous woman posing for a photo shoot while holding a bassoon. I think of her often.

I also sometimes talk to people who don't work on the Roman empire. The following group has pulled me out of rabbit holes, reminded me to use smaller words, and caught all number of embarrassing mistakes: Mariana Beatriz Noé, Brookes Brown, David Builes, Anna Conser, Elspeth Dusinberre, Joe Fischel, Eduardo García-Molina, Emily Greble, Joel Harrington, Danielle Kellogg, Adriaan Lanni, Mitzi Lee, Ryan Malecky, Anthony Petro, Amy Pistone, Adriana Robertson, Matt Simonton, Will St. Clair, Julia Staffel, Brian Talbot, Ryan Thoreson, Kim Welch, and Maggie Wittlin.

Now, institutions. While the Executive Committee of the Association of Ancient Historians has provided invaluable moral support, my relationship with other organizations and centers has been somewhat more materialistic. I completed this manuscript on a research leave funded by the Loeb Classical Library and by Boulder's own Center for the Humanities and Arts. The latter grant came with an invitation to an extremely generative seminar in humanistic research, and accordingly I am grateful to the Center's director Jennifer Ho for both money and wisdom – my fellow participants (David Boonin, David Glimp, and Terri Wilson) just provided wisdom, but that's not nothing. Other expenses associated with this book were defrayed by generous grants from the Benson Center at the University of Colorado-Boulder and from the Kayden Research Fund at the same institution.

Slightly less competitive institutional support was offered by Bittersweet Café and Confections in Louisville, CO. I wrote about 80% of this book at one of three tables there, and could not have done it without their great coffee, wireless internet, and inexplicable playlists.

Finally, none of this happens if I don't have a shoulder to lean on. My husband (or fiancé, depending on print timelines) Jeffrey Daigle has made me laugh, watched me cry, and kept me sane for the better part of a decade. You are the best thing in my life, and I love you more than words can say.

Abbreviations

This book employs Oxford Classical Dictionary (OCD) abbreviations for Classical texts, in addition to the following.

Amb. de ob. Val.	Ambrose, *de obitu Valentiniani*: Angliviel de la Beaumelle, Laurent, Guy Sabbah, and Jean-François Berthet, eds. *Sur la mort de Valentinien II*. Translated by Guy Sabbah and Jean-François Berthet. Paris: Cerf, 2022.
AV	*Appendix Visigothica*: Krüger, Paul, Theodor Mommsen, and Wilhelm Studemund, eds. *Collectio librorum iuris anteiustiniani in usum scholarum*. Berlin: Weidmann, 1890.
BTRL	Borkowski, Andrew. *Borkowski's Textbook on Roman Law*. Edited by Paul du Plessis. 2nd ed. Oxford: Oxford University Press, 2010.
C.	*Codex Justinianus*: Frier, Bruceet al., eds. *The Codex of Justinian: A New Annotated Translation, with Parallel Latin and Greek Text Based on a Translation by Justice Fred H. Blume*. Cambridge; New York: Cambridge University Press, 2016.
Cons.	*Consultatio cuiusdam veteris iurisconsulti*: Krüger, Paul, Theodor Mommsen, and Wilhelm Studemund, eds. *Collectio librorum iuris anteiustiniani in usum scholarum*. Berlin: Weidmann, 1878/1890.

CTh.	*Codex Theodosianus*: Mommsen, Theodor, and Paul Meyer, eds. *Theodosiani libri XVI cum constitutionibus Sirmondianis: Et leges novellae ad Theodosianum pertinentes*. 4th ed. Dublin: Weidmann, 1970.
D.	*Digest*: Watson, Alan, Paul Krueger, and Theodor Mommsen, eds. *The Digest of Justinian*. 4 vols. Philadelphia: University of Pennsylvania Press, 1985.
de Pall.	Tertullian, *de Pallio*: Hunink, Vincent. *Tertullian, De Pallio*. Amsterdam: Gieben, 2005.
EDRL	Berger, Adolf. *Encyclopedic Dictionary of Roman Law*. 3rd ed. Philadelphia: American Philosophical Society, 1991.
HSS	Kunkel, Wolfgang. *Die römischen Juristen: Herkunft und soziale Stellung*. 2nd ed. Cologne; Vienna: Böhlau, 2001.
J. Inst.	Justinian's *Institutes*: Krüger, Paul, and Theodor Mommsen, eds. *Iustiniani institutiones*. Berlin: Weidmann, 1872.
LT	*Laudatio Turiae*: Flach, Dieter, ed. *Die sogenannte Laudatio Turiae: Einleitung, Text, Übersetzung und Kommentar*. Darmstadt: Wissenschaftliche Buchgesellschaft, 1991.
Nov. L.	Noailles, Pierre, and Alphonse Dain, eds. *Les Novelles de Léon VI, le Sage*. Paris: Belles Lettres, 1944.
PG	Lenel, Otto. *Palingenesia iuris civilis*. 2nd ed. Graz: Akademische Druck-Universität Verlagsanstalt, 1960.
RGDA	Cooley, Alison. *Res Gestae Divi Augusti*. Cambridge: Cambridge University Press, 2009.
RLC	Johnston, David. *Roman Law in Context*. 2nd ed. Cambridge; New York: Cambridge University Press, 2022.
TLL	*Thesaurus linguae latinae*. Leipzig: Teubner, 1907.
XII Tab.	*XII Tabulae*: Crawford, Michael. *Roman Statutes*. 2 vols. London: Institute of Classical Studies, 1996.

Introduction: Did Romans Have Law?

This book argues that conventional understandings of Roman law – as an impersonal decisional paradigm under which disputes were resolved through casuistically elaborated rules – are not quite right. They are not entirely wrong, either; certain sources, especially the legal compilations authorized by Justinian I (r. 527–565 CE), describe a "Roman law" that looks very much like what I have described and that came to exercise enormous influence over later legal systems. But the law that would eventually be taught in Europe's first law school in Bologna, or that men like Irnerius,[1] Henry de Bracton,[2] and Hugo Grotius[3] took as a historical exemplar,[4] is surprisingly hard to find in the period we imagine it to have governed.

[1] Irnerius of Bologna, generally considered the first of the Glossators (medieval professors who wrote and taught from copies of the Justinianic texts with explanatory glosses included), introduced the formal study of Roman law to Europe. See Ascheri, *Laws*, pp. 9–28; Whitman, *Legacy*, pp. 26–28.

[2] Bracton (and others whose writing survives under his name) wrote a series of treatises on English law of the thirteenth century, structured by explicit analogy with copies of the *Digest* that were then circulating. McSweeney, *Priests*; *infra* pp. 298–300.

[3] The writings of Grotius, who was trained in Roman law at the University of Leiden, provided the intellectual foundation for much modern international law. Nellen, *Hugo Grotius*; on the Roman foundations of Grotian jurisprudence more specifically Straumann, *Foundations*.

[4] On this exemplarizing process more broadly Tuori, *Ideals*.

Instead, Romans of the "Classical period"[5] experienced a less rulebound political order that featured many different ways of thinking about state power. Law was present in the world but was not the only way to solve problems, or even always the most authoritative and final. Rome at this time combined an ancient legal tradition, which had been understood as inherently just and linked to the aristocratic power-sharing arrangements of the Roman Republic, with a newer autocracy. These two orders coexisted but did not really compete, since even at their weakest emperors had more power to enforce their judgments than did legal experts. Accordingly, imperial Romans understood law in somewhat symbolic terms: as an older way of doing things that worked as a metaphor for other older ways of doing things. Emperors who worked through legal channels (as judges, as legislators, and even as litigants) demonstrated respect for Republican political tradition, while those who did not appeared as more novel or troubling figures.

This pattern arose haltingly and slowly, but its most consequential evolution dates to the Severan dynasty (193–235 CE). The Severan period saw rulers represented in state communications as quasi-functionaries: high-ranking officials whose decisionmaking followed the prerogatives and logics of an overarching institutional structure. That structure was organized according to legal rules, and accordingly it is in the Severan period that Romans began to tell stories about an imperial state that was headed not by a man who follows or does not follow the law, but by the law itself. This tendency continued, and even the more centralized late antique (by which I mean the mid third to mid sixth centuries) autocracy described itself in similarly bureaucratic terms.[6] Severan legal documents come down to us – mostly – as part of Justinian's grand regularizing project, but that project was not a historical chronicle and attributes to these texts a social role that they only came to exercise far later. The set of principles and

[5] A term Roman lawyers use (unlike other Classicists) to refer to the period roughly between the accession of Hadrian and the death of Severus Alexander. Jolowicz and Nicholas, *Historical Introduction*, pp. 6 and 405–20.

[6] I take "late antiquity" to begin with the death of Severus Alexander in 235CE. There is no one accepted boundary, and my own line is sharper than that drawn by (for example) Brown ("about 200"; *World*, p. 7), but one of the major arguments of this book is that late antique legality responded to changing political conditions in the wake of the Severan period.

institutional relationships that we now understand to make up "Roman law" were creatures of ideal theory, which became socially powerful – in the way that we now understand law to be socially powerful – with time.

Those principles and institutional relationships were rarely stated out loud, but are strongly implied in Roman legal discourse. That discourse represents law as a technical discipline that governs judicial outcomes according to predictable and impersonal rules. This vision of legal sovereignty was compelling to Roman legal authors: to emperors who benefited from appearing to be institutionally legitimated agents, to bureaucrats who understood Roman power in terms of their particular specialties, and to subjects who found law a more appealing or useful sovereign than the one they actually had. All of these people discussed a legal regime that never quite existed, but in doing so they laid the groundwork for contemporary legal regimes, which mostly do.

Two Kinds of Thinking About Hay

Justinian's compilation, the *Corpus Iuris Ciuilis* or "Body of the Civil Law," presents Roman law as a set of rules. Roman law appears in these documents as a mass of dazzlingly precise technical arguments, in which jurists – trained scholars who served as advisers in courts throughout the empire – applied (or advised others on how they should apply) systematic and impersonal principles to specific fact patterns. By contrast actual court records, generally from Roman Egypt, show litigants ignoring the rules and invoking the pity of a benevolent sovereign; literary historians describe tyrants upending legal systems on a whim; and inscriptions thank enlightened rulers for handing justice down to their grateful subjects.

The difference is best illustrated via example. One can imagine specialists in all of these different corpora of evidence confronting the question "what remedies were available for a farmer in the Roman empire whose crops were stolen?" The *Corpus* (more specifically its collection of juristic writing, called the *Digest*) answers the question with an excerpt of writing from the jurist Paul, who focuses on the maturity of the crops and the nuances of legal ownership.

It is established that a tenant, if he cultivates his land because of cash payment [i.e. if he is not a sharecropper], *may bring an action for theft against whoever stole his standing crops: since they would have begun to be his as soon as they were harvested.*

(D.47.2.26.1: Paul, ad Sabinum) constat colonum, qui nummis colat, cum eo, qui fructus stantes subripuerit, acturum furti, quia, ut primum decerptus esset, eius esse coepisset.[7]

Other documents tell a different story. For example, the papyrus *P. Mich.* VI.423 preserves a petition to the *strategos* (a high provincial official) from the Greek Egyptian Gemellus-called-Horion. Gemellus-called-Horion de-emphasizes the elements of theft Paul treats as legally salient in favor of a pathetic narrative involving blindness and witchcraft.

To Hierax-called-Nemesion, the strategos *of the Herakleides district of the Arsinoite nome, from Gemellus-called-Horion the son of Gaius Apolinarius. Antinoite.*

Lord, I petitioned the most glorious prefect Aemilius Saturninus and informed him that a man named Sotas, who despised me for my weak eyesight and had designs on seizing my property, had come up to me and attacked with violence and willfulness; I received a sacred reply authorizing me to appeal to the most powerful epistrategos. *Then, after Sotas had died, his brother Julius (also using the violence associated with that man) entered the fields I had sown and not only took off a large amount of hay, but also cut dried olive shoots and other plants from my grove near Kerkesoucha; I learned that these things had been done by him when I came to the grove at harvesttime. Furthermore, he was not then satisfied but returned with his wife and a man named Zenas, holding a* brephos [a preserved human fetus, used in magic] *and wishing to wickedly bind my harvester in order that he would stop his work after having reaped another part of my fields; they took my crops for themselves. Afterwards I went up to Julius, in the company of local officials so that there might be a witness to these events. They threw the same* brephos *at me again, in the same fashion, wishing to wickedly bind me in front of Petesouchos and Ptollas, village elders of Karanis who serve as its secretaries, and Sokras their assistant; still in the presence of those same officials Julius harvested the rest of my crops and took them with the* brephos *to his house. I recorded these events with the aforementioned officials as well as the tax collectors of Karanis. Accordingly, I am compelled to submit this petition and ask for it to be*

7 On sharecropping in Roman tenant agriculture, and how it would necessitate exclusion from these kinds of remedies, see Kehoe, *Rural Economy*, pp. 107–09.

registered and for myself to retain the right to sue them before the most powerful epistrategos *about their shocking deeds and about the tax due to the fisc from the crops from the public fields because of their wrongdoing.*

Ἱέρακι τῷ καὶ Νεμεσίωνι στρα(τηγῷ) Ἀρσι(νοίτου) Ἡρακ(λείδου) μερίδος παρὰ Γεμέλλου τοῦ καὶ Ὡρίωνος Γαίου Ἀπολιναρίου Ἀντινοέως. Ἐνέτυχον, κύριε, διὰ βιβλιδίου τῷ λαμπροτάτῳ ἡγεμόνι Αἰμιλίῳ Σατουρνείννῳ δηλῶν τὴν γεναμένην μοι ἐπέλευσιν ὑπὸ Σώτου τινὸς καταφρονήσαντος τῆς περὶ τὴν ὄψιν μου ἀσθενείας αουλομένου αὐτοῦ τὰ ὑπάρχοντά μου κατασχεῖν βίᾳ καὶ αὐθαδίᾳ χρωμενος καὶ ἔσχον ἱερὰν ὑπογραφὴν ἐντυχεῖν τῷ κρατίστῳ ἐπιστρατήγῳ· τοῦ δὲ Σω τελευτήσαντος, ὁ τούτου ἀδελφὸς Ἰούλιος καὶ αὐτὸς τὴν περὶ αὐτου βίᾳ χρησάμενος ἐπῆλθεν τοῖς ἐσπαρμένοις ὑπ' ἐμοῦ ἐδάφεσει καὶ ἐβάστασε οὐκ ὀλίγον χόρτον οὐ μόνον ἀλλὰ καὶ ἐξέκοψε ὑπὸ τοῦ ὑπάρχοντός μου ἐ[λ]αιῶνος ὄντος περὶ κώμην Κερκεσοῦχα ἐλαεϊνα φυτὰ ἀπεξηραμμένα καὶ ἐρίκινα, ἅπερ παραγενάμενος ἐνθάδε πρὸς τὸν καιρὸν τῆς συνκομιδῆς ἔμαθον ταῦτα ὑπὸ αὐτοῦ πεπρᾶχθαι, ἐφ' οἷς μὴ ἀρκεσθεὶς πάλειν ἐπῆλθεν μετὰ τῆς γυναικὸς αὐτοῦ καὶ Ζηνᾶ τινος ἔχοντες βρέφος βουλόμενοι τὸν γεωργόν μου φθώνῳ περικλῖσαι ὥστε καταλεῖψε τὴν ἰδ[ί]αν γεωργίαν μετὰ τὸ θερίσαι ἐκ μέρους ἀπὸ ἑτέρου μου κλήρου, καὶ αὐτοὶ σσυνεκομίσαντο. τούτων γενομένων ἐγενόμην πρὸς τὸν Ἰούλιον μετὰ [δ]ημοσίων ὅπως αὐτὰ ταῦτα ἐνμάρτυρον γένηται. Πάλιν τῷ αὐτῷ τρόπῳ προσσ[έ]ριψάν μοι [τὸ] αὐτὸ βρέφος βουλόμενοι καὶ με φθόνῳ περικλῖσαι πα[ρό]ντων Πετεσούχου καὶ Πτολλᾶ πρεσβυτέρων κώμης Καρανίδος διαδεχο[μ]ένων καὶ τὰ κατὰ τὴν κομμωγραμματείαν καὶ Σωκρᾶ ὑπηρέτου, καὶ τῶν δημοσίων παρόντων τὸ βρέφος ὁ ϊουλιος συνκομισάμενος τὰ περιγενόμενα ἐκ τῶν ἐδαφῶν γένη ἀπηνέγκατο εἰς τὴν οἰκίαν αὐτοῦ, ἅπερ φανερὰ ἐποίησα διά τε τῶν αὐτῶν δημοσίων καὶ πρακτόρων σιτικῶν τῆς αὐτῆς κώμης. διὸ κατὰ τὸ ἀναγκαῖον ἐπιδίδωμι καὶ ἀξιῶ τάδε τὰ βιβλίδια ἐν καταχωρισμῷ γενεσθο πρὸς τὸ μένειν μοι τὸν λόγον πρὸς αὐτοὺς ἐπὶ τοῦ κρατίστου ἐπιστρατήγου περὶ τῶν ὑπο αὐτῶν τετολμημένων καὶ τῶν ὑπὲρ τῶν ἐδαφῶν δημοσίων ἐκφορίων τῷ κυριακῷ λόγο διὰ τὸ αὐτοὺς οὐ δεόντως συνκεκομικέναι.[8]

These sources preserve two very different views of, or modes of engagement with, Roman law. One describes legal order as formal, systematic, rational, and coherent: the other merciful, ethical, and sublime. That difference has been heavily theorized for more than a century, since papyri from Roman Egypt (like *P. Mich.* VI.423) clearly record very different legal processes than those found in the *Corpus Iuris Ciuilis*. Following Mitteis we sometimes refer to these two

[8] *P.Mich.* VI 423 ll. 2–26. The *brephos* papyrus has received a fair amount of scholarly attention, but see particularly Youtie et al., *Karanis*, pp. VI.122–26 (original publication); also Bryen and Wypustek, "Eyes"; Frankfurter, "Fetus Magic." On this style of petition Crook, *Advocacy*, pp. 68–69.

legal paradigms as *Reichsrecht* (law of the kingdom, law on the books) and *Volksrecht* (law of the people, law on the ground).[9]

More recent scholarship has analyzed this duality through the lens of legal pluralism.[10] Legal pluralism identifies "bargaining and conflict between contending normative orders" in much of what we imagine as legal history; it argues that many legal regimes feature overlapping paradigms with their own claims to legal force, and that people living under those regimes are often quite sophisticated in seeking out advantage under different sets of rules.[11] Whether conceptualized in weak terms (as two recognizably legal systems imposed by the same sovereign upon different populations)[12] or strong (where "the law" interacts with other paradigms that work to structure a community's normative beliefs),[13] legal pluralism gives historians a theoretical framework with which to bridge the gulf between what a law-code says should happen and what people actually do.

The problem at the core of this book – the difference between Roman law as imagined by Gemellus-called-Horion, and that imagined by jurists like Paul – is almost classically pluralist, but most legal pluralists care more about what happens in a courtroom than I do. The pluralistic tradition emerged from legal sociology, and in the Roman context has been taken up by scholars of ancient judicial practice. Accordingly, much pluralist work takes legal or quasi-legal process as its object of study, with codified law serving as a foil.[14] By contrast, I am primarily engaged with the questions and assumptions of Roman *Reichsrecht*. I agree with the pluralists that law on the books

[9] Mitteis, *Reichsrecht und Volksrecht*. Also Dolganov, "*Reichsrecht* and *Volksrecht*"; Amelotti, "*Reichsrecht, Volksrecht, Provinzialrecht*."

[10] See, among many examples: Czajkowski, *Localized Law*, pp. 17–22; Alonso, "Customary Law"; Tuori, "Empires" (with Czajkowski, "Limits" serving as a useful clarification; Roman pluralism might have featured a variety of different decisional paradigms, but nevertheless expected them to be exercised within Roman fora and according to Roman procedural norms).

[11] See Hartog, "Pigs and Positivism," p. 935. For further discussion of individual litigants engaging strategically with pluralist regimes see, e.g. Scott and Fornias, "Friar"; Humfress, "Forum Shopping."

[12] As in e.g. Burset, *Empire of Laws*; Saksena, "Jousting"; Whewell, *Borders*; Beverley, "Resource"; Ford, *Settler Sovereignty*.

[13] E.g. Bryen, *Violence*; Hartog, "Pigs and Positivism." This distinction originates in Griffiths, "What Is Legal Pluralism?," p. 5; see also Merry, "Legal Pluralism," pp. 872–74 (differentiating "new" from "classic" legal pluralism along similar lines).

[14] On this duality, see Humfress, "Legal Pluralism's Other," pp.158–61.

did not serve the purpose it has historically been taken to serve in subjects' lives, but instead of asking what those subjects really used, I ask what law on the books was really doing. In an influential article on the value of doctrinal sources for critical historians, Gordon notes that "mandarin materials are among the richest artifacts of a society's legal consciousness."[15] The *Corpus Iuris Ciuilis* preserves an astonishing volume of "mandarin texts," produced by mandarins whose hopes and fears give Roman *Reichsrecht* its distinctive texture. Accordingly, the *Corpus* can help us better understand how Romans thought about the nature and function of law in their world – a set of beliefs that I will refer to hereinafter as Roman "legality."

That legality is my focus. This book is not a history of Roman law as the subject has traditionally been understood – I do not discuss doctrinal evolution at all, and while I consider innovations in legal argumentation and recordkeeping I use them primarily to show change in what people thought they were arguing about and keeping records of. I hope historians of Roman law in that more traditional sense will still find the book useful, since it is a history of the conditions and assumptions that make Roman law coherent, and thus Roman legal historiography possible. But it remains a political history, of how law worked in Roman political thought.

By that, I mean that I am interested in how law imagines Roman power. Roman legal discourse describes a system operating according to prospective and clear rules, which derive their authority from broadly legitimated institutions like the Senate; the epigraph to this book is a claim by Ulpian that imperial power was only valid because it was bestowed by a "kingly law" (*lex regia*). In practice imperial power came from a broad variety of sources, and Rome's idiosyncratically weak autocrats relied upon buy-in from other powerful social actors like the Roman aristocracy, wealthy provincials, or the army.[16] That

[15] Gordon, "Histories," p. 120.

[16] The sociologist Michael Mann uses Rome as his paradigmatic example of a weak autocracy: "Autonomous Power," pp. 188–89. Ando notes, by contrast, that the weaker top of the Roman state overlay a more traditionally robust network of elite supervision that worked on behalf of that state as part of its broader manifestation of infrastructural power: "Ambitions." My question is somewhat different than Ando's; Ando's account explains why the Roman state was able to persist through long periods of extreme political instability (also: *Century*) but that persistence might be of little use to an emperor who had died in a coup.

buy-in was not guaranteed, and the unwritten rules that governed imperial politics were complex. Roman subjects – particularly the elites whose views are overrepresented in literary sources – sometimes understood those rules as a system of virtues. Good emperors act one way and live, bad emperors act another way and die.[17] At other times, imperial selection might be determined by military strength, palace intrigues, or even the result of an auction.[18] At all times, however, imperial politics were unpredictable and potentially violent.

That chaos is hard to find within the *Corpus Iuris Ciuilis*, whose structure and logics tell a very different story about imperial power. The result is an odd bifurcation within imperial historiography, which this book seeks to address. Many historians of the Principate and Dominate[19] find law forbidding and artificial, since it describes a different world from the one in which they are interested, and the *Digest* in particular is tough to square with the realities of the emperor's social and judicial role.[20] By contrast, scholars of the *Corpus* (who frequently work in law faculties) may be more interested in the fictive and influential constitutionalism that survives within those books than in the world of their authors. Accordingly, the majesty they sometimes attribute to Roman legal thinking can seem more like a misapprehension of imperial history than the aesthetic or philosophical judgment it actually is.[21]

[17] This account of imperial virtue is perhaps most closely connected to Carlos Noreña (*Imperial Ideals*), but for slightly different understandings of this process of negotiation and consensus-building Lobur, *Consensus*; Ando, *Ideology*.

[18] Like the one that led to the installation of Didius Julianus in 193 CE: Dio Cass. 74[73].11 [Xiph.].

[19] More terms of art. Roughly speaking, Roman political historians use the term "Principate" to refer to that subset of the imperial period in which the emperor was formally presented as simply another elite citizen with extraordinary persuasive power: a *ciuilis princeps*. E.g. Wallace-Hadrill, "Civilis Princeps." By contrast, the "Dominate" refers to the later era in which emperors were more frequently addressed as master, or *dominus*. The boundary is blurry, but I tend to think of the Principate as ending with the death of Severus Alexander in 235 CE and the Dominate as beginning with the accession of Diocletian in 284; this book uses those terms accordingly.

[20] On those realities Tuori, *The Emperor of Law*; Millar, *Emperor*, pp. 228–59.

[21] E.g. Schiavone, *Ius*, p. 65 ("E l'accanimento prescrittivo, messo in contatto, attraverso il sapere dei suoi sapienti, con lo spessore del mondo sociale e delle nuove realtà politiche ed economiche di una città in piena espansione, avrebbe ben presto portato al formarsi di una tradizione intellettuale straordinariamente vivace e sottile"), p. 194

I aim to resolve the problem by understanding Roman *Reichsrecht* as an archive of political imagination. The *Corpus Iuris Ciuilis* tells stories about the world that did not so much govern readers' encounters with law – the experience of litigants, as recorded in other media, suggests that they often did not – as help readers make sense of or accept those encounters. Imperial and legal sovereignty could not easily coexist, but Romans frequently used the structures and institutions of "law talk"[22] to think through problems of imperial power. This process was influenced by the conventions of Roman legal thought, and influenced those conventions in turn. The political crises of the Severan period and beyond necessitated new stories about imperial legality, but that legality is neither as straightforward nor as old as it appears.

Slouching Towards Bologna

Since I am arguing that the *Corpus Iuris Ciuilis* is part of the history of imperial representation, I should first clarify how I understand legal texts to engage in representation. While this particular capacity of law has not traditionally featured within doctrinal scholarship, it has been an object of intense interest within other branches of legal studies. This interest began in the early twentieth century, in a "legal realist" movement that understood adjudication as politically charged and often nondoctrinal, but the realists nevertheless treated law as a coherent object of study that they saw as affected by outside forces.[23] It was only in the 1970s and 1980s that scholars began to examine law using the broader toolset of critical theory and to situate it within larger discourses of cultural power.

The work that came out of this engagement – commonly known as Critical Legal Studies, or CLS – can be thought of not as a rival to realism but as a fusing of realist ideas about law with poststructuralist analysis

("L' autoisolamento dei custodi del *ius* in un universo di sole forme, di proporzioni e di compatibilità definite e nascoste, e il conseguente disciplinamento a partire da quelle astrazioni, sprigionava infatti un'immensa forza ordinante, una presa incomparabile sulla realtà della vita, collocata (provvisoriamente) da parte solo per essere meglio padroneggiata.").

22 Kennedy, *Critique*, p. 134.

23 See Desautels-Stein and Moyn, "Domestication," p. 198; Zaremby, *Realism*; Kalman, *Yale*; Gordon, "Histories," pp. 60–61.

of knowledge and society. Accordingly, while CLS is sprawling in its approach and critiques, it orbits around a few core descriptive and social commitments.[24] The most important of these for my project is Unger's critique of "formalism," defined as "[a] commitment to, and therefore also a belief in the possibility of, a method of legal justification that can be clearly contrasted to open-ended disputes about the basic terms of social life, disputes that people call ideological, philosophical, or visionary."[25] Like Unger, I see law as one of many discourses people use to contest social questions, and the separation between them as one of genre more than anything else.[26] Law is one language with which to tell stories about the world, which plays a particular role in organizing both Roman and contemporary society but which cannot be separated, or studied in isolation, from those societies. In more recent years, a growing strand of scholarship has considered how law and other forms of narrative work together to structure the symbolic order undergirding social life.[27] For specialists in contemporary law like Cover (who developed the concept of legal narrative studies), legal sociologists like Fitzpatrick, or more explicitly normative theorists like Matsuda, legal narratology offers a new angle on the world in which we live.[28]

Romanists do not have it so easy. Laws – or texts produced and transmitted in explicitly legalizing milieux – make up an enormous part of our evidentiary corpus, and we often rely on their testimony in imagining the world to which they responded and over which they purported to govern. As a result we often take that testimony as fact, without quite meaning to. Nobody thinks that when Constantine I (r. 306–337) claims that he will personally hear every complaint lodged against his administration he is speaking the literal truth, but we often imagine imperial or juristic writing as regularized, general, and

24 Kennedy, *Critique*, pp. 8–11; Tushnet, "A Political History"; Unger, "Movement."
25 *Ibid.*, p. 564.
26 In addition to Unger, this conception of genre also follows Miller's ("Social Action," p. 163) account of generic structures as combining both formal and pragmatic conventions. On law as genre in the Roman context see Bryen, *Violence*, pp. 3–4.
27 Again, much of this work comes from sociology or cultural history: e.g. Lowrie, "Force"; Adams, *Popular Culture*; Brooks and Gewirtz (eds.), *Law's Stories*.
28 Fitzpatrick, *Mythology*; Matsuda, "Looking"; Cover, "Nomos," "Violence"; also Tait and Norris, "Origins."

socially powerful because it represents itself in such a fashion.[29] This book argues that we can enrich the history of Roman law by approaching these narratives critically, and by adopting a less legalistic understanding of how legal texts worked in the Roman world.

That shift in perspective requires reckoning with what we mean when we talk about narrative. Law is a narrative mode of speaking, in the sense that it operates using paradigmatically narrative forms where actions lead to consequences.[30] When Section 18–4-102 of the Colorado Revised Statutes states that "[a] person who knowingly sets fire to, burns, causes to be burned, or by the use of any explosive damages or destroys, or causes to be damaged or destroyed, any building or occupied structure of another without his consent commits first degree arson" it presents its prohibition as a description of events, and so do the cases that interpret it. Legislation speaks in a general and prospective mode, and adjudication retrospective and specific, but both involve people doing things and thus include material explaining the factual predicate of a given judicial process.[31]

These narratives are an important part of how law structures a world. But law's influence on people often extends beyond the claims made within these narratives to other murkier or less factual commitments. Roman law is a good example of this extension. Legal texts do not explicitly assert the legality that seems to mark Classical Roman culture, but the reader nonetheless comes away thinking that laws are the things that mattered there. This idea is transmitted through broader features of the world surrounding the text – through what Genette would call its epitext[32] – that often postdate its creation in a narrow sense. The passages of Paul I cited above do not look like law only because they describe legal processes; they look like law because they are collated with other similar texts that we call law, because other people engaged with those texts in the ways that we expect people to engage with law, and because those texts have been transmitted and read and taught as part of later histories of law. None

29 *CTh*. 9.1.4; I discuss this particular constitution in greater detail *infra* pp. 235–37.

30 See Gelbach, "Dynamic Dilemma," pp. 4–14; Constable, *Bond*, pp. 50–52; Scarry, *Pain*, pp. 296–304.

31 This distinction between "legislative" and "adjudicative" reasoning follows Davis, "Problems of Evidence," pp. 402–10.

32 Genette, *Paratexts*, pp. 344–70.

of that work is *narrative*, exactly, but it helps represent Rome's legal world – to us and to Romans themselves.

So what should we call it? When I try to wrap my head around this particular kind of slippery-but-potent ideological messaging, I have found it useful to look to people writing in less formalist or theoretical modes. In particular, Joan Didion's writing on journalism and memoir (other genres that are explicitly narrative, but that do a great deal to shape readers' worldviews outside of that narrative process) offers an account of representation-through-storytelling that emphasizes function over form.

> We tell ourselves stories in order to live. The princess is caged in the consulate. The man with the candy will lead the children into the sea. The naked woman on the ledge outside the window on the sixteenth floor is a victim of accidie, or the naked woman is an exhibitionist, and it would be "interesting" to know which. We tell ourselves that it makes some difference whether the naked woman is about to commit a mortal sin or is about to register a political protest or is about to be, the Aristophanic view, snatched back to the human condition by the fireman in priest's clothing just visible in the photo behind her, the one smiling at the telephoto lens. We look for the sermon in the suicide, for the social or moral lesson in the murder of five. We interpret what we see, select the most workable of the multiple choices. We live entirely, especially if we are writers, by the imposition of a narrative line upon disparate images, by the "ideas" with which we have learned to freeze the shifting phantasmagoria which is our actual experience.[33]

The difference is small, but meaningful. Didion downplays the mechanics of representation and focuses instead on its effects. A story, here, is something people tell in order to accomplish a goal. Didion's stories help the people who hear them, and perhaps more importantly the people who write them, reconcile to their conditions; they make contingency legible, and life fair.[34] Didion's own discussion of stories precedes an account of late-sixties Los Angeles marked by paranoia and dissociation, and what makes the world of "The White Album" so scary is the lack of a coherent story that can structure or explain it.[35]

Rome was scary too. This book examines the legal discourse of a brutal autocracy, a frightening and nonsensical world; most of the

[33] Didion, "The White Album" 11. [34] *Ibid.*, pp. 34–37. [35] *Ibid.*, pp. 44–45.

writers I discuss died violently, and the ones who survived had very good reason to worry. Roman legal literature talks around that worry by describing a political order that made more sense than the ones its authors inhabited, and by offering technical guides that have the imaginative and fabulative qualities of Didion's captive princess.[36] In other words, Roman law did not so much offer narratives that described Roman reality as tell stories that refashioned reality into something more palatable. These texts have come down to us as a law-code, but should not be understood as separate from other stories that Romans told to themselves and each other.

That said, law is not the same as poetry. Roman law worked differently than other kinds of writing, on an audience that had been acculturated to different kinds of reading; because this book is so concerned with how Romans read legal stories, it is worth taking a moment to clarify what is so special about the stories that law tells.

Law talks in multiple registers. This point is basically uncontested within legal historiography, since any close reading of a legal text reveals different modes of speech that interact with the world in ontologically distinct ways, but scholars have tended to imagine these modes in dichotomy. For example, Austin contraposes the "performative" commands of law with "constative" assertions about the state of the world, and Constable notes that actual legal documents like statutes or case dispositions frequently employ "nounlike" statements of fact and "verblike" statements of law in tandem.[37] By contrast, I find it more helpful to think of law as communicating in three distinct modes. While command and description are both important to how law works in the world, they are not the whole story. In particular, both Roman and modern legal texts often employ a third register. Their audience walks away with certain ideas about the world that these texts never constate, but that they strongly imply to anyone who reads them in the way they have been taught to read law. I call this register "constructive," and thinking through its operations helps us understand not only what Roman law did for Romans but what it appears to have done for us. This triad is not

[36] On the unreality of Imperial Latin literature see Haynes, *Make-Believe*, pp. 19–28; Bartsch, *Actors*.

[37] Constable, *Bond*, pp. 20–21; Austin, *Words*, pp. 3–7.

perfect – categories always blur at the margins, and apply differently in different legal systems – but it introduces terminology I will use going forward and may be helpful in contexts outside of this book.

The *normative* register is probably the one that first springs to mind when you read a legal text. It is a story in the jussive or potential, telling the reader how they ought to act in order to stay on the good side of a sovereign or what they can do to alter their relationships with that sovereign. Examples might include *do not set houses on fire*, and *once you have reached the age of eighteen you may enter into the kind of relationship that might change your obligations to the state*, and *pay the government 37% of all income over $578,125*.[38] If there is any kind of cross-cultural definition of law, what separates legal texts from others is their capacity to speak in this register and to do so with authority. Positivistic definitions of law (like Shapiro's Planning Thesis, or Hart's secondary rules) treat law's ability to structure the world as its constitutive feature,[39] but natural lawyers like Fuller or Dworkin also invest law with a special moral force that derives from its normative capacities.[40] In particular, law's normative stories alter the world in ways that other kinds of commands do not. I might tell my child not to litter, for them to follow or ignore; by contrast, a law imposing a fine for littering meaningfully changes the world at the moment of its enactment. Law's normative stories *act*; they "verb" in Constable's formulation and perform in Austin's.

One might expect these kinds of legal stories to become less interesting when the sovereign who tells them becomes less powerful, and accordingly when they become less salient as social agents. Because of Roman law's influence on later systems, however, legal scholars remain concerned with how Roman doctrines developed over time, and how they might have come together to form a coherent system. These questions are not my questions, but they are the questions that law trains its readers to ask, and that the *Corpus Iuris Ciuilis* contemplates answering. The texts that come down to us appear as a system of interlocked commands, before they appear as anything else.

38 That latter command comes from America's Internal Revenue Service, as preserved at 26 C.F.R. 601.602.

39 Hart, *Concept*, pp. 94–99; Shapiro, *Legality*, p. 195.

40 Dworkin, *Law's Empire*, pp. 93–94; Fuller, *Morality*, pp. 39–40.

That said, while law acculturates its readers to look for and interpret its normative claims those are not the only claims it makes. Law also speaks descriptively, telling factual (or apparently factual) stories about the world. These claims can take a variety of forms. An American court might issue an opinion that relies in part on the assertion that certain practices were or were not widespread in earlier historical periods,[41] or that records certain fact claims about litigants' lives in its prefatory material,[42] or a Roman emperor might describe a prior state of affairs in the context of his own legal production.[43] This feature of legal speech is less distinctive; obviously, other genres of writing contain assertions of fact. But law trains us to read those assertions differently. The organizational structure of legal writing subordinates fact claims to normative reasoning, presenting them as explanatory or prefatory to the speech that matters. To give an example: while Sallust might deploy his factual account of the conspiracy of Catiline in the service of a broader project of moral instruction or political philosophy (as he states at *Cat.* 4), he still writes in a primarily descriptive register for an audience that is presumed to be interested in learning the facts as he describes them. By contrast, legal writing does not appear to contemplate being read for its facts. A reader of an imperial rescript presumes its descriptive elements to be true (in a different way than might, say, a reader of Propertian love elegy) but also unimportant, since they appear mainly as aids to understand the legal holding.

This odd hermeneutic helps law engage in different kinds of representation than do other texts. Modern Romanists often read legal texts for their descriptive claims, and those claims contain

41 For example, *New York State Rifle and Pistol Association* v. *Bruen*, 142 S. Ct. 2111, 2135–56 (2022); *Lawrence* v. *Texas*, 539 U.S. 558, 567–74 (2003).

42 This drafting practice is absurdly common, but to choose one example *EEOC* v. *Abercrombie and Fitch Stores*, 575 U.S. 768, 770 (2015) briefly describes the religious identity of a prospective Abercrombie employee who was turned away due to religious discrimination: "Samantha Elauf is a practicing Muslim who, consistent with her understanding of her religion's requirements, wears a headscarf." It is easy to imagine a point in the future where this might be the only record of Ms. Elauf's religious practices to survive.

43 For example, at C.11.4.1pr. Arcadius and Honorius describe a persistent social practice that their constitution aims to discourage: "many men maintain their own ships under the names and accounts of other owners" (*Multi naues suas diuersorum nominibus et titulis tuentur*).

valuable information. For examples of this work one thinks of administrative historians like Corcoran and Coriat who reconstruct imperial legal production on the bases of references to that production that survive in the law, or of legal sociologists like Czajkowski, Connolly, Eckhardt, Kelly, and many others.[44] But one of the reasons why these texts seem so useful is that their fact claims seem uncontroversial. In certain cases, that allows legal documents to make highly contestable claims about the world in the context of table-setting for a legal argument. These claims can be productively studied within histories of imperial representation but serve a unique function within those representational programs because they recede into the background of the texts in which they appear.

Finally, law tells stories in a third register. Because law speaks as if it governs reality, it primes its reader to look to law to better predict how their reality will unfold and accordingly to look at their reality as something that law actually governs. This priming is implicit – laws do not begin with "as a law, I exercise control over social life" – but can be very persuasive, particularly when a law is read by people who do not inhabit a given culture and who use law to understand how it worked. I call this register *constructive*, since law in this mode operates less by making assertions than by constructing a world within the imagination of its reader in which those unasserted claims appear to be true.

For example, suppose that tomorrow the Boulder City Council were to pass a law forbidding hail on Fridays. That law is obviously silly, but should also strike you as in some important way *mistaken*. It offers an account of the world that feels inaccurate, even though the Council never explicitly claims to control the weather. That is because the law in question constructs a world in which it works the way we expect law to work (i.e. in which the Boulder City Council is able to prevent hail), and because that constructed world is meaningfully different from the one in which we live. This law does not say anything false but strongly implies it, and does so using a rhetorical strategy that is unique to performative texts like law.

[44] Czajkowski and Eckhardt, "Law, Status and Agency"; Kelly, *Social Control*; Connolly, *Lives*; Coriat, *Le prince législateur*; Corcoran, *Tetrarchs*.

Of course, the Boulder City Council will never pass this law. While the above example might clarify the *mechanics* of constructive storytelling it does not explain the stakes; real people use lawlike utterance to construct worlds all the time, in ways that are subtler but speak to more legibly human concerns. Here, a useful (if somewhat grim) example comes from international human rights law. Savvy observers understand documents like the Universal Declaration of Human Rights, adopted by the General Assembly of the United Nations in 1948, as effectively hortatory and as opening new rhetorical or organizational possibilities to actors hoping to make change on the ground.[45] But the Declaration is not written as a hortation, and represents itself as something like a rule. For example, Article 9 reads in its entirety "No one shall be subjected to arbitrary arrest, detention or exile."

Both of the examples above issue commands over a field that the writer does not have the practical authority to alter in the ways that the document makes it appear. But both imply that the writer does possess that authority; while few Boulderites or later historians would read the law against hail and picture an omnipotent municipal government, the Declaration makes certain kinds of conduct appear to be *illegal* rather than simply wrong, and thus the General Assembly of the United Nations appear to exercise powers that it does not possess in the quite the way it seems to. We can see why the Assembly might wish to be seen as exercising such powers, and why it might further human welfare for them to be seen as exercising such powers; it creates that impression, however, through the rhetorical device of construction.

That device works only because these texts look like texts that perform in the world, and thus posit a world in which they could. To be more specific, while I have referred to these lawlike utterances as misleading neither one makes false assertions *per se*. Instead, they are what Austin would call "infelicitous."[46] They do not affect the world as do other similar utterances, and thus do not succeed in the regulatory work they seem to attempt. There are a number of ways for a performative utterance to be infelicitous; any performative utterance depends on the existence of an institutional framework that

[45] See, e.g. Grugel and Peruzzotti, "Domestic Politics."
[46] Austin, *Words*, pp. 13–15.

the utterance might serve to alter, and a predictable mechanism by which the alteration occurs. For example, a rabbi saying "I now pronounce you man and wife" has a legal effect only if the rabbi inhabits a jurisdiction in which rabbis are allowed to marry couples, and where that marriage is understood as legally significant, and furthermore if they are addressing a couple that is otherwise permitted to marry. If any of those three conditions fail, the rabbi's statement "I now pronounce you man and wife" is infelicitous and has no more effect than it would for me to say the same in an audio version of this book.

The laws I described above – the law against hail and the Universal Declaration – work similarly. They have no performative effect because there is no "accepted conventional procedure" by which they could do what they appear to do;[47] there is no mechanism by which the Boulder City Council can prevent hail or by which the General Assembly of the United Nations can exercise legitimate force against those who contravene the Declaration. Accordingly, the laws are not false so much as absurd. That said, most people read texts as if they are not absurd. Since these utterances depend on certain conditions to perform in the way that they look like they should, the reader assumes (often subconsciously) that such conditions hold. These assumptions are an important part of how law works in the world, but are difficult to find in a legal text; they instead inhabit worlds that the text builds around itself, in which it works the way it says it does.

This unreal quality can sometimes be hard to see, especially if laws are our main piece of evidence for dispute resolution in a given time and place. But when the world that a legal text constructs is obviously inapt, that accordingly opens up productive avenues for historical inquiry. For Romanists, this phenomenon is most evident in how legal communications change from the third to the fourth centuries. From about the fourth century on, imperial legal writing becomes much more voluminous and, frankly, histrionic. Late-antique law makes wildly inflated claims about the emperor's power, importance, and relationship to his subjects.[48] These claims help us think about the

[47] *Ibid.*, p. 14.

[48] I discuss this phenomenon in greater detail *infra* pp. 232–38, but for a brief introduction Eich and Eich, "Verlautbarungsstil."

rhetorical force of later law, and recent work shows how law shaped perceptions of emperors and administrators during this period. For example, Dillon considers how Constantine fashioned his own image as a transformational ruler through legal rhetoric, whereas Lenski describes the same ruler but focuses more on the dialogic representational process that occurred between petitioner and sovereign.[49] For the later fourth century, Drijvers considers law as an important aspect of the emperor Jovian (r. 363–364 CE)'s representational program, and – the first and likely progenitor of these studies – Schmidt-Hofner's analysis of the legislation of Valentinian I (r. 364–375 CE) argues that Valentinian's relative productivity in lawmaking was part of a broader attempt to portray the emperor as an active and responsive administrator.[50] Legal texts from earlier periods do not employ this same rhetorical strategy, and do not exist in nearly the same volume; accordingly, historians like Tuori and Christoforou who consider emperors-as-lawmakers in earlier periods analyze more obviously ideological media of communication like portraiture.[51] I stand within that methodological tradition – this book begins by analyzing legal discussion in other genres of communication before moving onto more specific discussion of legal documents in its later chapters – but even seemingly bland or straightforward legal communication can do representational work.

That matters, because Romanists have a great deal of seemingly bland legal communications and they allow us to tell stories that might otherwise remain obscure. For example, histories of Roman political theory, like Clifford Ando's *Imperial Ideology and Provincial Loyalty in the Roman Empire* or Carlos Noreña's *Imperial Ideals in the Roman West*, often focus on state communications because those communications are so comparatively well preserved.[52] It was rare for subjects of the empire to openly discuss political desiderata, but understanding the political valence of legal talk opens up new archives

[49] Lenski, *Cities*, especially pp. 12–15; Dillon, *Justice*.

[50] Drijvers, "Jovian"; Schmidt-Hofner, *Reagieren*.

[51] Christoforou, *Imagining*; Tuori, *The Emperor of Law*. Hekster, "Imperial Justice?" raises an important caveat to these analyses, however: namely, the relative paucity of explicitly legal imagery in imperial portraiture.

[52] Ando, *Ideology*; Noreña, *Imperial Ideals*.

from which we can perceive that discussion. Bryen's work finds these conversations in the legal documentary record,[53] but codified law preserves a different set of actors with different, and influential, concerns. My methodology ventilates the unreality at the heart of Roman law, but also shows how central law can be to histories of Roman thinking about the imperial state.

To summarize that methodology, then. In order to read law "properly" one must assimilate a number of paratextual assumptions about the legal regime within which that law operates, and those assumptions did not necessarily hold when "Roman law" was written. Roman legal texts seem to presume a coherent and socially powerful law, which was itself an object of political imagination throughout the imperial period. As a result, laws of the imperial period construct a world around themselves that was perhaps more influential than it was ever quite real. In his discussion of Constans (r. 337–350 CE) Woudhuysen mentions a danger in the use of legislation as historical archive: "It has always been worryingly easy to see government being carried on as normal in the Code and thus conclude that such and such an emperor, condemned by our other sources, was a good administrator and cannot have been so bad really."[54] The *Corpus Iuris Ciuilis* tells us what it meant for Roman government to "carry on as normal," and constructs the administrative paradigm within which we understand Roman law to have operated. This book treats that construction as a rhetorical project, and (hopefully) helps us better understand why that project was so world-changingly successful.

Cicero and the Talking Law

The project I describe took the shape it did because Romans of the imperial period found law extremely helpful to think with, and one reason for that is that Romans of earlier periods had invested law with tremendous symbolic weight. In particular, Romans imagined law as inherently moral and antiautocratic – these features of Roman legal thinking predate the documents I discuss in this book, but do a great

[53] E.g. *Violence*, "Judging." [54] Woudhuysen, "Uncovering," p. 162.

deal to inform the context in which those documents were produced and consumed.

The most famous example of this view of law is the story Rome told about its first written law-code, the Twelve Tables. According to the accounts of the historian Livy (3.31, 34, 57) and the jurist Pomponius (D.1.2.2.4: Enchiridion), soon after the establishment of the Roman Republic a committee of ten men was charged with writing down the laws of the Roman state for public display.[55] Previously Roman law had been viewed as a kind of sacral arcanum, the province of a college of priests, but the Tables made law into something visible and spectacular.[56] The Tables survive only in quotation (as at, e.g. Gell. *NA* 20.1.45) but are described by later sources as central to Romans' understanding of their own state. They were posted in the central Forum of the city, were at one point memorized by schoolchildren,[57] and were the subject of juristic commentary long after they had ceased to function as statutory law.[58] The Tables – or more broadly the codified, prospective legal order that traced its genealogy thereto – functioned as a near-metonym for Republican political arrangements. For example, Livy transitions from his account of the monarchic period to the early Republic with "I will now describe peacetime and wartime deeds of a free Roman people, their annual magistracies, and the majesty of their laws which was greater than that of their men" (2.1.1: *Liberi iam hinc populi Romani res pace belloque gestas, annuos magistratus, imperiaque legum potentiora quam hominum peragam*). These arrangements were nominally democratic and marked by frequent invocations of the "Roman people" (*populus Romanus*),[59] but should be better understood as an aristocratic system in which major decisions were informally negotiated by leading families. Accordingly, Republican nostalgia – a recurring theme in the early

[55] The public display of legislation was not unique to Rome; monumental legislation is attested in many ancient states throughout Western Asia, but a closer contemporary parallel to the Twelve Tables might be the public posting of laws in Classical Greek city-states. See Gagarin, *Writing*, pp. 67–92; Lanni, *Courts*, p. 144 n. 109; Thomas, "Writing, Law, and Written Law."

[56] Lehne-Gstreinthaler, *Iurisperiti et oratores*, pp. 24–61; Mitchell, "Roman Priests."

[57] Cic. *de Leg.* 2.59.

[58] For example, 28 fragments survive from Gaius' commentary on the Twelve Tables, written in the second century CE: *PG Gaius* 418–45.

[59] See Russell, "Populus."

parts of this book, since that nostalgia frequently engaged with legal concepts – is mostly an elite trope. But notions of the ideal state, or more precisely of the ideal sovereign, guided how elite Romans thought about law. Those thoughts left their mark on the *Corpus Iuris Ciuilis*, and thus on our modern legal world.

The clearest explanation of how law worked in Republican political theory comes from Cicero. This fact is not shocking; Cicero was a politician and jurist who wrote quite a bit, and we should not take him as representative of median Roman values.[60] But Cicero's account of political goods spends more time on law than do others from the Republican period,[61] and it treats law differently than a modern reader might expect. For one thing, while most ancient and modern descriptions of law treat its value as essentially instrumental Cicero views law as a *bonum in se*, which good men ought to seek out and cherish for its own sake (1.48: *per se igitur ius est expetendum et colendum*).[62] This vision differs sharply from modern positivistic justifications of law, in which law is a good thing because it serves human flourishing,[63] but also from other ancient accounts. Compare Aristotle's consequentialist argument for legal sovereignty at *Rhet.* 1354b:

The legislator's judgment does not regard the specific circumstance, but rather the general or future circumstance, whereas the assemblyman or juryman judge matters that are present and clearly defined: for them, friendship and hatred and private interest are often involved, with the result that they can no longer properly consider the truth, but instead private pleasure and pain cast shadows on their judgment.

ἡ μὲν τοῦ νομοθέτου κρίσις οὐ κατὰ μέρος, ἀλλὰ περὶ μελλόντων τε καὶ καθόλου ἐστίν, ὁ δ' ἐκκλησιαστὴς καὶ δικαστὴς ἤδη περὶ παρόντων καὶ ἀφωρισμένων κρίνουσιν: πρὸς οὓς καὶ τὸ φιλεῖν ἤδη καὶ τὸ μισεῖν καὶ τὸ ἴδιον συμφέρον συνήρτηται πολλάκις, ὥστε μηκέτι δύνασθαι θεωρεῖν ἱκανῶς τὸ ἀληθές, ἀλλ' ἐπισκοτεῖν τῇ κρίσει τὸ ἴδιον ἡδὺ ἢ λυπηρόν.

[60] For Cicero's juristic career, Lehne-Gstreinthaler, *Iurisperiti et oratores*, pp. 289–314.

[61] The clearest example being Sallust, whose histories of the Catilinarian conspiracy and Jugurthine War both highlight the decadence of late Republican Rome and contrast it to a largely imagined past marked by political and personal virtue. Connolly, *Life*, pp. 65–113; Kapust, *Republicanism*, pp. 27–80; Kraus and Woodman, *Historians*, pp. 10–50.

[62] Edelstein and Straumann, "Liberties," p. 1046.

[63] E.g. Shapiro, *Legality*, pp. 193–94.

For Aristotle lawmaking is a superior mode of decisionmaking, but nevertheless a better means to a desirable end. Cicero, by contrast, sees it as necessarily moral and thus predicts Lon Fuller's (much later) account of law's "inner morality."[64] Cicero also predicts the (much later) jurisprudence of Ronald Dworkin, by linking ideal law to ideal governance and ideal governors. Dworkin sees law as a negotiation between several different registers of public good, and adjudication as occasionally requiring judges to evaluate several competing rationales that might influence the disposition of a hard case.[65] Dworkin acknowledges that these requirements are demanding, and that most people cannot meet them; for a legal system to reliably instantiate Dworkin's constitutional values it would need judges of superhuman wisdom and deliberation, if not necessarily modesty.[66] Cicero agrees that judges are critically important, but his ideal decisionmakers are less super- than inhuman.

The laws shall govern the magistrates, as the magistrates govern the populace: indeed it could be said that the magistrate is a talking law, or the law a mute magistrate.

Leg. 3.2: Ut enim magistratibus leges, ita populo praesunt magistratus, vereque dici potest, magistratum esse legem loquentem, legem autem mutum magistratum.

Other Romans had drawn this link between the character of the state and the character of its representatives. For example, Ennius, one of the earliest Latin writers to survive, claimed that "Rome stands on ancient customs and on her men" (*Moribus antiquis res stat Romana virisque*).[67] But Cicero's account focuses less on the magistrate's moral imagination than on his obedience to broader quasi-ethical constraints. The magistrate is not a talking law (*legem loquentem*) because he internalizes the law's virtue, or because his thinking reflects virtuous qualities, but because he stays in line. The

64 Fuller, *Morality*, p. 42; Edelstein and Straumann, "Liberties," p. 1046 (noting that Cicero stands "completely outside the inherited Hellenistic views").

65 Dworkin, "Hard Cases," pp. 1082–96.

66 *Ibid.*, p. 1083: I discuss Dworkin's ideal judge, whom he names "Hercules," in greater detail *infra* p. 188.

67 Lowrie, "Roman Law and Latin Literature," p. 71; Nethercut, "Revaluation," p. 446; Elliott, *Architecture*, p. 41.

relationship between law and the magistrate is supervisory (*praesunt*), with the ideal magistrate subordinating his individual decisionmaking to the communal will as embodied by the laws. This subordination might not seem all that controversial, since it is arguably central to our understanding of what it means to have a legal system. But given the political breakdowns and extralegal violence of the late Republic, we can see why *leges loquentes* might be so desirable. Cicero frames his desire for orderly public life as a rule-of-law theory, and (as Edelstein and Straumann argue) he conceives of *libertas* in terms of legal regularity, as opposed to participation or consent.[68]

That focus makes Cicero's *libertas*, more than other glosses of the term, into the kind of good an emperor can provide. This book focuses on imperial Rome for a reason; the sources of Roman law, which come almost entirely from the imperial period, use that law to think through the distinctive paradoxes of Roman imperial sovereignty. Emperors of the Principate existed in a kind of permanent state of exception. Imperial powers were broad but undefined, and coexisted with an older set of political conventions that governed in name only.[69] That disjunct between appearance and reality was a problem for many Romans living under the Principate, especially the elite Romans who had exercised power under the earlier regime. If the "restored republic" of Augustus[70] was defined by meaningful elite participation in political decisionmaking, then it was a lie – other ways of thinking about *libertas* opened up more room for negotiation, or at least for plausible flattery. Emperors could promise to act like *leges loquentes*, subordinating their decisionmaking to higher normative orders, and because law had historically occupied such an important role in the Roman political imaginary it served as a potent metaphor for that subordination.

Romans of this period used law to think about other problems, and that process gave Roman law its distinctive and unreal character. The

68 Edelstein and Straumann, "Liberties," pp. 1038–39.

69 The concept of the "state of exception" (*Ausnahmezustand*) comes from Karl Schmitt, who defines it as a circumstance marked by suspension of legal order. Giorgio Agamben notes that absolute rulers necessarily exist in a state of exception, and the extreme informality of political order under the Principate exacerbated the problem. Schmitt, *Theology*, pp. 5–15; Agamben, *Eccezione*, pp. 88–91.

70 See the essays collected at Mineo and Hurlet (eds.), *Principat*; Galinsky, *Culture*, pp. 42–79.

figure of the talking law has never existed; laws do not talk, and judges are people. But its shadow looms large over Roman law, however hard it might be to find in Roman history.

* * * * *

Now, at long last, it is time to say what this book actually *does*. It consists of seven chapters in three parts and proceeds roughly chronologically. That schema has costs and benefits. I am tracking discursive tendencies that coexisted for much of Rome's history, and while they wax and wane over time a chronological approach may make things seem more directional than they are. It is, however, worth the risk. For one thing legal systems, particularly ones as historicizing and nostalgic as the current object of study, are strongly path-dependent. Quirks of legal writing in the third century CE take on outsized importance in the sixth, and those causal links can be hard to isolate in a more thematic argument. More broadly, the history of Roman legality is a history of crises, of "eventful temporalities" that shifted Roman thinking.[71] Those shifts are more visible in a diachronic history, even if they worked upon an ethical and social substrate that persisted over time. I also hope such a structure is less confusing. Not everyone who cares about Roman law comes to it with a knowledge of imperial history, and the political evolutions of the Principate and Dominate are easier to explain when placed on a timeline.

The book argues one basic point: that "Roman law" is better understood as a metaphorical language in which Romans talked about their state than as a law-code in the way it now appears or in the way law now more or less works. I also hope to validate some core methodological commitments, which are not unheard of in Roman legal history but which have perhaps found less purchase there than in other subfields: that Roman administration worked in tandem with state and imperial representation,[72] that people experienced Roman government in largely symbolic terms,[73] and that those symbolics exercised world-changing power independent of changes in people's material conditions.

Part I of this book discusses Roman law in the Principate. While we have relatively few records of Roman legal practice or education before

[71] Sewell, "Three Temporalities," pp. 262–64. [72] See Ando, *Century*, pp. 177–78.
[73] See Noreña, *Imperial Ideals*, pp. 300–02.

Gaius' *Institutes* in the late second century, a substantial epigraphic, literary, and artistic corpus survives that records elite concerns; that corpus records major changes in how elites understood law to relate to their lives, as well as actual regulatory shifts that were in many cases of only secondary importance to those changes of understanding.

Chapter 1 focuses on the role of law in the accession and politic of Augustus *né* Octavian, Rome's first emperor (r. 31 BCE–14 CE). Since Romans tended to associate legal supremacy with Republican political virtue, Augustus had to be carefully positioned as both an enforcer and abrogator of Roman laws in order to maintain his position. Accordingly, Augustan Rome saw a complex messaging program that included Augustus sacrificing his own daughter to an ascendant moral/legal order.

Chapter 2 considers how later emperors and their interlocutors developed a new discursive type: the "emperor who obeys the law." Both Vespasian (r. 69–79; the first "successful" emperor outside of the Julio-Claudian dynasty) and Titus (r. 79–81; the first successor to an emperor outside of the Julio-Claudian line, as well as the first emperor to succeed his biological father) presided over enormous changes to the legal framework of the Principate. Vespasian's "authorization" by the Senate was inscribed in bronze, taking the fiction of senatorial rule that originated in the Augustan period and expressing it in the physical medium and generic form most closely associated with Republican legislation. Similarly the Edict of Titus (which renewed, *en masse*, all privileges granted by his late father) regularized a system of bequests that had previously been understood through the symbolic language of beneficence, while also assimilating dynastic succession to ancient principles in the Roman law of obligations and persons. These changes would become standard tropes of imperial representation, as shown by Pliny's panegyric to Trajan (r. 98–117). Emperors could represent themselves as obeying law in order to comply with ethical notions of ideal governance even in the absence of real constraint.

Chapter 3 considers the rise of the rescript system over the second century CE and beyond. The emperor Hadrian (r. 117–134) initiated a series of legal reforms designed to centralize adjudicative power in the imperial bureaucracy. I argue that Hadrian inaugurated a model of lawmaking that derived its legitimacy from the distinctive personal qualities of the lawgiving sovereign, and which replaced the elaborate ritual praxis of earlier Roman law with a new symbolic system centered on different goods (like meritocracy and efficiency) that were broadly valued within political rhetorics of the early second century.

The system of enlightened judgeship Hadrian inaugurated would last for another seventy-five years or so, but the Severan period (193–235) posed new challenges and made Hadrianic legality untenable. Part II of the book discusses how both emperors and jurists of that time responded to its particular dynamics, and how those responses imprinted themselves upon the *Corpus Iuris Ciuilis* (whose constitutive documents largely date from this period and after).

Chapter 4 focuses on how imperial legal writing developed in the late Severan period, and particularly how it came to derive its force less from the personal qualities of a lawmaker than from that lawmaker's position within suprapersonal frameworks that had their own claims to legitimacy. I focus on two features of constitutions associated with the child ruler Severus Alexander (r. 222–235): his apparent reissuance of legal opinions issued by his disgraced predecessor Elagabalus (r. 218–222) under his own name, and the unusual tendency of Alexander's rescripts to describe him as following the opinions of his dynastic forebears. I argue that both of these practices depict the emperor not as "obeying the laws" (like Augustus and Titus) or granting attention to grateful subjects (like Hadrian), but as fulfilling an institutionally specified role in creating and interpreting Severan legal order.

Chapter 5 examines juristic writing of the same period. Nearly all of the juristic writing that makes up the *Digest* comes from the Severan jurists, in particular from Papinian, Ulpian, and Paul. These three men held high positions in the imperial bureaucracy and even – in one case – likely exercised imperial power. That melding of imperial and juristic careers gave rise to a distinctively "Severan" jurisprudence, which I argue has influenced our understanding of juristic work more broadly. I discuss these jurists' tendency to treat the consequences of specific legal interpretations as integral to evaluating their goodness, which appears quite suddenly in Severan juristic writing and suggests that jurisprudence changed to match the evaluative frameworks applied by other actors within imperial bureaucracy. I also note how jurists of this period cited "sacred constitutions" or other anonymized imperial authorities in support of their claims, rather than to specific documents with specific authors. This practice reflects a similar depersonalizing process to that visible in Alexander's writing, but here jurists subsume the imperial lawgiver into institutional, rather than dynastic, continuities.

The Principate Severus Alexander ruled would never return, and Part III of this book discusses how the analytic moves of the early third century were received over the course of the late-antique period. In addition to the imperial administration organizing along more frankly autocratic lines, the late-antique world was marked by a growing and increasingly powerful imperial bureaucracy. These changes drove shifts in legal culture, and led to the codification of a very specific version of "Roman law," which differed in important ways from that of earlier periods but which relied for its legitimacy on imagined connection with those periods.

Chapter 6 considers how legal thinking adapted to the realities of the fourth and fifth centuries. In particular, constitutions from this period were more institutionalizing in how they described imperial legal authority, and those constitutions were then compiled into novel archival forms (multiauthorial *codices*, organized by subject matter) and interpreted by a growing corps of experts. These changes looked back to the juristic treatises of the Severan period, and made the bureaucratic legality for which Roman law now appears to stand tenable, while laying the groundwork for Justinian's final codificatory project.

That project is the focus of Chapter 7. I argue there that the *Corpus Iuris Ciuilis* reflects Justinianic prerogatives, at a deeper level than textual redaction. Justinian presents a coherent, knowable, and static law-code as a backdrop for his own extraordinary munificence, and accordingly his compilation highlights texts that are well suited to that image. I focus specifically on the dearth of explicit conflict between rescripts within the *Codex Justinianus*, and on the comparative isolation of legal principles from other kinds of literary endeavor that might originally have been represented in juristic corpora.

Finally, I conclude the work by discussing Roman law's later reception. The bureaucratic impersonality of "Roman law" has come to stand for a set of values that would have likely read as foreign to its original writers and experts. This metonymic process is perhaps most apparent in Roman legal scholarship of the mid twentieth century.

Nazis and their victims, particularly refugee scholars like Fritz Schulz, used "Roman legal order" as a barely suppressed metaphor for liberal conceptions of the rule of law. The Roman law we have was embodied in the pronouncements of autocrats and the philosophical debates of their functionaries, which themselves became symbols of a liberty that none of their authors had ever known.

As I hope the summary above has made clear, this book deals with a fairly nightmarish textual tradition; as a result, editions matter. All citations to the Latin of the *Digest* refer to Watson et al. (1985), and the *Codex* Frier et al. (2016). It happens that one of our most thorough and reliable historiographical accounts of both the Augustan and Severan periods, that of Cassius Dio, has also had a difficult transmission. I rely on Boissevain (1955)'s and Cary (1927)'s divisions of books, and (following current scholarly practice) indicate the source of individual fragments in brackets when needed. All English translations are my own, unless otherwise specified. All errors are my own, or are loved as if they were.

PART I

NEVERTHELESS, WE LIVE ACCORDING TO THE LAWS

1

Augustus and the Birth of Imperial Legality

Augustan governance meant many things.[1] Later commentators – a category that includes ourselves, but also writers like Suetonius, Tacitus, and Cassius Dio – tend to see the Augustan period through the lens of what came after, as the genesis of a remarkably stable political system built on the meticulous pretense of consensus rule.[2] That tendency should be resisted. Scholarship in recent years has complicated this image of the "Age of Augustus," showing real contestation at all levels of society around the meaning of the Augustan settlement.[3] This contestation took many forms, but much of it was hermeneutic. Different actors shared a corpus of ideologically freighted symbols, narratives, and ideas but interpreted it according to their own idiosyncratic desires and commitments.[4]

This chapter considers how Augustus and his interlocutors used law to talk about power. While the sources preserved in the *Corpus Iuris Ciuilis*

[1] On the concept of "governance" as a catchall for moves made by both public and nonpublic actors that direct the resources and residents of a given polity see Tani, *Dependency*, p. 12 n. 35; Jensen, "Governance," *passim* but especially p. 381.

[2] On the role of consensus in the post-Augustan period, see (among many others) Hurlet, "L'idéologie dynastique"; Rich, "Consensus Rituals"; Lobur, *Consensus*; Flaig, *Herausfordern*. On the role of pretense and doublespeak in imperial political discourse see Bartsch, *Actors*, pp. 67–68.

[3] I think in particular of Cooley, "Invention"; Morrell, Osgood, and Welch (eds.), *The Alternative Augustan Age*; and Pandey, *Poetics of Power*.

[4] See Langlands, *Exemplary Ethics*, p. 120; Wallace-Hadrill, "Mutatio Morum," pp. 13–14.

only discuss Augustan legal innovations through centuries of hindsight, Augustan literature reveals an elite that was both knowledgeable of and engaged with Rome's ancient legal institutions.[5] These institutions exercised an affective power far beyond their role in adjudicating disputes. Law and legal talk represented aristocracy, tradition, and fixity in a world where all three were under threat. At the same time, Augustan *auctoritas* engaged with the forms of law while negotiating what those forms could include or entail. By examining what different people meant when they talked about Augustus and the law, we can better understand not only the *Denkwelt* of the Augustan period but also the tropes of autocratic legality that emerged in that period and would shape later Romans' understandings of imperial power.

That examination reveals a persistent notion of ethical sovereignty, which interacted with but did not necessarily submit to "the law." Our sources describe an Augustus who used law as a potent metaphor for tradition and aristocratic virtue, but when legal dictates clashed with virtue they describe him choosing the latter. These tropes positioned Augustus within a quasi-legal network of ethical constraint, even as they freed him from legal restrictions as traditionally understood.

Tropes are not laws, of course, and nor are they coherent. This story of Augustan legality differs from the one that is usually told; it downplays changes to positive law in favor of tracking legal thought in other genres.[6] But these glimpses of Augustan culture tell us something important about how Romans thought with law. The Principate was an inherently extralegal institution, if it can be called an institution at all, and while later sources take as a given that emperors would be closely involved with Roman legal development that entanglement was not inevitable. It grew out of habits of mind that can be traced in comic poetry, in popular narratives of Augustan mercy, and in unlucky women abandoned on small islands; these anecdotes add up to a powerful, and surprising, story about emperors and law.

[5] On the centrality of law to the education of elite Romans see Harries, "Legal Education"; on the prevalence of "lawspeak" in Augustan poetry see Gebhardt, *Sermo Iuris*.

[6] For a few examples of more traditionally "legal" historiographies of the period Gulina, "Cognizione"; Hurlet, "Origines"; Tuori, *The Emperor of Law*, pp. 68–125.

In telling that story, I explore four different moments in Augustus' reign and what they can tell us about how that reign was understood in legal terms. First I examine a poem by Horace, published a year after the Battle of Actium, that offers a window into elite views of the emergent Principate and its relationship to legal culture. Second, I discuss an *aureus* (gold coin) minted two years later, which refers to Augustus as "restor[ing] *leges et iura*" to Rome. I then move to two important events from later on in the Augustan period: the strange story of Vedius Pollio and his man-eating lampreys, and Augustus' condemnation and exile of his daughter Julia for violating his own laws against adultery. Taken together, these events show the gradual development of an idea that would become extremely important in Roman political thought: that a "good" emperor existed within overarching decisional frameworks that dictated his actions, and that law could serve as a potent metaphor for those frameworks even under emperors who were empowered to suspend it.

Finally, a note on language. This chapter will spend a great deal of time discussing things that "Augustus" thought or planned. We have no way of knowing what Augustus, as a person, thought or planned. Augustus was to some extent an avatar, for the broader bureaucratic or political factions that Morrell has smartly called "Team Augustus."[7] Frustratingly, we cannot be sure how much. Political rhetoric of the Principate tends to portray the emperor himself as playing an outsized role in state functions, perhaps as a result of a broader conflation of emperor and government.[8] That would change, and in the latter chapters of this book I argue that the increasing acceptance of bureaucracy in portrayals of the imperial court affected Roman concepts of legal supremacy. But for now, our sources describe an emperor making decisions on his own (or with a close team of advisers) that were probably somewhat less unitary in practice.[9] The line between man and machine is impossible to draw precisely, and "Augustus (or those working behind the scenes on his behalf)" is awkward. So when I refer to Augustus – or to later emperors in subsequent chapters – please insert that parenthetical as needed.

[7] Morrell, "Magpie," pp. 12–13.

[8] See, for example, Sen. *Clem.* 3.5 (comparing the relationship between the emperor and his subjects to that between the mind and the body).

[9] The classic treatment of this paradox is Kantorowicz, *Bodies*, particularly pp. 336–83.

Law and Laughter, After Actium

By 30 BCE, Octavian ruled the world. His victory over Mark Antony at Actium in 31 had destroyed his only real rival for control of the Roman empire, and Antony's alliance with the Egyptian queen Cleopatra had allowed him to recast his victory in civil war as the conquest of a foreign threat.[10] The young warlord was now in charge, and while everyone seems to have agreed that Octavian would control Roman politics for some time going forward, it was not clear exactly how he would do so or what framework he would employ.[11] Strongmen had dominated Rome for almost a century, but that domination took slightly different forms at different points; Marius had insisted on consulships, for example, and Sulla ruled as dictator. Furthermore, different autocrats had very different tastes for bloodshed, and no one knew how far the new purges might run. Rome's political elite, which had exercised tremendous power during the period of aristocratic rule called the Republic,[12] were waiting for information.[13]

They got poetry. That year Horace, a client of Octavian's associate Maecenas,[14] published his second book of satires. Horatian satire is gentle by the standards of the form but it retains the capacity to

[10] The actual events of the Battle of Actium are difficult to piece together. Our three main sources (Velleius Paterculus, Plutarch, and Cassius Dio) agree on key details; in each the conflict ended decisively when Cleopatra's ships suddenly fled the field of warfare. Vell. Pat. 2.85.3, Dio Cass. 50.15, Plut. *Ant.* 66.3–67.1. This inexplicable retreat, however, is always attributed to some combination of "Oriental" (in the sense of Saïd, *Orientalism*) weakness and the obvious superiority of the young Octavian. It is not difficult to see how both themes, which dominate official narratives of Augustus' rise to power, might distort later accounts of the fight. Lange, "The Battle of Actium," p. 615 is correct that "the clear consensus of our sources" is that Cleopatra inexplicably retreated from a close battle and that Antony inexplicably followed her; the nature of our sources, however, makes it impossible to say whether that consensus reflects reality.

[11] Our ancient sources, particularly Dio, describe a gradual but orderly accretion of powers; see Swan, *Succession*, pp. 13–17. Cooley, "Invention" rightly calls this narrative into question, and suggests rather more contemporary uncertainty about the "constitutional sentiment" (p. 75) of Augustan rule than is visible in the accounts of later authors.

[12] But see Flower, *Roman Republics* (noting the difficulties of this conventional periodization).

[13] To my mind the clearest account of this uncertainty remains Zanker, *Macht*, pp. 96–98.

[14] Horace describes his relationship with Maecenas in extremely status-asymmetric terms, and emphasizes the latter's generosity in providing him with a country house

disturb,[15] and the book begins with a supremely unsettling meditation on Octavian, violence, and law.

Horace's satires might seem like a strange place to start a legal history, and generally speaking this book will not spend much time on poetry. But one of the quirks of the Augustan period is that its dramatic changes in Roman legality are often best commemorated in sources that are not obviously "legal" or "historical." Augustan literature reflects anxieties about the nature and function of Roman power, and those anxieties were sometimes channeled into the language of law. From that perspective, Horace's *Sat.* 2.1 is an important monument in the history of imperial legality. It establishes what elite Romans thought their new regime might mean for law, and what that regime's approach to law might mean for them. *Sat.* 2.1 suggests that imperial power might be ontologically incompatible with legal sovereignty as it had traditionally been understood; it also suggests, however, that emperors might be better.

Horace starts the poem in a place of humorous despair, unsure how to write good satire without violating Roman laws against libel:

> *There are those to whom I seem too harsh when I write satire,*
> *and for whom I seem to stretch my work beyond what law permits;*
> *another group thinks that whatever I have written lacks nerve,*
> *and that a thousand verses like mine could be written in a day.*
>
> (*Sat.* 2.1.1–4) Sunt quibus in satura videar nimis acer et ultra (1)
> legem tendere opus; sine nervis altera quidquid
> conposui pars esse putat similisque meorum
> mille die versus deduci posse.

Ultra legem literally means "beyond the law," but here its sense is difficult to pin down. While Roman law had prohibited "evil poetry"

and enslaved servants; see *Sat.* 1.6.47–125. On Horace's connections with Maecenas see Weeda, *Credentials*; Skinner, "Horace, Catullus, and Maecenas."

[15] For example, *Sat.* 1.4 begins with an attack on Lucilius (the forefather of Latin satire) himself; the language is mild by later standards but nevertheless suggests not only that Lucilius was derivative but that his work in that specifically Roman genre merely imitated Greek models. See Freudenburg, *Satires of Rome*, pp. 17–20; LaFleur, "The Law of Satire," p. 1807. Later satirists like Persius and Juvenal, of course, were far more scabrous and have influenced our contemporary understanding of the genre today. See (for example) Goh, "It All Comes Out"; Nappa, *Making Men Ridiculous*; Geue, *Anonymity*; Bartsch, *Persius*; Uden, *Invisible*.

(*mala carmina*) since the Twelve Tables,[16] *lex* can also denote generic or literary boundaries, and Horace could be breaking rules of good taste as easily as the rules of Roman statute. Furthermore, an entirely separate group of readers (*altera pars*) sees Horace's poetry as just criminally boring.[17] Horace heightens this semantic tension by asking the jurist Trebatius Testa what he should do, and Testa responds that he should just be quiet (4–5: "*Trebati, | quid faciam? Praescribe.*" "*Quiescas*").[18] Again, there are many ways to read Testa's advice. While the obvious implication is that Testa worries about Horace's liability or his poetry's quality, commentators like Lowrie and Tatum have suggested that Testa represents a broader tension between how law and poetry structure their worlds.[19] More on that later, though; at the outset of *Sat.* 2.1 all we know is that law, and lawyers, want Horace to stop talking.

Horace does not stop talking. Instead, he argues that his satires are his only line of defense against harm (47–56) and stand within a proud Lucilian tradition (62–79). The poem ends when Horace finds an argument to which Testa cannot respond: If Octavian likes my poetry, who cares about the law? In the face of power Testa concedes, and while Horace fails to convince the jurist that his poetry is legal he successfully demonstrates that legality no longer matters in Octavian's Rome. That much is obvious, and scholars have noted the authoritarian implications of *Sat.* 2.1.[20] But a close reading of the poem suggests that the choice between law and autocracy is not an easy one. In *Sat.* 2.1 suspending the law means, or perhaps permits, engaging with the world in other fashions. Octavian does not so much

[16] The prohibition is partially preserved at *XII Tab.* VIII.1; Crawford, *Roman Statutes*, pp. II.580–81.

[17] See Lowrie, *Writing, Performance, and Authority*, p. 333; Tatum, "Ultra Legem," p. 694.

[18] *Sat.* 2.1.4–5. While none of Testa's work survives, he was an influential legal expert in the period; Cicero dedicated his *Topica* to Testa, and both Maecenas and Augustus sought his legal advice (D.24.1.64, *J. Inst.* 2.25 pr.). See Lehne-Gstreinthaler, *Iurisperiti et oratores*, pp. 264–89; *HSS* I.44; Wieacker, *Römische Rechtsgeschichte*, pp. 612–13; Bauman, *Transitional Politics*, pp. 123–36.

[19] Tatum, "Ultra Legem," pp. 689–90.

[20] Lowrie, "Slander and Horse Law," pp. 418–20 describes the close of the poem as resting on Augustus' power to suspend the law; McGinn, "Satire and the Law," pp. 97–98 refers to it as the rise of a "new order" in which Augustus takes his place above traditional Roman legal authorities.

violate legal norms as transcend them, and Horace's "dialectic between satire and the law" shows how Romans could reconcile *ius* and the Principate.[21]

To understand what Horace means when he talks about the Principate, though, we must understand what he means when he talks about law. For such a legalistic poem *Sat.* 2.1 is not terribly concerned with legal rules, and the actual standard for libel does not appear until its last five lines. Instead, Horace engages with law as a way of thinking and speaking. Horace represents himself as uncertain and verbose – confessing his failings in the eyes of the Roman public – against a Testa who is taciturn, confident, and archaic. Testa's first two statements in the poem consist of one word each (*quiescas* on 5, *aio* on 6) and are followed by a series of imperatives at 2.1.8–10. In that passage – which includes multiple instances of the future imperative (*transnanto/habento*), which had fallen out of nonlegal use by this time[22] – Testa demands that Horace engage in old-fashioned remedies to cure his insomnia, or failing that to write old-fashioned praise poetry. Ironically, he does so with the imperative *aude*: "*Dare* to speak of the accomplishments of victorious Caesar," hardly a daring thing for a poet to do.[23] Unless Testa is more sarcastic than he appears elsewhere in the poem his advice reflects a poor literary imagination, and the jurist seems as unaware of the evolution of Latin poetry as he is of the evolution of the Latin language itself.[24] If we consider Testa from this perspective his attachment to law reads very differently, and so does the new order that will supersede it and him.[25]

[21] Lowrie, "Slander and Horse Law," p. 406.

[22] Freudenburg, *Horace, Satires: Book II*, p. 57; Pinkster, *The Oxford Latin Syntax*, p. I.513. The future imperative is common in Cato and still appears regularly in Plautus, but by this time was limited to specific genres (particularly statute) and a few limited forms (*scito, memento*). While *habento* continues to be attested after Horace, it is one of very few future imperatives that do; the *transnanto* in particular makes Testa sound either extremely old-fashioned or like, quite literally, a talking law. On Roman understandings of legal speech as not just specialized but archaic, see Mantovani, *Les juristes écrivains*, pp. 71–72.

[23] Freudenburg, *Horace, Satires: Book II*, p. 58. A darker interpretation is available, of course; to speak of some of Caesar's behavior in the civil war would be very daring indeed. But in the context of Testa's other advice, the suggestion of praise poetry is not ambiguous. See also Clauss, "Allusion and Structure," pp. 200–01.

[24] See Lowrie, *Writing, Performance, and Authority*, p. 338.

[25] There is real irony in Horace presenting Octavian as a novel break with Testa's archaism, given the old-fashioned tendencies of later Augustan messaging (on

Having established the archaism of Testa's worldview, Horace next attacks its fairness. For example, at 2.1.47–56 Horace describes satire as his only means of self-defense in a world dominated by those more powerful than he. The thrust of the passage is self-deprecating, with Horace comparing himself to desperate animals at 52–56; that said, Horace is only desperate because he is threatened. At 2.1.47–49 Horace makes explicit that legal process is one of the threats that drives him to satire.

When Cervius is mad he brandishes laws and the judge's urn,
Albucus' Canidia, poison against those whom she opposes,
And Turius a great evil, should you contest anything before him in court.

Cervius iratus leges minitatur et urnam, (47)
Canidia Albuci, quibus est inimica, venenum,
grande malum Turius, siquid se iudice certes.

The archaic formalities of Testa's advice (mimicked by Horace's *siquid*) have here given way to a more dangerous reality, in which the discursive structures of law are as deadly as a witch's poison and no more just. These intimations of death and destruction are not novel incursions into the poem's world, and Horace has previously admitted to some fear that his imperial listener might "kick" the poet who upset him.[26] But the threats posed by law are far more direct. Horace describes them in less figurative language, as a constraint on his daily life. The legal world with which *Sat.* 2.1 engages is presented to readers as one that is not necessarily any less brutal than that of poetry or that of politics.

Of course, the poem ends firmly in that latter sphere, and Horace concludes it with his most programmatic statements on what Octavian means for law. When Testa warns Horace that the ancient prohibitions of the Twelve Tables will harm him financially, the poet invokes the protection of a higher power. (I should note that, since the last words of the poem offer two possible meanings, I leave them untranslated here and discuss further immediately below.)

which see among many others Galinsky, *Culture*; Zanker, *Macht*). But Horace wrote in 30 BCE, and it is not clear how strongly this archaizing strain in Augustan representation presented itself at that time.

26 *Sat.* 2.1.20; Lowrie, *Writing, Performance, and Authority*, pp. 344–45.

"But nevertheless you should be careful, lest by chance
Ignorance of the sacred laws should hurt your business interests:
If a man writes bad songs about another, there is law and judgement."
"Indeed, if they're bad; but what if someone writes good ones,
praised by judge Caesar? If a man's crimes
are worthy of reproach should he stay whole?"
The tablets will be erased by laughter, tu missus abibis.

(*Sat.* 2.1.80–86) 'sed tamen ut monitus caveas, ne forte negoti
incutiat tibi quid sanctarum inscitia legum:
si mala condiderit in quem quis carmina, ius est
iudiciumque.' 'esto, siquis mala; sed bona siquis
iudice condiderit laudatus Caesare? siquis
opprobriis dignum latraverit, integer ipse?'
solventur risu tabulae, tu missus abibis.

The law is not on Horace's side – what if the emperor is?

As throughout *Sat.* 2.1, Testa represents the perspective of the law, and that perspective is expressed in symbols as much as rules. In particular, the vision of law Testa offers is strikingly impersonal; instead of describing Horace being punished, or powerful actors like those Horace mentions at 47–49 using the law to accomplish their goals, Testa asserts that *ius* and *iudicium* merely *are*. They govern human relations but do not arise from them, and spring from text into the world. The text of the Twelve Tables is laconic; its judgments are mechanical and its lines are bright. If evil song, then punishment.

Horace counters with a more personal and individuated vision of justice. When *iudex Caesar* decides that Horace's poems are good (*bona*), he employs the evaluative techniques of a reader who decides to praise (*laudatus*) a given poet's work.[27] Those techniques allow Octavian to consider aspects of Horace's poetic program that the law ignores but readers do not: namely, whether his targets deserve (*dignum*) the abuse they get.[28] Horace can worry about whether his poems are *good*, rather than whether they are evil. Octavian appears at the end of *Sat.* 2.1 as a more attentive and thoughtful audience than Testa and his colleagues have ever been.

[27] *Ibid.*, p. 335 ("Aesthetically good poetry trumps legally bad poetry, that is, defamation.").

[28] See LaFleur, "The Law of Satire," p. 1823.

The last line, however, hides a barb. The speaker of 2.1.86 (*solventur risu tabulae, tu missus abibis*) is ambiguous. The standard reading has Testa responding to Horace and straightforwardly conceding defeat ("The tablets will be erased by laughter, and you will be freed and leave the courtroom"), but the change of speaker is not necessary. The same Latin could just as easily quote Horace, describing Testa's fate under a regime with no use for legal formalities ("The tablets will be erased by laughter, and you will leave when you are sent away."). Both readings emphasize the uselessness of law in the face of Octavianic power,[29] but depict that power very differently. Furthermore, *tabulae* is famously ambiguous.[30] While the term can indicate the tablets that were used for indictment under the praetorian system,[31] Horace never refers to a formal indictment. He does, however, quote the *XII tabulae* four lines above. The instrumental *risu* draws a direct conflict between the sovereign's emotional, individual reaction to a poem and the more straightforward reading practice indicated by law and its *tabulae*.[32] It is left to the reader to determine whether Horace sees Octavian's laughter as superseding the indictment, the foundational documents of Roman legal order, or the latter by means of the former. Horace gives us no answer to the question, and leaves this final claim about Octavian's relationship to law unspecified.

This lack of specification is the defining feature of *Sat.* 2.1's conclusion. Octavian has all the power; that much we know. But the exercise of his power leads, alternately or simultaneously, to something like a pardon and to something like an exile. If *tu missus* describes Horace, then Octavian's supremacy over Roman law is a tool for mercy, and for protecting the vulnerable poet from an archaic and dangerous legal regime. If *tu missus* describes Testa, however, then we are confronted with Octavian's ability to hurt those he dislikes, to "kick" as Horace put it before. In one world *missus* is a kindness, in the other it is a threat, and Horace leaves his reader with no way to

29 Thus Freudenburg, *Satires of Rome*, p. 105 ("Horace says the magic word, 'Caesar.' And with it his legal worries disappear.").

30 See Freudenburg, *Horace, Satires: Book II*, p. 79; Lowrie, *Writing, Performance, and Authority*, p. 346.

31 On the role of *tabulae* in Roman legal procedure see Meyer, *Legitimacy and Law*, pp. 112–20.

32 Pinkster, *The Oxford Latin Syntax*, pp. I.874–75; Plaza, "Solventur."

situate themselves between the two. We have already seen Octavian have strong personal reactions to poetry, but the subjectivity that marks his own reading practice has become universal and inescapable.

A poem that begins in confusion thus ends the same way. Horace starts *Sat.* 2.1 unsure of how his poetry will be evaluated, and concludes it unsure of practically everything else. This progression feels sinister, to us; we want to live in worlds defined by clear rules and find Octavian's unpredictability disturbing. Thus Freudenburg, for example, tells his reader that the end of the poem is "*really* every bit as offensive as you think it is."[33] Horace's attitude, though, is not as clearly horrified as we might like. While Horace is aware of the commitments that Octavianism violates, he gives us no evidence that he is attached to them. Octavian's reading – his taste in poetry – is never questioned, and while his standards are different than Testa's that difference is nothing to mourn.

In *Sat.* 2.1, Octavian can hurt. That potential for violence underlies the humanistic practices within which Horace seeks refuge, and line 86 shows the fragile boundary between victims and victors in the new regime. But Octavianic brutality accompanies ways of living that are nevertheless superior to Testa's own mechanistic cruelties. If we take *Sat.* 2.1 at its word and reckon with its insistence that the rule of law is not always a good thing, we can see new ways of understanding legality in the chaos of 30 BCE. Horace suggests simultaneously that Rome's relationship to Octavian is incompatible with its historical attachment to legal order, that that legal order has served as a tool of repression from which a poet might be grateful to be freed, and that whatever succeeds it might permit new kinds of public and literary freedom while also opening the door to unspoken atrocities.[34]

* * * * *

Why does *Sat.* 2.1 matter, though? We can all agree that the poem is not helpful to the present project if taken as a window into

[33] Freudenburg, *Satires of Rome*, p. 108.

[34] Cf. Pandey, *Poetics of Power*, p. 28 (describing the possibility of Augustan repression visible in much literature of the period). 2.1 suggests that state repression was not a new phenomenon in Roman literary culture and offers a vision (however early and however insincere) of Octavian/Augustus as defending, rather than constricting, frank speech. On how the emperor affected Horace's "satiric voice" see Freudenburg, *Satires of Rome*, p. 87.

Horace's interiority. Leaving aside questions of *persona* – or of whether the author himself would endorse the commitments and worldview of the poem's narrator[35] – Horace was one person. He was a person, however, who knew his audience better than we do. We do not have first-person accounts of the Augustan period that we can trust, but we can assume that Horace thought his readers would understand what he was doing. Horace wrote jokes about law, despotism, and jurists for an audience whose anxieties were more familiar to him than they are to us, and his artistic choices reflect presumptions about that audience that are historically valuable in their own right.

Taken that way, *Sat.* 2.1 tells us quite a lot. At the most superficial level, it assumes a very high level of sophistication around law. The poem orbits a legal prohibition that is not even summarized until its end, and the legalistic tics of its diction are never flagged at all. Horace is a deeply allusive poet and we should not assume every reader understood his references, but he here shows us how Augustan poets and readers could use law as a distinctly Roman index of cultural competence. More importantly Horace takes law as a natural symbolic and metaphoric language with which to discuss the aftermath of Actium, collapsing political with jurisdictional conflict.

In other words, Horace and his readers understood the story of the emergent Principate to be a story about law. Horace is less clear on how that story would develop, and highlights a feature of Octavianic sovereignty that later histories mostly elide. Horace does not say that the autocrat will uphold the law – an argument we might expect based on other imperial praise literature[36] – but that he will make better and more humane decisions than the law can. We do not need to take Horace at his word that he or anyone else believed this to be the case, but it is nevertheless meaningful that this argument made sense in 30 BCE. Later history conditions us to think of good emperors as

[35] On the Horatian *persona* see Freudenburg, "Horatius Anceps"; Harrison, "Confessions." On dialogue as a device within Horatian satire see Oliensis, "Fortunam."

[36] The most famous example of this rhetorical trope is probably Pliny's *Panegyricus*, discussed *infra* pp. 101–07.

working in concert with or submission to the law, but Horace shows us that this discursive tendency was not inevitable and was not unanimous in the earliest Principate. There are other ways to praise an emperor, and other ways to think about law, than what now seems universal.

Horace also predicts a very different relationship between emperors and jurists than the one that eventually developed. In *Sat.* 2.1 Octavian's justice renders Testa's moot; whether we read the last line as about exiling the jurist or simply overruling him, there is no place for Testa's approach in Octavian's world. In practice, however, the Augustan period was superficially friendly to jurists. I discuss jurists under the Principate in greater detail in Chapters 3 and 5, but legal experts like Labeo achieved prominence in this period and worked closely with the emergent imperial administration.[37] The second-century jurist Pomponius mentions that especially favored jurists were granted a "right of response" (*ius respondendi*), which allowed their opinions to guide the imperial court's view of the law.[38] Once again, this contrast shows us how unpredictable the Augustan period really was. In 30 BCE, Horace could describe imperial power as fundamentally incompatible with legal sovereignty; the two now strike us as mutually reinforcing aspects of the Principate, but that paradigm did not emerge until after Horace wrote and only looks obvious in retrospect.

In particular, this paradigm was inaugurated in the Augustan period but existed then as one among many. Over the course of Octavian's (later Augustus') reign, he would sometimes return to *Sat.* 2.1's script and portray himself as transcending the law to better serve justice. At other times, though, he would appear as something like a legal subject and submit himself to something like a legal order. These representational tendencies existed in tension, and different actors might highlight different features of the emperor in order to meet their own needs and to think through for themselves what having a *ciuilis princeps* might mean. My next section explores one remarkable case of this dialogic constitutionalism: a coin that commemorates the emperor restoring legal order through essentially extralegal means.

[37] *HSS* II.1; Bauman, *Lawyers and Politics*, pp. 25–55.

[38] I discuss the *ius respondendi* in more detail in Chapter 3, but for an explanation of Pomponius' account see Tuori, "Freedom."

Restoring the New Order

About thirty years ago, a new *aureus*-type appeared in an auction catalogue.[39] The coin was purchased by the British Museum, and a comparand was discovered in 2005 that removed all doubt about the *aureus*' authenticity.[40] Those initial doubts can be forgiven, however. *BMC* 22107001 is a very strange coin, whose iconography is far more explicitly "legal" than that of any other known imperial or provincial type.[41] The *aureus* itself is visible at Figure 1.1.

It was minted in Asia Minor, for use in broader trade (as opposed to the *cistophoroi* that were minted at the same time but were traded primarily within the province). Its obverse (heads, essentially) depicts a laureate bust of Octavian with the legend IMP CAESAR/DIVI F COS VI (*Imperator Caesar/son of a god, in his sixth consulship*). On the reverse, a togate Octavian sits and extends a scroll towards the left side of the image field. That reverse is accompanied by the legend LEGES

FIGURE 1.1 Augustan *aureus*. London: British Museum, BMC 22107001. Image: Trustees of the British Museum.

[39] Rich and Williams, "Leges et Iura," p. 169 n. 2.

[40] For scholarship doubting the authenticity of the Augustan *aureus* see Martini, "Falsifità," "Falsa emissione"; on the comparand see Abdy and Harling, "Two Important New Roman Coins," pp. 175–76.

[41] See Hekster, "Imperial Justice?," p. 254; Mantovani, "Principe e diritto," p. 45 n. 11.

ET IVRA P R RESTITVIT (*has restored the statutes and laws to/of the Roman People*).

The obverse iconography is unremarkable, but COS VI dates the coin to 28 BCE (an important year, as I discuss later). The reverse is more unusual. Legends are rarely so explicit, for one thing; by way of comparison, the *denarius*-type *RIC* 270 flanks a similar image with the text IMP CAESAR.[42] It is likely that the *aureus* is so wordy because the message it sought to convey could not be expressed through traditional numismatic iconography. Roman coins did not talk about law very often, so whoever struck the *aureus* did not have a set iconographic vocabulary with which to get their point across.

But what was that point? The *aureus* clearly references an event with which its audience was familiar, but in the decades since its publication scholars have argued about what exactly it is saying. While much of this debate is somewhat semantic,[43] the different translations offered by different commentators reflect real disagreement about what Octavian did in 28 BCE, and about the role of *leges et iura* in those actions and their reception. In what follows, I argue that the *aureus* reflects elite reaction to Octavian renouncing the triumviral powers he had previously held, and that it attempts to reframe that first emperor's public image through legal objects and rituals. It is difficult to tell how amenable Octavian was to this imagecrafting, but later practices suggest that debates over legal continuity would become an important part of the constitutional conversations we now refer to as the "Augustan settlement."

Whatever that settlement looked like, the *aureus* commemorates an important part of it. In his sixth consulship (again, 28 BCE) Octavian

[42] See Rich and Williams, "Leges et Iura," p. 176.

[43] The *aureus* was first published by Rich and Williams, who argue that the coin refers specifically to a restoration of earlier legal privileges that were abrogated during the triumviral period; "he has restored their laws and rights to the Roman people" (*Ibid.*, p. 182). Mantovani ("Principe e diritto," pp. 51–63) argues that the two terms do not so much indicate different classes of legal privilege as form a stock phrase indicating positive legal order, and Zehnacker ("Remarques") suggests that Augustus is not offering a scroll (representing the written law) to an unseen *populus Romanus* but instead offering a public reading. Rich reconsidered some of the claims made in the initial publication in "Making the Emergency Permanent," pp. 89–105; in particular, he concedes Mantovani's more limited claim about the meaning of *iura*, but maintains that the reverse image depicts Augustus gifting the law to the Roman people. Larger claims about the relationship of LEGES ET IVRA to Augustan constitutionalism remain unsettled, and I focus on those.

formally renounced the powers he had exercised during the triumviral period, purporting to restore Republican order and even delegating most provincial governance tasks back to the Senate. In return, that Senate gratefully voted him the title of *Augustus* (which I will use from here on out) among other honors, while continuing to follow the autocrat's "advice." In his later autobiography *The Accomplishments of the Deified Augustus* (*Res Gestae Diui Augusti*, or *RGDA*), Augustus describes this renunciation as part of a two-year process:

In my sixth and seventh consulship [i.e. 28 and 27 BCE], after I had already extinguished civil strife and become ruler of all things by universal consent, I transferred the res publica *from my own* potestas *into the judgment of the Senate and the Roman People.*

(34) In consulatu sexto et septimo, postquam bella ciuilia exstinxeram, per consensum uniuersorum potitus rerum omnium, rem publicam ex mea potestate in senatus populique Romani arbitrium transtuli.[44]

Other authors were more cynical. Tacitus describes the same event: "In his sixth consulship Augustus, secure in his power, undid the things he had ordered in the triumvirate and gave us the laws under which we enjoy both peace and prince." (*Ann.* 3.28: *sexto demum consulatu Caesar Augustus, potentiae securus, quae triumuiratu iusserat aboleuit deditque iura quis pace et principe uteremur*).[45] Cassius Dio's account of this period is far more detailed (taking up the greater part of Book 53) and largely reflects the idiosyncratic concerns of the third century, but he describes the exact decree that Tacitus does, with striking language.

Since [Augustus] had ordered many things both illegally and unjustly during periods of civic strife and civil war, as well as during his joint rule with Antony and Lepidus, he erased them all with a single edict.

(53.2.5) ἐπειδή τε πολλὰ πάνυ κατά τε τὰς στάσεις κἀν τοῖς πολέμοις, ἄλλως τε καὶ ἐν τῇ τοῦ Ἀντωνίου τοῦ τε Λεπίδου συναρχίᾳ, καὶ ἀνόμως καὶ ἀδίκως ἐτετάχει, πάντα αὐτὰ δι' ἑνὸς προγράμματος κατέλυσεν.[46]

[44] For a broader discussion of this trope in the *RGDA* see Cooley, *Res Gestae Diui Augusti*, pp. 39–40.

[45] See Woodman and Martin, *The Annals of Tacitus: Book 3*, pp. 258–59.

[46] Rich, *Settlement*, p. 134 discusses some possible procedural sequelae of the edict. It is impossible to effectively summarize recent scholarship on Cassius Dio's treatment of the triumviral and post-triumviral periods, but recent authors have seen Dio's fear of

Note the pairing of ἀνόμως (illegally) and ἀδίκως (unjustly). This juxtaposition is unusual in Dio, who uses νόμος (statutory or otherwise positive law) and δίκη (referring in Dio to law in a broader sense, or alternately to the virtue of justice) frequently, but almost never together.[47] While Dio does not name his sources for the events of Book 53, this odd locution specifically describes the subject of an edict, written and delivered in Latin, around the same time that an *aureus* was struck celebrating Augustus' restoration of *leges et iura*.[48] The relationship between *lex* and *ius* is not equivalent to that between νόμος and δίκη, but if a translator wished to preserve hendiadys in a translation from Latin to Greek or *vice versa*, these are the pairs they would likely use. Both documents likely derive this language from the same source, which traveled far enough to reach Asia Minor and was preserved into the early third century: probably the text of the edict itself. The language there cannot be definitively reconstructed, but Latin uses *contra leges*, *iura*, or both to express illegality/injustice.

That edict, then, led Dio to frame Augustus' renunciation of triumviral powers in legal terms. The same framing shows up somewhat less explicitly in the Tacitus passage quoted above and in the historian Velleius Paterculus, who claims that after Actium "force was restored to the laws, authority to judgments, majesty to the Senate, and the jurisdiction of magistrates was returned to its ancient form" (2.89: *restituta uis legibus, iudiciis auctoritas, senatui maiestas, imperium magistratuum ad pristinum redactum modum*).[49] But it vanishes completely from the *RGDA*, which describes the same events

civil war as both a reaction to his own times and a driving force in his account of the first century BCE. See, among others, Lange, "Perusia"; Lindholmer, "Exploiting Conventions"; Berdowski, "Interpretive Category"; Kemezis, "Senatorial Memory"; Peer, "Complexity"; Urso, "Cassius Dio's Sulla." This work builds of a rich – if less prolific – earlier tradition; see, for example, Gowing, *Triumviral Narratives*; Rich, *Settlement*.

47 The only real comparand – in a very long text – is at 41.54.2–3, where Dio claims that Pompey and Caesar "stole a great deal of money unjustly, and killed many of their friends illegally" (πολλὰ μὲν χρήματα ἀδίκως συλῶντι, πολλοὺς δὲ καὶ τῶν φιλτάτων ἀνόμως κτείνοντι). See also 4.17.9, referring to "laws weaker than weapons, and justice weaker than madness" (τούς τε νόμους τῶν ὅπλων καὶ τὸ δίκαιον τῆς ἀπονοίας . . . ἀσθενέστερα).

48 See Mason, *Greek Terms*, pp. 190–91.

49 My reading of this passage is greatly indebted to Cowan, "Hopes and Aspirations," pp. 42–45. See also Woodman, *Velleius Paterculus*, pp. 252–54 (connecting Paterculus' catalogue to specific events in the early Augustan period).

in solely political/constitutional terms, and from the roughly contemporaneous *Fasti Praenestini* of 8 CE.[50]

All told, different audiences represented Augustus' maneuver differently. To void actions taken contrary to *leges et iura* could be understood as a specifically first-order, legal intervention (changing people's rights and obligations) or a second-order constitutional one (changing the broader political structures that vested certain entities with the power to change rights and obligations). Law and politics collapsed, with the same action serving as a turning point in two concurrent histories.

The question remains of how that collapse took place. While Testa claimed to pronounce a law that was both archaic and suprapolitical, that law could not function in the ways shown here and in particular could not tell Augustus what to do. Understanding the *aureus*, then, requires us to get past Testa and to ask what different audiences might hear when Augustus talked about *leges et iura*. In these accounts, Augustus ceded sovereignty (to the Senate, or to "Rome" more broadly) by declaring actions that violated the law to be void. In 30 BCE Horace wrote as if law's power to order the world was very much in question; two years later an *aureus* could celebrate Augustus "restoring the law" with at least some presumption that its audience would find the claim legible. When Augustus voided his illegal actions he did not establish the rule of law as we understand it today, but he did set out some parameters for how law could work in imperial culture going forward.

First of all: in a fight between law and the emperor, the emperor wins. Both Tacitus and Dio refer explicitly to Augustus restoring legal order by voiding his previous illegal actions, but that restoration is voluntary. The primary criterion for assessing the validity of an action is whether it contravened the imperial decree, with law helping to gloss that decree's scope rather than determining validity in its own right.

Second: law remains a distinct (if subordinate) discursive framework that predates and survives under imperial governance.

[50] The *Fasti* are an inscribed calendar with glossary material written by the grammarian Verrius Flaccus. The *Fasti* inscription was restored by Mommsen in 1863 as commemorating the *restitutio* of the *res publica* (*CIL* I^2 231); Todisco, "I Fasti Praenestini" notes parallels between the *aureus* and the *Fasti*'s language of restitution, and in particular its framing of the *res publica* as restored to its proper owners.

These accounts of the "Augustan settlement," whether produced during or after that period, describe Augustus *interacting* with law. *Restituit* means "restored" and thus presumes something previously functional that has fallen into disuse; similarly, Dio's use of the pluperfect ἐτετάχει ("had ordered") implies that Augustus' actions had been illegal and unjust at the time they were taken. Roman law, then, was perfectly capable of existing as a form of normative reasoning without governing people's relationships to state power. That power could be mediated through legal methods or language, but those methods or language still existed if it was not.

Finally, law served as a metonym for "traditional" political order. Cowan notes that Augustus' voiding of "illegal actions" is described as *restitutio* in Paterculus and the *Fasti*, but pointedly not in the *RGDA*, and suggests that this language may have come from "below" as part of a broader attempt to persuade Augustus to follow republican governance norms.[51] Whether or not it was meant to persuade, though, the language of the *aureus* was produced by and for people who thought *LEGES ET IVRA* mattered. The audience for the coin was interested in legal supremacy, understood it as a good, and understood it as associated – some way, somehow – with prior ways of doing things.

I should note here what that audience was. Most inhabitants of the Roman empire never saw gold coins; this *aureus* traveled in narrow, wealthy circles.[52] By the same token, it is striking that this messaging occurs only on the "Roman" *aureus* and not on *cistophoroi* produced at the same time and place that were used for more local trade. This coin was meant for people with money, and with strong connections to networks that extended outside of Asia Minor.[53] That restriction may explain why the *aureus* uses imagery we rarely see in numismatics. If law was an elite pursuit, the restoration of *leges et iura* may have meant more to the kinds of Romans who used *aurei* – and who read Horace – than to the audience for other kinds of coins.[54]

51 Cowan, "Hopes and Aspirations."

52 See Metcalf, "Whose 'Liberalitas'?," pp. 343–45.

53 See Carbone, *Hidden Power*, p. 193.

54 The distinctly Roman/Latin valence of this discourse appears in the *RGDA* itself. As Cooley notes (*Res Gestae Diui Augusti*, p. 260), surviving Greek copies of the document describe Augustus not as handing over the *res publica* into senatorial control but as transferring κυριήαν, a far more generic term for ownership rights.

This interest in *leges et iura* only becomes more pronounced if we understand the phrase to refer to law in its everyday, rather than constitutional, sense. Mantovani has shown that the LEGES ET IVRA of the *aureus* is a specific locution that refers almost exclusively to positive legal conventions, and is not how Romans would describe the broader political commitments encompassed by something like the language of the *RGDA*.[55] Cicero, for example, describes *leges et iura* as proper objects of juristic study (*de or.* 1.253), Horace contrasts them with *senatusconsulta* in enumerating genres of legal text (*ep.* 1.16.42–43), and Juvenal's Laronia uses the term as a generic: "oh, the laws are under threat? Maybe you should start with the *Scantinia*" (2.43–44: *si uexantur leges ac iura, citari | ante omnis debet Scantinia*).[56] Mantovani uses these findings to argue against understanding the *aureus* as part of the broader constitutional discourse of 28 BCE. In that analysis Augustus restored neither rights nor republic to the Roman people, but merely the long-standing conventions of legal order.[57]

I agree with Mantovani that the restoration of 28 BCE would primarily implicate positive law, but I do not assume that audiences would have seen the "norme giuridiche" of which Mantovani speaks as compatible with all visions of Augustan sovereignty. To claim that *leges et iura* are enforceable is to imply, or to construct, a predictability and impersonality that earlier periods of one-man rule had failed to provide – either law decides who owns Ignotus' Hypothetical Villa, or a person does.[58] Thus back to *Sat.* 2.1; when Horace uses Augustus to shut Testa

55 Mantovani ("Principe e diritto," pp. 53–56) collects some forty-five examples of the phrase.

56 The *lex Scantinia*, while not well attested, appears to be a law forbidding certain kinds of sexual relationships between free Roman men and boys; Laronia accuses her targets of hypocrisy and sexual impropriety. See Williams, *Roman Homosexuality*, pp. 121–24.

57 Mantovani, "Principe e diritto," p. 65 ("*leges restituere* ... non significa affatto che si ridanno 'poteri' e nemmeno che si attua il ripristino delle funzioni tradizionali degli organi di governo 'repubblicani': indica invece il ristabilimento delle norme giuridiche, dopo un periodo di anarchia.").

58 The impersonality and generality that Octavian abrogated are sometimes thought of as necessary for the rule of law; see Fuller, *Morality*, pp. 38–39. I am personally somewhat more sympathetic to Shapiro's legal positivism than I am to Fuller's insistence on law as a moral system, but even Shapiro takes these qualities as inherent to a coherent system of social ordering through law. See Shapiro, *Legality*, pp. 392–400.

up, he acknowledges that the times in which he lives are lawless and inherently so. The idea that *leges et iura* could exist under an autocracy – and in fact, could derive their validity from that autocracy – was novel. The concept seems uncontroversial to modern readers of Roman law, given the conditions under which the sources of Roman law were written, but it would hardly have been obvious in 28 BCE. At that time, Augustus restoring *leges et iura* might have seemed rather different, and rather more like the grand and hollow promise Tacitus and Dio record.

Accordingly, Augustus' edict should lead us to question the division between private rights and public law. That division has its roots in juristic science, and Ulpian (who wrote in the early third century CE, two centuries after Augustus' death)[59] theorizes it explicitly at D.1.1.1.2 (Institutiones):

There are two components of this pursuit [legal study]: *the public and the private. Public law is that which considers the structure of the Roman state, private the interests of individuals: for there are some public goods and some private. Public law addresses cult, priests, and magistracies. Private law comes from the precepts of nature, from those of the nations, and from the civil law.*

Huius studii duae sunt positiones, publicum et priuatum. Publicum ius est quod ad statum rei romanae spectat, priuatum quod ad singulorum utilitatem: sunt enim quaedam publice utilia, quaedam priuatim. publicum ius in sacris, in sacerdotibus, in magistratibus constitit. Priuatum ius tripertitum est: collectum etenim est ex naturalibus praeceptis aut gentium aut ciuilibus.

That said, Ulpian's hard boundary between public and private is somewhat theoretical.[60] As a practical matter, individual rights rely on features of a state that we would now call constitutional or public. When jurists like Ulpian described an autonomous private law they were constructing a world in which private law could be autonomous, or imagining a state that might permit *leges et iura* to exercise supreme authority. This imaginative process is common in Roman legal texts, and makes them into something more daring than they first appear. Describing *ius priuatum* as separate and apart from the conditions of imperial sovereignty entails constructing a particular kind of imperial

[59] Ulpian is discussed in greater detail *infra* p. 192. [60] See Frier, *Rise*, pp. 283–87.

sovereignty without saying so out loud. Attending to this construction reveals new archives of political thought, even as it complicates our archive of Roman law.

Augustus here becomes similarly daring. By restoring private legal entitlements, Augustus could seem to restore the public-law conditions upon which those private legal entitlements had relied. This restoration was discretionary, because of the realities of Augustan power, but it gave his interlocutors language to describe a world in which it were not. The *aureus* praised Augustus for doing something he could not do, in terms that would only later become standard for describing imperial legal/political order. In retrospect it seems clear enough how Augustus could have restored the rule of law, because so much of our understanding of Rome's rule of law comes from sources that imagined it as the kind of thing an emperor might restore. But that idea was still being worked out.

* * * * *

Understanding this conceptual framework – which I call "Augustan legality" – as a new one explains many puzzling features of the *aureus*. The coin is verbose because it has to be; the ideas with which it played had not yet acquired iconography or vocabulary. That same logic explains its ambiguous reverse. Much ink has been spilled trying to gloss the exact meaning of Augustus' pose: Is he reading the laws *populi Romani* off a scroll to an unseen audience, or is he physically restoring the law – commonly understood as embodied by written text[61] – to the offstage *populo Romano*? To be blunt, I do not see this as a particularly important question. There is no reason to assume that the coin's original audience all understood its iconography in exactly the same way, or that they had to. Instead, we are better off thinking about unusual images in terms of core and peripheral meanings. Questions of what action Augustus intended to take with the scroll in his hand, or of the grammatical case of *P R*, are peripheral – by this I mean that whoever struck the *aureus* could tolerate a fairly high level of ambiguity about these points among even sophisticated viewers. One meaning or another might be

[61] See Meyer, *Legitimacy and Law*, p. 21 (on the "special relationship" between written documents and legal order).

intended, but far less effort was spent on clarifying these relationships than on other, more central, points. The "core meaning" of the reverse is expressed in its unabbreviated text (Augustus brought the law back) and in its juxtaposing of Augustus with other widely attested symbols like the magistrate's chair in which he sits[62] and the scroll he holds.

So, then, the *aureus* takes care to show Augustus as engaged with the written law, in the pose and with the *accoutrements* typical of a Roman magistrate. This is hardly strange, since Augustus was a magistrate; the coin was minted during his sixth consulship. But the pose is less associated with consuls than with praetors, the slightly lower-ranking officials who frequently heard disputes under Roman formulary procedure.[63] It would be a stretch to say that the coin calls Augustus a praetor – he wasn't, and it doesn't – but he is clearly presented as someone who might do the work of a praetor and hear complaints from aggrieved parties. We know very well that this is something Augustus did. The *laudatio Turiae*, for example, praises the deceased for intervening before Augustus on behalf of her husband.[64] But later traditions represent Augustus as straightforwardly adjudicating disputes, stripping other officials of an enormous jurisdiction. The next section of this chapter considers how that might have come to pass, and how the distinction between law and justice that Horace played with set the stage for broader reconceptualizations of Rome and its law.

Lampreys and the Higher Law

Suetonius' biography of Augustus, written in the early second century CE, paints him as a merciful – and busy – judge. In Suetonius' telling Augustus is constantly hearing cases, which he constantly tweaks in order to arrive at the fairest outcome.

He heard cases often and sometimes at night, with a litter taking the place of a tribunal if he was feeling weak or even in some cases resting at home. He gave law with care but also the greatest leniency, for example: it is said that if he

[62] Rich and Williams, "Leges et Iura," p. 176; Schäfer, *Imperii insignia*.

[63] See Zehnacker, "Remarques," p. 2. On the role of the *praetor* Kaser and Hackl, *Zivilprozessrecht*, pp. 172–75.

[64] See *LT* 11–18; Osgood, *Turia*, p. 55.

tried a defendant who was obviously guilty of parricide, lest that man be sewn up in the sack (a punishment not imposed upon parricides unless they confessed) he would ask them "surely you did not kill your father?" Furthermore, when all the signatories of a document were being held on account of false witness under the lex Cornelia, he gave to the jurymen not only the two tablets for "guilty" and "not guilty" but also a third urging that he pardon those whom the juryman felt had been induced to sign by fraud or error.

(*Aug.* 33) Ipse ius dixit assidue et in noctem nonnumquam, si parum corpore ualeret lectica pro tribunali collocata, uel etiam domi cubans. Dixit autem ius non diligentia modo summa sed et lenitate, siquidem manifesti parricidii reum, ne culleo insueretur, quod non nisi confessi adficiuntur hac poena, ita fertur interrogasse: "Certe patrem tuum non occidisti?" Et cum de falso testamento ageretur omnesque signatores lege Cornelia tenerentur, non tantum duas tabellas, damnatoriam et absolutoriam, simul cognoscentibus dedit, sed tertiam quoque, qua ignosceretur iis, quos fraude ad signandum uel errore inductos constitisset.

This account is not a fabrication, exactly, but it is a palimpsest. Suetonius describes events that probably happened (Augustus hearing cases, asking questions, engaging with some body of specified and empowered fact-finders or *cognoscentibus*) in the language of a juridical framework that would only become regularized later on.[65] The transition from a strongman who makes decisions to an emperor who delivers verdicts is a complicated one, and I do not aim to chart it exhaustively here. But Suetonius lived at a later point in that transition than did Augustus, and he describes Augustan adjudication through the lens of his own experience of what emperors were and did.

It is notable, however, that Suetonius cannot bring himself to describe Augustan lawmaking as a "regular" process. Instead, his justice is tempered by mercy, *diligentia* by *lenitas*, and the specific examples Suetonius gives demonstrate the latter. The stories that were passed down about Augustus as judge consistently highlight his willingness to tinker with rules to produce a fair outcome, in cases where rules and fairness were in manifest tension.

[65] See Tuori, *The Emperor of Law*, p. 89 ("Apart from these contemporary or near-contemporary accounts, most of the information on Augustus' jurisdiction comes from Suetonius and Dio, both of whom present an image of Augustus as a hard-working judge. A challenge is to evaluate whether they are depicting Augustus along the lines of the emperors of their own era, one of whose major tasks was jurisdiction.").

This tension comes up more often than it should. Most legal disputes are boring, after all, and even factoring in the greater survivability of "interesting" cases there are more ways than this for a case to be interesting. But a remarkable number of surviving stories depict Augustus as discarding legal prescription – often a legal prescription that vests decisionmaking power in traditional structures like the *familia* – in favor of superseding ethical commitments. In this section, I argue that the second part of the Suetonius passage above made the first part possible. The story of imperial jurisdiction was passed down as a history of mercy and fairness, of ethical norms overriding the impersonal strictures of the law.[66] Our own stories about Augustus and the law – particularly the legend of Vedius Pollio and his house of horrors, which I here discuss – highlight those exceptionalities. Pollio, with his man-eating lampreys, brings us from Horace's dream of mercy to the imperial courts that Suetonius and his readers knew as routine.

Specifically, sources describe Vedius Pollio as a vicious equestrian (i.e. a wealthy non-senator) who fed his slaves to specially trained lampreys before Augustus stepped in to stop him. Seneca's treatise *On Anger* (*de ira*) tells its reader that a person of truly great stature can calm the rage of his inferiors (or at least force them to pretend he has),[67]

As did the deified Augustus, when he dined at the house of Vedius Pollio. One of Vedius' enslaved boys had broken a crystal cup; Vedius ordered him to be seized and put to death in an unusual fashion. Vedius ordered that the boy be thrown to the enormous lampreys that he kept in a pool. Who would not think that Vedius acted this way on account of decadence? It was savagery.

The boy got free of Vedius' hands and flung himself at Augustus' feet, asking only that he be killed in another fashion and not become chum. Augustus Caesar was moved by the novelty of the torture and ordered that the boy be set free, that all of Vedius' glassware be broken while he watched, and that the lampreys' pond be filled in.

Thus did Augustus Caesar chastise his friend, making good use of his authority: "You order that human beings be snatched up from your dinner party and put to death in unheard-of ways? If your cup is broken, will men's guts be shattered too? You enjoy this so much, that you would order it in front of Augustus Caesar?"

[66] See Peachin, "Jurists and the Law," p. 118.

[67] Sen. *de ira* 3.40.2 (*nisi forte tanta persona eris, ut possis iram comminuere*).

(3.40.2–4) quemadmodum fecit diuus Augustus, cum cenaret apud Vedium Pollionem. Fregerat unus ex seruis eius crustallinum; rapi eum Uedius iussit ne uulgari quidem more periturum; murenis obici iubebatur, quas ingentis in piscina continebat. Quis non hoc illum putaret luxuriae causa facere? Saeuitia erat.

Euasit e manibus puer et confugit ad Caesaris pedes nihil aliud petiturus, quam ut aliter periret, ne esca fieret. Motus est nouitate crudelitatis Caesar et illum quidem mitti, crustallina autem omnia coram se frangi iussit complerique piscinam.

Fuit Caesari sic castigandus amicus; bene usus est uiribus suis: "E conuiuio rapi homines imperas et noui generis poenis lancinari? Si calix tuus fractus est, uiscera hominis distrahentur? Tantum tibi placebis, ut ibi aliquem duci iubeas, ubi Caesar est?"

Other authors support Seneca's account. Pliny the Elder uses the story of Pollio and his lampreys to illustrate the latter's feeding habits,[68] Tacitus mentions gossip about *Vedii Pollionis luxus*,[69] Tertullian uses Pollio as an archetype of pagan vice,[70] and Dio states explicitly that Pollio's cruelty had "entered into history" (ὥστε καὶ ἐς ἱστορίας λόγον ἐσελθεῖν) while adding the detail at 54.23 that Augustus later razed Pollio's house against the directions of his will. Ovid's *Fasti* supports Dio's claim and makes explicit what Augustus hoped to accomplish by this ostentatious destruction. Ovid explains how Augustus not only destroyed Pollio's house, but pointedly replaced it with a public gathering space – the Portico of Livia, which was famous enough to appear in later accounts of the beauty of Rome[71] and which contained a shrine to the Augustan virtue of *Concordia* (Concord).[72] In Ovid's telling, Augustus used Pollio as a tool of moral instruction.

> [Pollio's house] *was leveled to the ground, not for treason against the kingdom*
> *but because it seemed to harm Rome with its luxury.*
> *Caesar willingly destroyed such heights of construction*

[68] *NH* 9.77. [69] *Ann.* 1.10.5; see Syme, "Who Was Vedius Pollio?," p. 29.

[70] *De pall.* 5.6.2; Tertullian claims that Pollio would then consume the fish in order to indulge in a kind of paracannibalism, which is also suggested in Seneca's other treatment of Pollio at *Clem.* 1.18.2. Hunink (*Tertullian: De Pallio*, 274) suggests that Tertullian may have found this narrative especially useful in countering stereotyped accounts of Christian cannibalism.

[71] *E.g.* Plin. *NH* 14.11; Str. 5.3.8.

[72] On this deliberate rededication, see Newlands, *Playing with Time*, pp. 46–47; Flory, "Sic Exempla Parantur," p. 328. The Portico and accompanying shrine are discussed in greater detail – including a site map – at Carandini (ed.), *Atlas*, pp. 312–13.

and lost so much of his own inheritance;
thus is the censure performed and thus and are exempla *furnished,*
when the judge himself does what he encourages in others.

(*Fasti* 6.643–48) haec aequata solo est, nullo sub crimine regni,
sed quia luxuria uisa nocere sua.
sustinuit tantas operum subuertere moles (645)
totque suas heres perdere Caesar opes.
sic agitur censura et sic exempla parantur,
cum iudex, alios quod monet, ipse facit.

Note in particular Ovid's suggestion that the Portico, and the demolishment that made it possible, might serve as *exempla* to the Roman people. An *exemplum* is not quite an example, but is instead a kind of morally charged folktale that preserves the deeds of extraordinary Romans for later generations to consult in their own ethical reasoning.[73] Ovid, then, seems to contradict Dio's assertion that Augustus stripped Pollio of any monument (μνημόσυνον) in the city. Instead, he suggests that the story of Pollio would persist in the Roman imagination as part of the lore of the Portico itself. And of course, we know that story survived for centuries because we have it; Pollio appears in writers from Seneca to Adam Smith, out of all proportion to his accomplishments.[74] Even the literal erasure of Pollio's name (since he was not mentioned anywhere on the Portico) is a textual lacuna that comments upon, rather than hides, the memory of the non-honorand.[75] By stripping Pollio of his intended commemorative structures Augustus created new ones, and replaced the house of Pollio with a highly salient public monument that kept a version of his memory alive.[76] The tale of

[73] Langlands, *Exemplary Ethics*, pp. 29–36; Roller, "Exemplarity," pp. 3–4; Chaplin, *Livy's Exemplary History*, pp. 11–29.

[74] Dio describes him at 54.23.1 as "a man who had produced nothing worth remembering" (οὐδὲν μνήμης ἄξιον παρασχόμενος). Syme ("Who Was Vedius Pollio?") attempts to reconstruct Pollio's career on the basis of inscriptions found in Asia, and demonstrates that he was a "financial expert" (p. 29) but nevertheless one of many courtiers *cum* civil servants working at the time. On the afterlife of the Pollio story, see Africa, "Anecdotes."

[75] Newlands, "Contesting," pp. 227–29; Flory, "Sic Exempla Parantur," p. 328. This ostentatious refusal to remember has long roots in Roman commemorative practice; I discuss the idea in more detail in Chapter 4, but for Republican antecedents to Pollio's memory sanction see Flower, *The Art of Forgetting*, pp. 67–111.

[76] See Roller, "Demolished Houses," p. 164 ("[T]he trace of the demolished house and its owner clings like a contagion to all subsequent symbols connected with the site."); Milnor, *Domesticity*, pp. 61–62.

Pollio and his lampreys takes place entirely in a private house and would not have been difficult to suppress, but instead a fairly standardized account survives that flatters Augustus and is linked with an Augustan monument in the center of the city. We should assume, then, that that account was condoned (if not circulated) by organs of the nascent imperial state.

Why, though? What work did this particular story do? The Pollio narrative touches on thorny questions within imperial society, and helped its audience sort through their own relationship to power in their houses, their cities, and their state. At its most basic level, it is a fable about how to treat the people one has enslaved. Imperial Rome was a brutal slave society,[77] but Seneca suggests that making a human being into *esca* (bait) was a step too far.[78]

Stories like this are hardly unheard of in slave cultures, and one useful comparison might be the folklore that sprung upon around Delphine LaLaurie in America's antebellum South. Delphine LaLaurie was a wealthy white woman and enslaver in New Orleans, Louisiana. An 1834 house fire exposed that LaLaurie had been violently abusing and torturing her enslaved house staff, and a mob of New Orleans residents destroyed the house soon after. LaLaurie herself fled the country, but stories about her sadism and her slaves' suffering became a mainstay in American discourse about slavery. Abolitionists used the horrors of LaLaurie to demonstrate the evil of enslaving human beings, but advocates of enslavement still found her useful as a foil. By marking boundaries of acceptable discipline that existed entirely within elite discourse, these accounts could help

[77] See, for example, Coleman, "Fatal Charades." On the term "slave society," see Lenski and Cameron, *What Is a Slave Society?*; it is a vague and difficult criterion to employ, but I here use it to indicate, simply, a society in which enslaved labor was widespread and in which ideas of personhood had come to accommodate the practice.

[78] Cf. Mart. 4.56.6. While Seneca was famously horrified by other forms of execution (see *ep.* 7.3–5), the repeated use of *nouus* and *nouitate* suggest that Pollio's methods were worse and in some way unique. The exact nature of the violation, however, is not obvious. The answer may lie in the particular indignity of being eaten by a group of animals that are individually weaker than the victim; that indignity would be well captured by *esca*. Similarly, the relative privacy of the death – since most *damnationes ad bestias* occurred in spectacular contexts – may have rendered it unusual. Other logics are more universal. Being fed on by *murenae* would be slower than being devoured by lions and offer fewer opportunities for self-defense, and *murenae* look particularly alien and creepy.

enslavers understand themselves as decent and humane without having to reckon with the desires or preferences of their enslaved.[79]

Madame LaLaurie was punished for her transgression by informal community justice, however. Pollio faced the wrath of Augustus, who is depicted as enforcing community norms,[80] and at least in *de ira* that enforcement is remarkably formalized. Seneca's Augustus accuses Pollio of usurping certain kinds of decisional privilege that would come to be associated with the emperor himself, most obviously with *imperas* but also the phrase *tibi placebis*. Augustus ends the speech by explicitly accusing Pollio of making decisions when (or where) he should not be the decider: *ibi iubeas ... ubi Caesar est?* Pollio is thus guilty of both monstrosity and a kind of treason (a crime punishable, notably, by razing the offender's home).[81] Augustus and Seneca make clear that Pollio's decision was the wrong one, but also that it was *not his to make*. Pollio acts like an emperor, and a bad one. While Seneca uses the Pollio story to illustrate the relationship between emotion and power – and thus pays special attention to power and its gradations – the Pollio story frequently comes up in accounts of Augustan majesty. Dio mentions Augustus punishing him as only an emperor could, after all, and Tacitus includes his cruelty in a long list of Augustan follies occasioned by the emperor's funeral. The story of Pollio implicated Augustan authority, and in particular Augustus' authority to make decisions about how other people dealt with their enslaved property.

Pollio's fishpond thus became a site of jurisdictional conflict. The story illustrates not only how enslaved people ought to be punished but also who ought to determine how enslaved people ought to be punished: Does Pollio have jurisdiction over his own enslaved, or does Augustus have jurisdiction over enslavement more generally? The story is potent, however, because it casts Augustan action in two wildly different lights depending on which part the reader emphasizes. If we read the Pollio narrative as about slavery and cruelty, then Augustus upholds traditional ideas about how people should be treated against Pollio's perverse novelty. If the story is one about disciplinary authority, however, Augustus is the innovator. There is no Republican precedent for an intervention like that described, since Pollio's *potestas* over

79 See Brundage, "Shadow." 80 See Africa, "Anecdotes," p. 72.

81 Newlands, "Contesting," p. 233.

enslaved members of his household was not historically bounded by principles like those Augustus invokes against him here; the same *leges et iura* that Augustus had restored granted Pollio the power that Augustus here revokes.[82] These *leges et iura* changed over the course of the imperial period, and by the time Seneca wrote *On Benefits* (*de beneficiis*) a magistrate had been appointed to hear complaints by enslaved laborers against their owners (3.22.3). But Pollio's household management was not a matter with which a sovereign might usually be expected to concern itself. The nightmare of the lamprey makes Augustus' intrusion more palatable, and more traditional. The Pollio story plays different levels of normative ordering against each other, allowing its listener to recast circumscribing traditional property rights as vindicating traditional human decency.

* * * * *

Pollio's lampreys also reveal something important about how jurisdiction can change, or be changed. As Cover notes, the functioning of law in a society is inseparable from that society's broader sense of self: from the 'narratives' its inhabitants turn to in order to make their needs legible to each other.[83] Tuori has fruitfully applied this frame to questions of imperial jurisdiction, and tracked the slow triumph of the imperial judge through later literary accounts of emperors solving problems.[84] The story above demonstrates how Tuori's history might have worked in practice, and how it might have worked at the time. When Horace wrote about Augustus suspending law in the service of higher values, he played with a trope that would recur. A decree – likely widely circulated – described Augustus choosing to bound his actions through law when it suited him. A story was told at and by the Portico of Livia about Augustus

[82] See Lewis, "Slavery, Family, and Status," p. 152; Bradley, "Roman Slavery and Roman Law," pp. 491–92. In fact, Cassius Dio would later describe punishment as the distinct prerogative of the *dominus*: In Dio's account of the conspiracy of Cinna Magnus, Livia urges her husband Augustus to pardon Cinna while retaining the power to punish in other contexts, "as with slaves" (καθάπερ καὶ ἐπὶ τῶν δούλων). See Dio Cass. 55.18.2; Adler, "Conspiracy."

[83] Cover refers to these kinds of communities as *nomoi*, and sees them as united by commitments that function both as shared beliefs about the community and as more precisely defined rules members are expected to observe. Cover, "Nomos," pp. 12–18.

[84] Tuori, *The Emperor of Law*, pp. 2–3: ("[T]he emergence of imperial jurisdiction may be best observed through the manner in which it was discussed instead of through laws or legal practice").

infringing on another man's property rights out of deference to ethical traditions. These narratives did not come from nowhere, and as elite Romans used them to talk about their lives they built a web of symbolic and affective relationships that would inform centuries of imperial political discourse.[85] Hindsight presents an idea, iteratively refined over time, of the emperor as a guardian of broader ethical ideals against the vicissitudes of archaic law.[86]

Sex and the Imperial Subject

Of course, Augustus' best-known legal innovation took a more traditional legislative form. From 18 to 17 BCE Augustus passed laws[87] that sharply limited the marital and sexual choices available to Roman elites.[88] The broad strokes of the resulting regime are easy enough to reconstruct, even if its precise contours are not. Augustus required elite Roman men to marry and have children, with an elaborate set of punishments and rewards incentivizing stable and monogamous (for women, at least) sexual arrangements.[89] The punishments for adultery,

85 See Pandey, *Poetics of Power*, p. 10.

86 Morrell ("Magpie," p. 13) makes a similar claim in the specific context of Augustan legislative work.

87 Presumably under his tribunician power; Cooley, *Res Gestae Diui Augusti*, p. 143.

88 These restrictions were different for different subgroups within that elite, in ways that were likely explicit in the *lex* itself: Paul quotes it when stating that it only prohibited senators and their patrilineal descendants from marrying freed people. See D.23.2.44pr. (ad Legem Iuliam et Papiam); while Paul writes later, he would have had access to the statutory text as he did so. On the other hand, we know that Augustan marriage legislation was heavily contested in its own time, and that Augustus altered the law in response; further, equestrians were particularly vocal in their discontent (Dio Cass. 56.1.2; Suet. *Aug.* 34; Eck, "At Magnus Caesar, and Yet!," pp. 90–91; Evans-Grubbs, "Singles," pp. 111–20). So it is conceivable that Paul's senatorial restriction was adopted in response to equestrian pressure. Dio's claim (55.16.2) that Augustus "permitted those who wished, barring senators, to marry freed women" (ἐπέτρεψε καὶ ἐξελευθέρας τοῖς ἐθέλουσι, πλὴν τῶν βουλευόντων, ἄγεσθαι) suggests otherwise, but given the ahistoricity of Dio's statement (were they forbidden before?) I hesitate to take him as an authority on this particular question.

89 The earliest explicit reference to Augustus' marriage laws is a vague one; Horace's *carmen saeculare* refers to a "marital law that generates new life" (*prolisque novae feraci* | *lege marita*) (19–20). Ovid portrays Augustan restrictions on sexuality as extreme and coercive, but does so in metaphor, for example by describing Orpheus as a fool who insists on regulating sex and is killed for his efforts. See *Met.* 11.1–19; Ziogas, *Law and Love*, pp. 303–45; "Orpheus." For a reconstruction of the effects of the Augustan marriage legislation see Spagnuolo Vigorita, *Casta domus*, pp. 33–37.

in particular, were severe. Later commentators suggest that while only women caught in the act could be killed, those prosecuted afterwards faced property loss and relegation (a kind of exile).[90]

It is obvious enough that these laws about sex and marriage served a political purpose. The Augustan marriage legislation was meant as a representational tool, telling stories about Augustus' restorative project and moral reasoning that were all the more legible because they did so much work to change the world. When an emperor issued a statement emphasizing his commitment to family, or when that commitment was honored on a coin or a statue, it was easy enough to ignore. When that emperor cited his commitment as a reason for major legal overhauls, though, those overhauls proved its sincerity while increasing its salience.

Contemporary parallels illustrate the dynamic. For example, Milnor has compared the Augustan marriage legislation to the American Defense of Marriage Act (DOMA), which forbade states from recognizing same-sex marriages at a time when no state actually did so.[91] I find the parallel enlightening, but it merits some explanation. DOMA was signed into law in 1996, as part of a broader social panic around the looming threat of same-sex marriage, and stands as an absurd example of counterproductive sexual regulation. Like DOMA, the Augustan marriage legislation extended governmental power to an area previously outside its control;[92] like DOMA, it responded to a threat that only existed in the discursive "landscape" of the law itself;[93] and like DOMA, its commands and prohibitions were a tool to show that its promulgator meant business. Unlike DOMA, though, the *leges Iuliae* had immediate legal effects.[94] The

90 D.48.5.39.8 (Papinian, Quaestiones: quoting rescripts from Marcus, Commodus, and Pius). The passage of time is a concern, however, particularly given material in Justinian's *Institutes* that suggests prosecuted women were executed (4.18.4).

91 Milnor, "Landscape," pp. 7–8; on DOMA see George, *Family Matters*, p. 239.

92 Technically, DOMA usurped the authority of individual states (as opposed to the federal government) to regulate marriage, and only secondarily the authority of individuals to make their own marital arrangements. Both were substantial incursions, however, and the intricacies of late twentieth-century American federalism are beyond the scope of this book.

93 Milnor, "Landscape," pp. 22–23.

94 DOMA would become effectual. While the federal government has historically recognized all marriages solemnized by a state and assigned benefits accordingly, DOMA prevented same-sex couples married in states that permitted it from accessing

Augustan marriage legislation burdened a large swath of Rome's elite. Historiographic accounts of its passage describe both outcry and concrete changes in marital practice, neither of which we would expect from a symbolic dead letter or a law aimed at a powerless disfavored group.[95]

Here, the analogy breaks down. While DOMA purported to alter the world, it never did so for most people. While the law would come to burden same-sex couples and be struck down on that basis, supporters of DOMA were generally not in same-sex couples and thus experienced it purely as an expression of the government's ethical reasoning. While the law's impact on others remained important as proof that the government really *cared* about the sanctity of marriage, its primary role in the lives of most people – and particularly of its supporters – was as a communicative rather than binding force.

Augustus, however, bound. His laws intruded into private affairs at what appears to have been enormous social cost. Most historians have described the Augustan marriage legislation in terms of that intrusion, as a "sinister and cynical appropriation"[96] that cloaked greater supervision of elite households in the language of moral revival. I find this more than plausible, and my main argument in this chapter has been that Augustus' manipulations and abrogations of law were justified as instances of adherence to superseding normative orders. But the *leges Iuliae* are different, because Augustus confronted them as both enforcer and subject. Augustus publicly wrestled with many of the

those benefits. DOMA was finally struck down in a lawsuit filed by Edie Windsor, who faced tax penalties as a result of the federal government not recognizing her marriage to her late wife. *United States* v. *Windsor*, 570 U.S. 744 (2013). But no state recognized same-sex marriages at the time of DOMA's passage, meaning that the law did nothing until 2009 (when the legislature of the State of Vermont passed a marriage-equality statute).

95 Suetonius describes a "tumult of refusers" (*Aug.* 34: *tumultu recusantium*) objecting to the marriage laws, and a rash of betrothals between adult men and prepubescent girls intended to secure grooms the benefits of being engaged. Dio refers to public protest (54.16.3; τούτῳ καταβοήσεως) among senators. Tacitus states that the law had no practical effect but that the broad flouting of its provisions rendered elites vulnerable to purges: "the number of those in danger swelled" (*Ann.* 3.25: *multitudo periclitantium gliscebat*).

96 Milnor, *Domesticity*, p. 15; also Raditsa, "Legislation," p. 282. Galinsky (*Culture*, pp. 128–40) takes a far rosier view, suggesting that the law arose from sincere moral concern about the degradation of Rome's elite communities: in particular, about noble families disintegrating from loose marital and testamentary practice.

same quandaries his moral legislation imposed upon others, and some of the dark irony that scholars have noted in the misfortunes of the royal house (*domus Augusta*) may be better understood as its own form of potent – if costly, or because costly – representation.

Now, about that *domus*. As later historians describe it, Augustus' archaizing morals were not shared by his family. Multiple accounts claim that Augustus' daughter Julia was so flagrant in her adultery that Augustus himself was forced to condemn her before the Senate and, eventually, to deport her to an island. Our earliest version of events comes from Velleius Paterculus, who wrote under Augustus' successor Tiberius (r. 14–37 CE) and who provides the above narrative almost beat for beat.

A crisis, filthy to speak of and shameful to remember, erupted in the imperial house. For Augustus' daughter Julia, entirely heedless of her great father and husband [Tiberius] due to either decadence or lust, left nothing untried of those things which a shameful woman might either do or have done to her; the greatness of her fortune was measured out by her freedom in her crimes, claiming whatever she wished as if it were her right... Julia was exiled to an island and hidden from the eyes of her fatherland and parents, although her mother Scribonia voluntarily joined her as a comrade in exile.

(2.100.2–3, 5) foeda dictu memoriaque horrenda in ipsius domo tempestas erupit. Quippe filia eius Iulia, per omnia tanti parentis ac uiri immemor, nihil, quod facere aut pati turpiter posset femina, luxuria libidineue infectum reliquit magnitudinemque fortunae suae peccandi licentia metiebatur, quidquid liberet pro licito uindicans... Iulia relegata in insulam patriaeque et parentum subducta oculis, quam tamen comitata mater Scribonia uoluntaria exilii permansit comes.

As with the story of Pollio's lampreys above, versions of the Julia narrative survive in multiple sources and are remarkably consistent.[97] In this case, however, it is easy enough to see how a unified account might survive. Unlike Pollio, Julia's fate was determined in public and

[97] Fantham, *Julia Augusti*, pp. 138–46 collects all textual accounts of the fall of Julia. Some of these stories also reference a granddaughter of the same name. Suetonius, for example, claims that Augustus "relegated the Julias, both daughter and granddaughter, fouled by all manner of wickedness" (*Aug.* 65: *Iulias, filiam et neptem, omnibus probris contaminatas relegavit*), and Tacitus mentions Augustus having exiled his granddaughter to an island after condemning her for adultery (*Ann.* 4.71: *convictam adulterii*). However, the younger Julia appears less frequently in our sources, and we know very little about how her guilt was discovered or advertised.

was a matter of public record. While Paterculus omits this point nearly all later commentators refer to Augustus condemning Julia with some sort of written document: Seneca says he "publicized the shame of his household" (*flagitia principalis domus in publicum emisit*) (*Ben.* 6.32), Pliny the Elder cites "letters of that god" (*litterae illius dei*) that complain (*gemunt*) about Julia's affairs (*NH* 21.9), and Dio writes that "upon learning what Julia had done, Augustus became so angry that he could not keep the scandal at home, and instead informed the Senate" (55.14: τότε δ' οὖν μαθὼν τὰ πραττόμενα τοσούτῳ θυμῷ ἐχρήσατο ὥστε μηδ' οἴκοι αὐτὰ κατασχεῖν ἀλλὰ καὶ τῇ γερουσίᾳ κοινῶσαι). Suetonius goes into slightly more detail, claiming that Augustus "notified the Senate about his daughter by means of a letter read out in the Senate by a *quaestor* in his absence, and was so ashamed he withdrew from society for a long time, even considering having her killed" (*Aug.* 65: *de filia absens ac libello per quaestorem recitato notum senatui fecit abstinuitque congressu hominum diu prae pudore, etiam de necanda deliberauit*).

Like with Pollio, we here see private events rendered extremely public. The accounts above gloss over Augustus' reasons for announcing Julia's disgrace. Suetonius suggests that he was too distraught to proclaim it himself but takes as a given that a grieving father would naturally notify the Senate of his scandal. I do not. Without delving into Augustan psychology – a fool's errand – it should be easy enough to see that other options were available, and that Julia's fall is so well known because they were not chosen. Even Dio, who emphasizes the secret immorality of the *domus Augusta* in other settings, does so by highlighting instances where Augustus tried and failed to conceal that immorality.[98] Here, he announced it.

The exile of Julia is one of many well-attested stories about Augustan morals. But it also articulates a distinctive – and distinctly Roman – attitude towards legal order. As part of his moral legislation, Augustus had put forward the Julian Law on Restraining Adultery (*lex Iulia de adulteriis coercendis*) about fifteen years before Julia's condemnation. While our clearest source on the *lex* is the vastly later *Digest*,[99] D.48.5.1 excerpts an Ulpianic commentary (*de Adulteriis*)

98 See Langford, "Dowager Empresses," p. 437; Kemezis, "Paradigm."

99 Specifically, D.48.5.

that explicitly addresses the Augustan law.[100] So we can reasonably assume that the second- and third-century jurists whose writings make up D.48.5 were engaged with something they understood to be an Augustan document, and that document lays out a plan of action strikingly similar to that undertaken by Augustus. The *Digest* makes clear that, while the law permitted the killing of women caught committing adultery under certain circumstances,[101] its primary mechanism was a formal trial. Men who learned that their wives had been unfaithful were expected to publicly accuse them of adultery, with strict rules surrounding the timing of the accusation and strict penalties for men who dared to forgive their spouse.[102] But if a husband was unable or unwilling to expose his wife's infidelity, the law assumed that her father would step in.

D.48.5.4.1 makes clear that the *lex* privileged fathers as accusers over other interested parties.[103] While husbands were still expected to take the lead in a prosecution for adultery, the wife's father had an explicit role in the process that no other family member – including grandfathers, who are never mentioned as being able to step in as *patresfamilias* – or concerned citizen could usurp. Julia's husband, the future emperor Tiberius, was in Rhodes at the time and in no position to prosecute; the *lex Iulia* did not demand that Augustus publicly chastise his daughter, but designated that as a preferred course of action for a Roman legal subject. When Augustus wrote a letter denouncing his daughter's adultery and read it to the Senate (which retained the capacities of an adjudicative body), he was doing what a good Roman father was supposed to according to the rules he himself had laid out.[104] While Tacitus notes that Augustus went beyond the strict requirements of the law (*Ann.* 3.24: *suasque ipse*

100 The treatise *On Adultery* (*de Adulteriis*) states "this law was put forward by the deified Augustus" (*haec lex lata est a diuo Augusto*).

101 See, for example, D.48.5.23.4 (Papinian, de Adulteriis).

102 See Treggiari, *Roman Marriage*, pp. 277–90.

103 Specifically, it states that third parties are only allowed to accuse a woman of adultery after her husband and father have failed to act: "the power to accuse is granted to others after the husband and father; for after sixty days are made available to the husband and father, four actionable months are given to others" (Ulpian, Disputationes: *Extraneis autem, qui accusare possunt, accusandi facultas post maritum et patrem conceditur: nam post sexaginta dies quattuor menses extraneis dantur et ipsi utiles*). See Evans-Grubbs, "Singles," pp. 109–10.

104 On senatorial adjudication Talbert, *Senate*, pp. 460–80.

leges egrediebatur) he acknowledges that Augustus acted in such a way as to recall the law, using the tools made available by it and subjecting his family to the same panoptic scrutiny that surveilled other elite Roman households.[105]

In doing so, Augustus followed an extant script. Later historians saw Augustus' condemnation of Julia as an ironic marker of his legislation's failure,[106] but Romans told all kinds of stories about fathers who condemned children for violating generally applicable rules, and those stories suggest a different reading of Augustus' actions. Probably the most famous example is recorded in Livy 7.8, where the consul Titus Manlius orders his son to be executed for violating battlefield orders and engaging in single combat. Livy describes the filicide as a disturbing (20: *tam atroci imperio*), testament to the grim severity of early Rome (25–26: *exempli ... tristis*). But it does not demonstrate Manlius *père*'s inability to control his family, and in fact says quite the opposite. The consul understands that his son's disobedience forces him to choose between family and state, lamenting that he "must either forget the *res publica*'s interests or [his] own" (16–17: *aut rei publicae mihi aut mei obliuiscendum sit*) before choosing the republic and killing his son.

Langlands has argued, and I agree, that these stories are not altogether positive.[107] There is danger in reading exemplary history as facile moral instruction, and it is not clear whether Titus Manlius' actions reflect extraordinary piety or dangerous fanaticism. But they are not those of a hypocrite, and they are not unique. Romans in this period were exposed to a number of accounts of historical figures punishing their own children for endangering their community.[108] The

105 On the discursive linkage between Rome and the *domus Augusta* see Dettenhofer, *Herrschaft und Widerstand*, pp. 172–80.

106 For example, Cassius Dio takes the incident as proof that "men in control know everyone else's affairs better than their own" (55.13: οἱ γάρ τοι τὰς ἡγεμονίας ἔχοντες πάντα μᾶλλον ἢ τὰ σφέτερα γιγνώσκουσι). See also Edwards, *Immorality*, p. 61 ("[Julia's] licentious behaviour flagrantly undermined [Augustus'] attempts to reform Roman morals.").

107 Langlands, *Exemplary Ethics*, pp. 112–18.

108 Harris, "A Roman Father's Power" provides an exhaustive list of Roman stories about fathers killing sons. Particularly salient here are Lucius Brutus putting his sons to death for conspiring to bring back the Tarquins (p. 82; see e.g. Plut. *Pub.* 6), the dictator Postumius Tubertus punishing his sons for desertion (*ibid.*; Diod. Sic. 12.764.3, Liv. 4.29.5), and the Torquatus story above. On the role of the father's

resonance of this trope is easy enough to understand, and it shows up in other folkloric traditions as well; one thinks of the binding of Isaac.[109] Stories about parents sacrificing their own children for the benefit of a higher power – like a god or a state – concretize a set of anxieties around communal identity. They force their protagonists to choose between two important affiliations, they offer space to think through the demands of suprafamilial identity, and they acknowledge the conflict between familiality and citizenship. The father-as-magistrate, in particular, holds two simultaneous social positions, which impose different but absolute duties of loyalty. He must act either as a general, or as a patriarch.[110]

Remarkably, Augustus is neither. The stories I mention above center fathers making their own, difficult, decisions. Augustus had that agency, in the practical sense that he could have easily hidden or put up with Julia's affairs, but he is not presented in later accounts as *choosing* to turn her in. Instead, Augustus is described as doing the expected thing. Even Tacitus only ascribes to Augustus the narrow choice to exceed legal baselines (and given that the *lex Iulia* authorized the killing of adulterous wives, Tacitus could fairly be questioned here). Instead, Augustus more closely resembles the "talking law" that Cicero claimed magistrates should aspire to be and that I discussed in my Introduction. Augustus applied the law to his own family and – inasmuch as it surveilled Roman husbands and fathers – to himself, making a public and much-discussed scene out of doing what it asked. In reading the fall of Julia as evidence for the failure of the *leges Iuliae*, Cassius Dio appreciates that they could not tame human nature.[111] But if we take the more cynical view, that the *leges Iuliae* were meant to bring family units into a closer relationship

magistracy in explaining the necessity of filicide, *ibid.*, p. 90. Shaw ("Raising and Killing Children," pp. 56–77) raises an important cautionary note, and suggests that these stories do not reflect any kind of retrievable social fact; nevertheless, the recurrence of the trope suggests that the question of how a father should treat disloyal or treasonous children was meaningful to Roman audiences.

109 An episode in the Book of Genesis where God orders Abraham to sacrifice his son: *Genesis* 22:1–19.

110 See Thomas, "Vitae Necisque Potestas," pp. 157–58.

111 See Cooley, *Res Gestae Diui Augusti*, p. 144 (taking Julia's fall as "particularly embarrassing" in light of the Augustan marriage legislation); Kemezis, "Paradigm," pp. 278–81 (reading Dio as arguing that the *leges Iuliae* were unable to remake the aristocracy as Augustus wished them to, even if later demographic shifts and the rise of provincial elites like himself would accomplish the same goal).

with the nascent imperial state, the Julia story illustrates not their impotence but their supremacy.

A father turning his daughter over to the Senate for condemnation under a generally applicable law is not a hypocrite for doing so. He is a citizen. The normative principles at stake with Julia are not so different than those animating the Manlius narrative, but the demands of the state are here far more specific and far more quotidian. Other famous filicides took place in circumstances marked by the abrogation of legal order, like battlefield discipline or civic unrest.[112] Augustus, however, worked through third parties according to a process much like the one for normal fathers of normal adulteresses.

That process was more normal because it was more legal. Tacitus draws the most explicit connection between Julia's adultery and the *lex Iulia de adulteriis*, but other accounts link Julia's behavior to Augustus' lawmaking[113] in ways that suggest that they, too, understood the latter to govern the former. Augustus publicly condemning Julia as fathers were expected to do, then, suggested that his laws governed *him*.[114]

They did not, of course. Augustus was not driven by fear of punishment, and merely chose to obey the law. But that obedience can mean something, even as performance. Augustus wrapped a piece of Roman cultural mythology in newer language of legal subjecthood. Family governance was a matter of state concern now, and Augustus allowed that concern to extend to his own family by acting as the law said he should. In doing so, Augustus started a trend. Later authors throughout the Principate would play with the trope of "the *princeps* who obeys the law," understanding imperial obedience to legal rules as a matter of ethics or respect.[115] An emperor who chooses to act like a legal subject does not abrogate his sovereignty in any meaningful sense, but he makes that sovereignty easier to ignore and suggests that the broader organizing principles of the law govern his actions.

112 For example, one widely circulated story described a senator killing his son for supporting the Catilinarian revolt. Harris, "A Roman Father's Power," p. 85; Dio Cass. 37.36; Sall. *Cat.* 39.5; Val. Max. 5.8.5.

113 E.g. Dio Cass. 55.12 (referring to Julia as misbehaving "even on the *Rostra*" (καὶ ἐπ' αὐτοῦ γε τοῦ Βήματος)).

114 Cf. Evans-Grubbs, "Singles," p. 109 ("Those men, whose own reputation was most affected by the sexual conduct of an adulteress, were supposed to channel their anger through the courts.").

115 Discussed further in Chapter 2, but see J. *Inst.* 2.17, Plin. *Pan.* 36.2–4, 65.1.

As for Julia, she drops out of the story here. While we hear about changes to the conditions of her confinement she would never return from her exile, even after death; Augustus' will cut her out of the family mausoleum.[116] But she did valuable work.

* * * * *

It would be nice if the examples I discussed in this chapter told a coherent story, but they seem – at first – to contradict each other. Viewed from some angles the Augustus of this chapter is a quasi-constitutional monarch, of the sort at which Augustan representation frequently aimed.[117] While this Augustus' observance of legal norms is more discretionary than his interlocutors might prefer, he rules a world where Roman law still governs most people most of the time. At other times Augustus appears as a transformational figure, upending a sclerotic political paradigm metonymized by law. From one perspective Augustus restores order, from another he smashes it. That polyvalence is the norm in Roman imperial history, since emperors meant different things to different people and were described accordingly.[118] The tension between accounts of the emperor as omnipotent sovereign and as custodian of a more institutional order – between "priest-king"[119] and paper-pusher – gives this book its title. But Augustus is unusual in how strongly his legal program hit these two dissonant notes.

That may arise from a broader tension in how Romans thought about absolute power. Straumann has noted the persistence of "emergency powers" in Republican political thought; Romans had a coherent and commonly told story of individuals being granted near-absolute authority at times of crisis,[120] and that particular account of emergency closely resembles Schmitt's state of exception.[121] As both Julius Caesar and Giorgio Agamben remind us, however, the state of exception is a dangerous place for a sovereign to occupy.[122] Rome's history of

116 Suet. *Aug.* 101.3; Bond, *Trade and Taboo*, pp. 2–3.

117 See, as examples out of a vast corpus, Levick, *Augustus: Image and Substance*; Wallace-Hadrill, "Civilis Princeps."

118 Christoforou, *Imagining*, pp. 4–5.

119 Lendon, "Legitimacy," p. 57.

120 Straumann, *Crisis and Constitutionalism*, pp. 63–117.

121 See Tuori, *The Emperor of Law*, pp. 69–73.

122 See Agamben, *Homo Sacer*, especially p. 120 (describing how a modern politics conducted in the state of exception "loses the intelligibility that still seems to us to characterize the juridicopolitical foundation of classical politics"). On the relationship

dictators was also a history of assassins, and any stable political order that Augustus could inaugurate would necessarily run on something other than an extraordinary man.

Usually, we imagine that other thing as law. After all, in Weber's typology of legitimate authority the most "modern form of administration" (*modernen Form der Verwaltung*) is the rational, which is so intimately tied up with law that Weber uses *rationale* and *legale Herrschaft* interchangeably.[123] But if there is any throughline to Augustan legality at all, it is not the supremacy of law but the supremacy of ethics. Augustus follows the law (on the *aureus*, in the edict commemorated by the *aureus*, or in condemning his daughter) because following the law is the right thing to do, and when it is not (with Pollio or Horace) he does something different. The story that survives is one in which law is a potent symbol – of old ways of doing things, of political equality, of regular order – that Augustus uses as he talks through other problems.

This hierarchy is perhaps most obvious in Augustus' own account of his lawmaking. In his autobiography Augustus claims to have used legislation as a tool for improving public morality:

With laws passed on my authority I restored many exempla of our elders that were falling out of fashion, and myself handed down exempla of many things for imitation by our descendants

(*RGDA* 8) Legibus nouis me auctore latis multa exempla maiorum exolescentia iam ex nostro saeculo reduxi et ipse multarum rerum exempla imitanda posteris tradidi

The story Augustus tells is primarily one of moral instruction, with law serving as a tool – literally, an instrumental ablative – to accomplish his broader goals. While the procedural realities of Augustan lawmaking are left vague (*me auctore*), it is not clear whether they were hidden or just unimportant, since Augustus is speaking in a different register.[124] Instead of law, Augustus emphasizes an epochal progression of which he is only one (important) part. In Weberian typology, the story told

between Agamben's and Schmitt's account of the exception and its relationship to legal order, see Dyzenhaus, *The Constitution of Law*, pp. 38–40.

[123] Weber, *Wirtschaft und Gesellschaft*, pp. 124–25.

[124] Cooley, *Res Gestae Diui Augusti*, pp. 143–44 takes this passage as referring specifically to the Augustan revival of the *census*.

here is one of tradition as much as charisma. Augustus subsumes himself within broader transtemporal ethical frameworks even as he stands apart from and above his contemporaries. Those frameworks included the political institutions with which Augustus claimed to work, but also the broader social notions of right and wrong to which Augustus presented himself as subject. Law – a politically developed, institutionally mediated framework for separating right from wrong – was an especially powerful medium for these various performances.

The performance, though, remained the important thing. An easy trap when we examine legal changes that alter the world is to assume that they were designed to alter the world, or to evaluate their success and failure on the basis of that alteration. Laws do more than that. They are, as Milnor has put it, a "medium of representation" that political actors use to position themselves within the symbolic systems of their world.[125] Augustus is a momentous figure in the history of Roman law, but his interventions in that sphere can only be understood in the context of a broader evolution in Roman concepts of sovereignty. Law was an instrument, in the syntax of the *RGDA* and of Roman elite culture, through which the intellectual transformations of the Augustan period could occur. But these changes did not stop, and the Principate was never static. Later emperors, who did sovereignty differently, would do law differently as well.

[125] Milnor, "Landscape" p. 8.

2

The Emperors Who Obeyed the Law: Vespasian, Titus, Trajan

For an absolute ruler, it is surprising how often Augustus appears in our sources – and in the previous chapter – as just following rules. That tension will persist, in different forms, throughout this book. Emperors will combine an extravagant suite of powers with performative submission to overarching normative orders, both legal and not. The story of those combinations is the story of Roman imperial sovereignty, and of Roman law besides.

But later emperors treated legal order very differently than did Augustus, in ways that our sources tend to obscure. The "emergen[t] 'age of Augustus'" I described in Chapter 1 was strikingly extraconstitutional by the standards of later imperial politics.[1] Its namesake engaged with law as a guide to his actions, rather than as a binding or sovereign agent. Augustus does not describe himself, and is not described by others, as subject to law in any traditional sense; Cassius Dio describes him being formally released from legal authority.[2] Later emperors, however, remained *soluti legibus* but frequently described their relationship to law as one of (fraught, contingent) obedience. One well-known example gives Part I of this book its title: *J. Inst.* 2.17 claims that "the deified Severus and Caracalla would often say in their rescripts: 'although we

[1] Cooley, "Invention," p. 84.

[2] Dio Cass. 53.28.2 (πάσης αὐτὸν τῆς τῶν νόμων ἀνάγκης ἀπήλλαξαν). Brunt ("Lex de Imperio Vespasiani," pp. 108–09) argues that this claim is anachronistic, followed by Rich (*Settlement*, p. 164); see Tuori, "Appearances," p. 940.

have been released from the laws, nevertheless we live according to the laws'" (*Diui quoque Seuerus et Antoninus saepissime rescripserunt: "licet enim," inquiunt, "legibus soluti sumus, attamen legibus uiuimus"*).

While the theatrics of the *solutio legibus* date (possibly) to Augustus, Severus and Caracalla reference an ideal – the "*princeps* who obeys the law" – that emerges later.[3] This ideal becomes more formal over the course of the Principate, and in particular during the Flavian period. We have reason to think that earlier Romans wished to imagine the emperor as a legal subject; for example, the Neronian *Apocolocyntosis* (literally the "Ascent to Gourdhood": a freewheeling, invective account of the late Claudius being punished for his misrule)[4] subjects its protagonist to a literal and formally precise trial in the underworld.[5] But it is under Vespasian, the first Flavian emperor and head of the first non-Julio-Claudian dynasty, that emperors begin to describe themselves as *legally* empowered or constrained. This representational shift affected how Romans thought about emperors, but also how they thought about law. Vespasian's son Titus continued what his father began in more ways than one. The Edict of Titus, which confirmed Vespasianic grants *en masse*, inaugurated a new way of thinking about imperial decisions that applied legal models to what was previously a regime of favors and personal gifts.

It is not a coincidence that both Vespasian and Titus innovated in this space. Both of them faced crises of legitimacy, and we can fruitfully understand the Flavian period *tout court* as marked by broader shifts in how a newly transdynastic Principate was presented and received. But the Principate that emerged from these negotiations was more legalistic than the one that had entered, and both rulers used existing legal norms and structures to reframe imperial sovereignty in newly bureaucratic terms. By the second century CE, Pliny the Younger could talk about emperors on trial as part of a panegyric; Trajan appeared in a court, and abided by its judgments, as part of a newly established paradigm of emperors obeying laws. This paradigm lasted for a long

[3] On this disjunct in the Domitianic context Daube, "Princeps Legibus Solutus."
[4] Eden, *Apocolocyntosis*, pp. 8–12.
[5] See Bexley, "Saturnalian Lex," p. 49 ("The audience, rather than Claudius, assumes the role of judge"); Paschalis, "Afterlife," p. 209; Robinson, "In the Court of Time," p. 236 ("Now the arbitrary prosecutor has become the untrustworthy defendant").

time – arguably until Constantine – even though it makes little sense on its face.

This chapter argues that emperors who claimed to obey the law did not do so in any traditionally meaningful fashion but instead used legality as a medium of performance. Legal forms and practices held deep symbolic weight within the elite Roman imaginary, but by their very nature could not effectively constrain an emperor. Instead, they offered a script that emperors could use to demonstrate fidelity to older ways of doing things and respect to particular stakeholders invested in legal order. We often imagine legal performance as extraordinary, as ritual gestures or forensic spectacles that make their participants part of something over and above everyday life. Here, by contrast, extraordinary rulers used the scripts of law to make themselves look like everybody else. Law made the strange familiar, and helped Romans imagine a political order for themselves that could constrain unconstrainable men like Vespasian, Titus, and Trajan.

Importantly, law did all of this without operating in the way we expect laws to operate or binding in the way we expect laws to bind. The three case studies I discuss in this chapter all involve law that functions primarily as rhetoric. Returning to Austin the laws that purported to govern Vespasian, Titus, and Trajan lacked felicity; their commands were not enforceable, and thus did not alter Roman reality in the way that we might expect of legal utterance. But, as discussed above, infelicitous utterances like these could rhetorically posit a different world. They constructed a legality around themselves in which they had the power they claimed to exercise. That rhetoric was the point, and in showing how much Romans cared about ineffectual laws, this chapter challenges our notion of what effects law is supposed to have.

The Power of Vespasian's Law

Vespasianic rule appears more stable in later sources than it actually – probably – was. An odd passage in Suetonius' *uita* demonstrates this tension; it describes Vespasian responding to a serious threat in language that suggests Suetonius is not aware of how serious it was. Suetonius describes the victorious Flavian as *so sure of his and his sons' destiny that after constant conspiracies against him he dared to tell the Senate that either his sons would succeed him, or nobody would.*

(*Vesp.* 25) tam certum eum de sua suorumque genitura semper fuisse, ut post assiduas in se coniurationes ausus sit adfirmare senatui aut filios sibi successuros aut neminem.[6]

Suetonius presents this anecdote as widely known (*conuenit inter omnis*) and Dio records something similar at 66[65].12.1 [Xiph.]. That said, when Suetonius takes the line as evidence of Vespasian's confidence (*tam certum*) his interpretation is hard to justify. The last four emperors prior to Vespasian – Nero, Galba, Otho, and Vitellius – had all died without successors.[7] If Vespasian actually said this, as Suetonius' reference to universal awareness suggests, it is not obvious why any contemporary listener would hear it as Suetonius did and take that last clause as absurd. Vespasian was not saying that *of course* his sons would succeed him, with an alternative outcome being unthinkable or silly; instead, he was threatening the Senate with another civil war if they refused to accept a hereditary dynasty.[8] That threat should not shock us, and Osgood has demonstrated how Augustan messaging around *pax* (peace) made similar, if somewhat more implicit, claims.[9] But Suetonius treats Vespasian's *adfirmatio* as evidence that he had no reason to worry about his tenure, when it actually served as a logical strategy for maintaining that tenure in the face of *coniurationes*.

Suetonius' odd reading shows us not only how Vespasianic rule might have looked to its subjects (unsteady, contestable) but also why it might not appear that way in the historiography of the second century CE. To Suetonius, the idea of Vespasian not having a successor really would have sounded ridiculous.[10] Suetonius knew how the story ended, with

[6] See Jones and Milns, *Suetonius: The Flavian Emperors*, pp. 89–90.

[7] See Morgan, *69 AD*.

[8] Dio makes this valence clearer, describing Vespasian's claim as a reaction to abuse (βλασφημῶν) from the praetor Helvidius Priscus. Dio also describes Vespasian as upset to the point of tears (δακρύσας) rather than confident. See Osgood, "Ending Civil War," p. 1693; Levick, *Vespasian*, pp. 85–86; Murison, *Rebellion and Reconstruction*, pp. 158–59.

[9] Osgood, "Ending Civil War," pp. 1688–92.

[10] It is perhaps no coincidence that Dio wrote his more cynical account in the early third century CE; Dio, unlike Suetonius, was no stranger to contested succession or civil war. See, among many others: Bertrand, "Cassius Dio and the Roman Empire"; Kemezis, *Greek Narratives*, pp. 104–49.

Vespasian dying of natural causes (*Vesp.* 24) and being succeeded by his biological sons Titus and Domitian. Much like Augustus, Vespasian inaugurated a dynasty that seems stable in retrospect. Unlike Augustus, however, Vespasian stands in contrast to his younger son, an archvillain of later historiography. Suetonius begins the *uita Vespasiani* by saying that the *gens Flauia* was "in no way a source of woe for the state, although it is obvious that Domitian [Vespasian's younger son] justly paid the price for desire and bloodthirst" (1: *rei publicae nequaquam paenitenda, constet licet Domitianum cupiditatis ac saeuitiae merito poenas luisse*). Similarly, Tacitus (*Hist.* 4.51–52) describes Vespasian hearing reports that Domitian was "transgressing the boundaries of his youth and the rights of a son" (51: *terminos aetatis et concessa filio egrederetur*) and only forgiving Domitian because of an impassioned speech by Titus. The contrast between Domitian and his virtuous father and brother benefits the latter two. Since Domitian's reign appears in later authors as a hive of conspiracy and mistrust,[11] those same authors have reason to downplay the intrigues with which Vespasian and Titus had to contend.[12]

How does the threatening Vespasian of *Vesp.* 25, then, become the kind of figure Suetonius and Tacitus remember? In this section, I argue that the *lex de imperio Vespasiani* (The Law Regarding Vespasian's *Imperium*), a monumental inscription from early in Vespasian's reign, shows us how that transformation might have looked and the role that law – both as a genre of document, and as a set of ideas about how such documents might bestow imperial legitimacy – played in bringing it about.[13]

First, the basics. Our surviving text of the *lex de imperio Vespasiani* comes from the *lex*'s final tablet, which was not found *in situ* but which

[11] *E.g.* Iuv. 4; Plin. *Pan.* 48–49; Freudenburg, *Satires of Rome*, pp. 215–34.

[12] Tacitus' longer account does provide some detail on possible sources of the *assiduas coniurationes* mentioned by Suetonius; in particular, he describes (*Hist.* 4.38) Vitellian holdouts throughout the city of Rome. For more potential conspiracies in Suetonius, see Jones and Milns, *Suetonius: The Flavian Emperors*, p. 89.

[13] *ILS* 244 = *CIL* VI.31207. Brunt argues ("Lex de Imperio Vespasiani," p. 104) that the *lex* must have been written before January 9 of 70, the date on which Galba's memory was restored (*Hist.* 4.40.1); Levick disagrees ("The Parts and the Whole," pp. 18–19) and suggests that omitting Galba's name would be politically wise even after his restoration. Mantovani suggests ("Vagum imperium," p. 137) that the *lex* commemorates a senatorial grant of powers to Vespasian, commemorated at Tac. *Hist.* 4.3.5, that took place on December 20 or 21 of 69.

was large and imposing enough (at 1.64 m height, and 1.13 m width) to clearly indicate public display.[14] The *lex* is easy to excerpt – nine discrete paragraphs survive – but large parts of its communicative power come from the effect of the document as a whole, both as a text and as material object. Accordingly, Figure 2.1 shows the *lex* in its current home in the Musei Capitolini; I next reproduce those nine paragraphs in their entirety (and use facing translation to avoid presenting non-Latinate readers with a wall of gibberish).

Let him be permitted [to strike] a treaty with whomever he wishes, as was permitted for the deified Augustus, Tiberius, and Claudius

. . foedusue cum quibus uolet facere liceat ita, uti licuit diuo Aug(usto), | Ti. Iulio Caesari Aug(usto), Tiberioque Claudio Caesari Aug(usto) Germanico

And let him be permitted to convene the Senate, to give reports there, to refer matters there, and to make senatusconsulta through reportage and motion, as was permitted for the deified Augustus, Tiberius, and Claudius

utique ei senatum habere, relationem facere, remittere, | senatus consulta per relationem discessionemque facere liceat | ita, uti licuit diuo Aug(usto), Ti. Iulio Caesari Aug(usto), Ti. Claudio Caesari | Augusto Germanico

And when the Senate is in session according to his desire or authority or order or mandate or in his presence, let its authority over all things be maintained and respected, as if it had been announced and was held in accordance with the law of the Senate

utique cum ex uoluntate auctoritateue iussu mandatuue eius | praesenteue eo senatus habebitur, omnium rerum ius perinde | habeatur seruetur, ac si e lege senatus edictus esset habereturque

And that the case of those men whom he has recommended to the Senate and people in their candidacies for office, power, imperium or curatio of any matter, and to whom he has promised and given his support, should be considered more than usual by all in the assemblies

utique quos magistratum potestatem imperium curationemue | cuius rei petentes senatui populoque Romano commendauerit | quibusque suffragationem suam dederit promiserit, eorum | comitis quibusque extra ordinem ratio habeatur

[14] Dimensions: Crawford, *Roman Statutes*, pp. I.549–53. For a recent reconstruction of the *lex*'s lost material see Purpura, "Tavola perduta"; for a discussion of the difficulties involved with these reconstructions see Bruun, "Riflessioni."

FIGURE 2.1 The *lex de imperio Vespasiani*. Rome: Musei Capitolini, NCE2553.

And that he shall be permitted to move or extend the boundaries of the pomerium when he considers it best for the state, as was permitted for Claudius

utique ei fines pomerii proferre promouere, cum ex re publica | censebit esse, liceat ita, uti licuit Ti. Claudio Caesari Aug(usto) | Germanico ; |

And that whatever he considers to fall to the advantage of the state and the majesty of divine or human, public or private circumstances, he shall have the right and power to do and accomplish, as had the deified Augustus, Tiberius, and Claudius

utique quaecunque ex usu rei publicae maiestateque diuinarum | humanarum publicarum priuatarumque rerum esse | censebit, ei agere facere ius potestasque sit, ita uti diuo Aug(usto), Tiberioque Iulio Caesari Aug(usto), | Tiberioque Claudio Caesari | Aug(usto) Germanico fuit ; |

And that Imperator Caesar Vespasian should be released from whatever laws and plebiscites it has been written that the deified Augustus, Tiberius, and Claudius were unbound by; and whatever was proper for the deified Augustus, Tiberius, or Claudius to do according to any law or proposal, should all be permitted for Imperator Caesar Vespasian Augustus

utique quibus legibus plebeiue scitis scriptum fuit, ne diuus Aug(ustus), | Tiberiusue Iulius Caesar Aug(ustus), Tiberiusque Claudius Caesar Aug(ustus) | Germanicus tenerentur, iis legibus plebisque scitis imp(erator) Caesar | Vespasianus solutus sit ; quaeque ex quaque lege rogatione | diuum Aug(ustum), Tiberiumue Iulium Caesarem Aug(ustum), Tiberiumue | Claudium Caesarem Aug(ustum) Germanicum facere oportuit, | ea omnia imp(eratori) Caesari Vespasiano Aug(usto) facere liceat ; |

And that those things which were done and decrees which were ordered by Imperator Caesar Vespasian Augustus under his order or mandate prior to this proposed law should be treated as just, and considered as though they were done upon the command of the people or the plebs.

utique quae ante hanc legem rogatam acta gesta | decreta imperata ab imperatore Caesare Vespasiano Aug(usto) | iussu mandatuue eius a quoque sunt, ea perinde iusta rataq(ue) | sint, ac si populi plebisue iussu acta essent. |

Sanction

Sanctio

If anyone should act or has acted under color of this law against laws or proposals or plebiscites or senatusconsulta, or if he has as a result of this law not done something that it would be proper for him to do according to a law or proposal or plebiscite or senatusconsultum, let it not work to his disadvantage, nor let him be made to owe anything to the people on its account, nor let any action or judgment lie for anyone regarding such a matter, nor let anyone allow a case to be pled before him on such a matter.

Si quis huiusce legis ergo aduersus leges rogationes plebisue scita | senatusue consulta fecit fecerit, siue quod eum ex lege rogatione | plebisue scito s(enatus)ue c(onsulto) facere oportebit, non fecerit huius legis | ergo, id ei ne fraudi esto, neue quit ob eam rem populo dare debeto, | neue cui de ea re actio neue iudicatio esto, neue quis de ea re apud | [s]e agi sinito.

The *lex de imperio Vespasiani* is hard to pin down. The question of its formal legislative character (namely, whether the document's repeated *uti*-clauses, typical of *senatusconsulta*,[15] conflict with the *sanctio*'s self-identification of the *lex* as *lex*) is long-standing[16] but something of a red herring. Mantovani has argued that the text we have is that of a *senatusconsultum* that was transformed into *lex* by comitial passage,[17] while Lucrezi and Hurlet have argued that this document, like the Tiberian *lex* commemorated on the *Tabula Hebana*, reflects the blurring boundaries between *leges* and *senatusconsulta* that accompanied the Principate.[18] Crawford argues that any resemblance is artificial, since the indirect commands of *senatusconsulta* – unlike those of the *lex* – employ secondary sequence.[19]

In practice I take Crawford's philological observation as dispositive, but law is more than its formalities. The repeated *uti*-commands of the *lex*

[15] Compare, for example, the repeated subjunctive commands of the *S.C. de Cn. Pisone Patre* (The *Senatusconsultum* de Gnaeus Piso Sr.), preserved at ll. 71–123 (translation and commentary at Cooley, *The Senatusconsultum de Gn. Pisone Patre*, pp. 120–24, 190–217).

[16] For a recent example, Pani refers to the document as a hybrid "*s. c./lex*" on the basis of the twin forms; "Costituzionalismo," p. 107.

[17] Mantovani, "Vagum imperium," p. 138.

[18] Lucrezi, *Aspetti*, pp. 92–94; Hurlet, "Légitimité," p. 265; also Brunt, "Lex de Imperio Vespasiani," p. 95. The *Tabula Hebana* was first published at Oliver and Palmer, "Text of the Tabula Hebana" and extended by González, "Fragmento."

[19] Crawford, *Roman Statutes*, p. I.550.

de imperio Vespasiani, even if not formally marking it out as a *senatusconsultum*, signified law to an audience used to *senatusconsulta* and positioned the *lex* within a genre of state speech to which both *senatusconsulta* and *leges rogatae* belonged. Notably, later authors (most famously Ulpian) are unanimous in referring to these kinds of enactments as *leges regiae* (kingly laws).[20] The *lex de imperio Vespasiani* was probably the first of these, although we cannot say for sure; it seems hard to imagine that a document so focused on analogizing its provisions to prior grants would not reference an earlier *lex regia* if one existed.[21]

A thornier question, however, is what the *lex de imperio Vespasiani* actually did. On the one hand it appears to authorize imperial rule, in the same way we might imagine an American law to authorize enforcement actions taken by the head of an administrative agency. When jurists describe imperial power they refer to it as legally authorized in just this way – I provide two examples of the phenomenon below.

What pleases the emperor has the force of a law, inasmuch as the populus *grants all of their* imperium *and* potestas *to him, and confers it upon him, by means of a* lex regia *which has been passed regarding his powers.*

(D.1.4.1pr.: Ulpian, Institutiones) Quod principi placuit, legis habet uigorem: utpote cum lege regia, quae de imperio eius lata est, populus ei et in eum omne suum imperium et potestatem conferat.

[20] Mantovani, "Vagum imperium," p. 126. *Leges regiae*, specifically, is only attested in Ulpian but other authors (all writing far later) will refer to imperial power as authorized by some sort of *lex*. E.g. C.6.23.3 (Severus Alexander); Gai. *Inst.* 1.5.

[21] Cf. Ferrary, "Pouvoirs," pp. 150–51, claiming that these precedents argue against the idea that "ce fut un document unique." To my mind, Ferrary is uncontroversially correct as to content. As Brunt notes ("Lex de Imperio Vespasiani," pp. 95–107) the basic powers afforded by the *lex* were not novel in 69 CE, and the absence of perfectly specific enumerating clauses from a document as fragmentary as this one probably does not mean much. That said, while the *lex*'s surviving material insists on its similarity to prior grants it is circumspect about the mechanism by which those grants were extended (simply repeating *licuit*), to an extent that would be odd if the mechanism had not changed. Lucrezi makes a similar claim ("Mito," p. 158), but on the grounds that a transdynastic *lex regia* would make no sense in the constitutional discourse of the first century CE. Either way, the document is simply too fragmentary to answer the question with confidence, particularly given the late date of our other sources for *leges regiae*.

An imperial constitution is an imperial ruling, contained in a decree or an edict or a letter. Nor has it ever been doubted that such a thing takes the place of a law, since the emperor has himself taken his imperium *by means of a law.*

(Gai. *Inst.* 1.5) Constitutio principis est, quod imperator decreto uel edicto uel epistula constituit. Nec umquam dubitatum est, quin id legis uicem optineat, cum ipse imperator per legem imperium accipiat.

That said, Ulpian's and Gaius' claims quickly fall apart in the context of Vespasian. Leaving aside the events of 69 CE – in which Vespasian won a civil war that had previously elevated three short-lived emperors – the *lex*'s own language makes clear that Vespasian had been acting as emperor for some time before its passage. If Vespasian's "acts and decrees" (para. 8: *acta gesta decreta imperata*) lacked legal force prior to the *lex*, that says more about legal force as a criterion for evaluating Vespasianic action than it does about Vespasianic action itself. This *lex regia* simply did not alter the world in the way that we expect laws to alter the world.[22]

That basic mismatch makes the *lex de imperio Vespasiani* an excellent test case for the taxonomy of legal storytelling I discussed in my Introduction. To refresh: Laws speak in a normative mode (the prohibitions, commands, and regulations we tend to associate with law), a descriptive mode (the specifically factual claims that survive in legal texts), and a constructive (the murkier, less explicit second-order commitments that arise from laws' implied relationship to the world in which they exist).

When I say that the *lex de imperio Vespasiani* did not work as we expect laws to work, what I mean is that it is hard to read normatively. While the *lex* claims to intervene in the operations of Roman governance, it ratifies a state of affairs that already existed and that only a fool would subject to legal challenge. In fact, it is difficult to imagine any kind of legal process hinging on the existence or precise interpretation of the *lex*. That difficulty does not render such precise interpretations impossible, in ancient or modern interpretive milieux;[23] these interpretations may even correctly predict how an

[22] See Ando, "Origins and Import," pp. 930–31.

[23] E.g. Mantovani, "Les clauses 'sans précédents'" (arguing that the "*clauses sans précédents*" of the *lex* simply acknowledge the comparatively informal nature of the powers they confer, and that the drafters' decision to not include grants to prior

ancient specialist would have applied the *lex de imperio Vespasiani* to hypothetical scenarios in which the legality of imperial action was determinative. But the *lex* was not designed to be read in such a way, because it does not contemplate such scenarios, and accordingly its drafting is imprecise in places where precision could matter.[24]

Leaving aside the question of statutory form I described above, paragraph 6 renders almost all of the *lex* redundant.[25] That paragraph, which empowers the emperor to do whatever he thinks best, is a transplant from a Republican tradition of wide-ranging emergency powers that superseded the enumerative processes of "normal" Roman law and of the remainder of the *lex*.[26] The normative stories that laws usually tell – of specific things that one can or cannot do, under pain of state violence – here become incoherent, even if the formal characteristics of the *lex* train its reader to expect them and to try and make them work.

So what stories does the *lex de imperio Vespasiani* tell instead? If we consider the *lex* as speaking in a descriptive mode, we can see it making fact claims about the world. Paragraphs 1, 2, 5, 6, and 7 all reference prior emperors being permitted to take certain actions. While each reference appears in a subordinate clause that nominally limits the paragraph's grant of authority,[27] the all-encompassing paragraph 6 renders such a limit unworkable. Instead, these references are part of the point. The *lex de imperio Vespasiani* informs its reader of certain regularities in imperial relations with the Senate, about which its drafters would like that reader to know. That information makes the

emperors in paragraphs 3, 4, and 8 should not be taken as arbitrary but as instead reflecting a subtle deployment of imperial precedent and formalizing rhetoric).

24 Thus Pani, who argues ("Costituzionalismo," pp. 102–03), against Brunt's account of paragraph 6 as syntactical "nonsense" ("Lex de Imperio Vespasiani," p. 113 n. 106) on the grounds that the *lex*'s authors would have been too careful to produce such slapdash drafting. The argument flips on its head. If these careful drafters were willing to produce something too unclear for traditional applications of legal texts, they likely did not foresee such applications. On the *lex*'s lack of detail see also Bruun, "Riflessioni," p. 43.

25 See Ando, "Origins and Import," pp. 930–31.

26 Straumann, *Crisis and Constitutionalism*, pp. 63–117; the concept of legal transplants is developed by Watson, *Legal Transplants*.

27 For instance, one could theoretically imagine the *ita licuit* ... clause in paragraph 1 only authorizing Vespasian to use his diplomatic powers in the same way that his predecessors had.

lex appear as a chronicle of prior imperial history, and in cases where the chronicle has no reason to mislead it can be reliable; for example, Claudius really did expand the *pomerium*.[28] The fact that earlier emperors got to do certain things, and that those permissions form the basis of the current emperor's powers, were far more important for imperial transition than the *lex*'s present-focused commands.

Two aspects of the *lex*'s descriptive account, however, complicate its self-representation as a historical source. The first is obvious – Augustus, Tiberius, and Claudius were not the only emperors in the world. Vespasian inherited a position whose powers had been renegotiated rather violently the year before, but Nero appears nowhere in the *lex* and neither do Caligula, Galba, Otho, or Vitellius. The history that appears in the *lex de imperio Vespasiani* is manicured, selecting particular instances of imperial grant as exercising normative force in the present, and consigning the rest to oblivion. It is tempting to describe this cull in the language of memory sanctions, which Flower defines as "deliberately designed strategies that aim to change the picture of the past."[29] But we can also understand it as a more regularized process inherent to the *lex*'s style of argument. Peachin's account of "exemplary government" in the *lex de imperio Vespasiani* urges us to think of Augustus/Tiberius/Claudius (and their compliant senates) not as binding precedents but as hortatory *exempla*: as a select corpus of historical figures and events that the *lex*'s authors, readers, and nominal subject might use to think through problems of imperial governance.[30] Exemplary reasoning creates and reasons from potted histories, since we do not take everything that happened in the past as worthy of imitation.[31]

[28] A ritual boundary of the city of Rome; see Mignone, "Pomerium," pp. 439–42.

[29] Flower, *The Art of Forgetting*, p. 2; see also Hedrick, *History and Silence*, pp. 93–94. Roman memory sanctions are now generally categorized (following Vittinghoff, *Staatsfeind*) as *damnatio memoriae*, and I discuss them further *infra* pp. 156–61.

[30] Peachin, "Exemplary Government," p. 77 ("[*E*]*xempla* contributed, and did so roughly on a level with acts that we would comfortably categorize as statutory [e.g. decrees of popular assemblies, *senatus consulta*, or formal edicts issued by emperors], to what we would perceive as the constitutional foundation of the imperial government").

[31] Roller, *Models*, pp. 17–23; "Exemplarity," pp. 3–4; also Liv. pr.10: "This is a particularly useful part of the study of affairs, namely that you see the evidence of every *exemplum* laid out on a grand monument; then you may choose what to imitate for yourself and your state, then what to avoid as shameful in its development and

Accordingly, it is unclear whether the *lex*'s drafters erased these earlier rulers from an administrative record presenting itself as complete, or from a morally charged narrative presenting itself as selective.

That ambiguity brings me to my second point about the *lex* as a history. Law is by its nature a historiographic endeavor that makes claims about the past, but it does so for prospective reasons – in support of prescriptions upon legal subjects in the present and future.[32] Law presumes that the judgments of a past period (that of drafting) are necessarily salient to problems that will arise at a later date, and thus primes its reader to bring the past into their present. That orientation lets law tell especially plausible stories about the past, since it does not appear to go out of its way to tell them, and they instead appear as simple predicates to normative argument. A reader of the *lex de imperio Vespasiani* could absorb its descriptive assertions without necessarily even realizing they were there. Furthermore, anyone hoping to use the law – unlikely here, but easy to imagine for other kinds of legislative speech – would recapitulate its claims about the world as they invoked the rules that those claims underlay.

This melding of historiography and command reflects some distinctly Roman ways of looking at the world. The *lex de imperio Vespasiani* describes past states of affairs and then imitates them; it treats the Augustan, Tiberian, and Claudian settlements as *exempla* from which to reason. This exemplarizing tendency, which I briefly discussed in the context of Augustan marriage law, informed how Romans approached normative problems in other aspects of their lives.[33] It fits especially well with legal hermeneutics as we understand them to exist today, but "thinking through particulars" was quite natural to the *lex*'s intended audience and only secondarily a distinctive feature of legal documents.[34] The *lex de imperio Vespasiani*, however, reverses the usual reasoning tendencies of exemplary thought. In most accounts of exemplary reasoning, the reasoner accesses a broadly accepted corpus of descriptive accounts in order to solve a tricky or controversial

result." (*hoc illud est praecipue in cognitione rerum salubre ac frugiferum, omnis te exempli documenta in inlustri posita monumento intueri: inde tibi tuaeque rei publicae quod imitere capias, inde foedum inceptu, foedum exitu, quod uites*).

[32] See Tushnet, "Following," pp. 793–804.

[33] Langlands, *Exemplary Ethics*, pp. 88–111; Morgan, *Popular Morality*, pp. 122–59.

[34] Lowrie and Lüdemann, *Thinking through Particulars*; Langlands, "Mediating," p. 69.

normative problem. Here, the *lex*'s normative claim (that the sitting emperor can be an emperor) is banal, while the descriptive account that qualifies it more closely resembles the kind of message an emperor like Vespasian might want to get out. The fact claims nested within the *lex de imperio Vespasiani* built an exemplary chain that could link Vespasian with his Julio-Claudian forebears, and that could bridge the interregnum of 69 CE. That linkage appears in the *lex* as senatorial approval and legal empowerment. The *lex* represents the Senate granting Vespasian the power to act as an emperor, and thus implies (without quite stating it) that it matters whether or not the Senate has granted Vespasian the power to act as an emperor.

This is the constructive story that law tells. Legal writing is unusual in its capacity to change the world; in Austin's parlance, laws work as performative utterances on behalf of the state.[35] So when a document identifies itself as a law we expect it to perform, and thus imagine the society around it as one in which it could. The *lex de imperio Vespasiani* holds itself out as a law, and as a powerful one. It takes the form of a gorgeously crafted monumental bronze inscription, employing the generic structures of *leges* and *senatusconsulta* and peppered with the archaic language (*uti*, *huiusce*, *esto/debeto/sinito*) of Roman statute.[36] Documents like the *lex de imperio Vespasiani* held both symbolic and practical power in many fields of Roman social life; by publicly posting the *lex* Vespasian and his Senate could give the impression that imperial politics was one of them.

That impression, more than anything else, is the point of the *lex de imperio Vespasiani*. When Ando refers to the document as part of a "continuous exchange of flatteries" his point seems uncontroversial; the Senate gives Vespasian powers and he gives them respect in exchange.[37] But the mechanics of that latter flattery are subtle. The *lex de imperio Vespasiani* does not explicitly claim that the approval it records is necessary for Vespasian's rule to be legitimate but constructs a world in which that appears to be the case. For example, the *sanctio* analogizes the *lex* to other statutes that really did govern and bind state

35 On performative utterances, Austin, *Words*, pp. 4–7.

36 On the quality of the *lex*'s craftsmanship Levick, "The Parts and the Whole," p. 16; Crawford, *Roman Statutes*, p. I.549 ("one of the most elegantly inscribed of all Latin inscriptions").

37 Ando, *Ideology*, p. 160.

power.[38] In permitting a law to be publicly posted that authorized his rule, Vespasian effectively pretended to subject his rule to legal authorization without having to make any statement to that effect.[39]

By subsuming himself within senatorial and legal order, Vespasian could transcend dynastic conceptions of sovereignty that might otherwise have caused some trouble.[40] Specifically, the *lex de imperio Vespasiani* writes Vespasian into a history of imperial, rather than Julio-Claudian, governance. The constructive story of the *lex* is a story in which Rome's traditional lawmaking bodies exercise meaningful control, and in which the emperor exercises broad powers on their behalf as a sort of agent. Those traditional lawmaking bodies had predated Augustus and outlasted his successors; a world in which they conferred legitimacy on imperial action would experience 69 CE as less of a break than it had been in practice, and imperial action as less of an object of contestation than it actually was.[41]

Of course, the *lex de imperio Vespasiani* was not the only public monument to link Vespasian with Julio-Claudian predecessors. To give just a few examples: Suetonius records Vespasian restoring the Augustan Theater of Marcellus and completing a temple to the now-deified Claudius, and Noreña has argued that Vespasian's "Temple of Peace" (*Templum Pacis*) deliberately recalled Augustus.[42] But the *lex* spoke in a different language. It directed its viewer's attention towards clauses delineating the precise boundaries of Vespasian's power, and away from the tenuous basis of that power itself. That project was successful – so successful that scholars today still read the *lex* as an expression of legal supremacy.[43] But if the *lex de imperio Vespasiani* is a part of the history of Roman constitutionalism, that has implications for what we understand the constitutionalism of the Principate to mean.

[38] Compare, for example, the *sanctio*-clause in the *lex Irnitana*; González and Crawford, "The Lex Irnitana," p. 181.

[39] See Levick, "The Parts and the Whole," pp. 21–22 (noting that the law's precedents "imply that Vespasian was not free to act as Gaius or Nero had done" before acknowledging that "[i]n truth they were a pleasing fig leaf, or rather a set of emperor's new clothes, leaving the emperor restricted only by his own *pudor*").

[40] Levick, *Vespasian*, p. 86. [41] See Waters, "Second Dynasty," pp. 212–13.

[42] *Vesp*. 9.1, 19.1 (with deification at *Cl.* 45); Noreña, "Medium and Message"; also Levick, *Vespasian*, pp. 73–74; Schmidt, "Claudius und Vespasian," p. 87; Isager, "Vespasiano e Augusto."

[43] See, e.g. Lucrezi, *Leges super principem*, p. 259 (crediting Vespasian with the invention of "una nuova forma di egemonia del *princeps* sulla società").

Within the Principate, formal or institutionally mediated concepts of sovereignty coexisted with ones that were more individual and charismatic. An emperor could present himself as a god on earth, a conquering hero, or an employee of the state. Different stories might resonate with different audiences at different times, or might fit better with the details of particular imperial careers. Vespasian, a man with dynastic ambitions but no dynastic claims, benefited from the more abstract links drawn by the *lex de imperio Vespasiani.* And since statutes necessarily apply abstract concepts to different people in similar ways, a statute could draw those links while seeming to do the different and more granular work that we generally expect from legal speech. The legalistic, transdynastic world of the *lex* appears to be a backdrop for its grants of power, while actually functioning as its primary communicand.

* * * * *

The distinctive messaging work of the *lex de imperio Vespasiani* makes it an important part of the history of Vespasianic representation. Whether the *lex* is simply the first *lex regia* to survive or a new invention, it responded to a new kind of legitimacy crisis that Vespasian was eventually able to overcome.[44] That said, the *lex de imperio Vespasiani* is also an important document in the history of Roman law. If we imagine that history in normative terms as a historiography of doctrine, the *lex* has very little for us, but law did more. The *lex de imperio Vespasiani* shows us how Roman elites conceived of law as a symbolic, as well as a practical, order. Legal symbolics could make Vespasian look like his predecessors, and fit him naturally into the precedential discourse of the statute.

That dynamic will recur throughout this book. Romans living under the Principate had a variety of frameworks available to them with which to understand said Principate. Different people might understand their sovereigns, and different sovereigns might wish to be understood, as charismatic outliers or bureaucratic agents or

[44] Vespasian was not the first non-Julio-Claudian emperor, but merely the first one to reign longer than a few months. Notably, his predecessors in 69 CE seem to have engaged in their own elaborate accession rituals; the records of the Arval Brethren show multiple sacrifices connected to the short-lived emperor Otho. Ando, "Origins and Import," p. 921; Scheid, Tassini, and Rüpke, *Commentarii Fratrum Arvalium*, pp. 99–107.

dynastic placeholders. Each of these stories sites the legitimating feature of imperial sovereignty in a slightly different place. Vespasian (who could claim no dynastic tie with Augustus) here appears as a subject of senatorial approval, who derives his legitimacy from his position within the related institutional frameworks of senatorial and legal order. It is not a coincidence that that representation happened in a statute. Legal discourse was old, and so was the Senate. Legal discourse treated different people similarly, and Vespasian benefited from being treated like Augustus, Tiberius, and Claudius. The fact that that representation happened in a statute that did no legal work is, in some ways, immaterial. Legality is as much a set of generic tropes as it is a characteristic of state actions.

Predictability, Paternity, and the Emperor Titus

These tropes did not die when Vespasian did. In fact, the brief reign of Vespasian's elder son Titus offers another example of legal symbolism marshaled against a crisis of legitimacy. That crisis is easy enough to understand, if we begin with the observation that imperial power did not generally pass from father to son. One imagines the Principate as dynastic – any undergraduate survey will reference the "Julio-Claudian," "Flavian," and "Severan" periods.[45] But this schema of quasi-familial quasi-continuity masks a surprising lack of direct filiation, at least until quite late in the game. The Principate records only three instances of sons succeeding their fathers (Titus, Commodus, and Caracalla). By contrast it was relatively common practice for emperors to adopt their successors, and while those adoptions often happened within broader kinship networks they were always of adults and were understood to coexist with traditional family ties.[46] For example,

[45] Even the exception proves the rule; the period between 96 and 193 is sometimes referred to as one of "adoptive emperors," following Gibbon and highlighting its pseudofiliative succession practice (on which see Hekster, *Emperors and Ancestors*, pp. 11–12; "All in the Family"), or as the "Nerva-Antonine" (as at, e.g. Rebeggiani, "Expansion"), which highlights the dynastic rule of the Antonines from 136 to 192. The *Cambridge Ancient History* splits the difference, calling the last four emperors of this period "The Antonines." See Birley, "Hadrian to the Antonines."

[46] For a more detailed discussion of imperial adoption Hekster, *Emperors and Ancestors*, pp. 78–95.

Marcus Aurelius begins his *Meditations* with gratitude to his "begetter" (γεννήσας) Marcus Annius Verus (1.2) as well as to his adoptive "father" (πάτηρ) Antoninus Pius (1.16); notably, while Marcus preserves the fiction that Antoninus is his father, his other familial identifiers track biological paternity (e.g. referring to Verus *père* as his grandfather at 1.1, rather than the emperor Hadrian).[47] These adoptions were not taken entirely literally, and more closely resemble a "meritocratic" appointment process than the heredity that put Titus on the throne.[48]

We can thus begin to understand why Vespasian might have relied on threats in support of Titus' claim. Suetonius' biography of Titus, while extremely complimentary,[49] mentions that "hardly any man became emperor with so much hostile rumor or so little support" (6.2: *non temere quis tam aduerso rumore magisque inuitis omnibus transierit ad principatum*). If Suetonius is right, then Titus took the throne while facing intense public suspicion. Either way, however, we know that Titus – the first emperor to succeed his father, and the first non-Julio-Claudian to accede peacefully – faced novel challenges in justifying his reign.

That novelty may explain some enormously consequential administrative shifts. Both Dio and Suetonius claim that Titus was the first emperor to confirm prior imperial decisions *en masse*. First Dio:

47 On Verus, *HA*, *Pius* 4.2.

48 Unfortunately, we have no explicit discussion of the merits of adoption over heredity as a succession principle until decades after Titus' death (and specifically until the Trajanic period, when that discussion gained a panegyric cast). But for evidence of how Romans would come to describe heredity and adoption see Tac. *Hist.* 1.16 (in which Galba, announcing his adoption of Piso, claims that "under Tiberius and Gaius and Claudius we were like the patrimony of one family: that we are beginning to be chosen [as emperors] will stand in the place of liberty; and with the fall of the Julio-Claudian house adoption will find the best man. For it is a matter of luck to be born and raised by emperors, and nothing more: the judgment of adoption is untainted and, if you should wish to choose a successor, he is indicated by *consensus*" (*sub Tiberio et Gaio et Claudio unius familiae quasi hereditas fuimus: loco libertatis erit quod eligi coepimus; et finita Iuliorum Claudiorumque domo optimum quemque adoptio inueniet. nam generari et nasci a principibus fortuitum, nec ultra aestimatur: adoptandi iudicium integrum et, si uelis eligere, consensu monstratur*); Dio Cass. 69.20.1–5 [Xiph.] (in which Hadrian expounds on the virtues of adoptive succession on meritocratic grounds). For Hadrian's speech as implicit commentary see Davenport and Mallan, "Hadrian's Adoption Speech."

49 E.g. Suetonius calls Titus "the love and delight of humankind" (*Tit.* 1: *amor ac deliciae generis humani*).

[Titus] also established many other things aimed at people's stability and safety; for he promulgated a decree confirming all those things that had been given to anyone by previous emperors, so as not to incur effort from petitioners one after the other, and expelled informers from Rome.

(66[65].19.3 [Xiph.]) πολλὰ δὲ καὶ ἄλλα πρός τε τὸ ἀσφαλὲς καὶ πρὸς τὸ ἄλυπον τῶν ἀνθρώπων κατεστήσατο: καὶ γὰρ γράμματα ἐξέθηκε βεβαιῶν πάντα τὰ ὑπὸ τῶν προτέρων αὐτοκρατόρων δοθέντα τισίν, ὥστε μὴ καθ' ἑκάστους σφῶν αἰτοῦντας αὐτὸν πράγματα ἔχειν, τούς τε μηνυτὰς ἐξήλασεν ἐκ τῆς πόλεως.

Likewise, Suetonius:

[Titus] was most kindly by nature; although from a Tiberian practice all previous emperors would not honor grants (beneficia) *given by their predecessors unless they themselves had granted the same benefits to the same petitioners, Titus was the first to confirm all prior grants in one edict and he did not permit them to be sought from him again.*

(*Tit.* 8.1) Natura autem beneuolentissimus, cum ex instituto Tiberi omnes dehinc Caesares beneficia a superioribus concessa principibus aliter rata non haberent, quam si eadem iisdem et ipsi dedissent, primus praeterita omnia uno confirmauit edicto nec a se peti passus est.

The accounts are strikingly similar.[50] While Dio does not rely heavily on Suetonius as a source,[51] both authors understand Titus' edict as fulfilling nearly identical social functions. Both refer to the edict as specifically preventing later petition, and both present it as evidence of Titus' good nature (Dio juxtaposes it with the expulsion of informers, and Suetonius with Titus' *natura beneuolentissim*[*a*]).[52] In practice, while we should probably take both authors at their word that this change occurred under Titus, they are less reliable as to why. A decree regularizing imperial grants could serve several different purposes. It saved time and expense for both emperor and subject, but also helped those grants perform some of the organizing or planning functions previously associated with

[50] Also Aur. Vict. *Caes.* 10.2: "Finally, although it was customary for grants of prior emperors to be confirmed by their successors, as soon as Titus took the throne he voluntarily granted those things to their possessors with an edict" (*Denique cum concessa per priores principes firmari ab insequentibus mos esset, simul imperium cepit, talia possidentibus edicto sponte cauit prospexitque*).

[51] See Gowing, *Triumviral Narratives*, pp. 39–50; Manuwald, *Cassius Dio und Augustus*, pp. 258–68.

[52] On the punishment of *delatores* see Coleman, "Parade"; Rutledge, "Tradition." On *delatores* in later discussion of Domitian see Powell, "Juvenal and the Delatores."

statutory law. Perhaps most importantly, by making imperial transition less salient – by minimizing the disruption to legal and social order that attended an emperor's death – the edict reframed Titus' sovereignty in more obviously dynastic terms and subsumed his own rule into a new story of Flavian continuity.

The Edict of Titus represents a turning point in the history of Roman law. It introduced a principle – that the statements of one emperor were presumed to remain valid under the next one – without which the rescript system as we know it could not have developed. But it is also a watershed in the history of Roman thinking about imperial power. It uses the structure of law and legal change to restructure Roman ideas of what having an emperor meant, and further demonstrates how the framework we now call "Roman law" grew out of changing approaches to imperial sovereignty and representation.

I begin with the practical impact of the edict. To raise an obvious point, the Edict of Titus saved a great many people a great deal of time. While Rome's system of imperial grants and petitions was not as developed as it would become under Hadrian, emperors still regularly offered privileges and favors. When those grants became void upon an emperor's death, recipients of imperial *beneficia* were forced to engage in a complicated and expensive process of petitioning for renewal. This repetitioning process could impose enormous costs, inconvenience, and uncertainty upon those who had relied upon an emperor's goodwill. For example, *CIL* X.8038 (=*FIRA* I.72) records Vespasian confirming a grant that Augustus had made to the Corsican *Vanacini* and whose validity appears to have been meaningfully uncertain prior to the *Vanacini*'s embassy.

I confirm the beneficia *granted to you by the deified Augustus after his seventh consulship, which you have retained into the reign of Galba.*

Beneficia tributa uobis ab diuo | Augusto post septimum consulaltum, quae in tempora Galbae retilnuistis, confirmo.[53]

The next paragraph dates the embassy of the *Vanacini* to October 12 of 77. In other words, the beneficiary status of this community had been unsettled for nearly a decade; while Galba (r. 68–69) had likely confirmed Augustus' grants, Otho and Vitellius had not, and it took

[53] Commentary at Zucca, "Esterzili."

eight years plus a personal embassy for Vespasian to settle the matter. Not every community could manage that sort of expense whenever an emperor died. In fact, even the *Vanacini* could only resolve the matter in the context of other business, since the prior paragraph discusses a boundary dispute that was probably the actual reason for the embassy. Asking small communities to send ambassadors to Rome every few years – or few months – could be catastrophic, and leaving legal rights in limbo until they did so even worse.

These confirmations were no picnic for the incoming emperor, either. Suetonius' Latin frames the edict as prohibiting requests (*nec a se peti passus*). In a passage that is otherwise complimentary, it is striking that Titus here does not permit petitions, as opposed to simply rendering them unnecessary. That prohibition suggests that the edict was intended, at least partially, to save the emperor's time as well as his subjects'. Dio's Greek is a bit more laconic, but it is notable that both Titus (αὐτὸν) and his petitioners (αἰτοῦντας) take mirrored forms as parties spared from trouble.

These practical advantages, however, do not themselves explain either historian's framing. Each describes the edict in the language of charity and benevolence, beyond what its conveniences would necessarily support. These choices make more sense in light of the ideological valence of what Titus did. We have already seen that elite audiences had strong affective attachments to law as a tool for social ordering, and the Edict of Titus rendered imperial decisionmaking more closely coterminous with law. A *beneficium* that must be renewed upon the death of its benefactor is necessarily personal, denoting a change in the relationship between two individuals, and that relationship only survives as long as those individuals who make it up. By contrast, *beneficia* that survive the transition seem to connect their recipient to something more abstract and stable. That abstraction and stability was closely linked with law as a symbol, since Roman legislation did not sunset upon the death of its promulgators. Making *beneficia* look more like legal grants, as the Edict of Titus did, made rule by *beneficium* look more like the rule of law.[54]

[54] For an intriguing parallel see Tac. *Ann.* 4.37. Tiberius explains that he had previously authorized the construction of a temple in Asia to himself and his family because Augustus had done the same, and Tiberius claims that he followed Augustus' example

In fact, the Edict of Titus was an arguably necessary precursor to the imperial regime with which "Roman law" is most closely associated. I discuss the rescript system further in the next chapter, but briefly: Starting under Hadrian we begin to see evidence of a quasi-centralized bureaucracy through which petitioners could ask the emperor questions about the interpretation of legal rules, and get answers they could use in disputes that might arise decades or centuries after his death.[55] This correspondence practice presumes that the documents it generates would outlast imperial transition, for both practical and conceptual reasons. As a practical matter imperial rescripts could take the form of rules, and voiding large bodies of rules upon an emperor's death would create obvious problems.[56] As a conceptual one, the rescript system imagines imperial writing as occupying a similar generic space to other sources of law. For example, when Papinian lists the sources of the *ius ciuile* he cites "laws, plebiscites, *senatusconsulta*, imperial decrees, and the authority of the learned" (D.1.1.7pr., Definitiones: *legibus, plebis scitis, senatus consultis, decretis principum, auctoritate prudentium*) as equally binding.

No other document in Papinian's list relies upon its author being alive. If we imagine emperors as Horace imagined Augustus, as extraordinary figures whose desires and virtues can abrogate legal order, their abrogations should only last as long as their desires. Imagining emperors as Papinian does, though, as sources of a disembodied *ius*, means constructing a *ius* that includes their opinions. That latter framework presumes an emperor's words to mean something after he dies. It is under Titus that they were formally understood to do so.

That said, it is important to remember that the *beneficia* Titus addressed were not laws in the traditional sense, even if they took on that character in later periods. They were promises, made by a person whose promises mattered more than the law. And there was nothing unusual about a son keeping his father's promises. If we understand imperial accession to be like any other testamentary event – i.e. a death – then the Edict of Titus seems rather less revolutionary. The Roman law

as part of a broader tendency to "consider his words and deeds as if they were law" (*omnia facta dictaque eius uice legis obseruem*).

55 Connolly, *Lives*, pp. 22–38; Sirks, "Request"; Crook, *Consilium Principis*, pp. 56–65.

56 Sautel, "Usurpations," pp. 474–75.

of persons clearly imagines that a son who took on his deceased father's estate also took up his obligations. Roman heirs could refuse to inherit a parent's insolvent estate via the "right of abstention" (*ius abstinendi*), but if they did not they absorbed the estate along with its debts.[57] While our clearest sources for this legal principle date from after the Flavian period the practice is attested before it, in the late Republic. Cicero mentions at *Phil.* 2.44 that Mark Antony went bankrupt as a result of his father's debts (*"Patris," inquies, "ista culpa est."*) and suggests that fulfilling these obligations constituted filial *pietas*.[58]

This transfer of obligations should be understood not as reflecting distinctively Roman concepts of "debt" or "contract," but instead distinctively Roman concepts of "death" and "personhood." A son in power (*filius in potestate*) had sharply limited rights of contract and was considered under law as an agent of a larger unit headed by the *paterfamilias*. Romans had historically understood fathers' power over their children to be nearly absolute; upon a father's death, though, the son would step into his legal position and assume his role at the head of the *familia* as an economic and social entity. Per D.28.2.11 (Paul, ad Sabinum): "no inheritance is considered as having taken place; as if they were already the owners [of the property], since they are considered as like owners even when their father is alive" (*nulla uideatur hereditas fuisse, quasi olim hi domini essent, qui etiam uiuo patre quodammodo domini existimantur*).[59] This account of Roman family law is, to be clear, somewhat clichéd. Romans knew that children – especially adult children – had agency and found extreme expressions of paternal power archaic and creepy.[60] But this account of personhood nevertheless informed what succession meant. An heir did not just receive his father's property but instead stepped into his father's social position, inheriting his rights, taking on his obligations, and assuming his role in a whole network of dependencies and relationships.

57 See *BTRL* pp. 213–14. Not all heirs had the right to abstain, exactly; a testator could manumit an enslaved person in their will on the condition they serve as a "necessary heir" (*heres necessarius*). While some protections were available to the enslaved heir of an insolvent estate, they were quite different in structure. *Ibid.*, p. 232.

58 Cicero makes this point in a sarcastic rejoinder to a strawman argument; Cicero pictures Antony complaining about having to take on his father's debt and refers to that complaint as "a defense full of piety" (*pietatis plena defensio*).

59 See *BTRL* pp. 214; Roller, *Constructing Autocracy*, p. 238.

60 See Thomas, "Vitae Necisque Potestas," pp. 144–210; Curran, "Ius Vitae Necisque."

These relationships would be especially fraught for a son like Titus. When Tiberius made grantees petition individually for their *beneficia* to be renewed, he differentiated imperial grants from the quotidian obligations that he faced as Augustus' heir. Tiberius thus separated imperial and family business, putting the former into a novel conceptual space. By treating Vespasian's *beneficia* as his own, Titus merged the two. Titus not only regularized the relationship between emperor and subject by analogizing it to that between law and citizen but also regularized the relationship between emperor and successor by analogizing it to that between father and son. The Edict of Titus put *beneficia* at the intersection of contractual rights and legislation, and they would occupy that space – much to the consternation of legal authorities who wanted a cleaner break – for centuries.[61] But the contractual, persistent nature of these *beneficia* depended upon imperial stability, and Titus described that stability in a language of family and inheritance that Romans already had to hand.

That said, this change was symbolic more than it was legal. In practical terms Titus maintained absolute discretion over which *beneficia* would persist and which would not, since the edict simply established a new default rule.[62] Whereas previous *beneficia* had been presumed to lapse upon an emperor's death (but his successor could renew them), under Titus Vespasianic *beneficia* were presumed valid (but Titus could void them). The edict was not exactly infelicitous – it renewed *beneficia* that exercised power in the social world – but it was unreliable. It created rhetorical expectations over and above its legal effects, and those rhetorical expectations mattered.

To be more specific, the Edict of Titus can be understood as part of a broader messaging program common to both Titus and his father. As already discussed, Vespasian faced novel challenges in legitimating his authority; Titus, who had not himself won a civil war and whose claim to the throne sprung from biological descent, faced even more. While Flavian historiography makes it hard to determine exactly how people felt about Titus, we can see a years-long effort to legitimate Titus' succession of his father. For example, Vespasian and Titus celebrated

[61] On later anxieties around the arbitrary nature of imperial grants see *infra* pp. 276–77.

[62] For more discussion on the effects of changing default rules Sunstein, "Switching."

a highly unusual joint triumph after suppressing the Jewish revolt.[63] My instinct is that this work happened for a reason, and responded to pushback from an audience that "Team Vespasian" knew better than we do. But either way, the work was happening. The Flavian bureaucracy tried hard to legitimate Titus, by making him appear as a co-ruler who could step in upon his father's death with as little disruption as possible, and the edict fits with that project. Tiberius' earlier practice of renewing *beneficia* individually had been enormously disruptive but worked to reinforce petitioners' bonds and debts to Tiberius as a person. The Edict of Titus made accession smoother by drawing beneficiaries into a relationship with the Flavians as a family, one that remained in power.

It also, and finally, prompted those beneficiaries to see Titus as they might see other Roman legal subjects. A son who took on his father's property as Titus had was not only expected to honor that father's promises as a matter of etiquette, but was bound by them as if he had made them himself. We have already seen how that *boundedness*, that impression of existing within and being subject to existing constraints, worked as a desideratum within imperial political discourse. We have also seen law working as a potent metaphorical language for expressing that boundedness. The Edict of Titus is nowhere near as explicit as the *lex de imperio Vespasiani* in portraying the emperor as subject to the laws, but in both cases the framework within which the emperor appears to be constrained is a legal one.

This idea of the emperor as following the laws, as discharging the same (or similar) obligations that everyday Romans were compelled to by statute and *ius ciuile*, differs from the Augustan attitude towards law that I discussed in the previous chapter. That difference may reflect broader changes in how Romans thought about imperial sovereignty. Max Weber's account of how authority survives at moments of succession describes a "routinization of charisma" (*Veralltäglichung des Charisma*). Specifically, over time a charismatic leader gives way to a more institutionally mediated governing framework that might invoke

63 The triumph is recorded at Dio Cass. 66[65].12.1 [Xiph.]; Joesph. *BJ* 7.123–57; Suet. *Tit.* 6.1. On Titus being represented as a sort of co-ruler during this time, see *ibid.* ("From then on Titus did not cease from exercising participation in, and even guardianship over, the empire" (*Neque ex eo destitit participem atque etiam tutorem imperii agere*); Tarel, *Titus*, pp. 193–224; Jones, *The Emperor Titus*, pp. 77–113.

that leader as a legitimating historical actor without overturning existing systems as that leader themselves once did.[64] The transformational outsider's account of legitimacy dies with them, and successors necessarily justify their authority with different arguments and stories. Those stories may be dynastic, or they may ground themselves in broader narratives of administrative continuity. The edict merged the two, using law and legal arguments to highlight an emergent dynastic claim. These two discourses – dynasty and law – will recur over the course of this book, but while Romans sometimes understood them to exist in tension they could also work in concert as they do here. Law and family were two ways to ground an individual emperor's authority in something bigger and more legitimate than the man himself. Accordingly, the language of imperial legality, like the language of dynasty and filial succession, emerged at moments when emperors needed to justify their authority.

* * * * *

Titus did not have very long to put this representational tendency into practice. He died suddenly in 81, and was succeeded by his brother Domitian.[65] Domitian himself was assassinated in 97, which inaugurated a roughly century-long period of adoptive – rather than dynastic – succession.[66] It is perhaps not a coincidence that our most explicit account of "the *princeps* who obeys the law" comes from that period, and that it lays out a surprisingly complex paradigm for how law and the Principate could coexist.

Law as Imperial Etiquette: The Case of Pliny

Pliny's *Panegyricus*, the subject of the final section of this chapter, is a tough read. A speech delivered in 100 CE by Pliny the Younger to thank Trajan for honoring him with a consulship, the *Panegyricus* is relentless in its praise. That repetitive and fulsome prose makes the

64 Weber, *Wirtschaft und Gesellschaft*, pp. 770–72; see also Kantorowicz, *Bodies*, pp. 383–84.

65 For more on this succession Griffin, "The Flavians," pp. 54–56.

66 Domitian's own representational program is not easy to discern, given the memory sanctions that followed his death. However, sources like the poetry of Statius (on which see Newlands, *Poetics of Empire*) and surviving architecture (Conlin, "Assemblages") represent Domitian as a divinely favored, charismatic ruler who nevertheless engaged with earlier Julio-Claudian models.

Panegyricus somewhat challenging, and it is not necessarily clear what historians should do with it. For some time the dominant view has been that of Bartsch, who assesses the *Panegyricus* as a camp text *avant la lettre*: as a gifted orator's attempt to express sincere gratitude in a communicative milieu whose insistence on constant, insincere gratitude made that job impossible.[67] Other recent work has highlighted the *Panegyricus*' rhetorical brilliance and impact, while evaluating Pliny's specific fact claims as more or less plausible historical data.[68] These readings can coexist. The *Panegyricus* can be well-made and influential without being compelling to a modern audience, but its naked supplication to Trajanic authority gives it a historical value all its own. Like other Classical praise literature,[69] the *Panegyricus* serves as a record of what kind of imperial qualities might be considered praiseworthy. While the *Panegyricus* does not command any particular credibility when it claims that Trajan "loves peace" (16: *pacem amas*), it suggests that Pliny's audience (including Trajan) understood such a claim as flattering and accordingly that it identifies a desirable characteristic in a ruler. Conversely, the *Panegyricus* abuses Domitian by accusing him of political acts and moral attributes that we can then understand to be bad in Pliny's world. In short, the *Panegyricus* is a useful tool for understanding the paradigm with which elite Roman subjects made sense of the early second century.[70]

It is striking, then, how large a role law and legal processes play in that paradigm. Part of an emperor's job is to supervise a social order

67 Bartsch, *Actors*, p. 149 ("[I]n large part, the *Panegyricus* is an obsessive attempt to prove its own sincerity"); see also Gibson, "Unending Praise," pp. 122–23. I follow Sontag's definition of "naïve camp" at "Notes on Camp," pp. 282–83 as denoting a piece of art that so earnestly demands a particular reading (and so utterly fails to justify that reading) as to generate unintended hermeneutics.

68 Shannon-Henderson, "Deification"; Innes, "Rhetorical Theory"; Noreña, "Self-Fashioning"; on the facticity of the *Panegyricus*, see Roche, "Thanksgiving," pp. 14–18.

69 On which see Gibson, "Contemporary Contexts." On the instructional role of the *Panegyricus* Gibson, "Unending Praise," pp. 133–36.

70 "Roman" is intentional. While we have other examples of praise literature from this rough period, they are written in Greek for a largely Greek audience. I discuss Aelius Aristides' praise of Rome *infra* pp. 132–33; on Dio Chrysostom's rhetorical tropes see Strazdins, *Fashioning*, pp. 37–40; Jackson, "Dio Chrysostom"; Pernot, *Epideictic Rhetoric*, pp. 44–45; Whitmarsh, *Greek Literature and the Roman Empire*, pp. 186–90.

that includes law, and accordingly panegyricists tend to reference law as one of the public goods for which they are grateful. Pliny's contemporary Dio Chrysostom, for example, will call the ideal king "a judge more lawful than a duly chosen jury" (3.5: νομιμώτερος μὲν δικαστὴς τῶν κατὰ κλῆρον δικαζόντων). Pliny innovates, however, by describing Trajan as a litigant and not a judge. In his telling, Trajan is such a good autocrat that he pretends not to be one at all; he allows citizens to challenge his actions in court, and sometimes even to win.

But the honor of the laws persists, and no blow is struck against the public interest: no one's punishment is lessened but vengeance is increased, and the only difference is that now it is not informers but laws that are feared. But perhaps you do not manage the imperial fisc with the same prudence as your own accounts? On the contrary it is even greater, since you believe yourself to be granted greater leeway with your own funds than with the public's. It is said to your agents, and even to your procurators: Come to court! Approach the bench! *For a tribunal has been set up for imperial business, equal to all others except as regards the magnificence of its litigant. The fisc's judge is assigned by lot: we are allowed to reject him, and to exclaim:* Not this one! He is too afraid, he does not understand the blessings of our new era! Not that one either! He likes the emperor too much! *Empire and liberty use the same courtroom: and the special monument to your glory is that your fisc often loses: something which can only occur under a good emperor.*

(*Pan.* 36) Manet tamen honor legum, nihilque ex publica utilitate conuulsum: nec poena cuiquam remissa, sed addita est ultio, solumque mutatum, quod iam non delatores, sed leges timentur. At fortasse non eadem seueritate fiscum, qua aerarium, cohibes. Immo tanto maiore, quanto plus tibi licere de tuo, quam de publico credis. Dicitur actori, atque etiam procuratori tuo: In ius ueni: sequere ad tribunal. Nam tribunal quoque excogitatum principatui est, par ceteris, nisi illud litigatoris amplitudine metiaris. Sors et urna fisco iudicem assignat: licet reiicere, licet exclamare: Hunc nolo, timidus est, et bona seculi parum intelligit: illum nolo, quia Caesarem fortiter amat. Eodem foro utuntur principatus et libertas. Quae praecipua tua gloria est, saepius uincitur fiscus; cuius mala caussa nunquam est, nisi sub bono principe.

Pliny here uses the language of legal supremacy – *non delatores, sed leges timentur* – but frames that supremacy almost entirely in procedural terms. Pliny does not emphasize law's ability to constrain imperial action; while he seems to describe a world in which those constraints exist and guide the tribunal's decisions, substantive legal protections matter less than the phrases and gestures that symbolize legal order. Under Trajan, the rule of law means being able to say *in ius ueni!* to an imperial agent, and then drawing a judge's name from an urn. Later in the speech Pliny will make this ritualistic legality explicit, by praising Trajan for participating in the kinds of rituals that actual legal subjects are compelled to undergo.

On the rostra, as well, you subjected yourself to the laws with a similar reverence; those laws, Caesar, which no one wrote for the emperor. But you wish for yourself no greater license than that given to us, with the result that we want even more for you. For the first time I hear, and know, not that the emperor is above the laws but that the laws are above the emperor and that the same restrictions apply to the emperor as to other consuls. He swears upon the laws, with the gods watching (for who else would they watch?), in the presence of those who must swear the same oath, knowing that no one needs to be more scrupulous about keeping his word than the man to whom it falls to prevent others from lying. Similarly, on the point of finishing your consulship you swore that you had done nothing contrary to the laws.

(*Pan.* 65) In rostris quoque simili religione ipse te legibus subiecisti: legibus, Caesar, quas nemo principi scripsit. Sed tu nihil amplius uis tibi licere quam nobis: sic fit, ut nos tibi plus uelimus. Quod ego nunc primum audio, nunc primum disco; non est princeps super leges sed leges super principem idemque Caesari consuli quod ceteris non licet. Iurat in leges attendentibus dis (nam cui magis quam Caesari attendant?), iurat obseruantibus his quibus idem iurandum est, non ignarus alioqui nemini religiosius quod iurauerit custodiendum, quam cuius maxime interest non peierari. Itaque et abiturus consulatu iurasti, te nihil contra leges fecisse.

Trajan performs legal subjecthood, in the most literal sense of being *legibus subiectus*, in public. Accordingly, he raises questions about what it means to perform with law. Most accounts of legal performance center law's ability to set out particular spaces, gestures, or utterances as distinct from those of ordinary life. In the ancient context we often think of legal proceedings as a site of spectacle, in which everyday power relations are superseded by the distinctive practices of the courtroom. Thus Lanni describes the Athenian popular court as a venue for the *demos* to impose their ethical notions upon a more stratified society, Bablitz treats the behaviors of Roman trial advocates as complex and ritually significant, and Stone Peters considers courtrooms from ancient

Greece to early modern England as in dialogue with other forms of theatrical entertainment.[71]

Historians of more recent legal regimes often take these practices to constitute not so much a spectacle as a kind of performative citizenship. Put differently, in these regimes courtroom behavior could demonstrate suitability for membership within a given political unit. Gross describes a legal culture in the post-Civil War American South that defined white men as "civic being[s] who voted, *served on juries*, and mustered in the militia"; citizenship is something one does, and courtrooms are one place in which one does it.[72] People with more tenuous claims to belonging used these legal rituals to construct a civic identity, and Welch describes Black litigants of the antebellum period who mastered litigation in order to situate themselves within a hostile polity.[73]

Trajan fits better into this contemporary model, and these later accounts of legal performance help us understand what Pliny is using law to say. Pliny describes a legal order that is ritual and only ritual: oaths and urns that do nothing beyond setting certain procedures apart as special.[74] But that order purports to govern a man whose whole life is special. Trajan does not use legal forms in order to set himself apart from the polity, in the way that law sets itself apart from everyday activity. Instead, he uses them to set himself under the polity, in the way that other consuls and other litigants exist under the sovereignty of the law. For example, Pliny asserts restrictions on Trajan's conduct (*non licet*) of which there is no evidence. No remedy is available for one who believes that Trajan has acted contrary to the laws in his tenure as consul, at least not like those which might be available against Pliny.[75] That lack of constraint is a necessary feature of imperial sovereignty, and Pliny acknowledges that no one imagines laws applying to a man in Trajan's position (*nemo principi scripsit*).

[71] Stone Peters, *Law as Performance*, pp. 9–11; Bablitz, *Actors and Audience*, pp. 187–92; Lanni, *Courts*, p. 178.

[72] Gross, *What Blood Won't Tell*, p. 53 (emphasis added).

[73] Welch, *Black Litigants*, p. 14.

[74] This sense of "ritual" follows Bell (*Ritual Theory, Ritual Practice*, p. 74) in describing ritual actions as those that are "distinguish[ed] and privilege[d] ... in comparison to other, usually more quotidian, activities."

[75] On the *Panegyricus*' exaggerated connection between Pliny and Trajan as fellow consuls, see Noreña, "Self-Fashioning," pp. 35–38.

But a good emperor acts as if he is legally bound, and even seems to voluntarily concede in circumstances where a legal subject would be compelled to do so: i.e. after his case has failed (*uincitur fiscus*).

Pliny suggests that these performances help narrow the space between *principatus* and *libertas*, literally placing them in the same forum (*eodem foro*), and thus make the former resemble the latter. The law here appears as a set of rules for Trajan to follow, but those rules function as ethical hortations rather than the coercive, state-backed restrictions that Roman law placed upon others. This moral valence makes Pliny's job easier – complying with ethical hortations is praiseworthy, in a way that following the law to avoid a penalty is not[76] – but also gives the *leges* to which Trajan subjects himself an odd tinge. For Trajan following the law is like calling your mother, not like paying your taxes.

That said, you should still call your mother. Law remains part of the normative framework by which a good emperor evaluates his actions, and by which other inhabitants of the Principate evaluate an emperor's actions and determine whether he is a good emperor or not.[77] Trajan follows the law because good emperors follow the law, and having a good emperor is almost like liberty. This vision of imperial sovereignty differs starkly from the one contained in *Sat.* 2.1, which I discussed in the previous chapter. Horace views the emperor as entirely unconstrained, and thus as an escape from the quaintness and cruelty of law. Pliny, by contrast, views Trajan's omnipotence as unsettling, and praises him for acting in accordance with a law from which he is effectively exempt.

Each author is diametrically opposed in how they moralize the problem of emperors and law, and accordingly each recommends different solutions to it. But both agree on why having an emperor is a problem for legality, and on how an emperor's existence changes what we understand law to mean. Once law gets too close to an emperor's person (close enough that he might take an interest and make his own judgments), it becomes symbolic and somewhat brittle. If we imagine what gives a prescription its distinctively legal character

[76] The analogy to Kant's prudent shopkeeper is obvious but somewhat anachronistic; a similar argument for the greater goodness of actions taken without a mind to punishment or reward might be the Gyges narrative of Pl. *Rep.* 2.

[77] On this evaluative practice as a specifically senatorial prerogative see Kemezis, "Vox Populi, Vox Mea?"

to be its power to alter the world, that power vanishes if the emperor disagrees. What remains are ritual phrases, like Pliny's *in ius ueni!* or Horace's archaic imperatives, that only have power if the emperor wants them to. Neither author, accordingly, spends much time on what law says about the world, since that matters very little for the world in which they live. The more pressing question, instead, is "what does an emperor's treatment of law say about himself?"

For all its legal niceties the *Panegyricus* does not have much to say about Roman law. It talks, instead, about Trajanic sovereignty. And the version of Trajan that appears in that speech is beautiful and somewhat sinister. He is a god who graciously pretends to be a man, and an absolute ruler who graciously pretends to follow the law. Pliny states this paradox most openly at *Pan.* 24: "we are ruled by you and subject to you, but in that way that we are subject to laws" (*regimur quidem a te, et subiecti tibi, sed quemadmodum legibus, sumus*). *Regimur*, with its connotations of *reges regentes regna*, is an ugly word for a man like Pliny to say. While Greek panegyricists like Dio Chrysostom seem to feel no anxiety about referring to the emperor as a king or *basileus*, for a Latin speaker to call an emperor *rex* would mean accusing him of high-handedness, tyranny, and even of rejecting Roman values.[78] *Regimur a te* walks right up to that line, but Pliny dodges the bullet by analogizing Trajanic and legal orders. The rule of Trajan is like – not quite the same as, not similar enough to allow one to articulate the relationship in more specific terms than *quemadmodum*, but nevertheless *like* – the rule of law.

* * * * *

Pliny's rhetorical exertions demonstrate the problem that emperors like Vespasian and Titus used law to try and solve. Since Augustus, emperors had existed outside of legal order, but the emperors whose engagements with law I have tracked in this chapter had reasons to worry about how they were perceived. Even Trajan, whom Pliny describes as owing his tenure to a military revolt that forced Nerva to adopt him as heir,[79] knew what happened

[78] See Noreña, *Imperial Ideals*, pp. 315–17; Wallace-Hadrill, "Civilis Princeps," pp. 41–44.

[79] After describing the revolt in vague terms at *Pan.* 5–6, 7 refers euphemistically to Trajan's "new and unheard-of path to the throne" (*nouum atque inauditum ad principatum iter*).

to Domitian.[80] Pliny, moreover, takes pains to remind Trajan of what happens to tyrants. By abusing Domitian for ruling badly, Pliny warns Trajan of the consequences of ruling badly. Emperors like Vespasian, Titus, and Trajan responded to these pressures with a broad representational program, of which law was an important part, in which they voluntarily abided by constraints that other Romans experienced as binding rules. Those constraints were often symbolic (like the somewhat incoherent *lex de imperio Vespasiani*, or the Edict of Titus analogizing succession to a legally scrupulous inheritance), but symbols are important in the history of the Principate.

This account of emperor as legal subject innovated on the Augustan model. While Augustus made a show of subsuming himself within existing frameworks and systems of rules, he called attention to the discretionary nature of his obedience to law. By contrast, the three emperors shown here appear to act as normal legal subjects do. They rely on powers granted to them by *leges* or *senatusconsulta*, they take on their fathers' obligations and commitments, they send their agents to court and hope they win. This new model of imperial representation, of "the *princeps* who obeys the law," would persist for centuries. When Severus Alexander claims in a rescript that "nothing is as befitting of *imperium* as living according to the laws," he uses law as a metaphor for rejecting tyranny and observing traditional organs of legitimate authority.[81]

But the law is a metaphor before it is a law. On the one hand, it is hardly uncommon for law to offer a symbolic vocabulary that extends beyond the narrow jurisdiction in which it exercises legal force. On the other, we typically understand the symbolics of law as deeply bound up with its practical function. Legal order is impressive because it affects the world, with the rhetorical and performative aspects of law intended to support that project. In this chapter, law has been rhetoric and rhetoric alone. When law gets too close to an imperial subject it loses

80 Suetonius (*Dom.* 17) records Domitian being stabbed in his genitals (*inguina*) by an assassin.

81 C.6.23.3. As Lucrezi notes (*Leges super principem*, p. 176), this phrase strikingly resembles the language of Justinian's *Institutes* discussed *supra* pp. 75–76. Furthermore, Justinian refers to Severus and Caracalla making this claim *saepissime*, suggesting a trope of which this rescript may be a later example. I discuss the problem further *infra* p. 180.

its normative capacity; the fact that law remained such an important aspect of imperial representation in this period implies that it was doing a lot more than normative readings would suggest. Law gave sovereigns a language with which they could talk about themselves like they were subjects, and gave subjects a conceptual framework within which they could construct a tolerable politics.

3

Letters from a God: Hadrian and the Rescript System

In this chapter I discuss the centralization of legal work within the imperial court that took place under Hadrian and his successors. This centralization took many forms and had many consequences. Institutional structures that had helped earlier Romans understand the law withered, and other discursive spaces emerged in which to produce or communicate legal certainty.

But those spaces served other purposes as well. They were venues in which subjects could bring their problems to the attention of the emperor, and the emperor could demonstrate his own interest and solicitude. Hadrian's administrative program transformed him into a supreme and competent court of last resort, while also transforming law from something outside of imperial authority into a language through which people could invoke that authority for themselves. This newer vision built on Greek paradigms, which imagined law as a good provided by a sovereign rather than as something that was sovereign itself.[1] Accordingly it made law into a proper object of euergetism, or status-asymmetric generosity performed by powerful men.[2] Rather than law being something that the emperor ought to be a subject of, law here became something that an emperor ought to provide to subjects. The clearest example of this normativity is an anecdote, preserved in Cassius Dio, where Hadrian

[1] Tuori, "Greek Tyranny." [2] I define euergetism more closely *infra* pp. 117–18.

encounters a woman who demands a hearing as the price of sovereignty.

When he [Hadrian] passed a woman on the road who had need of something or other, he first told her "I have no time"; then when she shouted back "then don't be emperor" he stopped and spoke with her.

(69[68].6.4 [Xiph.]) ἀμέλει γυναικὸς παριόντος αὐτοῦ ὁδῷ τινι δεομένης, τὸ μὲν πρῶτον εἶπεν αὐτῇ ὅτι 'οὐ σχολάζω,' ἔπειτα ὡς ἐκείνη ἀνακραγοῦσα ἔφη 'καὶ μὴ βασίλευε,' ἐπεστράφη τε καὶ λόγον αὐτῇ ἔδωκεν.

This never happened.[3] But Dio isolates the core of a promise that legitimated imperial authority and shows how legal processes could work to fulfill it. Importantly, Hadrian's interlocutor does not demand results – she demands time. Dio does not say whether Hadrian granted her request, because the grant itself is not part of the bargain. Instead, Hadrian is expected to listen and to consider her narrative, to enter into a kind of intimacy with his subject whether or not he agrees with her at the end of it.[4] This expectation is a common feature of contemporary legal systems and explains how these systems can appear legitimate to subjects even when they lose in court. Merry refers to this "legal entitlement" as a "right to protest" and Tyler as "procedural justice" but both describe litigants who expect to be taken seriously and listened to.[5] This chapter shows how emperors and their officials came to use legal process to perform that script.

It is striking that so much of this change occurred under Hadrian. While Hadrian came from the Latin-speaking western empire (specifically what is now Spain)[6] he maintained the persona of a cosmopolitan philhellenist. It might not shock, then, that Hadrian's

[3] As Millar notes (*Emperor*, pp. 3–4), this colloquy is a trope in Greek historiography; cf. e.g. Plut. *Reg. et imp. apophth.* 179 C–D (describing a subject approaching Philip II), *Demetr.* 42.4 (Demetrios Poliorketes).

[4] See Bryen, *Violence*, pp. 89–125.

[5] Merry, *Getting Justice*, pp.179–81; Tyler, *Why People Obey the Law*, pp. 163–65.

[6] Oddly, while administrative communication took place in Latin throughout the Roman West, the *uita Hadriani* (3.1) suggests that Hadrian "devoted himself to the study of Latin" (*Latinis operam dedit*) as an adult, in order to increase his mastery and fluency (*usque ad summam peritiam et facundiam*). The text leaves unclear whether Hadrian was trying to minimize a Spanish accent (cf. *HA*, *Sept. Seu.* 19.9 on Septimius Severus' African accent, which he never fully suppressed) or improve his facility with the Latin language – the latter would suggest that a wealthy family of Italian origin (per Hadrian's autobiography: see *HA*, *Hadr.* 1.1) did not speak Latin at home.

reforms rendered imperial governance more legible within Greek models of benevolent kingship. Imperial legality of the first century CE reflected a Roman understanding of laws as suprasocial and unchanging, like the system of virtues an emperor might be expected to embody. Hadrian and his successors linked law more closely with the sovereign's own will, generosity, and solicitude.

The legal system that arose in the second century CE mixed Greek and Roman influences, and told different stories about emperors and empire to different viewers. Historians of other aspects of imperial Rome have discussed this refractive quality in Roman political representation, and how "Rome" and "emperors" served diverse and somewhat incoherent symbolic functions.[7] But that polyvalence is an important part of how Roman law got to be the way it is. Some audiences expected a law that was reasoned and philosophically coherent, others a law that was authoritative, centralized, and straightforward. They all, however, expected law from the emperor. Accordingly processes from this time that strike us as inherently legal (like the rescript system) can be understood not in terms of an autonomously developing "legal thought" but instead in terms of imperial performance. Hadrian and his successors made themselves legal authorities, to borrow Fergus Millar's famous line, by using law to do the kinds of things emperors did.[8]

This chapter argues that the massive changes to Roman legal process that took place during and after the reign of Hadrian brought law into line with other kinds of imperial storytelling. I begin by explaining how Roman legal production became more centralized under Hadrian, and why that centralization might have been more visible to later than to contemporary viewers. I next consider how legal communication came to serve as an important venue for imperial representation according to many different paradigms of the same. Imperial control of Roman law looked sometimes like a philosophers' salon and sometimes like a traffic court, but it always offered subjects the chance to experience the emperor's judgment for themselves.

[7] See e.g. Mazurek, *Isis*, pp. 13–17; Dench, *Cultures*, pp. 47–73; Noreña, *Imperial Ideals*, pp. 245–99.

[8] Millar, *Emperor*, p. 6.

Hadrian's Revolution

Hadrian transformed the administration of the Roman empire. Our major Classical accounts of Hadrian's reign – Cassius Dio and, most likely, Marius Maximus (via the *HA*) – come from the third century CE, and they mainly emphasize his interest in travel and comparative indifference towards military expansion.[9] Without necessarily endorsing their claims about Hadrian's personality, the third-century biographers can be taken at face value that Hadrian brought the empire back within defensible borders and that he spent a great deal of time outside of Italy. As they describe Hadrian's itinerary, both Dio and Maximus refer only in passing to shifts in legal policy. The *HA* mentions that Hadrian "established an imperially funded communications system, lest local officials be burdened by the effort" (*Hadr.* 7.5: *cursum fiscalem instituit, ne magistratus hoc onere grauarentur*), and Dio that "he judged cases together with the foremost men, sometimes in his palace and sometimes in the Forum and sometimes in the Pantheon and in other places besides (69[68].7.1 [Xiph.]: ἐδίκαζε μετὰ τῶν πρώτων τοτὲ μὲν ἐν τῷ παλατίῳ τοτὲ δὲ ἐν τῇ ἀγορᾷ τῷ τε Πανθείῳ καὶ ἄλλοθι πολλαχόθι).

By contrast, historians writing in the fourth century place more weight on Hadrianic administrative reforms. For example, the *Epitome de Caesaribus* notes that Hadrian "arranged the public and imperial bureaucracies, as well as the army, into the form which persists today barring a few changes made by Constantine" (14.11: *Officia sane publica et palatina nec non militiae in eam formam statuit, quae paucis per Constantinum immutatis hodie perseuerat*).

The Hadrianic revolution was clearer in retrospect. Later Romans would come to associate Hadrian with certain reforms that really came into being more gradually. But Hadrian oversaw real changes to how Roman law was produced and applied, without which Severan and late-antique legalities would make no sense. Before I describe how these changes worked within the empire of the second century, I here explain what Hadrian did and how we know about it. I focus on three particularly consequential evolutions of the Hadrianic period:

[9] Dio Cass. 69.5.1 [Xiph.], 69.9.1 [Xiph.]; *Hadr.* 5, 10, 13.5 ("hardly anyone else traveled so much imperial territory so quickly" *nec quisquam fere principum tantum terrarum tam celeriter peragrauit*); see also Birley, "Hadrian's Travels."

stabilizing the Praetor's Edict, formalizing the imperial cabinet or *consilium*, and the growing use of imperial correspondence to answer legal questions via what is often called "the rescript system."

The Perpetual Edict

Later historians frequently mention Hadrian regularizing the Praetor's Edict, or the list of actions that Roman legal subjects could bring in court. These references are laconic and brief, but suggest that Hadrian's jurist Salvius Julianus fixed the provisions of the edict into a perpetual form which could only be amended by imperial constitution (i.e. by a written statement attributed to the emperor; I will use this term quite a bit going forward).[10] After discussing the prior edict, as well as our evidence for its alteration under Hadrian, I discuss what this change might have meant for imperial legal culture of the second century.

In Republican times, Roman adjudication had been left in the care of the praetor. Praetors were high-ranking senatorial officials, generally subordinate only to consuls, who served one-year terms. In any given year two praetors would split the docket, with one (the *praetor urbanus*) hearing cases within the city of Rome, the other (*praetor peregrinus*) cases involving those outside the city.[11] At the beginning of his term (the Kalends of January, i.e. January 1) the praetor published an edict listing all of the actions he would recognize as valid in the coming year.[12] In practice, we should assume that praetors did not rewrite the edict every year but instead worked off of and altered existing lists of actions.[13]

[10] This definition follows Ulpian's at D.1.4.1pr. (Institutiones): see *supra* p. 84.

[11] This is a somewhat vague framing, and intentionally so: the exact contours of the peregrine's jurisdiction in the Republican period, and how those contours changed over time, are hard to discern. See Brennan, *Praetorship*, pp. 85–89; Daube, "The Peregrine Praetor."

[12] Brennan, *Praetorship*, pp. 130–33.

[13] Eberle collects (at "Edicts," pp. 242–59) the existing evidence for Republican edicts and shows enormous variation in different praetors' fidelity to existing models. While the edict is usually discussed as praetorian, in practice provincial administrators (proconsuls, propraetors, and eventually *praefecti*) served similar functions. The Flavian *Lex Irnitana*, for example, commands that local magistrates display the edict of the provincial governor (ch. 85). Johnston, "Three Thoughts," pp. 64–67; González and Crawford, "The Lex Irnitana," pp. 176, 230–31.

Praetors continued into the imperial period and, at first, remained responsible for the edict. However, in practice Aurelius Victor's claim that the edict in this time was "displayed in a changing and chaotic fashion by the praetors" (*Caes.* 19.2: *uarie inconditeque a praetoribus promebatur*) probably misses the mark and praetors, who were at least informally chosen by the emperor, did not go so rogue. The edict was already under loose imperial control, and we have no evidence of radical changes to it in the earlier Principate.

It was Hadrian, though, who regularized the edict and took it out of praetorian hands. The sources for this process are numerous, and span different genres.[14] Epigraphic evidence makes clear that the jurist Salvius Julianus was recognized for providing some kind of extraordinary service to Hadrian; a Tunisian inscription (*CIL* VIII.24094 = *ILS* 8973) commemorates Julianus' career and claims that "the deified Hadrian doubled his quaestoral salary on account of his extraordinary learning" (*diu*[*u*]*s Hadrianus soli salarium quaesturae duplicauit propter insignem doctrinam*).[15]

Other sources explain what made Julianus so special. Both Eutropius and Aurelius Victor identify Julianus with the establishment of a permanent edict, albeit in a somewhat roundabout fashion. Eutropius refers to the short-lived emperor Didius Julianus (r. 193) as "grandson of Salvius Julianus, who composed the Perpetual Edict under Hadrian" (8.17: *nepos Saluii Iuliani, qui sub diuo Hadriano perpetuum conposuit edictum*). Aurelius Victor, by contrast, confuses the two entirely and describes Didius as "[A] man with a lineage that was noble, and outstanding in the urbane study of law; for he was the first to put the edict, which previously was displayed in a changing and chaotic fashion by the praetors, into a settled order" (*Caes.* 19.2: *Genus ei pernobile iurisque urbani praestans scientia; quippe qui primus edictum, quod uarie inconditeque a praetoribus promebatur, in ordinem composuerit*).[16]

[14] For discussion of the sources for Hadrian and the Perpetual Edict, see especially Tuori, "Hadrian's Perpetual Edict," pp. 220–24; also Robinson, *Sources*, p. 12; Jolowicz and Nicholas, *Historical Introduction*, pp. 356–57.

[15] See Kunkel, "Lebenszeit," pp. 200–01.

[16] The *HA*'s biography of Didius Iulianus also mentions this familial link: *Did. Iul.* 1.1. On the plausibility of the *HA*'s evidence *HSS* II.36.

Legal sources are less confused. The *CTh.* preserves Theodosius referring to "the edict of the deified Hadrian" (4.4.7pr.: *edicto diui Hadriani*) and to the "grant of the edict that was established by the deified Hadrian" (11.36.26: *edicti per diuum Hadrianum conditi beneficium*). Later, Justinian would call Julianus "a man of the greatest authority, who organized the praetorian edict" (C.4.5.10.1, 530: *Saluium Iulianum summae auctoritatis hominem et praetorii edicti ordinatorem*) and claim that he "most subtly established the laws and the Perpetual Edict" (*Tanta* 18: *ipse Iulianus legum et edicti perpetui subtilissimus conditor*).[17] These references are brief, and late; the only contemporary testimony for the edict is a laconic reference to Julianus' extraordinary learning, and Guarino has argued that Hadrian's creation of the Perpetual Edict is a late-antique myth.[18] By contrast, I follow Tuori and Honoré.[19] These references are too generically diverse to arise from a simple misunderstanding, and *CIL* VIII.24094 provides good evidence that something unusual happened while Salvianus was *quaestor* that justified doubling his salary. The most logical explanation is that Salvius Julianus oversaw the fixing of the edict into a new and unchanging form.

That said, Guarino has a point. It is striking how little Julianus' and Hadrian's contemporaries cared about the Perpetual Edict, given its outsized role in late-antique legal discourse. The clearest explanation is that those living in the second century saw Hadrian as simply ratifying the *status quo ante*; we have no reason to think that the edict was changing radically, or changing at all without imperial approval, before Hadrian got involved. Even so, commentators writing within the more centralized and bureaucratic legal milieux of the fourth through sixth centuries understood Hadrian as inaugurating their own legal order.[20] The Perpetual Edict put into words an understanding of imperial legislative supremacy that had come about more gradually and thus seemed to create that supremacy out of thin air for later readers.

[17] Tuori, "Hadrian's Perpetual Edict," pp. 221–22.
[18] Guarino, "Leggenda," pp. 253–54; see also Cancelli, *Codificazione*; Tuori, *Ideals*, p. 143.
[19] Tuori, "Hadrian's Perpetual Edict," p. 223; Honoré, *Gaius*, p. 47.
[20] See Guarino, "Leggenda," p. 255.

So if the Perpetual Edict did not meaningfully change the development of new causes of action in the second century, what did it do? On this reading, the change was primarily symbolic. The praetorian edict was a republicanizing fiction, siting legal authority in the elected official who had once held the real thing and in the rituals that surrounded his investiture. A perpetual edict tells a different story, de-emphasizing magistrates and highlighting imperial supervision. Instead of a praetor choosing to grant relief in specified circumstances, the edict describes justice as Hadrian's prerogative and draws litigants into relationships of dependence with the imperial lawgiver.

Notably, the edict does so without actually tying anyone's hands. Like the Edict of Titus described in Chapter 2, the Perpetual Edict can be thought of as simply changing a default rule. In earlier periods, the praetor's list of remedies was voided and reformed every year; even if it happened to look exactly the same after this reformation, that reconstitutive ritual discourages legal subjects from seeing the list as stable. By contrast, the Perpetual Edict was presumed to last until altered. In practical terms the available remedies could shift, but the edict now more closely resembled other Roman legal texts in that it set out a baseline that did not require renovation.

Viewed in this light, the Perpetual Edict symbolized a changing understanding of how emperors engaged with law. It also, importantly, symbolized a law that was fixed. Hadrian and Julianus constructed a law that was perpetual and reliable, laying the groundwork for praetors (or emperors) to succeed each other with minimal disruption. We saw in the previous chapter how this stability could serve as a political desideratum, and how law was a particularly potent metaphorical language with which to communicate that stability. By offering a perpetual and unchanging set of legal remedies, Hadrian could make continuity itself into an imperial gift.

That gift can be thought of as part of a longer tradition of benefaction by great men. The Roman *urbs* and Greek *polis* alike relied upon leading citizens undertaking civic functions at their own trouble and expense. These acts of generosity confirmed the benefactors' elevated status in their communities and drew beneficiaries into relationships of informal dependence. We commonly call this tradition *euergetism* after the

Greek, since Greek city-states had more formalized accounts of euergetic action; the practice persisted, however, well into the Roman period.[21] Making the edict into a public good linked closely with the emperor and his promise to intervene – making it into a list of Things The Emperor Will Do For You, If You Ask Him To – meant making law euergetic. While previous emperors had engaged with law as an impersonal tradition with sacred components, Hadrian represented it as fixed and as under his benevolent control. That control was a public good over and above anything someone might win in court; settling the law was something that the sovereign, and only the sovereign, could accomplish.

The Right of Response and Juristic Centralization

Settled law required settled interpretation. Earlier periods had left the clarification of ambiguous rules up to councils (*consilia*) organized by individual praetors and populated by jurists (like Horace's Testa, discussed in Chapter 1) who offered guidance on an informal basis. These jurists also answered legal questions from the public, and published guides to the law as a quasi-literary project. This workflow changed over the course of the second century, and once again that change is linked with Hadrian. Jurists slowly entered into closer relationships to the imperial court, with implications not only for the emergent juristic profession but for the law jurists sought to explain.

As far back as Augustus, we can see imperial attempts to control juristic claims to authoritative knowledge. Leaving aside the literary fiction of *Sat.* 2.1 our best evidence for these attempts is Pomponius' *Enchiridion*, a second-century history of juristic practice whose excerpts make up nearly all of D.1.2. Pomponius describes Augustus bringing legal authority under his control through a system of grants:

> *Massurius Sabinus was in the equestrian order, and was the first person to respond publicly* (publice respondere). *For after this privilege* (beneficium) *began to be given, it had been granted to him by Tiberius Caesar. Just to clarify, before the time of Augustus the right to respond publicly was not given*

[21] The literature on euergetics in Mediterranean governance is too vast to summarize, but see e.g. Wen, *Communal Dining*; Maehle, "Munificence"; Zuiderhoek, *The Politics of Munificence*; Veyne, *Le pain et le cirque*, pp. 477–693; Saller, *Personal Patronage*. On the specific role of euergetism in Greek political economies, see Osborne, "Initiative"; Ma, *Antiochos III*, pp. 182–214; Gauthier, *Bienfaiteurs*.

by principes, *but instead those who had faith in their own studies would respond to those seeking advice. Furthermore, they did not necessarily give sealed opinions, but often wrote the judges themselves, or alternately those who had consulted them would give witness in court. The deified Augustus was the first to rule that individuals could respond to queries under his authority, in order that the law might be held in greater esteem* (ut maior iuris auctoritas haberetur). *And from that time this privilege began to be sought out. Thus our great emperor Hadrian, when men of praetorian rank were seeking permission to respond on his behalf, said in a rescript that this privilege was customarily not asked for, but taken upon oneself; and that therefore he would be delighted if anyone who had faith in their abilities would prepare himself for responding to the people.*

(D.1.2.48–49: Pomponius, Enchiridion) Massurius Sabinus in equestri ordine fuit et publice primus respondit: posteaque hoc coepit beneficium dari, a Tiberio Caesare hoc tamen illi concessum erat. Et, ut obiter sciamus, ante tempora Augusti publice respondendi ius non a principibus dabatur, sed qui fiduciam studiorum suorum habebant, consulentibus respondebant: neque responsa utique signata dabant, sed plerumque iudicibus ipsi scribebant, aut testabantur qui illos consulebant. Primus diuus Augustus, ut maior iuris auctoritas haberetur, constituit, ut ex auctoritate eius responderent: et ex illo tempore peti hoc pro beneficio coepit. Et ideo optimus princeps Hadrianus, cum ab eo uiri praetorii peterent, ut sibi liceret respondere, rescripsit eis hoc non peti, sed praestari solere et ideo, si quis fiduciam sui haberet, delectari se populo ad respondendum se praepararet.

Unfortunately, no one knows what Pomponius meant. Tuori rightly notes that the *ius respondendi* is "beset by controversy and doubt";[22] the text of Pomponius is damaged,[23] and there is no reason to assume that Pomponius was himself entirely familiar with a scheme that had already been phased out and was only rarely used while still on the books. But the rough outline remains visible, and reminiscent of the "restoration" of *leges et iura* described in Chapter 1. Augustus claimed to esteem existing organs of legal contestation of authority, but *chose* to esteem them, and in doing so reaffirmed his position as outside of and analytically above that of legal order.[24] Augustus did not banish

22 Tuori, "Freedom," p. 296, with an extensive bibliography on the *ius* and its problems at pp. 295–96 n. 2; see also Robinson, *Sources*, pp. 7–9.

23 On the various reconstructions of this passage, see Kunkel, "Wesen."

24 Both Gaius' and Justinian's *Institutes* make this point explicit at I.7 and 1.2.8 respectively, claiming that the unanimous opinion of some subset of jurists who had been ratified by the emperor (*quibus permissum erat iura condere*) could bind

the jurists, as Horace implied he might, but instead tried to fold them into a broader legal apparatus within which the emperor could honor chosen jurists by permitting them to state the law (i.e. by putting the enforcement organs of imperial justice behind their statements, and thus making them similar to law in their ability to alter the world).[25]

This apparatus did not last. Pomponius describes Hadrian simply refusing to grant the *ius respondendi*, and in fact the few references we have to jurists responding *publice* all predate Hadrian's reign.[26] That said, Hadrian's biographies frequently mention his engagement with trained jurists, in language that seems to fit awkwardly with Pomponius. The *HA* claims that Hadrian judged with the help "not only of his friends, but also jurists like Celsus, Iulianus, Neratius Priscus, and others" (*Hadr.* 18.1: *non amicos suos aut comites solum sed iuris consultos et praecipue Iuuentium Celsum, Saluum Iulianum, Neratium Priscum aliosque*), and the "first men" Dio mentions (69[68].7.1 [Xiph.]: τῶν πρώτων) as assisting Hadrian were probably jurists as well. If Hadrian had simply dismissed jurists of his period and left them to their own devices, as *quis fiduciam sui haberet* implies, what were they doing on his council? Similarly, Crook notes that jurists had served on *consilia* throughout the earlier Principate; the *uita* implies that the practice was novel, but what the *HA* describes as an innovation on prior custom is, at most, an intensification of existing practice.[27]

This problem resembles that found in historiography of the Perpetual Edict. Pomponius (writing relatively soon after Hadrian's death) describes a change in the relationship between emperor and jurist that is otherwise hard to find in the record, while the *HA* describes a long-running practice as if Hadrian had invented it. So how can we square the rhetoric of transformation with the reality of

judges as effectively as other sources of law; once again, however, that that binding was established by imperial constitutions.

[25] For lawgiving as an honorable profession, and that honor being mediated by imperial recognition, see, e.g. Eunap. *VS* 500; Gell. *NA* 13.10. On the role of honor in organizing the growing imperial bureaucracy see Lendon, *Honour*.

[26] E.g. Plin. *ep.* 6.15.3. While some authors like Gellius (*NA* 13.10.1) and Ulpian (D.3.1.1.3) wrote after Hadrian's consolidation they describe *responsores* (Nerva and Labeo, respectively) from the pre-Hadrianic period. On these two jurists see *HSS* II.1, II.13.

[27] Crook, *Consilium Principis*, pp. 58–59.

gradual accretion? While it is possible that Hadrian was simply less important than the historians take him to be, a small detail in the *uita* suggests how Hadrian could have innovated in his treatment of jurists, and how that innovation could accord with the evidence of both Pomponius and the *HA*.

Specifically, the *uita Hadriani* mentions that Hadrian was assisted by "Celsus, Iulianus, Neratius Priscus, and others, *all of whom the senate had approved*" (18.1: *aliosque quos tamen senatus omnia probasset*). A senatorial hearing was not the norm for consiliar advisers, who served in a more casual capacity,[28] and other members of the *consilium* participated at the emperor's pleasure.[29] By contrast, these particular appointments were accompanied by some kind of process ratifying a given jurist's fitness to consider legal questions. It seems unlikely that the consular Marius Maximus, on whose biographies the *HA* probably relied, would have invented an unusual senatorial procedure out of thin air,[30] and if these hearings really did happen they can explain both why Hadrian unwound the *ius respondendi* and why later historians would remember him as nevertheless assimilating jurists into the imperial bureaucracy.

The *ius respondendi* was as much an honor as it was a job. Whether or not we understand the *ius* to have been a major part of imperial engagement with jurists in practice, the role later authors describe it as performing is primarily one of recognition. Accordingly, if the new procedure referenced by the *HA* for ratifying jurists as *consiliarii* took the *ius*' place, it did so by providing similar opportunities for approbation and display. A senatorial hearing could easily accomplish those goals. While a hearing on the fitness of Hadrian's preferred adviser would be necessarily ceremonial, the work that hearing was meant to do (elevate its subject within economies of juristic prestige, demonstrate imperial commitment to meritocratic appointment procedures, ostentatiously collaborate with senatorial elites) was the kind of work that ceremonies do well.[31] Tuori is

28 *Ibid.*, p. 60.

29 For an example of how emperors could simply dismiss members of their *consilium* see Dio Cass. 78[77].17 [Xiph.]; Davenport, "Cassius Dio and Caracalla."

30 On Maximus' background and career *PIR*² *M* 308; Hoët-Van Cauwenberghe, "Marius Maximus"; Birley, "The Consular Biographer," pp. 2694–703.

31 On the importance of the senate in imperial ceremonial, Talbert, *Senate*, pp. 354–71.

correct that we will probably never know exactly what the *ius respondendi* did or how Hadrian altered it.[32] But that is because the *ius respondendi*, and Hadrian's replacement thereof, fit better into histories of communication and ceremony than they do into histories of legal change. Augustus preserved a fiction of juristic independence while making imperial approval into the highest honor a practitioner could receive.[33] Hadrian replaced the Augustan grant with an extremely public and well-compensated appointment, making imperial employment into the apex of a juristic career (and thus making the jurists on his *consilium* necessarily the most prestigious and influential).

In some ways, this story is old hat. The rough outlines of Hadrian's innovation can be seen in many other technical fields over the course of the Principate, from oratory[34] to medicine[35] to literary production.[36] Imperial approval was a powerful sign in the symbolic order of the Roman Mediterranean, and a growing bureaucracy created more opportunities for the imperial administration to signify its approval of a particular expert by paying him for his expertise.[37] But there are some key differences in how Hadrian dealt with the jurists versus other experts, and those differences tell us something important about how Romans thought about law.

For one thing, it is striking that Hadrian here used the Senate as his venue. Even when the emperor's control over Roman life was unquestioned, law in particular channeled its rituals into an older language of aristocratic sovereignty. An emperor who did other things on his own – and who had a complex relationship with the Senate as a body – saw engaging with jurists as a senatorial prerogative.[38]

32 Tuori, "Freedom," pp. 336–37.

33 See Carboni, *La parola scritta*, p. 31; Robinson, *Sources*, p. 34.

34 Dolganov, "Law as Competitive Performance," pp. 75–98; Strazdins, *Fashioning*, pp. 301–02; Künzer, *Konkurrenz*, pp. 249–91; Gleason, *Making Men*, pp. 21–25.

35 Salas, "Medicine as Competitive Performance," p. 124; Nutton, *Ancient Medicine*, pp. 171–73.

36 See Newlands, *Poetics of Empire*, pp. 260–84; Barchiesi, *The Poet and the Prince*, pp. 214–15.

37 See Noreña, *Imperial Ideals*, pp. 300–02.

38 Dio (69.23.3 [Xiph.]) describes the Senate refusing to deify Hadrian upon his death, but in other contexts, most notably the speech adopting Pius at 69.20 [Xiph.] but also the character sketch at 69.7 [Xiph.], Hadrian is portrayed as more deferential. See Davenport and Mallan, "Hadrian's Adoption Speech," pp. 641–42. On law as associated with senatorial, and not imperial, sovereignty Nörr, *Rechtskritik*, p. 55.

Second, our sources do a terrible job of explaining how Hadrian transformed the *ius respondendi* because they were not designed to commemorate the relationships with which he interfered. The *ius respondendi* was an artifact of a period in which *principes* had different tools available with which to pick winners, and it withered as a result of imperial centralization and bureaucratization. The people who wrote about Hadrian looked back from a politic that was further along in that process. Marius Maximus and Cassius Dio were deeply enmeshed within an imperial court that paid jurists for their expertise, and that had done so for awhile; they understood the history of jurists as a history of imperial bureaucrats.[39] By contrast Pomponius, a historian of the juristic profession, imagines jurists as a genealogy of learned men and thus does not articulate changes to how they engaged with other centers of power.[40] These two histories had run on parallel tracks, which Hadrian brought together by making jurists into (unusual, senatorially approved, Republicanish) advisers.

In doing so, Hadrian also brought fixity to the process of legal interpretation. Jurists could and did disagree on legal questions, with Pomponius mentioning a division between schools that went back to the Augustan jurists Labeo and Capito.[41] How one views those conflicts depends on how one views law. On the one hand, disagreements are not necessarily concerning if we understand jurisprudence to be a kind of ethics; both reasonable people and professional ethicists disagree on those all the time.[42] But if law is a sovereign actor upon which people

39 On that court, and the specific roles of these two historians within it, Christol, "Destins croisés."

40 For example, the long excerpt from Pomponius' *Enchiridion* that makes up D.1.2.2 ends with a list of powerful jurists of the last half-century: "Cassius was followed by Caelius Sabinus, who exercised great power in the Vespasianic period: Proculus was followed by Pegasus, who was then the city prefect: Sabinus was followed by Iavolenus Priscus: Pegasus by Celsus: Celsus was followed by his son and Neratius Priscus, who were consuls (Celsus twice): Iavolenus Priscus by Aburnius Valens and Tuscianus, then Salvius Iulianus." (*Cassio Caelius Sabinus successit, qui plurimum temporibus Vespasiani potuit: Proculo Pegasus, qui temporibus Vespasiani praefectus urbi fuit: Caelio Sabino Priscus Iauolenus: Pegaso Celsus: patri Celso Celsus filius et Priscus Neratius, qui utique consules fuerunt, Celsus quidem et iterum: Iauoleno Prisco Aburnius Valens et Tuscianus, item Saluius Iulianus*). I discuss Pomponius in greater detail *infra* pp. 281–88.

41 See Frier, "Juristic Literature," pp. 181–82; Liebs, "Rechtsschulen," pp. 198–214; Stein, "Two Schools."

42 This is, notably, very much not how Romans saw legal questions. Jurists consistently approach legal problems as difficult-but-solvable and as having one right answer that

base their behavior, then legal controversies become unsettling from a reliance perspective. Most people do not want the interpretation of wills to hinge upon the correct response to the trolley problem, and people who have built their lives around law might like its interpretation to be predictable.[43]

A world of rival jurists who disagreed on major questions in the law would struggle to provide that good. We can imagine the *ius respondendi* as an initial attempt to provide that fixity, but a unitary system through which jurists spoke in Hadrian's voice would do so more effectively. Even in cases that required adjudicators to act in the absence of clear guidance,[44] Hadrian's staffing practice rendered any disagreements internal to a process that necessarily generated definite outcomes.

Once again, parallels with the Edict of Titus are apparent. Titus made imperial *beneficia* into something stable and reliable, and Hadrian appears in our sources as doing the same for both edictal law and juristic interpretation. Those latter two, however, were not so obviously amenable to imperial control. Titus, by definition, made the same grants and conferred the same privileges as his predecessors. Hadrian, by contrast, brought under his aegis legal institutions that had predated the Principate. Similarly, when Titus ratified his father's promises he was stepping into the familiar position of the Roman heir. Hadrian claimed for himself the prerogative to decide what the law was and what it meant, and in doing so he told a different story. Tuori has noted resonances between this novel juridical persona and Greek conceptions of the lawgiving tyrant, in that both used the relationship between judge and petitioner to reproduce status differences between emperor and subject.[45] This euergetic legality became clearer in

can be discerned through sufficiently careful enquiry. Frier, "Juristic Literature," pp. 180–81; Bretone, *Ius controversum*, pp. 834–43.

[43] Cf. Yiftach-Firanko, "Law in Graeco-Roman Egypt," p. 545 (discussing the benefits of "legal certainty" in helping individuals understand and predict their legal obligations); Bretone, *Ius controversum*, p. 779. The "trolley problem," a classic thought experiment developed by Philippa Foot ("Abortion," pp. 8–9), asks whether it is ethical to divert a trolley onto a track with one person tied to the tracks (therefore killing that person) in order to save the lives of multiple others.

[44] On the inevitability of cases forcing adjudicators to go beyond existing law Hart, *Concept*, pp. 124–36.

[45] See Tuori, "Greek Tyranny," p. 114.

retrospect, and most people living in Hadrian's Mediterranean would probably not have seen replacing the *ius respondendi* with senatorial acclamation as a watershed moment. But it made possible the legalities of later Rome, and articulated how jurists could coexist with a man whose word was law.

The Rescript System

Those jurists needed something to do. Hadrian's biographers, writing a century or more after the fact, take as a given that legal questions would cross an emperor's desk. That was not as much of a given in earlier Roman history. Before Hadrian, the evidence for legal argument in front of an emperor is surprisingly thin on the ground. Suetonius describes Augustus sitting in judgment but probably retrojects Trajanic practice,[46] and Claudius is commemorated in Seneca's *Apocolocyntosis* (12.3.19–22) and Suetonius' biography (*Cl.* 14) as judging occasional hearings and doing it badly.[47] These cases are unusual and freewheeling, governed less by rules than by the complex ethical system within which imperial action was categorized as tyrannical or fair. By contrast, a new kind of imperial judge emerged in the Hadrianic and post-Hadrianic periods. This judge clarified points of law within a defined institutional context, for grateful questioners far away. That change was in some ways downstream of the administrative evolution mentioned above, since Hadrian and his successors had more staff than before and could thus take more requests. But it also reflected changing conceptions of what being an emperor meant, and of the kinds of goods an emperor might be expected to provide. In this period we see the refinement and widespread adoption of new kinds of imperial legal writing, which could interpret unclear law for private petitioners.

I refer to the *rescriptum*, literally a "written reply" and commonly referred to in Anglophone scholarship as a "rescript."[48] No literary

[46] *Aug.* 33; further discussion *supra* pp. 55–56.

[47] See Bexley, "Saturnalian Lex," pp. 54–55.

[48] On the generic distinctions between different types of imperial replies – *libelli*, *subscriptiones*, *rescripta*, et cetera – Arcaria, *Referre ad principem*; but note Coriat's caution (*Le prince législateur*, pp. 77–101) that these distinctions are somewhat artificial. Riedlberger discusses (*Prolegomena*, pp. 26–77) the evolution of this typology in the late-antique period.

source mentions the invention of the rescript – the closest is Aurelius Victor's laconic mention of the *officia publica* – but vast numbers of them survive in Roman legal literature. Surviving collections of imperial correspondence – the largest of which being the *Codex Justinianus* and the *Codex Theodosianus* – include these brief replies, with the earliest (C.6.23.1, discussed in greater detail below) attributed to Hadrian.

Similarly, the jurists of the *Digest* frequently cite imperial legal opinions and frequently describe them as *rescripta*. Those juristic citations are another window into imperial writing, and they suggest that Hadrian oversaw real changes in the quantity and generic form of legal writing that emperors produced. As for quantity: of the 1,255 citations to imperial constitutions that survive in the *Digest*, only 63 cite any emperors before Hadrian.[49]

[49] For a full list of the citations see Appendix 1, but the 63 I refer to are: D.1.2.2.32 (Pomponius, Enchiridion, citing Augustus, Tiberius, Claudius, and Nerva); D.1.2.2.49 (Pomponius, Enchiridion, citing Augustus and Hadrian); D.1.7.8 (Modestinus, Regulae, citing Claudius); D.1.15.1 (Paul, de Officio Praefecti Vigilum, citing Augustus); D.2.12.9 (Ulpian, de Officio Proconsulis, citing Trajan); D.4.4.3.4 (Ulpian, ad Edicum, citing Claudius); D.5.3.7pr. (Ulpian, ad Edictum, citing Trajan); D.8.3.35 (Atilicinius as preserved in Paul, ad Plautium, citing Caesar); D.14.2.9 (Volusius Maecianus, ex Lege Rhodia, citing Augustus); D.16.1.2pr. (Ulpian, ad Edictum, citing Augustus and Claudius); D.23.2.14.4 (Paul, ad Edictum, citing Augustus); D.26.7.12.1 (Paul, ad Edictum, citing Trajan and Hadrian); D.27.1.17.6 (Callistratus, de Cognitionibus, citing Trajan); D.28.2.26 (the *Pauli Sententiae*, citing Augustus); D.28.5.1pr. (Ulpian, ad Sabinum, citing Trajan); 28.5.42(41) (Pomponius, ex Variis Lectionibus, citing Claudius); D.29.1.1pr. (Ulpian, ad Edictum, citing Titus, Domitian, Nerva, and Trajan); D.29.1.24 (Florentinus, Institutiones, citing Trajan); D.29.5.10.1 (Paul, ad Senatusconsultum Silanianum, citing Trajan); D.34.9.5.20 (Paul, de Iure Fisci, citing Trajan); D.36.1.31(30).5 (Marcianus, Institutiones, citing Trajan, Hadrian, and Caracalla); D.37.12.5 (Papinian, Quaestiones, citing Trajan); D.37.14.5pr. (Marcellus, Institutiones, citing Claudius); D.37.14.7pr. (Modestinus, de Manumissionibus, citing Vespasian); D.40.1.14.1 (Paul, ad Plautium, citing Augustus); D.40.2.21 (Modestinus, Pandectae, citing Augustus); D.40.8.2 (Modestinus, Regulae, citing Claudius); D.40.15.4 (Callistratus, de Iure Fisci, citing Nerva and Claudius); D.41.4.2.8 (Paul, ad Edictum, citing Trajan); D.47.11.6.1 (Ulpian, de Officio Proconsulis, citing Trajan); D.47.14.3.3 (Callistratus, de Cognitionibus, citing Trajan); D.47.21.3.1 (Callistratus, de Cognitionibus, citing Nerva); D.48.2.2.1 (Papinian, de Adulteriis, citing Vespasian); D.48.3.2.1 (Papinian, de Adulteriis, citing Domitian); D.48.5.1 (Ulpian, de Adulteriis, citing Augustus); D.48.5.39(38).10 (Papinian, Quaestiones, citing Claudius); D.48.10.14.2 (Paul, Quaestiones, citing Claudius); D.48.10.15pr. (Callistratus, Quaestiones, citing Claudius); D.48.13.5.4 (3.7) (Marcianus, Institutiones, citing Trajan and Hadrian); D.48.16.10.2 (Papinian, de Adulteriis, citing Trajan); D.48.16.16 (Paul, de Adulteriis, citing Domitian); D.48.17.5.2 (Modestinus, Pandectae, citing Trajan); D.48.18.1pr.

By contrast, Hadrian is cited (either as sole authority or together with one or more of his successors) 128 times,[50] and the numbers increase from there.[51] The nature of these citations also changes with Hadrian. When earlier emperors appear in the *Digest* it tends to be in a "legislative" mode, following Davis;[52] the emperor has made an affirmative, prospective change to Rome's existing legal system and the jurist is now explaining what that change means. For example, Paul refers to punishments imposed upon those who have committed testamentary fraud by the "edict of the Deified Claudius" (*edict*[*um*] *diui Claudii*).[53]

(Ulpian, de Officio Proconsulis, citing Augustus and Hadrian); D.48.18.1.11 (Ulpian, de Officio Proconsulis, citing Trajan); D.48.18.1.12 (Ulpian, de Officio Proconsulis, citing Trajan); D.48.18.1.19 (Ulpian, de Officio Proconsulis, citing Trajan); D.48.18.1.21 (Ulpian, de Officio Proconsulis, citing Trajan); D.48.18.8pr. (Paul, de Adulteriis, citing Augustus); D.48.19.5pr. (Ulpian, de Officio Proconsulis, citing Trajan); D.48.22.1 (Pomponius, ad Sabinum, citing Trajan); D.49.14.1.3 (Callistratus, de Iure Fisci, citing Titus); D.49.14.13pr. (Paul, ad Legem Iuliam et Papiam, citing Trajan); D.49.14.16 (Ulpian, ad Legem Iuliam et Papiam, citing Trajan); D.49.14.42pr. (Valens, Fideicommissa, citing Trajan); D.49.14.42.1 (Valens, Fideicommissa, citing Trajan); D.49.14.49 (Paul, de Tacitis Fideicommissis, citing Trajan); D.49.16.4pr. (Arrius Menander, de Re Militari, citing Trajan); D.49.16.4.5 (Arrius Menander, de Re Militari, citing Trajan); D.49.16.4.12 (Arrius Menander, de Re Militari, citing Trajan); D.50.4.18.30 (Arcadius Charisius, de Muneribus Ciuilibus, citing Vespasian); D.50.7.5(4).6 (Marcianus, Institutiones, citing Vespasian); and D.50.12.14 (Pomponius, Epistulae et Variae Lectiones, citing Trajan and Pius).

50 Furthermore, these citations appear in a wide variety of authors. Hadrian is cited forty-six times by Ulpian; thirty times by Callistratus; twenty-one times by Paul; eleven times by Papinian; twelve times by Marcianus; five times by Modestinus; four times by Tryphoninus; three times by Arrius Menander and Pomponius; twice by Iunius Mauricianus and Saturninus; and once by Arcadius Charisius, Celsus, Gaius, Macer, Papirius Iustus, and Scaevola.

51 For example, Antoninus Pius is cited 235 times, Marcus and Verus (as the *Diui Fratres*) 133 times, and Marcus as sole ruler an additional 110 times beyond that. I discuss these rates of citation, and what they can tell us about the politics of the second and third centuries, *infra* pp. 213–14.

52 Davis, "Problems of Evidence," pp. 402–10; *supra* p. 11.

53 D.48.10.14.2 (Paul, Quaestiones): "A husband manumitted a dotal slave and wrote a legacy to himself in the freedman's will. It was asked what the wife was entitled to under the *lex Iulia*. I responded that the husband ought to be pronounced to suffer a penalty under the edict of the deified Claudius as should an emancipated son, even though both are permitted to seek *possessio bonorum* if passed over in a will." (*Maritus seruum dotalem manumisit et in testamento eius legatum sibi adscripsit. Quaesitum est, quid mulier ex lege Iulia consequi possit. Respondi: et patronum incidere in poenam edicti diui Claudii dicendum est et filium emancipatum, licet praeteriti possint petere possessionem bonorum.*).

By contrast, Hadrian often appears as an intervenor in specific questions, replying (*rescripsit*) to named questioners about what the law already is, and accordingly applying it to events that have already happened. For example:

The deified Hadrian replied to Flavius Proculus that, when one who is alleged to be property of the imperial fisc sues for liberty, judgment ought to be given in the presence of the usual agents of the fisc; and freedom suits of this sort that were not decided in the presence of fiscal agents are hereby void.

(D.49.14.3.9: Callistratus, de Iure Fisci) Diuus Hadrianus Flauio Proculo rescripsit, cum in libertatem proclamat qui ex bonis ad fiscum pertinentibus esse dicitur, iudicium dari praesentibus et agentibus etiam his, qui negotiis fisci solent interuenire: et huiusmodi liberales causae, si non interueniente fisci aduocato decisae sint, in integrum restituuntur.

The retrospectivity is the tell. Callistratus does not describe Hadrian as making an affirmative, prospective legal change. Instead, Hadrian says what he understands the fisc's procedural rights to *have already been* under existing law at the time Flavius Proculus wrote. Hadrian simply explains the meaning of law already on the books. While Hadrian was not the first emperor to clarify existing law in written documents,[54] this style of imperial writing became more common in this period and accordingly easier to integrate into a discursive landscape that was dominated by juristic treatises. Those treatises aimed to clarify what the law meant, and emperors were now doing the same kind of work.

This shift was only possible because of longer-term logistical and administrative developments. Salaried, equestrian positions like the *a libellis* (secretary of correspondence) developed over the preceding century[55] and slowly replaced an earlier paradigm in which administrative/governance work had been handled by either

[54] E.g. D.2.12.9 (Ulpian, de Officio Proconsulis): "The deified Trajan replied to Minicius Natalis that holidays only paused judicial business, but not matters of military discipline" (*Diuus Traianus Minicio Natali rescripsit ferias a forensibus tantum negotiis dare uacationem, ea autem, quae ad disciplinam militarem pertinet, etiam feriatis diebus peragenda*) In addition, D.48.16.15.1 (Macer, de Iudiciis Publicis) refers to a constitution that clarified the scope of the Neronian *senatusconsultum Turpillianum*. I discuss this constitution further *infra* pp. 206–10.

[55] For an excellent survey of the development of the equestrian civil service – which continued well into the Antonine period – see Davenport, *Equestrian Order*, pp. 302–18.

ambitious senators[56] or freedmen within the imperial *domus*.[57] This division conceptually matches onto a broader dichotomy of public and private service that structured much imperial political thought[58] – senators had historically run Roman public affairs, while enslaved and freed bureaucrats had run private estates. For members of this latter class to manage Roman social life offended an aristocracy who considered it public and thus theirs.[59] In practice this paradigm had never fully mapped onto the Principate,[60] but it was perhaps most awkward in contexts that required technical expertise. Law had historically been an elite pursuit,[61] and it is hard to imagine someone with the resources to pursue a legal education ever becoming an imperial freedman. In the mid second century, however, we see extremely prominent jurists without senatorial heritage or resources.[62] A salaried bureaucracy could integrate knowledgeable equestrians into the imperial administration on a full-time basis, better than older institutions like the Republican *consilium*.[63]

It remains murky how problems actually came to the bureaucracy's attention. Some of the first commentators on this problem – most notably Wilcken – argued that post-Hadrianic administration relied on something like a modern postal service transmitting queries to the imperial court,[64] but Williams has shown this to be unlikely. Petitioners still relied on informal connections in order to get their questions answered, outside of specific circumstances like an imperial visit to the provinces or officials kicking particularly hard questions

[56] Like Hadrian himself, who governed Pannonia Inferior under Trajan; *HA*, *Hadr.* 3.9. See also Talbert, *Senate*, pp. 372–407.

[57] See Carboni, *La parola scritta*, pp. 9–17; Weaver, *Familia Caesaris*.

[58] See e.g. Moatti, *Res publica*; Russell, *Public Space*.

[59] E.g. Tac. *Hist.* 2.95; Damon, "Potior," pp. 246–50.

[60] For example, Egypt, a wealthy province that played a crucial role in securing Rome's urban food supply, had been run by equestrian *praefecti* since the Augustan period; see Brunt, "Administrators."

[61] See Frier, *Rise*, pp. 140–71.

[62] Harries, "Iurisperiti," pp. 89–90; *HSS* pp. 272–89.

[63] See Davenport, *Equestrian Order*, pp. 79–83 (on equestrian administration in the Augustan period), pp. 302–18 (on its expansion over the second century); Millar, *Emperor*, pp. 83–101.

[64] Wilcken, "Propositio"; "Kaiserreskripten"; see also Honoré, *Emperors and Lawyers*, p. 33; "The Severan Lawyers," p. 164 (referring to the rescript system as developing into "a scheme of free legal aid").

upstairs.[65] Nevertheless, correspondence was cheaper than embassies, and more regular than the *beneficia* that those embassies might receive.

That regularity mattered. The rescript offered the possibility of extraordinary action, and the emperor maintained the power to declare exception and abrogate the rules that governed life below him. But in practice, a complex administrative structure staffed by legal experts was better equipped to clarify the law than to suspend it. For example, C.6.23.1, the only Hadrianic rescript to survive in the *Codex Justinianus*, represents itself as simply applying existing principles to a complicated inheritance case.

It is not appropriate to contest the free status of witnesses in this particular case, when they occupied the position of free men by universal agreement as the will was being signed and when nobody has objected to their status up until this point.

(n.d.) Testes serui an liberi fuerunt, non oportet in hac causa tractari, cum eo tempore, quo testamentum signabatur, omnium consensu liberorum loco habiti sunt nec quisquam eis usque adhuc status controuersiam mouerit.

We can see that some of the practices associated with the rescript system had not yet come into being; for example, the document is undated. But C.6.23.1 shows what Hadrian could use rescripts to do. Hadrian here addresses a question (the validity of a specific will) that was too minor to adjudicate via embassy, but that was also a little too difficult to be left to the discretion of lower officials. C.6.23.1 sets two legal principles against each other; the testimony of enslaved witnesses is suspect, but at the same time those who would be harmed ought to object in a timely fashion. There is no guarantee that two judges or two *consilia* would come to the same decision, and by making a definite (*non oportet*) statement Hadrian can offer clarity to subsequent litigants.[66]

The nature of that clarity, however, would have been different for litigants of that time than it appears for us today. While the question clearly arose from a specific dispute, Hadrian avoids settling that dispute and instead states a general principle for lower officials to

[65] Williams, "Procedure," pp. 93–98. Those visits, however, gave locals the opportunity to bring their questions directly to the emperor's attention in a fashion much closer to what Wilcken and Honoré describe. See Connolly, *Lives*, p. 108.

[66] See Coriat, "Technique," pp. 333–42.

apply.[67] That conditional quality – if the facts are X, the outcome is Y – will persist as a hallmark of the rescript form, and a holdover from earlier Roman judicial processes. Under traditional Roman formulary procedure questions of law were 1) argued before an official, who then 2) provided a *formula* dictating the legal outcome if certain alleged facts were proven to be true; finally, a subsequent process would 3) determine if the *formula* applied.[68] Hadrian here steps into the traditional role of the praetor and delegates fact-finding to men on the ground.[69] Like the praetor, Hadrian had access to trained experts who could help him formulate a principle that would make sense if broadly applied.

This hypothetical structure was so closely linked with Roman legal practice that it persisted as a signifier of "Romanness" well into the medieval period. As Jasper and Fuhrmann note, the medieval papacy made heavy use of correspondence in asserting its own sovereignty from the fourth century on;[70] this rescript system would become an important avenue of legal development and particularly of what we might call the pope's appellate authority.[71] The decretal letters (*decretales epistulae*) that responded to these appeals were extremely socially powerful,[72] but kept the one limitation – that legal guidance contained therein would only be dispositive if the facts of the petition were verified – of the Classical Roman *rescriptum*. For example, in a letter from 1184 or 1185 Pope Lucius III overturns a marriage annulment but does not simply reunite husband and wife; instead he orders that judges below "hear the case more closely" (*audiatis attentius*) in order to determine whether the facts of the case merit annulment.[73] This strict separation of "facts" and "law" seems natural to us now, but it originates in a particular quirk of imperial correspondence which itself looks back to early Roman legal practice.[74] Accordingly it shows how thin the

67 See Coriat, *Le prince législateur*, pp. 338–39.

68 Metzger, *Outline*, pp. 21–26; Kaser and Hackl, *Zivilprozessrecht*, pp. 151–382.

69 See Wankerl, *Appello ad principem*, p. 243.

70 Jasper and Fuhrmann, *Papal Letters*, pp. 7–28; also Kikuchi, "Authority at a Distance," p. 13.

71 Larson and Sisson, "Papal Decretals," pp. 164–65; Duggan, *Decretal Collections*, pp. 20–21.

72 Southern, *Making*, pp. 137–39.

73 X.2.13.10; Larson and Sisson, "Papal Decretals," pp. 169–70.

74 For a more detailed discussion of the interrelationship of Classical Roman law and the decretal system, see Eichbauer and Brundage, *Medieval Canon Law*, pp. 79–83.

boundary between "legal" and other modes of thinking really was for Romans, and how practices specific to Roman literary and political culture have survived into our own time through inherited legal custom.

* * * * *

One reason for this survival is that, unlike earlier adjudicators, Hadrian issued judgments that outlived him. C.6.23.1 survives as part of a Justinianic compilation, put together about four centuries after Hadrian wrote, and the idea of the emperor as a final authority on questions of law became a standard feature of Roman government. But it was hardly inevitable. We have seen how earlier accounts of Roman legal order grounded that order in Republican symbolics and associated law with liberty, sacrality, and archaic speech. By contrast the rescript system made law into something the emperor gave, authoritative and stable in the same way he was.

Rescripts and the Language of Power

Accordingly, rescripts became one of the primary media through which emperors could be depicted as authoritative and stable. As discussed in Chapter 2 Roman legal texts, which trained their audience to read them closely and seriously, were uniquely powerful storytelling tools. Lenski – writing about constitutions produced within the different political context of the early fourth century – explains how imperial legal correspondence invited emperor and subject into a collaborative meaningmaking process. Per Lenski, the emperor Constantine used constitutions to "talk his subjects into talking themselves" into the affective relationships that underlay imperial power.[75]

In Hadrian's case, the image of the emperor that is constructed by his legal writing is supreme and polyglot. Hadrian appears as knowledgeable enough about Roman law to identify and choose between competing principles, and also powerful enough to enforce his choice. This account of imperial sovereignty makes more sense within Greek than Roman understandings of kingship. As the orator Aelius Aristides later put it in his panegyric *Eis Rōmēn* (Upon Rome),

[75] Lenski, *Cities*, p. 15 (discussing Constantine using legal correspondence to promote Christianity).

a world in which "it is easy for the central authority to manage the whole kingdom via letter" (33/336: εὐμάρεια πολλὴ καθημένῳ πᾶσαν ἄγειν τὴν οἰκουμένην δι' ἐπιστολῆς) is a world in which "should something need to happen, you only have to think about it and it is done" (31/335: κἄν τι γενέσθαι δέῃ, ἀπόχρη δόξαι, καὶ πέπρακται).[76] The emperor looks very different in Roman panegyric – consider Pliny's self-effacing, collaborative Trajan.[77] These hellenizing tendencies are visible in other aspects of Hadrian's representational program. For example, the Arch of Hadrian in Athens explicitly compares Hadrian to Theseus, the city's founding hero.[78] The rescript, which wedded a very Roman kind of legal argumentation to a comparatively Greek account of legal authority, fit with other Hadrianic stories.

It also fit later political realities. While the rescript system as we know it grew out of Hadrianic administrative shifts, that system did not fully emerge until after Hadrian's death. As mentioned above, only one rescript of Hadrian's makes it into the *Codex*; the imperial constitution as we now understand it appears under Hadrian's successor Antoninus Pius (r. 138–161). It makes sense that changes in staffing and organization would have a gradual impact on the functioning of a large bureaucracy, and also that later Roman historians would look back and see Hadrian as a sharper break than he was. But the rescript system they inherited proved extremely flexible in adapting to different accounts of imperial legitimacy – it could tell a variety of stories about imperial power depending on the needs of promulgators, functionaries, and recipients.

The remainder of this chapter will consider how other versions of the legal reply, issued by emperors who ruled after Hadrian but before the upheavals of the mid third century, represented their authors. The vast majority of these surviving rescripts look roughly like Hadrian's example – short, conditional statements of legal principle. It is not entirely clear how much this tendency arises from

[76] On Aristides as Roman panegyricist see Pernot, "Aelius Aristides and Rome"; *La rhétorique de l'éloge*, pp. 80–84; on the Roman Oration, see Oliver, "The Ruling Power," pp. 879–85; on the Oration's hellenizing approach to state administration, see Tuori, *The Emperor of Law*, pp. 199–207.

[77] On the character of Trajan in Pliny's *Panegyricus*, see *supra* pp. 101–07.

[78] Mazurek, *Isis*, pp. 10–11; Boatwright, *Cities*, pp. 146–47; Adams, "Arch," p. 11; Boatwright, *City*, pp. 203–12; Oliver, "The Athens of Hadrian," p. 124.

house style and how much from later redaction,[79] but in cases where imperial writing survives via unusual transmission methods we can see a much greater diversity of form. For example, Ulpian preserves a rescript of Pius' successors, the Deified Brothers (Marcus and Verus: r. 161–69) that does not so much set out a rule as transcribe the debate that produced it.[80]

The Deified Brothers wrote the following in a rescript: "we have learned from those more learned than ourselves that it has been doubted for some time, whether a grandson may seek possession of the estate of his grandfather's freedman against the tablets[81] *if the grandson's father had accused his own father's freedman, at a time when he was of sufficient age to do so, of a capital offense, and also that Proculus (obviously no minor authority on legal matters) had believed that a grandson ought not to be granted possession in such circumstances. We also followed his opinion, when we replied to the petition of Caesidia Longina: but Volusius Maecianus, our friend on account both of his old and well-founded expertise in the Civil Law, and besides on his scrupulous attention, was induced by the authority of our rescript to affirm in our presence that he did not believe a different answer was appropriate. But when we discussed further, with Maecianus himself and with our other jurist friends in attendance, it seemed better to say that the grandson was excluded from his grandfather's freedman's estate by neither the letter nor the spirit of the law or the Edict, on account of his father's status or reputation: this was not only the view of the majority of the jurists in attendance, but also that of our friend Salvius Julianus, a most excellent man."*

(D.37.14.17pr., ad Legem Iuliam et Papiam) Diui Fratres in haec uerba rescripserunt: "Comperimus a peritioribus dubitatum aliquando, an nepos contra tabulas auiti liberti bonorum possessionem petere possit, si eum libertum pater patris, cum annorum uiginti quinque esset, capitis accusasset, et Proculum, sane non leuem iuris auctorem, in hac opinione fuisse, ut nepoti in huiusmodi causa non putaret dandam bonorum possessionem. Cuius sententiam nos quoque secuti sumus, cum rescriberemus ad libellum Caesidiae Longinae: sed et Volusius Maecianus amicus noster ut et iuris ciuilis praeter ueterem et bene fundatam peritiam anxie diligens religione rescripti nostri ductus sit ut coram

79 See Johnston, "Interpretation," p. 153 ("Crudely stated, the aim of Justinian's compilation is the abstraction of functional rules from casuistic material not promisingly formulated for that purpose."); Nörr, "Rescriptenpraxis," pp. 6–8.

80 For further discussion of this document, see Babusiaux, "Zitate," pp.250–53; Sirks, "Request," pp. 123–25.

81 I.e. upon a showing that the original will was deficient. D.37.4; Vacca, "Bonorum possessio contra tabulas."

nobis adfirmauit non arbitratum se aliter respondere debere. Sed cum et ipso Maeciano et aliis amicis nostris iuris peritis adhibitis plenius tractaremus, magis uisum est nepotem neque uerbis neque sententia legis aut edicti praetoris ex persona uel nota patris sui excludi a bonis auiti liberti: plurium etiam iuris auctorum, sed et Salui Iuliani amici nostri clarissimi uiri hanc sententiam fuisse."

This rescript does a great deal more than state a legal principle. The principle is there, if one reads closely – even though a man who wrongly accuses his father's freedman of serious crimes forfeits certain rights against that freedman, those rights persist in the man's offspring.[82] That said, Marcus and Verus include a great deal of information that is irrelevant to that normative story. As the thirteenth-century *Glossa Ordinaria* puts it, "this law is verbose but its intention is light" (*lex ista est uerbosa, tamen eius intentio est leuis*).[83] If what matters is the rule, why do we need to know which jurists were in the room at which time?

Instead, we should understand these details as working in descriptive and constructive registers. The rescript makes specific factual claims about how legal questions were decided in the court of the Deified Brothers; legal experts are brought in to debate close questions, informed by but not necessarily deferring to earlier juristic writing. The Brothers themselves participate in this debate (*tractaremus*), but their role remains purposefully obscure. They follow majority rule,[84] but do so at their own discretion and with the knowledge that jurists in the room will hesitate to contradict the *religio* of imperial opinion.[85]

The image this rescript puts forward of Antonine deliberation matches that preserved in more explicitly narrative sources. Cassius Dio describes Pius engaging in leisurely examination and argument,

82 For the rights of a Roman *manumissor* against their *liberti*, *BTRL* pp. 103–05.

83 *Glo. Ord. ad* D.37.14.17pr., v. *diui*.

84 The reasoning of the rescript – which tracks the majority rule of a chosen subset of jurists, while also noting the view of the most eminent among them – bears a remarkable resemblance to the heuristic adopted by Valentinian III 250 years later, in the Law of Citations. I suspect this is a coincidence, but it may reflect broader tendencies in how emperors resolved disagreement between juristic authorities; these disagreements rarely surface in surviving imperial legal writing, which makes any hypothesis hard to prove or disprove. I discuss the Law of Citations *infra* p. 255.

85 See Gualandi, *Legislazione*, p. 10.

spending a great deal of time on each case "in order to precisely identify the just outcome from every angle" (72[71].6.1 [Xiph.]: ὥστε πανταχόθεν τὸ δίκαιον ἀκριβοῦν). But by attaching this story of deliberation and collaboration to a legal judgment, the rescript preserved at D.37.14.17pr. constructs a world where those procedural virtues are important to the functioning of the Roman legal system. The writer imagines future grandsons citing it in court, and encourages them to ground their arguments in both the rescript itself and the juristic *consensus* for which it speaks. The emperor remains as a source of legal certainty, since most (*plurium*) is not all; the rescript settles the question differently than would at least some of the people in the room where it was drafted. But it can only do so because it comes from a legitimate authority. The Deified Brothers' legitimacy, at least among the kinds of people who cared about technical legal documents, rested on qualities like collaboration, expertise, and deference. Accordingly, the rescript emphasizes those over and above its actual normative claim.

The rescript of the Deified Brothers comes to us as part of a very specific juristic tradition. Ulpian quotes it because it flatters him and his profession, and given his later career it is not shocking that Ulpian would tell a story about Roman law in which emperors listened to jurists.[86] It is unique within our surviving archives, however, and in all likelihood the bulk of imperial legal correspondence looked very different. Most imperial responses were short, to the point, and not interesting enough to attract the attention of compilers.

When these responses survive they do so in papyri like *P. Col.* 123, a collection of imperial replies posted in Alexandria on March 14 of 200 that are commonly referred to as the *Apokrimata*. These replies did not come about through regular order, exactly; the emperor Septimius Severus and his son/co-ruler Caracalla were visiting Egypt and were thus more accessible to Egyptian petitioners than they ever would be again. But those irregularities, or extraordinary circumstances, are hard to find in the text. Instead, *P. Col.* 123 records imperial legal work as brisk and bureaucratic.

86 I discuss Ulpian's career in more detail *infra* p. 192, but in brief: Ulpian served as a legal adviser and potentially regent for the child ruler Severus Alexander. Dio Cass. 80[80].2[Xiph].; Honoré, *Ulpian*, pp. 14–36.

In Alexandria

Copies of responsa posted in the Stoa of the Gymnasium. Year 8, Phamenoth 18. Imperator Caesar Lucius Septimius Severus Pius Pertinax Arabicus Adiabenicus Parthicus Maximus Augustus and Imperator Caesar Marcus Aurelius Antoninus Augustus.

(1) To Ulpius Heraclanus, also called Callinicus.
We revoked penalties imposed upon Alexandrians or Egyptians when we assigned a definite time (of remission).

(2) To Artemidorus, also called Achilles.
Having placed yourself in agreement with the decisions (rendered), too late you take umbrage at the judgments (given).

(3) To the Aurelii Artemidorus and Anoubion and others.
Comply with the opinions rendered.

(4) To Cil-dis, also called Midas, through Philocrates, his son.
Since you feel decisively that the instrument of sale of the mortgages was unjustly voided, the prefect of the province will issue the order that you regain possession of the plots seized by force without an agreement.

(5) To -thalge, daughter of Ambrelus, through her son, Abdomanchus.
Women are not forbidden to obligate themselves for loans or to exact payment on behalf of others.

(6) Likewise published in the same Stoa.
To Apollo, son of Harnektotes, and others.
The (edicts) regarding investigations. A general edict has given consideration to Egyptians.

(7) To Aurelius Sarapion.
Some time ago we forbade that inheritances from the mother's side come down in succession.

(8) To Proclus, son of Apollonius.
It is not just that the heirs written in wills – the wills may even be said to have given rise (to them as heirs) – have been ejected from their right of possession. Those who have introduced the cases will

take care to summon those who are being charged if, indeed, the affair is of the type of case requiring jurisdiction of a special judge.

(9) To Cronius, son of Heraclides.
Transient sicknesses do not afford relief from municipal liturgies. Those who are physically sick are subject to liturgical services if they are mentally capable of conducting their household affairs.

(10) Likewise (i.e. also posted in the Stoa).
To Dioscorus, son of Hephaestion, and to Pieseis, son of Osiris, and others.
We have forbidden that you pay money in place of grain.

(11) To Isidorus, son of Dius.
His Excellency, Fulvius Plautianus, prefect of the camps and our household companion, will conduct the investigation of the audacious actions (emanating) from Comon. In respect to Apion, the tax collector, if he is not involved with Comon in the charges (against him, Comon) you will have the prefect of the province as your judge.

(12) To Isidorus, also called Heraclides, through Apollonius.
Although you gave a deed of cession in the matter of your paternal inheritance and you do not have the assistance (arising) from minority status, you assert that, under the law of sales, confiscation has been applied against your estate. Comply.

(13) To -elatheus, son of Caerenus.
If you take guardians for orphans outside of the (regular) order, in respect to their properties a judge of special delegation will be given against those assigned (i.e. against the guardians).[87]

No one has ever called *P. Col.* 123 verbose. While D.37.14.17pr. provides so much detail that its holding is difficult to discern, the thirteen decisions contained in the papyrus offer no holding at all. Instead, they simply intervene, or decline to intervene, in specific cases. One reason that these documents look so different is the different administrative processes that generated them. D.37.14.17pr. begins

[87] Translation: Westermann and Schiller, *Apokrimata*, pp. 9–10. For a detailed bibliography of *P. Col.* 123 up to 1978 see Oliver, *Greek Constitutions*, pp. 451–52. For more contemporary discussion, see Tuori, "Greek Tyranny," pp. 115–16.

with the emperor facing a general legal question (*an … accusasset*), whereas replies like "comply with the opinions rendered" (l.12: τοῖς ἐγνωσμένοις πίθεσθαι) suggest that Severus and Caracalla were being asked to overturn specific administrative rulings.[88] Another reason is their very different transmission. The rescript quoted in D.37.14.17pr. was preserved within a scholarly tradition that was particularly interested in legal questions, and that cared about rescripts primarily as sources of general law. By contrast *P. Col.* 123 survives through different archival practices. Westermann and Schiller suggest that the document may have been kept by a scribe interested in official phrasing, but the answers are too brief to be of interest to academics.[89] In practice we should assume that the vast majority of imperial rescripts looked more like *P. Col.* 123, since the archives kept by jurists were so much more selective. D.37.14.17pr. and documents like it were fascinating outliers, but most responses were simple and brief.

That said, *P. Col.* 123 still tells a coherent story about imperial power. While the emperor maintains the ability to make exceptions to general rules he rarely does so; eight of the decisions simply state an uncontroversial legal principle and apply it. The circumstances of *P. Col.* 123's production and effect on the world – an imperial visit to Egypt with accompanying pomp,[90] petitioners of varying means begging the sovereign for help,[91] that sovereign granting possession of land (l.18: χωρίων) with a word – prime its reader to imagine Severus and Caracalla as nearly omnipotent. But the world constructed by *P. Col.* 123 is nevertheless orderly and predictable, governed by the same processes that hold when the emperor is not in

88 I should acknowledge that the rescript of the Deified Brothers does not explain how this question got to court in the first place, merely how the jurists framed it after it arrived (*comperimus a peritioribus*). It is not clear whether the question was posed by a lower-level adjudicator seeking imperial guidance, or a loser in that adjudication who sought victory on appeal. Even in the latter case, however, that appellant raised a question of law, and no evidence suggests *P. Col.* 123's *Aurelii* did the same.

89 Westermann and Schiller, *Apokrimata*, pp. 99–101. Katzoff, "Intended Use" provides an excellent overview of broader debates about the original archival context of *P. Col.* 123.

90 See Millar, *Emperor*, pp. 28–40.

91 While *P. Col.* 123 does not preserve the language of the petitions to which Severus and Caracalla responded, a number of imperial petitions survive from Roman Egypt and employ a rhetorical style emphasizing the petitioner's powerlessness and vulnerability. See Bryen, *Violence*, pp. 133–34.

town.[92] Even when granting Cil-dis' request in case 4, Severus and Caracalla direct the prefect only to return properties that he determines to have been seized by force (l.18: πρὸς βίαν). The image that survives in *P. Col.* 123 is one of powerful sovereigns, subordinating their judgment to general law.

These documents construct a world around themselves in which emperors fill a variety of roles. The emperor sometimes acts as an adjudicator, sometimes as a legislator, and sometimes as a messenger; the Deified Brothers report the outcome of a juristic deliberation and in doing so ratify its contents, while Severus and Caracalla simply inform their petitioners of their legal obligations. This final role might be surprising, but we have already seen emperors use legal work to portray themselves as part of a broader ethical and political system. The generic form of the rescript, which is produced within a depersonalized institutional context and appears to its audience as disembodied writing rather than a monument or speech, was especially well suited to these kinds of messages. Given how Romans had historically thought about law, imperial legality was a kind of paradox – the rescript resolved it by collapsing emperor and law into a single system.

Viewed in this light, D.37.14.17pr. and *P. Col.* 123 have more in common than they seem. Both D.37.14.17pr. and *P. Col.* 123 were legal documents, but they were produced by someone with the power to suspend the law. They existed within an institutional milieu that their existence necessarily threatened. That tension between autocracy and law had existed for centuries, and not only in Rome,[93] but here we begin to see a shift in how Roman legal actors resolved it. These documents portray the emperor not as outside the law, nor subject to the law, but as foundational to it; they cast the Roman legal system as an emanation of imperial will. That legal system looks different in each case, and one story of reasoned debate among experts bears little resemblance to another story of fixed and authoritative rules. Both, however, come from the imperial center.

The rescript system ratified (and was ratified by) a particular relationship between emperors and laws that was hardly inevitable. It

[92] See Tuori, *The Emperor of Law*, p. 247 ("The emperor here is nothing but a bureaucrat, an unfriendly character familiar from your local tax office.").

[93] See e.g. Ma, *Antiochos III*, pp. 168–70.

was an idiosyncratic hybrid of an older model, in which legal order existed outside of and parallel to imperial politics, with one in which law was a sovereign's wishes made manifest. This chimera emerged under an emperor with particular interests in Greek culture, but it outlasted him and went on to generate the documents, jobs, and institutional frameworks that later commentators would understand as Rome's legal legacy. The emperor said what the law was, with the help of experts but on his own authority, and subjects who obeyed the law obeyed him.

* * * * *

Post-Hadrianic legality, then, based the legitimacy of law on the legitimacy of the emperor. The emperor's legal judgments rested on his wisdom, his decency, and his ability to kill anyone he wanted. That might be surprising, given the afterlife of Roman law; rescripts have exercised authority in times and places where emperors did not. But this vision of law also fits awkwardly into the later Roman world. The second century CE was a period of remarkable stability in Roman imperial politics, when everyone generally agreed on who the emperor was. Gibbon's claim that "If a man were called to fix the period in the history of the world, during which the condition of the human race was most happy and prosperous, he would, without hesitation, name that which elapsed from the death of Domitian to the accession of Commodus" is a bit much,[94] but things looked very different in the third century. The time between the assassination of Commodus (193) and the rise of Diocletian (284) is marked by civil war, frequent coups, and weak leaders. Romans struggled to respond to these changes, and to articulate a coherent reason why anyone should listen to the emperors who ruled under those circumstances.

As they did so, however, they imagined new accounts of law that could survive imperial instability. The first half of the third century sees enormously consequential developments in Roman legal thought. Emperors and jurists in this time tried to make imperial constitutions into documents that could exercise power on their own, without emanating from a broadly accepted sovereign. They succeeded. The form of the rescript system stayed roughly the same, but its story of the

[94] Gibbon, *Decline*, p. 90.

emperor as the foundation of all law subtly changed. In this time of political chaos, different actors came to describe law in a newly impersonal language: as deriving its authority not from ancient ritual practice or the moral sensibilities of a god on Earth, but from something like a state, for which emperors spoke. Part II of this book tracks the origins of that shift, in boys and men who used the language of law to tell stories of a world less violent than their own.

PART II

LAW WITHOUT ORDER

4

Inheritance, Authority, and Alexander

The legality that emerged from the Principate lasted about as long as the Principate did. Documents like *P. Col.* 123 commemorate a particular relationship between emperor and law, in which the emperor expresses his autocratic, unbounded power as a system of rules.[1] That expression looked different in different contexts, but by the third century CE legal work was closely related to imperial sovereignty; law had become less an independent normative order than a complex articulation of imperial will. For example, in his biography of Septimius Severus (r. 193–211), Cassius Dio describes the emperor hearing cases in a room specially decorated with the imperial horoscope.

Severus knew this [the time of his death] particularly due to the stars under which he had been born, for he had placed them on the ceilings of the rooms in the palace in which he would hold court so that they could be seen by all, with the exception of the portion showing the hour – as they say – of his seeing the light; for he carved this differently on each side.[2]

[1] Some of the research contained in this chapter – particularly the sections entitled "Methodology: How to Do Things with Justinian" and "The Rule of Precedent" – was previously published in my article "Precedential Reasoning and Dynastic Self-Fashioning in the Rescripts of Severus Alexander," published in 2020 in *Historia* volume 69.

[2] While Dio's account of Hadrian's activities is apocryphal, he at least claims to speak from firsthand experience of much of Severus' reign. See e.g. 76.4.1–7 [Xiph.]; Bering-Staschewski, *Zeitgeschichte*, pp. 51–77. On the importance of omens and horoscopes in Severus' self-representation, see Rubin, *Civil-War Propaganda*.

(77[76].11.1 [Xiph.]) ᾔδει δὲ τοῦτο μάλιστα μὲν ἐκ τῶν ἀστέρων ὑφ᾽ ὧν ἐγεγέννητο καὶ γὰρ ἐς τὰς ὀροφὰς αὐτοὺς τῶν οἴκων τῶν ἐν τῷ παλατίῳ, ἐν οἷς ἐδίκαζεν, ἐνέγραψεν, ὥστε πᾶσι, πλὴν τοῦ μορίου τοῦ τὴν ὥραν, ὥς φασιν, ἐπισκοπήσαντος ὅτε ἐς τὸ φῶς ἐξῄει, ὁρᾶσθαι: τοῦτο γὰρ οὐ τὸ αὐτὸ ἑκατέρωθι ἐνετύπωσεν.

While this scene provides our most detailed surviving evidence of painted designs in judicial space, both Dio and other historians describe emperors using public, ceremonially charged spaces for judicial performance.[3] The reason for this pomp is never made explicit, but it vests both decision and decisionmaker with a similar kind of imperial pixie dust. These spaces hosted the rituals and symbolics that Roman power used to talk about itself, with their scale and opulence serving as evidence of the grandeur that underlay the imperial state.[4] Those symbols mattered; emperors heard cases and made law in a messaging environment saturated with images of imperial *power*, but also generosity, wisdom, fairness, and solicitude. The commands that resulted from these processes (pay your taxes, leave the city, *follow the law*) would seem more correct – in all senses of the term – once endorsed by such an extraordinary figure.

So what happens when the emperor stops being extraordinary? Towards the end of the Severan period Roman imperial politics got violent, and weird. This period saw the collapse of social conventions that had governed second-century imperial selection and legitimation. In brief: Septimius Severus left the throne to his two biological sons, Caracalla and Geta;[5] the next year (212), Caracalla killed his brother and ruled alone for five years before being stabbed to death while defecating on the side of a road (217);[6] his prefect Macrinus, who had likely ordered the assassination, took over and ruled as the first

[3] See Ath. 4.148d; Dio Cass. 57.7.2, 60.4.3; de Angelis, "The Emperor's Justice," p. 136.

[4] On premodern constitutions resting on symbolic or ritual orders see Stollberg-Rilinger, *Clothes*, pp. 2–7. On these sorts of symbolic rule systems creating or structuring social life Giddens, *Constitution*, pp. 21–28.

[5] Pangerl, "Brüder"; Kemmers, "Shadow." On the systematic postmortem erasure of Geta see Krüpe, *Vernichtung*. Kemezis provides (*Greek Narratives*, p. 48) a valuable cautionary note on the actual novelty of hereditary succession within Antonine political culture.

[6] Dio Cass. 79[78].5 [Xiph.]; *HA*, *Ant.* 6–7; see also Hekster and Kaizer, "An Accidental Tourist?"

non-senatorial emperor before being deposed and murdered the next year (218) by a military coup.[7] That coup's financière – Septimius Severus' former sister-in-law Julia Maesa – put on the throne her grandson, the fourteen-year-old priest of a regional Emesene cult to a sacred stone known as Elagabal.[8] This teenager (who ruled under the name "Antoninus" but who is conventionally known as Elagabalus, and whom I will call by that name going forward)[9] based his claim to power, as best we can tell, on two different arguments. Elagabalus justified his rule by claiming to be the illegitimate child of Caracalla,[10] but also by invoking his special relationship with the god Elagabal.[11]

Neither took. After an initial period of concord between the child ruler and the Senate, relations went south. Historiographic sources attribute this decline to shocking displays of vice from the young *princeps* including cinaedism (effeminacy and anal receptivity),[12] lurid accusations of what we might now call transfemininity,[13] corruption,[14] and religious mania.[15] While the first few claims cannot be confirmed, Emesene religious imagery became far more frequent on coin issues later in Elagabalus' reign. For example, it was

7 Little is known about Macrinus due to memory sanctions (on which see Wood, "Too-Successful"; Sijpesteijn, "Macrinus' Damnatio Memoriae"), but see Scott, "Legitimization"; Baharal, "The Emperor Macrinus."

8 Emesa is roughly the site of modern Qoms, in Syria. On the Emesene cult of Elagabal see Rowan, *Under Divine Auspices*, pp. 164–218; Frey, *Untersuchungen*; Turcan, *Soleil*; Optendrenk, *Religionspolitik*.

9 On the various names of this emperor see Scott, *Emperors and Usurpers*, pp. 111–12.

10 Hekster, *Emperors and Ancestors*, pp. 18–21.

11 Icks, "Failed Legitimation"; Frey, *Untersuchungen*, pp. 101–06.

12 This is a very brief gloss on the role of cinaedism in Roman invective, and the biographers who accused Elagabalus of acting in this way invoked complex medical, ethical, and political stereotypes that were all bound up in the *cinaedus* trope. See Sapsford, *Performing*; Williams, *Roman Homosexuality*, pp. 172–218; Gleason, *Making Men*, pp. 64–81. I discuss Elagabalus' brief reign in more detail at Herz, "How to Do the History of Elagabalus," pp. 411–16.

13 See Betancourt, *Byzantine Intersectionality*, pp. 106–08; Chrysanthou, "Sex and Power," pp. 614–15; Icks, *Crimes*, p. 100.

14 The *uita Elagabali*, in particular, describes Elagabalus appointing ministers on the basis of no qualification other than "the enormity of their shameful parts" (12.2: *commendatos sibi pudibilium enormitate membrorum*). On these staffing practices as part of a broader thematic of corruption see Osgood, "Secret History," pp. 184–85.

15 A particular theme in Herodian at e.g. 5.6. See also Icks, *Crimes*, pp. 61–91; Dirven, "The Emperor's New Clothes"; Rowan, "Parasols"; Sommer, "Konstruktion," pp. 104–06.

only in late 219 that Elagabalus began to be represented on obverses in recognizably "religious" garb.[16]

Soon after in 221, Elagabalus' twelve-year-old cousin Severus Alexander entered the picture as his heir and adopted son.[17] While little is known about Alexander's public persona at this time, his traditionalist numismatic program seems to draw an explicit contrast between the cousins and thus suggests something less than familial unity.[18] At around the same time, rumors began to spread that it was Alexander, and not Elagabalus, who was Caracalla's illegitimate son.[19] Elagabalus would be dead within two years; the Praetorian Guard was paid to switch its allegiances from one cousin to another, and on March 11 of 222 they killed the emperor and his mother before proclaiming Alexander's accession.[20] In short, Julia Maesa installed her grandson on the throne, then hired men to kill him (and her own daughter) so she could try again.

Part II of this book considers what that chaos meant for law. The Severan period – and especially the late Severan period, after the murder of Caracalla – sees a near-total breakdown in existing paradigms of imperial representation and legitimation.[21] As a result, historians of Roman imperial ideology have taken a particular interest in how Severan emperors justified their rule.[22] But less attention has been paid to how these legitimacy problems affected legal discourse. Post-Hadrianic legality drafted off of post-Hadrianic sovereignty, subordinating legal order to the broader symbolics of a stable and

[16] Rowan, *Under Divine Auspices*, p. 211. Rowan argues that this may simply reflect the time it took for Elagabalus to arrive at Rome, which I find persuasive. That said, a delay nevertheless explains the Senate's initial belief that Elagabalus would be a more pliable or less idiosyncratic ruler.

[17] See Kemezis, "Fall," p. 378.

[18] See, for example, *RIC IV Sev. Alex.* 3, struck in 221, whose obverse portrait of Alexander is accompanied by a reverse image of traditional Roman sacrificial implements and the legend "Imperial Piety" (PIETAS AVG).

[19] Dio Cass. 80[79]19.4 [Xiph.]; Hdn. 5.7.3.

[20] This date is not perfectly secure: see *infra* p. 158.

[21] Kemezis, *Greek Narratives*, pp. 74–89; lo Cascio, "Age," pp. 137–42.

[22] The bibliography here is extensive, and readers with particular interest in the subject should consult Herz, "Precedential Reasoning," p. 105 n. 12. For present purposes, a few good recent treatments are Van Voorhis and Abbe, *Imperial Colors*, pp. 123–53; Rantala, *Ludi Saeculares*; Lusnia, *Creating Severan Rome*; Langford, *Maternal Megalomania*; Rowan, *Under Divine Auspices*; Faust and Leitmeir (eds.), *Repräsentationsformen*.

legitimated imperial lawgiver. When that lawgiver was replaced with a short-lived figurehead, that new world required new stories about legal authority.

It got them. Vast quantities of legal writing survive from the Severan period, in both rescripts and juristic treatises. That writing describes the relationship between emperors and law in different terms than what had come before. Both emperors and jurists at this time begin to describe the emperor as a kind of caretaker of law, someone who serves as the final authority on questions of legal interpretation but who does so from within an institutional order that extends above him. This curatorial account of imperial lawmaking would thrive in later periods, and appears to the contemporary reader as an uncontroversial norm in Roman legal thought. But a close read of Severan legal texts shows how unstable and contested this norm was at the time. Different actors told different stories of how Roman law worked, based on their own institutional positions and needs, and those stories only became coherent in retrospect.

In particular, the Severan period sees a sharp divergence in how emperors and jurists imagined the legal order into which they fit. Both site authority in entities greater than the sitting emperor, but the positivism we associate with Roman law is a specifically juristic invention. Imperial rescripts of the same time solved the problem in a different way, and looked to dynastic institutions as a source of legitimacy. This chapter considers the rescripts of Severus Alexander (the only late Severan ruler whose legal writing survives in any volume), and how Alexander's court used legal communications to tell a new story of dynastic precedentialism. This particular legality died when Alexander did,[23] but it shows how contingent the thing we call "Roman law" actually was. I discuss two innovations in Alexander's legal writing – the promulgation of rescripts written under Elagabalus with Severus Alexander's name, and Alexander's idiosyncratic tendency to cite prior imperial decisions in his own legal writing – and connect them to Alexander's broader representational program, before concluding with a closer treatment of one of Alexander's most famous rescripts, his discussion of imperial inheritance at C.6.23.3.

[23] Violently, of course, at the hands of another military coup in 235. Hdn. 6.8–9; Davenport and Mallan, "Emperorship"; Speidel, "Maximinus and the Thracians."

Relabeling of Legal Correspondence

The rescripts I discussed at the end of the last chapter do not go out of their way to justify their normative claims. When Severus and Caracalla decline to help their petitioners, or when the Deified Brothers say what the law is, their writing takes on a performative character. These documents do not so much make an argument to be evaluated as alter the world through the fact of their being written and publicized.[24] For all of the Brothers' deliberations, the nature of that deliberation is left obscure and the rule it produced is not up for debate. The authority of these documents rests on their signature, or on the fact that the man/men who signed them had the authority to state the law. If law is what the emperor says it is, his statements need little justification.

That relationship between authorship and legal validity, however, became scrambled in 222. Three rescripts survive from the beginning of that year that were authored under Elagabalus but relabeled as opinions of his successor Severus Alexander. Here I include not just the content of the rescripts but also their headings and dates – that administrative/indexing material is vital for the argument that follows.

Feb. 3, 222:

> Emperor Alexander, to Rufus.
>
> Whoever hurries to accuse of a public crime, shall not be granted an audience for that purpose, unless they have made a written claim beforehand and offered a bond for the bringing of the case.
>
> But if they were not present after the giving of bond, they should be told by an edict that they must come to try their case, and if they have still not been present, not only should they be punished extra ordinem, but furthermore they will be forced to pay any expenses which are associated with this matter and the expenses of coming to court.
>
> Posted three days before the Nones of February [February 3][25] in the consulship of Emperor Alexander [222]

(C.9.1.3) Imp[erator] Alexander A[ugustus] Rufo.

> Qui crimen publicum instituere properant, non aliter ad hoc admittantur, nisi prius inscriptionum pagina processerit et fideiussor de exercenda lite adhibitus fuerit.

24 Austin, *Words*, pp. 5–7.

25 The Nones of February took place on the fifth of that month, and Roman calendar reckoning was inclusive. Ergo, three days before the Nones would be the third of February.

Sin uero post satisdationem praesentes non fuerint, edicto admonendi sunt, ut ueniant ad causam agendam, et si non adfuerint, non solum extra ordinem puniendi sunt, sed etiam sumptus, quos in eam rem et circa ipsum iter ad litem uocati fecerunt, dependere cogentur.

P[rae]P[ositum] III [dies ante] non[es] Febr[uarii] Alexandro A[ugusto] Cons[ule]

Feb. 19, 222:

Emperor Alexander, to the soldier Aurelius Maro.

If your father has sold his home under compulsion by force, it will not be considered valid since it was not done in good faith: for a purchase in bad faith is void.

Therefore, if approached the governor of the province will interpose his authority on your behalf, especially if you state that you are prepared to repay to the buyer that which was given on pretext of price.

Decided eleven days before the Kalends of March [February 19] *in the consulship of Elagabalus and Alexander*

(C.4.44.1) Imp[erator] Alexander A[ugustus] Aurelio Maroni militi.

Si pater tuus per uim coactus domum uendidit, ratum non habebitur, quod non bona fide gestum est: mala fide enim emptio irrita est. aditus itaque nomine tuo praeses prouinciae auctoritatem suam interponet, maxime cum paratum te proponas id quod pretii nomine illatum est emptori refundere.

D[atum] XI [dies ante] K[alendas] Mart[is] Antonino et Alexandro cons[ulibu]s

Mar. 8, 222:

Emperor Alexander, to Octavius.

It is clear that, even if a seller specifically did not offer the right of eviction, an action on purchase lies once the object of sale is evicted.

Posted eight days before the Ides of March [March 8] *in the consulship of Emperor Alexander* [222]

(C.8.44.6) Imp[erator] Alexander A[ugustus] Octavio.

Non dubitatur, etsi specialiter uenditor euictionem non promiserit, re euicta ex empto competere actionem.

P[rae]P[ositum] VIII [dies ante] id[es] Mart[is] Alexandro A[ugusto] Cons[ule][26]

[26] See Coriat, *Le prince législateur*, pp. 105–06.

These rescripts address a variety of legal problems, but for our purposes their most important features are the heading and date. Each identifies itself as a statement of Severus Alexander, but each was finalized before Elagabalus was deposed/killed. The first and third are dated with *PP*, which means that they were "posted" on the indicated date; since Elagabalus was emperor until March 11, each document would have thus circulated as an opinion of Elagabalus taking the form in which it appears in the *Codex*. The second document is dated with *D*, meaning the opinion was "given" on February 19; this dating formula was specific to imperial archives,[27] which may explain why this document retains a reference to Elagabalus as one of the two consuls of 222. However, even the imperial archives were redacted at some point; given that Elagabalus was clearly alive when this document was produced, it is remarkable that the opinion is attributed to Severus Alexander alone.

These documents all purport to commemorate imperial speech but "misrepresent" their speaker. This misrepresentation was first noticed by van Sickle in 1928, who argued that it, along with other similar errors, meant "[t]hat for the student of history the headings of rescripts of the *Severi* in the Justinian Code are of very little value."[28] Ironically, these faked headings can be thought of as important historical documents in their own right. They are political fiction, but a potent example of Severan law telling stories about itself and its world.

Specifically, the rescripts of 222 erase Elagabalus from official legal reality and replace him with Severus Alexander. While we cannot be certain exactly when this erasure occurred, it can be dated with some confidence to Alexander's reign for three reasons. The first is simple motive. Alexander died without an heir, and it is by no means obvious who would benefit from attributing Elagabalic legal writing to Alexander during the long period of conflict that followed.[29] This is particularly true given the volume of alteration. While one can imagine a solitary opinion being altered over the course of a transmission period, no rescript survives from 222 that is attributed to Elagabalus

[27] See Corcoran, *Tetrarchs*, p. 28; Corcoran notes this archival tendency in the context of Diocletianic rescripts, as I discuss further *infra* p. 243.

[28] Van Sickle, "Headings," p. 277.

[29] On which see generally Drinkwater, "Maximinus to Diocletian."

or Antoninus.[30] Instead, it appears that all Elagabalic rescripts from 222 were relabeled as a unit. Figure 4.1 provides all surviving rescripts from 222–24 broken down by month.

While these numbers are far too small for any statistical confidence, there is no clear difference between the productivity of the last months of Elagabalus' reign and the first months of Alexander's. Instead, the major shift happens in September of 222, far too late to attribute to the change in ruler.[31] There is simply no evidence of any kind of selective cull, nor clear distinguishing characteristic that might make the surviving Elagabalic rescripts particularly worthy of transmission. Instead, the sources suggest a mass relabeling of the sort that would only make sense if it took place under his immediate successor.

Second, contemporary sources suggest that Elagabalus' memory was condemned early in Alexander's reign. Dio claims (80[79].21.2–3 [Xiph.]) that Elagabalus' administrative retinue and patron deity were immediately purged from the city of Rome, and the *HA* that his name was "erased on the order of the Senate" (*Elag.* 17.4: *erasum est senatu iubente*). This erasure is amply attested in the epigraphic record as well. For example, a statue base in the Antiquarium Forense originally honored both Elagabalus and his mother before the names were excised.[32] Assuming our ancient sources are correct, this purge happened soon after Elagabalus' death. Unless we believe that Elagabalus' rescripts continued to circulate under his own name for at least thirteen years, during which time the man himself was abominated and excised from all other official records, these documents had to have been renamed under Alexander.

Finally, this renaming accords with Alexander's treatment of Elagabal and Elagabalus in other media. To begin with architecture – Elagabalus is

30 Ironically, C.2.18.8 records a rescript of an "Antoninus" given July 27 of 218. Assuming the document is dated correctly it can be attributed to Elagabalus, but because Elagabalus used the same regnal name as Caracalla the compilers (and perhaps others besides) mistakenly attributed it to the latter. C.2.18.7 and .9 are both securely Caracallan, and the *Codex* groups rescripts by promulgating authority.

31 This burst of activity, which ends abruptly in September of 224, has been attributed to Ulpian's attainment of the sole praetorian prefecture by Honoré (*Ulpian*, p. 30). That ending date is approximately the period of Ulpian's death, and I believe (and plan to argue in more detail in later work) that they may be related. That claim is irrelevant, however, to the present project.

32 Varner, "Portraits, Plots, and Politics," p. 49; Bartoli, "Riccordi di Elagabalo," pp. 50–54.

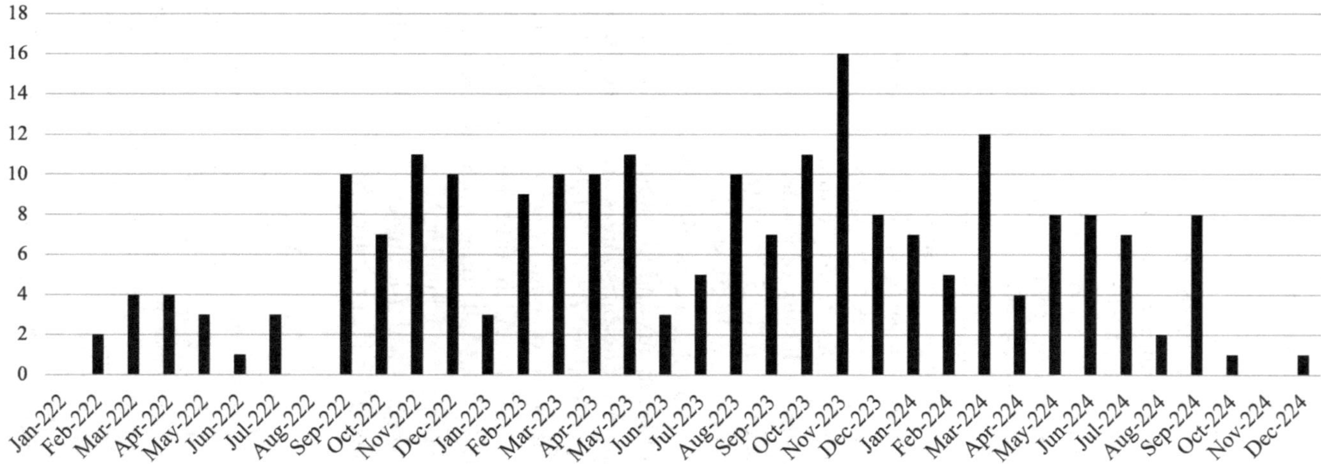

FIGURE 4.1 Extant rescripts of Elagabalus/Severus Alexander by month, 222–24. Data: Honoré, *Emperors and Lawyers*.

known to have inaugurated two separate temples to Elagabal: a large *Elagabalium* under excavation on the Vigna Barberini,[33] and a second monumental complex that is attested in Herodian but whose modern location is unknown.[34] While we cannot be certain of the afterlife of the second structure, the Vigna Barberini temple was rededicated under Severus Alexander to Jupiter Ultor (Jupiter the Avenger). Excavations of that temple show two building phases in rapid succession, and comparing temples visible on Elagabalus' and Alexander's coinage makes clear that the *Elagabalium* and Alexander's Temple of Jupiter were the same structure (Figures 4.2 and 4.3).[35]

FIGURE 4.2 Elagabalic coin reverse. Berlin: Staatliche Museen zu Berlin, Münzkabinett/Reinhard Saczewski, 18205364.

[33] See Aur. Vict. *Caes.* 23; *HA*, *Elag.* 3.4–5; Jer. *Ab Abr.* 296g (Helm); Villedieu (1997), *La Vigna Barberini.*

[34] Hdn. 5.6.6–7: κατεσκεύασε δὲ καὶ ἐν τῷ προαστείῳ νεὼν μέγιστόν τε καὶ πολυτελέστατον, ἐς ὃν ἑκάστου ἔτους κατῆγε τὸν θεὸν ἀκμάζοντος θέρους. Paterna (1996, "Il circo Variano" 846) locates this temple in the Sessorian Palace, based largely on structural parallels between there and the Vigna Barberini. By contrast, Palmer ("Trastevere," pp. 377–80) and Matern (*Helios und Sol*, pp. 33–34) have placed this second temple on the Juniculum Hill, based on the large number of inscriptions on that site referencing Elagabalic religious beliefs and practices. Rowan (*Under Divine Auspices*, pp. 202–03) notes, however, that the inscriptions honoring Elagabal from this site largely predate Elagabalus himself. Earlier, Optendrenk had argued (*Religionspolitik*, p. 87) that the same site was instead home to a temporary *Elagabalium*.

[35] On the building phases of the Vigna Barberini complex see Broise and Thébert, "Complexe religieux," p. 739; on the similarities between the *Elagabalium* and the temple of Jupiter Ultor see Woytek, "Aedes," pp. 213–16; Rowan, "Becoming Jupiter."

FIGURE 4.3 Coin reverse of Severus Alexander. New York: American Numismatic Society. Image: Clare Rowan.

FIGURE 4.4 Portrait of Severus Alexander, with visible recarving. Naples: Museo Archeologico Nazionale di Napoli, 5993.[36]

Portraits of Elagabalus suffered a similar fate. Most images of the young emperor were destroyed after his condemnation, as was common for victims of Roman memory sanctions.[37] That said, four statues of

[36] Other recarved portraits are catalogued at: Museo Nazionale Romano, Palazzo Massimo alle Terme, inv. 329; Musei Capitolini, Palazzo dei Conservatori, inv. 2457; and Nelson-Atkins Museum of Art, inv. 45–66. For more detailed description see Varner, *Mutilation and Transformation*, pp. 279–81.

[37] Krüpe, *Vernichtung*, pp. 40–55; Flower, *The Art of Forgetting*, pp. 83–85.

Elagabalus survive as recarved images of Severus Alexander. Figure 4.4 shows the most obvious alteration, from the Farnese Collection at the Museo Archeologico Nazionale di Napoli; Alexander's face has here been grafted onto a pre-existing heroic nude of Elagabalus. Similar portraits survive in Rome's Palazzo Massimo alle Terme and Centrale Montemartini, as well as the Nelson-Atkins Museum of Art in Kansas City.

While post-destruction reuse of this sort was not unheard of, it was rare; the last *princeps damnatus* whose portraits were remade was Domitian.[38] And even then, the standard practice was to simply modify the image with as little waste as possible. By contrast, whoever made the Naples portrait did not just alter the emperor's face (hardly difficult, given the similarity of their surviving portraiture), but attached an entirely new one to the existing head.

If recarving was unusual, grafting a new face onto an old sculpture was nearly unprecedented. So why do it? Varner has argued that the original Elagabalic visage was defaced immediately after his death and Alexander added years later.[39] This would certainly explain the need for a graft; if the statue were publicly defaced and left in that condition for several years, there would be nothing to recarve. But like rededicating the *Elagabalium* to a god of revenge, grafting Alexander's face onto a ruined portrait was an ostentatious act. These memory sanctions did not erase a historical narrative so much as comment on it. An audience that remembered the original sculpture's appearance and function would see these adaptations as visible, tangible proof that the former emperor had been fully condemned.

Something similar happened to Elagabalic rescripts. These documents were altered, but not comprehensively or well; instead of claiming to have been issued by Alexander on a plausible date, they make facially absurd claims about imperial chronology. This absurdity is plain enough to any historian who knows their dates; C.9.1.3 (dated to February 3, 222) and

38 Varner, *Mutilation and Transformation*, pp. 115–25. While images of Commodus were defaced, the earliest reworking of a Commodan image now extant is post-Severan; *ibid.*, pp. 139–40.

39 *Ibid.*, pp. 190–91. The nearest parallel (a portrait of Domitian whose facial features were removed and replaced with Nerva's) was likely defaced very soon after Domitian's assassination, making traditional recarving impossible. By contrast, the Alexander-type on the Naples portrait is not commonly used until 225.

C.4.44.1 (February 19) are clearly Elagabalic, C.8.44.6 (March 8, 222) is probably Elagabalic but a harder call,[40] and Alexander's court oversaw the creation of C.4.50.2 (March 20, 222) and everything after. However, relabeling is itself a communicative action. Given the relatively sophisticated audience at which these documents were aimed, reading them as a straightforward deception to straightforwardly unravel underestimates the intelligence of all parties involved.[41] Advocates who relied on these rescripts or recorded them for educational purposes would not be fooled, and would read these headings as establishing an official reality rather than simply reflecting events.

The question remains, though, of how Elagabalic speech could even fit into this official reality. If legal authority rested on the elaborate, ideologically charged process that made the ruler's pronouncements legitimate, and specifically on the virtues that made his opinions *the correct opinions*, how do we read legal opinions generated by a possibly transgender, definitely murderous teenage meteorite cultist? The same state organs that were damning Elagabalus' memory, and presumably issuing the kind of judgments upon him that would be reflected in scabrous biographies,[42] were also honoring his legal opinions, even if they required a change of name in order to do so.

Doing both simultaneously – damning the man, citing his words – entailed a subtle shift in thinking about law. The authority of these

[40] Our sources are not particularly clear on the precise date of Alexander's accession, and they enter into some conflict. Dio claims that Elagabalus reigned for three years, nine months, and four days from the Battle of Antioch; given that Dio elsewhere dates the Battle of Antioch to June 8, 218, this would indicate a death date of March 11, 222. Dio Cass. 78[77].39.1, 79[78].3.3[Xiph.]. By contrast, the *uita Alexandri Seueri* refers to Alexander addressing the senate as emperor *pridie Nonas Martias* (March 6): *HA*, *Alex. Seu.* 6.2. The Chronography of 354 lists Elagabalus' reign as – most likely – three years, eight months, and twenty-eight days from his proclamation, which occurred on May 16, 218. That said, assuming that the Chronography actually dates its reign from June 8 produces a date of transition (March 8) that is at least superficially plausible. See Butler, *Heliogabalus*, pp. 106–08. I personally follow Dio's chronology, largely on the evidence of C.8.44.6. It seems implausible that Alexander would have been in any position to hear cases so soon after a coup, but Elagabalus could easily have done so in the days before his death.

[41] Riggsby describes (*Legal World*, pp. 60–66) the formal education that those interacting with legal documents of the Severan period likely received; Schuol argues ("Rechtsschule") that the famous Roman law school in Beirut had been founded about twenty years before Alexander's accession.

[42] Put most bluntly by Syme, who called portions of the *uita Elagabali* "A farrago of cheap pornography" (*Emperors and Biography*, p. 2).

relabeled documents remained inseparable from imperial authority more broadly, but that authority rested less on virtue than on continuity. Explaining how this shift worked, however, requires briefly revisiting the stories told by more conventional imperial legal writing. When I say that an imperial rescript derives its authority from the implicit claim that its author is wise/fair/godlike/et cetera, that claim really comprises two subordinate assertions: first, that the signatory actually wrote or approved the order contained therein, and second that his personal qualities vest that writing or approval with some sort of normative force. Viewed in this light, the implications of Alexandrian relabeling become apparent.

Normally, one pictures that second claim about imperial goodness as the object of state messaging; the recipient of that messaging is to be convinced of the ruler's extraordinary virtue.[43] We cannot know if people who received that messaging sincerely believed it, but there is no reason to assume that even sophisticated readers were overly cynical about a faraway, omnipotent man who only appeared to them in idealized form.[44] By contrast, the relabeled rescripts make a claim that would have been more widely recognized as absurd. People might say that Severus Alexander had issued a legal judgment as *Augustus* on February 3 of 222; they almost certainly did if they ever used that judgment in court. But sophisticated audiences could not be expected to simply forget who was *Augustus* in February of that year, or who was *Augustus* when the opinion was first issued.

In other words: people might say that C.9.1.3 was an opinion of Alexander's but they would not believe it, at least until some time had passed. Nor would they believe – based on surviving evidence – that the actual issuer was a person worth listening to. But they listened regardless. These opinions were preserved, circulated, and cited because Alexander's court wanted them to be, and they were preserved, circulated, and cited under Alexander's name for the same reason. But to the extent anyone took them seriously, they did so

[43] See Noreña, *Imperial Ideals*, p. 45 (describing the "formidable ideological apparatus" available to Greek and Roman monarchies for communicating the virtue of a given ruler).

[44] For example, soon after Nero's death and condemnation an individual claiming to be Nero led a large popular revolt centered in Greece and Asia Minor. Dio Cass. 66.19.3; Tac. *Hist.* 2.8.

because they were told to, or because those opinions had been taken seriously before.

This relabeling, and its implicit claims about what it means to be a rescript "of" an emperor, cannot be divorced from those legal documents that seem to date more securely to Alexander's reign. Fairly soon after Alexander was installed on the throne, surviving documents suggest a flurry of adjudication; as Figure 4.1 shows, the number of surviving rescripts from Alexander's reign picks up sharply in September of 222, and continues until September of 224. The product of this activity mingled, in both *codex* and courtroom, with opinions put forward under another man entirely that were nevertheless to be treated the same. The only way to make sense of this commingling is to understand authorship to mean something very different for these rescripts. In his account of the politics of memory in later Rome Hedrick draws a distinction between "memory" and "representation" that is particularly relevant here. In Hedrick's parlance, the choice to *represent* Alexander as the author of these documents should not be understood as instantiating – or even as aiming to instantiate – the *memory* of his doing so.[45] Otherwise, there would have been some kind of attempt to render these documents plausibly Alexandrian in their official chronology. Instead, the rescripts disambiguate representation from remembered truth and proffer a new theory of authorship. These rescripts (really their headings) tell a story about the past in a descriptive register, but that story is not intended to remind anyone of anything true nor to convince anyone of anything false. Instead, these rescripts construct a new social reality in which they are linked with the current regime and in which that linkage determines legal validity.

"Regime" replaces "emperor" for a reason. Whatever virtue made a relabeled rescript deserving of obedience was not a personal virtue of Severus Alexander, nor of Elagabalus. Audiences knew the former had not produced the document they were citing, and had been told the latter had no virtue to speak of. A comparison to the Edict of Titus may be instructive. The effect of the Edict was not obviously different than this relabeling, since each led to the opinions of one emperor being treated as

[45] Hedrick, *History and Silence*, pp. 113–26; also Flower, *The Art of Forgetting*, p. 278 ("[I]n many cases, [memory sanctions] can be better described as the reversal of identity, rather than a simple loss of identity").

the opinions of another. But the Edict of Titus happened in public. Every *beneficium* of Vespasian remained Vespasianic in later discourse, even if it was the later opinion of Titus (that Vespasian's opinion should be respected) that lent it force. Similarly, to claim that Vespasian possessed the sorts of qualities that could legitimate his decisions was hardly controversial; Vespasian was deified and Titus was not subtle about his filiation.[46] By contrast, there was no public or official speech-act that we know of which validated Elagabalic rescripts. Instead, those rescripts were circulated in a new form, and the change that rendered them legitimate was private and anonymized. The machinery of imperial opinion thus receded into the background, with the documents themselves telling a story of imperial power in which the emperor served as an incoherent signifier.

Relabeling was thus an institutionalizing move, divorcing legal authority from authorial charisma or brilliance. The clearest sign of this new orientation lies in the selection criteria, or lack thereof, of the rescripts of 222. As discussed above there is no reason to suspect any process of selection, because the Elagabalic rescripts that survive share no obvious subject matter or decisional feature. They were, however, already law. While we have no contemporary commentary on the renaming of rescripts – for reasons that should be clear enough – continuity was a desideratum in Roman legal culture going back to the Twelve Tables.[47] Occam's Razor suggests it was a desideratum here as well, especially since no other can be found.

* * * * *

Admittedly, this analysis hangs rather a lot of weight on three oddly dated documents, but these documents are *impressively* odd. There was no precedent for this archival practice that we know of, and almost no successor to it.[48] However, Alexander's own legal correspondence

[46] See, for example, *RIC II Tit.* 435 (referring to Titus as "Son of the deified Vespasian" [DIVI VESP F]); Hekster, *Emperors and Ancestors*, pp. 55–56.

[47] Peachin notes (*Iudex Vice Caesaris*, p. 79) that this continuity did not arise from consistently applied rules but from the possibility of appeal; unreasonable decisions could be fixed by the reasonable emperor. One can see the problems such a framework might encounter in this period.

[48] Rescripts of the persecutor Licinius were likely relabeled and compiled into the *CTh* under Constantine's name. See Corcoran, "Hidden"; Barnes, "Three Imperial Edicts"; *infra* p. 254. No other case is known, however, and no similar practice has been found in the *Codex Justinianus*.

shows some of the same communicative strategies as does this relabeling. When read using careful statistical methods – which I explain immediately below – Alexander's rescripts contain another emergent historical narrative, this one centered on Alexander's heritage. On its own this tendency might be a minor idiosyncrasy in an idiosyncratic time, of interest to Severanists and no one else. But in conjunction with the relabeling of older rescripts, Alexander's legal correspondence suggests a concerted effort to use law to suggest continuity, and specifically to construct a "Severan law" that might deserve the respect that a Syrian adolescent and his powerful advisers could not otherwise easily claim.

Methodology: How to Do Things with Justinian

From here on out, there start to be numbers. As I mentioned at the beginning of this chapter, legal production explodes in the Severan period and accordingly Severan legal historiography is a somewhat different kind of project. While earlier periods demand that the historian find legal culture in nonlegal sources, or engage in close reading of scattered statutes, the sheer volume of Severan legal correspondence permits some different approaches. For one thing, the density of archival material permits a less diachronic approach; while Part I of this book maintained strict chronology in order to make sense of legal scraps, the remainder of this book will be at least somewhat more thematic. The other difference is that, once legal sources become thick on the ground, the legal historian gains the ability to employ quantitative methods and to actually consider something like an emperor's legal program[49] (or, for my purposes, rhetoric) as a whole.

Unfortunately, we do not have a representative sample of that program. The vast majority of surviving legal material from the Severan period and beyond comes down to us through compilations put together by Theodosius II (r. 402–450) and by Justinian. Theodosius only collected legal pronouncements from Christian emperors (i.e. post-Constantine: *CTh* 1.1.6.1), so the present inquiry focuses on the *Codex Justinianus*.[50]

[49] See Nasti, *L'attività normativa*; Soraci, *L'opera legislativa*.

[50] On the difference between how Theodosian and Justinianic compilers approached their texts see *infra* p. 253.

Justinian presents something of a problem, however. In his introductory constitutions (the pronouncements that vested each compilation with legal force, discussed in greater detail in Chapter 7), Justinian explicitly authorized his compilers to engage in "necessary addition or deletion" (*Tanta* 10: *adiectionem uel deminutionem necessariam*) in order to update the ancient text for a later audience. These edits, commonly called "interpolations," muddle the relationship between Classical text and Justinianic artifact.

The study of interpolations goes back centuries, but in its modern form is most closely associated with Gradenwitz, who inaugurated the practice of what is sometimes called "interpolation-hunting" (after Lenel) within the *Corpus Iuris Ciuilis*.[51] This strand of scholarship aims to identify likely Justinianic additions (most often, but not exclusively, to the *Digest*) on the basis of syntax and legal logic, in order to better determine the contents and language of the "lost" Classical text. Interpolation criticism changed enormously in the mid twentieth century following influential work by Kaser and Wieacker, which demonstrated that interpolation, regardless of Justinian's claims, consisted largely of shortening Classical juristic texts; the compilers stripped juristic fragments of context and of material they saw as extraneous, but almost never added anything in.[52] Most scholars now take as a given that the surviving text of a given fragment of the *Corpus Iuris Ciuilis* is probably close to the original text of the treatise or constitution it purports to quote. This point does not render interpolation harmless but shifts discussion of Justinianic alteration from the insertion of words to more subtle and complex "transposition[s] of context"[53] or unrepresentative excerpting practices.[54]

Justinian's compilers, however, were themselves working with imperfect copies. A substantial (if unknown) number of the alterations that survive in the *Corpus* can be chalked up to redactions that occurred over the long period between the composition of Roman legal texts and

51 Lenel, "Interpolationenjagd"; Gradenwitz, *Interpolationen in den Pandekten.*

52 Kaser, *Rechtsquellenforschung*; "Glaubwürdigkeit"; Wieacker, "Textkritik und Sachforschung"; "Zur gegenwärtigen Lage"; *Textstufen.*

53 See Johnston, "Interpretation," p. 152.

54 For further discussion see Babusiaux, "Défauts," pp. 24–28; Andrés Santos, "Interpolacionismo"; "Critica interpolazionistica"; Lokin, "Epilegomena."

the early sixth century. Wieacker demonstrated these problems of transmission (*Textstufen*) by comparing juristic fragments that were copied down at different points in the transmission period; that said, we will never know the exact scope of the changes.[55] These features of the Justinianic compilations make it largely impossible to say what third-century legal writing actually looked like to third-century readers. The texts we have survive because they were taken – by compilers, or by legal cultures in the long period between writing and compilation – as evidence for normative rules, and not for the other kinds of work that law can do.

That said, by adopting a proportional approach (i.e. by looking at how particular corpora of rescripts or juristic fragments differ from others in the same compilation) we can isolate particular tendencies and changes over time. Going forward, when I make claims about rhetorical features of particular authors/authorities in the *Digest* or *Codex*, I focus on how those features differ between one author/authority and another. I do that because, while compilers were likely quite comfortable editing the fragments that make up the *Corpus Iuris Ciuilis*, that editing process would not have differed substantially for different fragments. There is no reason to think, for example, that the compilers were more inclined to preserve a particular rhetorical trope in rescripts of Severus Alexander than in those of Caracalla. Accordingly, difference in the rate of survival of that particular trope can be taken as evidence for difference in how frequently different emperors used it.

To be clear, I refer only to documents that had already been selected for inclusion. Emperors who had been subjected to memory sanction were generally excluded from the *Codex Justinianus*,[56] and specific juristic treatises were more or less likely to make it into the *Digest* based on the reputations of their authors. But proportional analysis allows us to isolate diachronic change, even within a highly edited corpus. While interpolation concerns make it hard to say exactly how a document would have looked before the compilers got their hands on it, we can say how it differs from others that were preserved via the same process.

[55] Wieacker, *Textstufen*, pp. 72–92; also Connolly, *Lives*, pp. 37–38.
[56] On this practice see briefly Sautel, "Usurpations."

Of course, not every difference is meaningful. Anyone who has flipped a coin 100 times in a row knows that odd patterns sometimes emerge in a dataset through simple coincidence. Accordingly, when possible I subject my findings to what is called *chi*-squared analysis; this statistical tool helps us determine the chances of a given disparity coming about by accident. *Chi*-squared analysis uses the raw data of a particular statistical finding to determine whether the disparity is too great, and over too large a sample, to be coincidental. Accordingly, it determines whether a given finding is "statistically significant." To call a finding "statistically significant" does not mean that it is important – I am still writing about Roman law – but instead that it is unlikely to have happened by chance. When I reference statistical significance I will provide the relevant equations and confidence intervals in a footnote, but it can be taken to simply mean "nonrandom."

That said, I should offer a few caveats and methodological qualifiers before I move on to presenting quantitative material. First, the proportional approach I described above works well for the major juristic treatises – which were produced in a remarkably short period of time in the early third century CE, and thus have roughly similar transmissions[57] – but has dangers that I should acknowledge before applying them to the *Codex*. For example, the constitutions of Severus Alexander, which I discuss immediately below, had a much longer transmission period than those of someone like Leo I (r. 457–474) with accordingly greater opportunities for alteration. Fortunately, persuasive rhetoric is much more likely to drop out of imperial legal writing over the course of transmission than it is to be added in; accordingly, if Alexander's rescripts feature particular arguments that later ones do not, we can take that as good evidence of idiosyncrasy.[58] But as a general rule we should be cautious about equating documents that predated Justinian by centuries with those that did so by decades.

Finally, this procedure only works on corpora that were built according to uniform selection criteria. What that means, in practice,

[57] On the sudden efflorescence of juristic writing in this period (and the near-total collapse of juristic writing afterwards) see Babusiaux, "Zitate"; de Blois, "Influence"; "Roman Jurists."

[58] For evidence of this redactive tendency, compare *CTh.* 3.1.4 (a constitution issued jointly by Gratian, Valentinian II, and Theodosius I and codified under Theodosius II) with the much shorter version preserved at C.4.44.15.

is that quantitative arguments in this book will be restricted to the Justinianic archives.[59] While most Classical and post-Classical legal material comes down to us via the *codices*, some other documents survive via inscription or papyri and I have left these out for the sake of statistical clarity.[60] Uncodified material comes to us via a number of different, idiosyncratic methods of transmission and preservation, and that variety makes regression analysis impossible. I cannot be certain, for example, that the traits I am selecting for would not impact the likelihood of an inscription surviving differently than they would the likelihood of a rescript being included in the *Codex*. Considering uncodified material would increase the size of my datasets but would also introduce massive and unpredictable endogeneities into the same; accordingly, I stick to Justinian when making statistical arguments.

The Rule of Precedent

The method I just described reveals some startling tendencies in the Justinianic corpus. This section deals with one of the most striking: Severus Alexander's extreme and idiosyncratic tendency to cite legal opinions of his putative ancestors. Accordingly, I begin with an example of the form, in which Alexander addresses a question about inheritance law by following a constitution of Septimius Severus.

If you can prove in an action that your mother made excessive gifts-in-contemplation-of-death to your sister, according to the constitution of the deified Severus, my grandfather, you may make use of the reasoning of the lex Falcidia.

(C.6.50.6: Severus Alexander, 223) Si mortis causa immodicas donationes in sororem tuam matrem contulisse probare potes, legis Falcidiae ratione secundum constitionem diui Seueri aui mei uti potes.

We know little about this rescript's context. It is addressed *Samosatae*, but that personal name is unattested elsewhere and urban toponyms

[59] There is no reason why similar work could not be done on the imperial constitutions collected in the *Codex Theodosianus*, although the selection criteria for that compilation remain contested: see *infra* p. 275. This book does not mount any such arguments with the *CTh*, however, and accordingly I focus here on the material most important for my subsequent claims.

[60] E.g. *CIL* VIII(supp.).17639, discussed at Purpura, "Papiri," p. 207; Arcaria, *Referre ad principem*, p. 144.

are unusual in Greek.[61] *Samosatae* could be locative – we know Samosata was densely populated in the early third century – but C.8.45.1 (Severus Alexander, 223) was produced on the same day and addresses someone by the Latin name *Publicius*. Regardless of names, the rescript answers what must have been an explosive question: Could the *lex Falcidia* be invoked against a parent favoring one sister over another?

The emotional stakes of accusing one's dead mother of favoritism should be clear enough, but the tools used are fascinating in their own right. The *lex Falcidia*, a Roman inheritance statute dating to the late Republic, invalidated wills or, as here, testamentary gifts (*donationes mortis causa*) that gave away more than three-quarters of the decedent's estate to nonheirs.[62] We have reason to think its operations were somewhat obscure, since Cassius Dio – hardly unlearned in matters of law[63] – erroneously claimed that the *lex* permitted an heir to refuse an inheritance and walk away with only a quarter of the estate instead.[64] We know the petitioner (whom I call Samosata for ease of reading, even if her name was almost certainly different) was a Roman citizen, but she and her family may only have gained access to Roman law eleven years prior with the *constitutio Antoniniana* (*CA*).[65] Nevertheless, this woman benefited from the emperor himself intervening in her family dispute using the technical, finicky apparatus of a 250-year-old inheritance law.

We can imagine Samosata's – and her sister's – reaction to the rescript upon seeing it. But this is only part of the story told by C.6.50.6. The reasoning that the rescript employs is unusual, both as a matter of simple logic and within the broader corpus of imperial legal writing that survives. The document presents itself not as jurisgenerative – as affirmatively stating what Samosata's rights and obligations ought to be – but as simply interpreting Septimius Severus' prior order. C.6.50.6 explicitly hierarchizes, and not to the benefit of the sitting emperor;

61 Hornblower and Matthews, *Greek Personal Names*, pp. 86–87.

62 See D.35.2; *J. Inst.* 2.22; *RLC* 59.

63 Dio claims at 77[76].17.1 [Xiph.] to have advised Septimius Severus on legal questions, and was quite annoyed that Caracalla paid less heed to his counsel. See Davenport, "Cassius Dio and Caracalla."

64 Dio Cass. 48.33.5.

65 An edict of the emperor Caracalla, issued in 212 CE, that granted near-universal citizenship to inhabitants of the Roman empire; see *infra* pp. 235–36.

secundum positions Alexander as a follower, whose approach to the problem presented rests not on his own moral judgment but on that of his grandfather.

To be clear, this form of argument was common in other genres of Roman law talk – jurists used it all the time. While I discuss juristic engagement with imperial decisionmaking in more detail in Chapter 5, some examples may be helpful. Ulpian states that "one who has asked for a tutor for *pupillis* due to his friendship with their father, or who has held their current tutors in suspicion, has no action against them according to a constitution of the deified Severus (D.3.5.43, Disputationes: *secundum diui Seueri constitutionem*)." Similarly, Paul responds to a technical question (whether a *bona fide possessor* can be compelled to return the thing possessed, or merely its value) by simply quoting a Hadrianic *oratio*.

In the instant case we must determine whether it is the case that 1) the possessor is more deserving of being heard, should he wish hand over a good that has lost value, than the petitioner who wishes to receive the value, on the grounds that such a wish is inappropriate; or 2) that since the possessor has profited from a part of the inheritance he ought to return whatever he has gained from the price. The following can be found in a speech of the deified Hadrian on this subject: "Decide, *patres conscripti*, whether it is fairer for a possessor to not make a profit and return the price he received for another person's goods; on the grounds that the price of the sale can be reckoned to have come into the place of the inheritance goods and, in some ways, to have become part of the inheritance itself." *Therefore, it is best for the possessor to return both the good and whatever profit he made from its sale to the petitioner.*

(D.5.3.22: ad Edictum) An hic magis possessor audiendus sit, si uelit rem tradere licet deteriorem factam, non petitor, si pretium desideret, quod inuerecundum sit tale desiderium: an uero, quia ex re hereditaria locupletior sit, et id quod amplius habet ex pretio restituere debeat, uidendum. nam et in oratione diui Hadriani ita est: "dispicite, patres conscripti, numquid sit aequius possessorem non facere lucrum et pretium, quod ex aliena re perceperit, reddere, quia potest existimari in locum hereditariae rei uenditae pretium eius successisse et quodammodo ipsum hereditarium factum." oportet igitur possessorem et rem restituere petitori et quod ex uenditione eius rei lucratus est.

Hadrian's quote is subtle but clearly suggests his opinion of the case, and the language implies an open question (*numquid*) that his suggested reasoning entirely answers. But Paul's interpretation is rather more straightforward. Paul not only takes Hadrian's words as clearly indicating imperial opinion, but also views that opinion as dispositive (*oportet igitur*).

The *Digest* preserves over 1,200 juristic citations of imperial lawmaking.[66] By contrast, the *Codex Justinianus* contains only 82 such citations. This difference reflects the basic, second-order rules undergirding classical Roman law. Unlike the juristic treatises of the *Digest*, imperial constitutions simply needed to state *what* the law was, not *why* the law was what it was. As a result, they almost never include explicit argumentation.[67] For example:

The judge with jurisdiction is not unaware that a woman who alleges that she is pursuing retribution for the death of her son ought not be rashly permitted to accuse without first proving herself to be the victim's mother.

(C.9.1.9: Gordian III, 239) Non ignorat competens iudex eam, quae ultionem et mortem filii persequi adlegat, non temere ad accusationem esse admittendam, nisi prius matrem se esse probauerit.

No reasoning is given, none is needed. Gordian – or whoever wrote under his name – is empowered to simply state the responsibilities of the judicial bureaucrat hearing the case. Gordian posits the rule he states as literally incapable of contestation, as a fact that cannot be disputed but can only be known or not known (*ignorat*). If law is imagined as extending from imperial desire, to state that desire is to incontrovertibly state the law. If anything, this tendency against reasoning is even more visible in opinions that were not preserved for education or citation; as I discussed in Chapter 3, the decisions recorded in *P. Col.* 123 barely explain themselves at all.

So, emperors rarely cited precedent. After all citing precedent implies the need to cite precedent, or the possibility of argument over whether or not the imperial statement is in line with whatever authority it claims to interpret. Since rescripts emanated directly from the prevailing legislative authority and spoke on his behalf, no argument was necessary. The question, then, is why a rescript might use argumentative techniques

[66] See Appendix 1.
[67] Babusiaux, "Zitate," pp. 249–50: "Die kaiserliche Kanzlei teilt das Ergebnis mit; die Juristen berichten über die Entscheidungsfindung."

commonly associated with other, less authoritative forms of legal reasoning.

At the level of the individual document this question cannot be answered – we do not know enough about how any given rescript was composed – but the *Codex Justinianus* provides a very large sample of imperial correspondence in which some trends can be seen. Specifically, this sample allows us to contrast the argument styles used by the rescripts of different emperors. As Figure 4.5 shows, different emperors cited precedent – i.e. referenced prior imperial lawmaking, broadly defined, as influencing their decisionmaking – at vastly different rates. The most extreme outliers in this regard are Justinian and the subject of this chapter, Severus Alexander. While Justinian almost never relies on prior imperial decisions, Alexander does so approximately four times more frequently than the average. Alexander's correspondence gives us over 25% of surviving precedential citations within the *Codex*, even though it makes up only 7% of the *Codex* by volume.[68]

Justinian will be discussed in Chapter 7; his relationship to prior lawmaking may be the most idiosyncratic of any Roman ruler. But Alexander comes close. Alexander gives us the plurality of precedential citations within the *Codex*, but more importantly those citations are preserved out of all proportion to the number of his rescripts, as a whole, that survive. By way of comparison while Diocletian also provides a large number of precedential citations, this can be entirely explained by his high rate of preservation within the *Codex* generally.[69]

Alexander's correspondence not only makes unusually frequent mention of earlier emperors, but discusses a curated subset of them and does so in unusual language. For example, Alexander's reply to Samosata did not simply refer to a prior imperial constitution but specifically to "the constitution of the deified Severus, my

[68] For a list of imperial *constitutiones* citing prior imperial communications as precedential authority see Appendix 2.

[69] While Diocletianic rescripts provide 19.5% of our precedential citations that survive, they constitute 19.7% of the *Codex tout court*. In other words, Diocletian was slightly *less* likely than average to cite precedent, but his rescripts are so well represented in the *Codex Justinianus* that that subset still makes up a large proportion of the total sample.

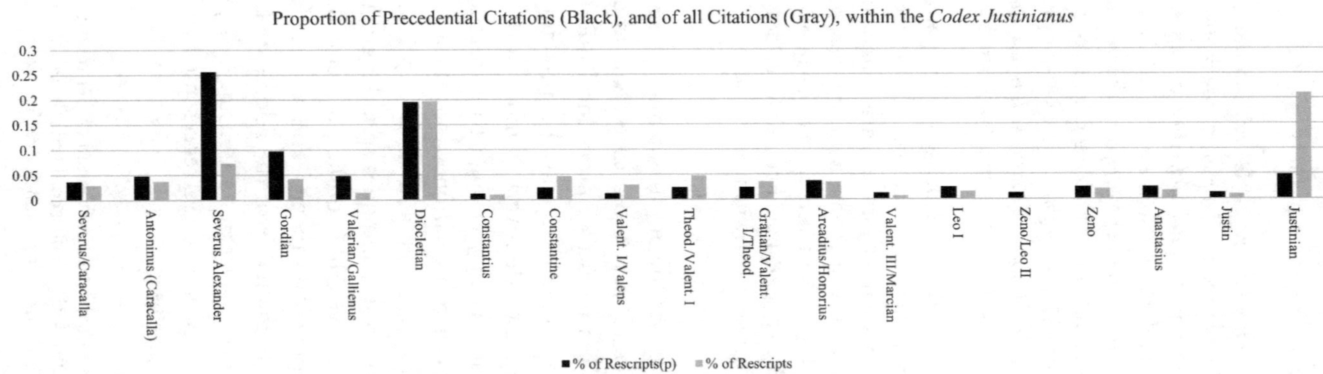

FIGURE 4.5 Precedential citation in the *Codex Justinianus*.

grandfather." The following example shows Alexander applying similar language to a very different set of facts.

Those things which both I and my father, the deified Antoninus, said in reply accord with the rules of right and reason. Nor are those replies distinct or in disagreement, since it matters very much whether a defendant asks for accounts to be provided with which he claims he can build a case, from one who seeks something and who can be kept off from the petition's objective through a defense of fraud – an outcome which the fairness of the case always demands – or whether the plaintiff is asking that accounts be produced by the one from whom something is sought, since in that case it is not appropriate that the petition be based on the accounts of the man who is being prosecuted.

(C.2.1.8: Severus Alexander, 225) Et quae a diuo Antonino patre et quae a me rescripta sunt, cum iuris et aequitatis rationibus congruunt. nec enim diuersa sunt uel discrepantia, quod multum intersit, ex parte eius, qui aliquid petit quique doli exceptione submoueri ab intentione petitionis suae potest, rationes promi reus desideret, quibus se posse instruere contendit – quod utique ipsa rei aequitas suadet – an uero ab eo a quo aliquid petitur actor desideret rationes exhiberi, quando hoc casu non oportet originem petitionis ex instrumentis eius qui conuenitur fundari.

Here, it is easier to reconstruct the argument than its social context. The question presented (can a party to a case demand access to the counterparty's accounts) is the sort of procedural query that could accompany most complex litigation, and the principle Alexander puts forward (that burdensome discovery is more fairly imposed on a plaintiff than a defendant) is easy enough to understand. But this document appears to answer a brazen question. Rather than simply laying out obligations, the rescript addresses a perceived conflict between two imperial authorities, and does so in language presuming that the audience itself perceives that conflict; it seems likely that the petitioner attempted to play Alexander's and Caracalla's opinions against each other.[70] While the name of the addressee (*Florus*) gives us little information, the question suggests a business dispute, and one in which the petitioner was well enough represented to be aware of earlier opinions on the same topic.

70 To be specific, the petitioner probably alleged that an earlier rescript of Alexander's overruled one of Caracalla's. While the conflict could run the other way, claiming that a sitting ruler's opinion was invalid due to conflict with his predecessors seems both legally and politically unwise.

Alexander's response to that petitioner is majestically testy – and unusually careful. Alexander takes great pains to present his opinion not merely as correct because of its emanation from the imperial pen, but also as according with external rules of moral reasoning (*iuris et aequitatis rationibus*, *ipsa rei aequitas*). Particularly notable is the accordance between Alexander and the rescripts of his father, the deified Antoninus. Alexander here presents his own reasoning as a logical extension not merely of his institutional predecessors, but also of his lineage and name.

That emphasis on family is a running theme of Alexander's citations to precedent. All but four cite emperors from whom he claimed descent: seven cite *diui parentes* (at C.2.40.1 (229), C.4.1.2 (223), C.6.21.6pr. (225), C.7.8.6 [n.d.], C.9.9.6.1 (223), C.9.22.2 (223) and C.10.60.1 [n.d.]); three cite Caracalla (C.2.1.8 (225), C.6.54.6 (225) and C.12.35.4 [n.d.]); one cites Septimius Severus (C.6.50.5 (223)); six cite Marcus (C.4.57.2 (222), C.4.57.3pr. (224), C.5.62.5 [n.d.], C.6.54.7 (225), C.7.11.3 [n.d.] and C.12.35.4 [n.d.]); and – most strangely – three of those cite Marcus acting jointly with Commodus (C.4.57.2 (222), C.4.57.3pr. (224), and C.6.54.7 (225)). Other emperors demonstrate no clear preference for citing family members or even recent predecessors. To give one example, Diocletian's authorities range from Claudius to Aurelian.[71]

I have already discussed Alexander's relationship to Caracalla and Septimius; he claimed to be the former's son and the latter's grandson. That said even biographies that otherwise favor the young emperor describe this claim as a transparent fiction, making clear that it was heavily contested in Alexander's own lifetime.[72] The repeated precedential linkages between Alexander, Marcus, and Commodus refer to an even more contested paternity. The Severan dynasty emerged from a brief civil war following the assassination of Commodus, and Septimius only successfully consolidated power after promising to forego dynasty and naming Clodius Albinus as his successor.[73] That promise was broken. Severus soon killed Albinus and appointed his own son as heir, reformulating imperial rule along the

[71] C.2.13.1.2 (293), C.12.62.4 [n.d.].
[72] See Hekster, *Emperors and Ancestors*, pp. 219–21.
[73] Dio Cass. 74.15.1 [Xiph.]; Birley, *The African Emperor*, p. 98.

dynastic lines he initially abjured. Severus' own nonimperial birth was no great obstacle to this, since starting in 194 he appears in inscriptions as "the son of the deified Marcus" (*diui Marci filius*).[74] Being the son of Marcus, however, meant also being the brother of Commodus, who had been assassinated just a few years prior. Awkwardly, Severus had previously linked himself to Commodus' successor, the anti-dynast Pertinax.[75] Dio records Severus' solution: restoring Commodus' reputation as part of a broader turn against the Senate.

And it shocked us most of all that he proclaimed himself to be the son of Marcus and the brother of Commodus, and he gave heroic honors to Commodus, whom he had recently been insulting. And in giving a speech before the Senate, while praising the austerity and harshness of Sulla and Marius and Augustus as safer, and reproaching the mildness of Pompey and Caesar as having brought about disaster for them, he launched into a defense of Commodus, attacking the Senate on the grounds that they had dishonored him unjustly, if they lived more shamefully than he. "For if it were terrible," he said, that that man killed beasts with his own hands, but then just yesterday one of you in Ostia, an old consular, publicly sported with a prostitute mimicking a leopard. But he fought, by God, and none of you fights: then how, and why, did some of you buy his shields and his golden helmets?"

(76[75].7–8. [Xiph.]) μάλιστα δ᾽ ἡμᾶς ἐξέπληξεν ὅτι τοῦ τε Μάρκου υἱὸν καὶ τοῦ Κομμόδου ἀδελφὸν ἑαυτὸν ἔλεγε, τῷ τε Κομμόδῳ, ὃν πρῴην ὕβριζεν, ἡρωικὰς ἐδίδου τιμάς. πρός τε τὴν βουλὴν λόγον ἀναγινώσκων, καὶ τὴν μὲν Σύλλου καὶ Μαρίου καὶ Αὐγούστου αὐστηρίαν τε καὶ ὠμότητα ὡς ἀσφαλεστέραν ἐπαινῶν, τὴν δὲ Πομπηίου καὶ Καίσαρος ἐπιείκειαν ὡς ὀλεθρίαν αὐτοῖς ἐκείνοις γεγενημένην κακίζων, ἀπολογίαν τινὰ ὑπὲρ τοῦ Κομμόδου ἐπήγαγε, καθαπτόμενος τῆς βουλῆς ὡς οὐ δικαίως ἐκεῖνον ἀτιμαζούσης, εἴγε καὶ αὐτῆς οἱ πλείους αἴσχιον βιοτεύουσιν. 'εἰ γὰρ τοῦτο ἦν' ἔφη 'δεινόν, ὅτι αὐτοχειρίᾳ ἐφόνευεν ἐκεῖνος θηρία, ἀλλὰ καὶ ὑμῶν τις χθὲς καὶ πρῴην ἐν Ὠστίοις, ὑπατευκὼς γέρων, δημοσίᾳ μετὰ πόρνης πάρδαλιν μιμουμένης ἔπαιζεν. ἀλλ᾽ ἐμονομάχει νὴ Δία. ὑμῶν δ᾽ οὐδεὶς μονομαχεῖ; πῶς οὖν καὶ ἐπὶ τί τάς τε ἀσπίδας αὐτοῦ καὶ τὰ κράνη τὰ χρυσᾶ ἐκεῖνα ἐπρίαντό τινες;'

Leopards aside, it is clear that under Septimius Severus there was a concerted effort to rehabilitate Commodus and that this effort included deification. Alexander took matters further by not just proclaiming his descendancy from Commodus but also holding up

[74] See *CIL* VIII.9317.
[75] Dio Cass. 74[73].4.1–5.5 [Xiph.]; Birley, *The African Emperor*, pp. 104–05.

his administrative acts as worthy of imitation.[76] This behavior was not repeated. While later emperors would cite the decisions of Marcus as guiding authority[77] Alexander's three references to Commodus (all to decisions made by him and Marcus together)[78] are his only appearance in the *Codex Justinianus*.

* * * * *

Alexander's legal correspondence, taken in full, tells an unusual story. It argues very differently than that of other emperors, and constructs a child ruler who agrees with and often follows rules set down by his ancestors. At the same time rescripts were circulating with clearly fictionalized attributions of authorship, and the question of who "wrote" imperial rescripts seems to have mattered less than ever before. The next section will explore in more detail why the legal correspondence of Severus Alexander reimagined imperial legality on impersonal and hereditary grounds. While the dynastic model Alexander put forward did not take root, it shows us what sort of political crisis faced legal actors in the late Severan period, and how those actors tried to use law to save themselves.

Law in a World of Children

Third-century imperial history can blur. Historians from Cassius Dio to Edward Gibbon have imagined the Severan period as something of a parade of horribles, and consequently Alexander's reign as a return to normalcy. Similarly, the *HA* changes sources after Elagabalus and its biography of Severus Alexander belongs to traditions of late-antique hagiography.[79] Accordingly, that biography presents Alexander as part of a tradition of virtuous child rulers that in fact postdated

[76] On legal citation as imitative, and thus as a form of exemplary reasoning, see Peachin, "Exemplary Government"; *supra* pp. 87–88.

[77] The latest of whom to be attested is Diocletian: C.9.41.11pr. (290).

[78] While the number is small, the total absence of decisions put forward under Commodus' sole authority is unlikely to be coincidental, since Commodus only ruled jointly with Marcus from 177 to 180 and then ruled alone until the end of 192. The most likely explanation is that Commodan constitutions were purged at some point in 193.

[79] Chastagnol, *l'Histoire Auguste*, pp. 549–61.There is an extensive bibliography on the dating of the *HA*, but for two recent treatments see Thomson, *Studies in the Historia Augusta*, pp. 49–53; Cameron, *Last Pagans*, pp. 743–82.

him.[80] Perhaps in consequence, our record of the late Severan moment glosses over what was likely a major shift in governance practice, and one that might explain the oddities of Severus Alexander's legal program.

I refer specifically to child rule. Alexander and Elagabalus both took the throne before turning fifteen, and were dramatically younger than any emperor before them. While contemporary historians are certainly aware of this fact, it is difficult to determine from extant sources exactly how it affected their public image. The accusations leveled against Elagabalus in later writing make it uncomfortable – to say the least – to think of him as a child during his reign;[81] Elagabalic portraiture, however, suggests that he was portrayed veristically even when that meant showing him as a boy. Similarly, both coins and portraiture from early in Alexander's reign present him as obviously pubescent (Figures 4.6 and 4.7).

FIGURE 4.6 Portrait bust of Elagabalus. Boston: Museum of Fine Arts, 1997.337.

[80] McEvoy, *Child Emperor Rule*; Bertrand-Dagenbach, *Alexandre Sévère*. On the *HA*'s use of historiographic tropes in the service of a broader and more innovative literary project see Rohrbacher, *Play of Allusion*.

[81] See Herz, "How to Do the History of Elagabalus," pp. 415–16.

FIGURE 4.7 Silver *denarius*, obverse image of Severus Alexander. Berlin: Staatliche Museen zu Berlin, Münzkabinett/Lutz-Jürgen Lübke (Lübke and Wiedemann), 18200791.

Dio and Herodian present Alexander's youth as an administrative hurdle, but one easily overcome through the use of advisers. Alexander's first official action in Dio is handing over power to Ulpian (80[80].1.1 [Xiph.]), and Herodian explicitly differentiates between the "appearance and name" (6.1.1: τὸ μὲν σχῆμα καὶ τὸ ὄνομα) of power that were given to Alexander and the actual administration (*ibid.*: ἡ μέντοι διοίκησις) that his mother and grandmother controlled.[82] But while Dio claims to speak from firsthand knowledge of Alexander's court, Herodian does not. Accordingly, if Herodian saw the emperor as too young to make decisions on his own then others likely did as well.

To be clear, Elagabalus and Alexander were hardly the last children to rule. Gordian III took the throne at thirteen in 238, and young emperors were common in the fourth century. But these two were the first, and their youth could have caused considerable anxiety within a symbolic system that still based imperial legitimacy on a set of virtues that fourteen-year-old boys could not be easily said to possess.[83]

Comparative evidence from later periods shows this anxiety. While Ambrose's funeral oration for Valentinian II (who was proclaimed *Augustus* at four and died at twenty-one) was delivered in the vastly

[82] On Dio's view of Severus Alexander as a young and passive ruler see Kemezis, "Vox Populi, Vox Mea?," pp. 47–48.

[83] See Kemezis, *Greek Narratives*, pp. 83, 86; Noreña, *Imperial Ideals*, pp. 37–100; Ando, *Ideology*, pp. 232–45.

different context of 392 CE, it emphasizes virtues like innocence, tranquility, and kindness (*tranquillitas pacifica, simplicitas, leuitas, innocentia*) that are all but unheard of in panegyric for mature leaders. Ambrose thus suggests that the traditional language of imperial virtue was effectively unavailable when discussing decisions one had made as a child.[84] McEvoy notes that child rulers in the later empire were not, as a rule, able to engage in meaningful administrative work; while this period's more advanced judicial bureaucracy could function under a figurehead, that was all the child ruler could reasonably be, making it difficult to base legal authority on his extraordinary wisdom or fairness. Returning to the third century, given how even positive commentators like Herodian describe Alexander we must assume that audiences would have rejected similar legitimating stories about the late Severan child monarchs. As a result, it should not be surprising that the imperial court developed new ones. Those for Elagabalus seem clear enough; the unprecedented cultic activity that marked Elagabalus' reign, and the unprecedented linking of Elagabal and Elagabalus, articulate a religious justification for rule where older models based on individual qualities might prove an odd fit. This strategy failed, however, and Alexander was represented to Roman audiences as a near-total opposite of his cousin – traditionalizing, continent, and pious. He was still, however, very young.

Accordingly, representation of Alexander tries new ways around the problem. While the imperial *consilium* was hardly a Severan innovation, both Dio and Herodian portray Alexander as dependent on bureaucrats and this dependence as a good thing. Herodian describes Alexander's female minders as guiding the court on a "wiser and more just path" (6.1.1: ἐπί τε τὸ σωφρονέστερον καὶ σεμνότερον). Specifically, they made Alexander completely dependent on a council of the wisest and most just men (6.1.2: σεμνοτάτους καὶ βίῳ σωφρονεστάτους; a theme becomes apparent), who were given veto power over the emperor's decisions. Herodian describes this subordination as an unalloyed good, moving the court away from hubristic tyranny and towards a more aristocratic mode of governance (*ibid.*: ἐκ τυραννίδος ἐφυβρίστου ἐς ἀριστοκρατίας). While the tropes are not new, Herodian does not depict an emperor who chooses to listen to his advisers, but one who is unable to act on his own and is a better ruler for it.

[84] Amb. *De ob. Val.* 68, 79; McEvoy, *Child Emperor Rule*, pp. 127–28.

If we take this account as representing an official (or officially accepted) account of Alexandrian governance, it differs sharply from how other *ciuiles principes* had been represented in the past. Alexander was a good emperor not because his personal preferences and virtues guided his actions, but because they did not; the boy ruler was kept safely away from a humming bureaucracy. This model of governance would become common, so common that when the *HA* says that Alexander "acted according to the opinion of whoever was most learned" (*Alex. Seu.* 31.1: *ex eius sententia qui disertior habebatur*), it reads as obviously reflecting late-antique political theory.[85] But in the 220s it had no real precedent, and there was no script for a child ruling well.

Viewed in this light, Alexander's legal moves make far more sense. Within a symbolic system that relied on imperial fitness to validate governmental action and that defined fitness using terms that obviously excluded the current ruler, Alexander's actions stood uneasily on his own (as opposed to his family's or state's) merits. This problem required a different theory of authority, which led to the sorts of argumentative shifts discussed above. Implicit in these changes is an idea that was novel in classical Roman law – that an emperor's legal opinion might be worth following even if the emperor who wrote it were not. By keeping things as they were before, Alexander could articulate a working theory of legitimation that did not rely on his specific charisma or virtue.

* * * * *

That theory is perhaps most apparent in the final document I discuss in this chapter. Like in the Samosata case above Alexander here answers a technical question about inheritance, but his rhetoric touches on broader questions about the emperor's place within Roman legality.

Many constitutions say that the emperor shall not claim an inheritance from a defective will. Although the law of imperium *has released the emperor from legal stricture nevertheless there is nothing more becoming of power, than to live according to the laws.*

(C.6.23.3: Severus Alexander, 232) Ex imperfecto testamento nec imperatorem hereditatem uindicare saepe constitutum est. Licet enim lex imperii

[85] Bertrand-Dagenbach, *Alexandre Sévère*, p. 189.

sollemnibus iuris imperatorem soluerit, nihil tamen tam proprium imperii est, ut legibus uiuere.

Once again, the normative claim is straightforward. While leaving bequests to the emperor was a common testamentary practice, those bequests did not trump the requirements of the Roman will. If those requirements were not met an estate devolved to its default heirs, imperial interest notwithstanding.

That said, C.6.23.3's rhetoric is more surprising than its holding. For one thing, the second half of the constitution – although (*licet*) law has freed (*soluerit*) the sovereign from legal obligation, nevertheless (*tamen*) it is best to live by the laws (*legibus uiuere*) – strikingly mimics the language of Severus and Caracalla that I discussed at the beginning of Chapter 2. Justinian describes the two emperors as "often say[ing] in rescripts: 'although we have been released from the laws, nevertheless we live according to the laws.'"[86] Severus and Caracalla use nearly identical language, with *licet* and a *soluo*-form preceding *attamen legibus uiuimus*. Justinian describes the claim as a frequently deployed trope (*saepissime*), and Alexander – who cited both men's legal opinions frequently – may be explicitly engaging with it. But because most rescripts are preserved as a source of normative rules, and not of broader claims about the nature of imperial sovereignty, it is difficult to track political nostra in the *Corpus*.

Similarly, C.6.23.3 evades a difficult problem through slippery phrasing. Alexander necessarily has a direct financial stake in the question before him, since he is the *imperator* whose inheritance rights are at issue, and everyone who has ruled on this question has done so while standing in the same position. Accordingly, the abstract rule with which the *constitutio* opens is misleading. *Constitutum est* implies imperial authority, but any emperor faced with this question would, by definition, not be stating a principle to apply to others. Instead, they would be like Alexander: heirs under an imperfect will, refusing to interfere with a testamentary process to which they were a party. By describing these refusals as *constitutiones* Alexander analogizes them to legislation, and paints his following of political *exempla* as obedience to law. If it was awkward for an emperor to resolve a dispute in which he

86 *J. Inst.* 2.17; *supra* pp. 75–76.

had an interest, C.6.23.3 hides that awkwardness by subsuming the dispute into what looks like a matter of legal logic.

That logic is complex. If Justinian's *saepissime* is right, Alexander's audience would have been used to emperors who claimed to live according to the laws. But C.6.23.3 offers two complementary glosses of the phrase. Alexander, like Severus and Caracalla before him – and like Vespasian, Titus, and Trajan before them – presents himself as a legal subject. He is under the same restrictions as everyone else, and cannot take bequests from a *testamentum imperfectum* for the same reason nobody else can. But Alexander also presents himself as a conscientious judge. Living according to the laws means obeying them both as constraints on one's behavior as a subject and as guides to one's decisionmaking as an adjudicator; here, Alexander does both. While the facts of the case suggest that the rule restricts what Alexander himself can inherit, C.6.23.3 constructs a world in which Alexander faces an abstract decision about the nature of inheritance and resolves it by observing precedential authority. While the Deified Brothers were portrayed as actively working to determine the good and using legal processes to do so, Alexander acts like his hands are tied.

Remarkably, he does not say by whom. In the examples of precedential reasoning I discussed above Alexander links himself with specific predecessors; he constructs a legal authority that resides not in his own young mind, but in the family to which he belongs and whose rule he continues and maintains. Not so here. *Constitutum est* instead sites legal authority in the act of imperial writing itself. We do not know which emperors made this decision and do not need to, since the fact of emperors having made this decision is enough. This is an unusual move within Alexander's corpus and merits some explanation. One possibility is that Alexander is referring to predecessors with whom he did not wish to be linked by name. Alternately, if C.6.23.3 alludes to Severus and Caracalla then those two might be the authorities in play. But an anonymous citation fits with the artificial naming conventions I discussed earlier in this chapter, and works as a claim in its own right. If *constitutiones* derive force from the simple fact of their being *constitutiones*, without anybody needing to know who the author really was, they begin to lose the character of imperial statements (always read with reference to their speaker and his personal qualities) and take on the character of other kinds of institutionally empowered speech.

Specifically, when we imagine communications that are empowered by general social convention we imagine laws and do so in a positivistic sense. Alexander here talks about *constitutiones* not as deeds of his predecessors but as positive law. This seems normal in retrospect – the *Corpus Iuris Ciuilis* treats rescripts and other kinds of imperial writing as law all the time – but is jarring here. Alexander describes himself not as an enlightened ruler but a conscientious member of a legal bureaucracy.

Ironically, members of that bureaucracy were more inclined to describe it in terms like that of C.6.23.3 than was Alexander himself. Alexander's rescripts (mostly) describe legal authority as a Severan prerogative, but the Severan jurists describe it as an institutional fact. That latter vision was better suited to the world, and dominates our own understanding of Roman law. But Alexander's citations and redactions are more than just a road not taken. They were an experiment in how law could adapt to a crisis that would not go away. The second century did not come back, and neither did its rules.

5

Juristic Reasoning, Citational Practices, and Law at the End of an Empire

From emperors, to jurists. When Severus Alexander claimed to follow his father's reasoning, he was not acting alone; like other emperors, Alexander employed a coterie of legal experts who helped in the production of legal correspondence. That said, Alexander's legal staff did not perfectly resemble that of Hadrian or the Deified Brothers, and one odd feature of the Severan dynasty is how closely it engaged with jurists. From Septimius Severus on, jurists occupied high offices at court, participated in palace intrigues, and exercised remarkable sway in administering broader Roman affairs.

At the same time, when not serving in the imperial court jurists of this period were writing the texts that now dominate our conception of what juristic literature was. In their free time men like Ulpian, Papinian, and Paul wrote treatises – long commentaries on the Perpetual Edict or on earlier juristic work – explaining how Roman legal principles ought to be applied in a variety of cases. The Severan jurists were not the first to engage in this kind of work, but they seem to have been nearly the last.[1] We have only scattered excerpts of post-Severan juristic texts, and four of the five jurists recognized as pre-eminent authorities by Valentinian III's Law of Citations (promulgated in 426) worked during this period.[2]

Severan juristic writing is thus an important chronicle of how trained administrators responded to crisis. These men inhabited

[1] See e.g. de Blois, "Influence." [2] *Infra* p. 255.

a dangerous political culture but wrote texts that described the Roman state in orderly and technocratic forms. Their story of Roman governance was compelling to later audiences, but clashes in surprising ways with other contemporaneous accounts of imperial governance. In Chapter 4, I described how Severus Alexander's legal correspondence paints him as a Severan caretaker, whose authority to pronounce the law derives from his dynastic position. Ironically, the same men who helped Alexander create those documents constructed a very different legal reality in the work produced under their own name. The law that survives in Severan juristic texts is institutional and impersonal, even if the world in which it operated was not. Instead of casting the emperor as one actor within a broader dynastic framework, the Severan jurists described him in bureaucratizing terms, as a man performing a job within a system whose legitimacy rested elsewhere. Between these two stories, the jurists' won. Roman law would come to fit their vision, and the guiding framework of the *Corpus Iuris Ciuilis* owes even more to the Severan jurists than their domination of the *Digest* might suggest.

This chapter proceeds in three parts. First, I explain how different jurists positioned themselves within the unstable Severan bureaucracy, and how that imbrication affected their approach to legal questions. I then discuss two hugely influential changes in legal reasoning that occurred over the course of the Severan period: a sharp increase in arguments that consider the consequences of a given juristic interpretation, and a radical shift in citation practices visible in the Severan jurists. These changes recast juristic interpretation as an important tool for providing public goods, while simultaneously minimizing emperors' role in shaping law to provide those same goods. The legality that appears in Severan juristic texts shaped the reality of later legal cultures, even as it misrepresented the world it claimed to describe.

Brilliant Cogs

The jurists who wrote at this time were not the same as those who had come before. Because so much of our juristic writing dates to the Severan period – and so much of the rest comes from Gaius, whose career is nearly unknown except for the *Institutes* of c. 160 – our understanding of juristic work is more static than it should be. Private actors had written scholarship on legal questions for centuries before Gaius picked up a pen,[3] and those actors were often described as doing the kind of work we now see as juristic, but they had different relationships to their state and (later) their emperor than did those who exemplify the genre for us today. This is not a book about the evolution of juristic writing over the imperial period,[4] but in order to explain how the Severan jurists innovated on earlier work it seems important to understand who the Severan jurists were, and how their self-conception differed from that of their forebears.

Jurists had always had an odd relationship with imperial power. As discussed in Chapter 3, Hadrian replaced an earlier system in which jurists worked outside of the imperial bureaucracy with one in which they helped write the legal replies that went out under his name. That change had enormous consequences for how emperors engaged with law, but also for jurists themselves as a professional class. Earlier *iurisperiti* ("legally learned men") had made their careers by responding to legal questions from both adjudicators and private parties, but imperial rescripts were more definitive and thus more reliable. As a result, question-and-answer struggled to compete with petition-and-response.[5]

At the same time, however, the rescript system produced a tremendous demand for legal expertise within the imperial court. Emperors were not necessarily trained in law – both Dio (79[78].11) and the *HA* (*Macr.* 4.3) refer to the short-lived emperor Macrinus'

[3] While we do not know exactly when juristic work began, Dionysus of Halicarnassus claims that when Romulus set forth the duties of *patrones* he included among them that of explaining the law (2.10: ἐξηγεῖσθαι τὰ δίκαια). One need not believe this quotation from Rome's mythical founder-king to see that Dionysus, writing in the Augustan period, understood juristic work as having a very long history and as deeply bound up with Rome's earliest social networks. For the early history of juristic practice Lehne-Gstreinthaler, *Iurisperiti et oratores*, pp. 17–81; Harries, *Cicero and the Jurists*, pp. 32–37.

[4] On which see, for scattered examples: Zetzel, *Critics, Compilers, and Commentators*, pp. 123–25; Harries, "Iurisperiti"; Schiavone, *Ius*; *HSS*, pp. 63–113; Peachin, "Jurists and the Law"; Bauman, *Lawyers and Politics*.

[5] The petition-and-response model of Roman governance is of course most closely linked with Millar, *Emperor* (also "Empire and City"; "Emperors at Work"), but on petition and response as a distinctive genre of civic speech Wankerl, *Appello ad principem*; Hauken, *Petition and Response*, pp. 258–89.

legal work as unusual and indicative of low status – but now promised to guide the development of a complicated legal system by deciding questions frequently and regularly.[6] Accordingly Hadrian and his successors required a new level of support in managing legal business, which led to new understandings of the juristic career. While jurists had always helped nonprofessional adjudicators like praetors with individual cases, that help is described in our sources as *ad hoc* and compatible with those other pursuits (like scholarly writing or answering questions from litigants) that gave one a reputation for *iuris peritio*.[7] The rescript system changed things. As Crook put it, Hadrian's consolidation of Roman legal authority necessitated "the creation of a professional nucleus within the *consilium*."[8]

This professionalization meant two things. On the one hand, imperial advising became a more formal affair, with jurists formally ratified to the position.[9] On the other, this advisory work became more impactful. Rescripts functioned as a kind of case law – by which I mean statements of law upon which nonlitigant actors might plausibly rely – in ways that earlier responses or adjudicative outcomes did not. As a result, jurists who advised an emperor in composing rescripts were helping to *make law* in a way that they had not previously on a large scale. The Hadrianic reforms necessarily standardized the law, and jurists were now invited into the rooms where that standardized law was produced.

The role they played there is less clear. It seems obvious that jurists lent their expertise in the drafting of rescripts, but what exactly was that expertise? If law is what the emperor wishes it to be, what would it mean to tell the emperor what he wished? Exploring this dynamic can help us better understand the delicate balance between law and whim that underlay post-Hadrianic rescripts, and how jurists' role in them changed over time. On the one hand, we might look at a document like *P. Col.* 123 (discussed in Chapter 3) and see very little evidence of reasoning whatsoever. We can assume that much of an emperor's "legal" work took a form something like this, hearing petitions that asked him to waive existing legal obligations and declining to do so.

[6] See Millar, *Emperor*, pp. 242–45.
[7] See Harries, *Law and Empire*, pp. 16–17.
[8] Crook, *Consilium Principis*, p. 59.
[9] See *HA*, *Hadr.* 18.1; Daalder, "Aequum Putavit Imperator," pp. 133–34; Coriat, *Les constitutions des Sévères*, pp. 203–04.

Managing these requests required extra pairs of eyes and ears, with sufficient training to catch irregularities that were brought to the emperor's attention via petition. In the absence of such an irregularity response could be straightforward, and if there were some sort of error that error could be corrected with only marginally more effort. One thinks of a document like C.3.42.4 (Severus Alexander, 230), stating that the *iudex* shall not be unaware (*iudex non ignorabit*) of what is presented as a settled legal norm (that had, presumably, not received enough attention earlier in the litigant's case).[10] Both kinds of production required a competent advisory staff, but would not substantially innovate on earlier juristic prerogatives. Composing these kinds of documents required knowing what the law already was, in an abstract sense.

Some cases, however, were harder. Instead of simply regularizing the law – ensuring broad concordance between legal outcomes and preexisting rules – emperors in this period sometimes had to innovate. The imperial court was now responsible for adapting existing principles to novel facts, or for determining proper outcomes in conditions of legal uncertainty. This kind of work is inevitable, since some disputes will always require an adjudicator to generate new law in resolving them.[11] Dworkin calls these disputes "hard cases" and notes the particular demands they place on judges. Hard cases require a judge to keep in mind not only an existing system of legal rights and responsibilities that might bear on any particular outcome, but also the broader institutional and normative paradigms within which an outcome might be evaluated.[12] Dworkin, of course, wrote in the context of an Anglo-American common law system, in which

[10] In full: "The judge will not be unaware that for any instruments of your claim, which you prove to have been in the possession of other parties and which those parties do not themselves present, you are entitled to the opportunity of attestation by oath" (*Non ignorabit iudex, instrumenta tui iuris, quae penes diuersam partem fuisse probaueris, si ab eisdem non exhibeantur, iurisiurandi in litem facultatem deferri tibi oportere*).

[11] Hart, *Concept*, p. 272 ("[I]n any legal system there will always be certain legally unregulated cases in which on some point no decision either way is dictated by the law.").

[12] Dworkin, "Hard Cases," pp. 1082–83. Dworkin analogizes a judge developing this paradigm to a referee understanding the "character of a game," and I find the analogy helpful. A game's character includes not only its formal rules but also the broader context within which the game is understood as pleasurable or fair.

legislative and judicial work are more analytically distinct than they were in imperial Rome.[13] Many of the objections he imagines a reader raising to the work of his ideal judge rest on the perceived prerogative of political actors in doing certain sorts of politically salient work, and those objections would obviously hold no purchase in the very different context of imperial legal writing.[14] But if anything, the emperor's broad adjudicative and legislative authority made hard cases harder. Jurists in the imperial court had to master policy and principle; emperors were asked not just for clarity but also for help, and the documents produced in reply could be fairly evaluated upon their ability to do both jobs.

This evaluative process was central to imperial politics within the Principate. The legitimacy of a given rescript rested upon the role it played within a defined system of actors and institutions, but also upon the intelligence and moral imagination of its imperial author. Dworkin calls his judge, who has to be a legal-expert-*cum*-political-theorist-*cum*-institutional-historian, "Hercules" because resolving difficult disputes fairly requires "superhuman" gifts.[15] Imperial representation in this period hit these same – usually metaphorical – notes.[16] As explained in Chapter 3, rescripts benefited from and helped to constitute an emperor's broader image. They were unusually tangible evidence of an emperor's knowledge and moral sensibility, and so needed to demonstrate those qualities.

We can see, then, what kind of help jurists might need to provide. The rescript system required emperors to demonstrate encyclopedic knowledge of existing law, to understand the implications of extending

[13] For an extreme account of how separation of legislative and adjudicative functions might work in modern polities, see Damaška, *Faces*, pp. 37–38.

[14] E.g. Dworkin's account at "Hard Cases," p. 1101 of the "argument from democracy," which holds that "elected officials have superior qualifications to make political decisions." In the post-Hadrianic system any popular conception of judicial qualification would be inseparable from broader claims of imperial legitimacy. An intriguing possible exception is the (much later) *uita Macrini* of the *HA*, which describes Macrinus trying to invalidate prior imperial correspondence "so that matters would be governed by law and not by rescripts" (13.1: *ut iure non rescriptis ageretur*; *infra* p. 276). The *HA*'s account is unreliable, however, and if Macrinus did attempt to position himself relative to law in such a way it ended rather badly for him.

[15] Dworkin, "Hard Cases," p. 1083.

[16] Commodus, of course, being a remarkable exception. See Meyer-Zwiffelhoffer, "Visionär," pp. 196–201; Hekster, *Commodus*, pp. 104–07.

or altering legal doctrines, and to clearly explain those changes to readers with different relationships to and training in law. Even in the superficially meritocratic environment of the second century, these were not skills an emperor could be reasonably expected to possess. Jurists, who were already trained in law and how to explain it to different audiences, fit well in this new bureaucracy. They could read incoming petitions, help resolve especially difficult questions, and even aid in drafting.[17] Furthermore, this help would be almost invisible. Accounts of second-century imperial legal work emphasize the emperor's own judgment, and the rescripts produced in his name intentionally obscured the contributions of others.[18] Jurists in the second century often served as secretaries *a libellis*, but whatever role they played in higher-level deliberations was not generally publicized.[19]

These dynamics changed with the rise of the Severans in 193. Severan emperors named jurists to high, and highly public, administrative positions. For example, Septimius Severus appointed the jurist Papinian as his *praefectus praetorio* (praetorian prefect, in charge of the emperor's bodyguards but also supervising a good portion of Roman adjudication via his oversight of the courts).[20] Unlike the relatively anonymous secretaries *a libellis*, who are

[17] Different historians have imagined that drafting process differently. Honoré (*Emperors and Lawyers*) takes a maximalist position, arguing that rescripts issued by the imperial court were drafted by the *a libellis* working alone or nearly alone, and accordingly that changes in the *a libellis* were marked by discontinuities of writing style (p. 56). The analysis upon which Honoré bases his reasoning has been criticized (as for example by Millar, "A New Approach" and Watson, "Review"). Furthermore, Connolly notes (*Lives*, pp. 55–57) that the sheer volume of legal writing suggested by documents like *P. Col.* 123, even if relatively straightforward, is effectively incompatible with a single juristic drafter. I follow Peachin's comparatively cautious approach; while it seems obvious that some sort of collaboration ("Prozess," p. 221: *Zusammenarbeit*) was the norm, the nature of that collaboration is concealed by our sources.

[18] This sort of obscuring is inevitable in any system that takes imperial legal work as reflecting the emperor's unique capabilities or judgment. If Dio sees legal opinions of Marcus, for example, as reflecting his special effort "to determine the just outcome from all sides" (72[71]6.1 [Xiph.]: ὥστε πανταχόθεν τὸ δίκαιον ἀκριβοῦν), that requires those opinions to be understood as the product of such effort.

[19] Crook notes (*Consilium Principis*, p. 68) the difficulty of reconstructing the presence of legal advisers in individual *consilia* off of surviving evidence.

[20] See e.g. *ILS* 2187. Further evidence of Papinian's praetorian prefecture is collected at *PIR*^{2} A 0388; *HSS* II.56; Liebs, *Hofjuristen*, pp. 52–54; "Jurisprudenz," p. 117. On Papinian's career more broadly Magioncalda, "Papiniano."

documented in specifically legal texts,[21] praetorian prefects were understood to have a greater sphere of influence. For example, Plautianus, who held the office before Papinian, was honored with public statues before he fell from grace as a result of broad corruption and favor-trading.[22] These accusations demonstrate the kind of power a praetorian prefect could hold and how well the Roman public, whom Dio describes calling for Plautianus to be removed, knew who was in that office at any given time.

Septimius' successor Caracalla was less friendly to legal professionals.[23] Even he, however, appointed a praetorian prefect with substantial legal training: Opellius Macrinus, who had Caracalla killed before taking the throne for himself. Macrinus' tenure was brief and difficult, as was that of his successor Elagabalus.[24] The next emperor, Severus Alexander, elevated jurists to very high positions. The best known is Ulpian, who served as something like a regent in addition to holding two different powerful prefectures,[25] but the jurist Paul served on both Septimius' and Alexander's *consilia* and may have also held a prefecture,[26] and Modestinus (the latest of the five jurists included in the Law of Citations) is attested as *praefectus uigilum* under Alexander

[21] Papinian's own tenure in this role, to give one example, is commemorated primarily by other jurists like Tryphoninus at D.20.5.12pr. (Disputationes) (referring to an imperial rescript being issued *agente Papiniano*).

[22] Dio Cass. 77[76].2–6 [Xiph.]; *HA*, *Sept. Seu.* 14; Krüpe, "Plautianus und Plautilla"; Bingham and Imrie, "Plot."

[23] Caracalla had Papinian killed, according to both Cassius Dio (78[77].4 [Xiph.]) and the *HA* (*Sept. Seu.* 21.8; *Ant.* 4.1). Dio also records Caracalla mocking Papinian's legal expertise, telling his soldiers that he deferred to them "as both accusers and judges" (ὡς κατηγόροις καὶ ὡς δικασταῖς) and empowering them to kill the jurist on that basis.

[24] On Elagabalic maladministration in biographies of the emperor (specifically Dio's) see also Chrysanthou, "Sex and Power," p. 608. Documentary evidence is fairly mixed. While some Elagabalic courtiers like P. Valerius Comazon enjoyed rapid and untraditional advancement through the ranks, their careers really skyrocketed under Macrinus, rather than Elagabalus, and Salway has convincingly argued that we should understand these appointments to reflect exigency rather than corruption or sexual favors. Salway, "Fragment," pp. 144–46; see also Mennen, *Power and Status*, pp. 168, 179 n. 179.

[25] For Ulpian's regency see Dio Cass. 80[80]1.1 [Xiph.]; Hdn. 6.1.4 (referring to a regent council of men trained in law [νόμων ἐμπείροις]); also Ferrary, Marotta, and Schiavone, *Ulpianus: Institutiones, de censibus*, pp. 3–35; Liebs, *Hofjuristen*, pp. 69–70.

[26] The *uita Nigri* suggests at 7.4 that Paul served as prefect under Elagabalus, and the *uita Alexandri* says at 26.5 that Paul was made *praefectum* by either Alexander or

and may have served as his *a libellis* besides.[27] Herodian goes even further and claims that Alexander's mother surrounded him with jurists in order to keep him away from bad influences (6.1.1), but his account remains dubious.[28] All told, it is clear that jurists played a greater and more public role in Roman politics during the Severan period than they ever had before.

It is less clear why jurists became so prominent. One answer may lie in broader shifts in court composition that mark the period. As Schöpe has argued on the basis of prosopographic evidence, the Severan court was more isolated from the senatorial class than were its Antonine forebears and accordingly more reliant on equestrian service.[29] That change had implications for juristic careers. While elite Roman education generally included some legal training,[30] jurists of this period appear to have gone through a more specialized process. Gaius' *Institutes*, written in the late second century, were intended for use in legal education, and Severan jurists frequently refer to mentoring relationships that resemble apprenticeships more than the tutoring a senatorial family might procure for their son.[31] This specialized training was not part of traditional senatorial careers, and jurists who entered the *consilium* generally did so by occupying equestrian positions like the *a libellis*. As equestrians became more generally prominent, it seems inevitable that jurists, who had historically worked closely with the emperor, would be

Elagabalus. For a speculative biography see Liebs, "Jurisprudenz," p. 151; more recently Brutti, *Decretorum*, pp. 24–31.

[27] The prefecture is attested at *CIL* VI.266. Modestinus' tenure as *a libellis* is more speculative, based on Honoré (*Emperors and Lawyers*, pp. 101–07) tentatively labeling Modestinus as the author of rescripts composed between October of 223 and October of 225. See also *HSS* II.72; Liebs, "Jurisprudenz," pp. 195–201.

[28] I discuss this account, and what it means for the changing public image of the emperor in the late Severan period, in more detail *supra* pp. 175–79.

[29] Schöpe, *Kaiserhof*, pp. 174–76. Cf. Davenport, *Equestrian Order*, p. 508; Mennen, *Power and Status*, pp. 49–133. Both Davenport and Mennen warn against understanding the changing face of third-century administration in terms of two monolithic classes. Even as the influence of the *ordo senatorius* writ large began to wane, a nucleus of senatorial power continued well into the fourth century, and similarly the equestrian professionals who rose to prominence in this period (including the jurists) were not representative of equestrians as a whole.

[30] See Harries, "Legal Education"; Riggsby, *Legal World*, pp. 57–66.

[31] On the *Institutes* see Wibier, "Transmitting Legal Knowledge"; Nelson, *Gai Institutiones*, pp. 395–423. Relationships between jurists are extremely well attested within the *Digest*. See, for example. D.47.2.52.20 (Ulpian, ad Edictum) (referring to "my student, Herennius Modestinus" [*Herennio Modestino, studioso meo*]).

overrepresented among this new cohort. We can see some evidence for this correlation between rank and expertise in the differing fates of the praetorian and urban prefectures; the latter, which was traditionally senatorial, did not feature in the Severan jurists' careers despite its broad adjudicative powers.[32] Under this theory, the rise of the jurists was essentially epiphenomenal to the broader flourishing of equestrians in Severan politics.

This argument does not explain Ulpian, though. C.8.37.4 (Severus Alexander, 222) describes Ulpian serving as Alexander's prefect of the grain supply in a document issued immediately after the coup, but historiographic accounts describe Alexander entrusting Ulpian with the government of the empire soon after. Dio is the most blunt when he claims that Alexander "delegated to a certain Domitius Ulpianus the praetorian prefecture and the other duties of empire" (80[80].1.1 [Xiph.]: Δομιτίῳ τινὶ Οὐλπιανῷ τήν τε τῶν δορυφόρων προστασίαν καὶ τὰ λοιπὰ τῆς ἀρχῆς ἐπέτρεψε πράγματα). Rescripts support Dio's account; C.8.37.4 preserves Alexander describing Ulpian as *amicus meus* and in C.4.65.4.1, issued in December of 222, Alexander calls Ulpian his *parens* and states that he had already been given the praetorian prefecture.[33] This relationship cannot be attributed solely to a fondness for equestrians. Instead, it looks more idiosyncratic – Ulpian had been close with Alexander (and his mother?) before he took the throne.

These two accounts join together into a coherent, if contingent, origin story for the Severan jurists. The broader rise of the equestrians elevated jurists to new levels of prominence and influence, and one of them picked the right side in an ugly succession dispute and briefly enjoyed the benefits. These dynamics combine to make the Severans' domination of our juristic literature seem more intentional than it may have been. Individual emperors might have been passionate about law – the *uita Septimii Seueri* begins with the toddler Septimius Severus making his playmates pretend to litigate before him in a mock court – but that does not imply a concerted dynastic attitude towards law as a form of social ordering.[34]

[32] On those powers see Ruciński, *Praefectus urbi*, pp. 62–66, 110–57.

[33] Specifically, he refers to "Domitius Ulpianus, praetorian prefect and my parent" (*Domitium Ulpianum praefectum praetorio et parentem meum*).

[34] The *uita* describes Septimius Severus refusing to participate "in any game except that of judges" (1.4: *nullum alium inter pueros ludum nisi ad iudices exercuit*).

What does distinguish the Severans is their discomfort with, or unsuitability for, the discourses of imperial legitimation that had governed the second century. That era's public narrative of meritocratic selection and senatorial collaboration was replaced with shifting dynastic and religious claims that were less successful.[35] As mentioned above, Severan emperors died violently and with bad reputations; the period witnessed broader breakdowns in a political order that would not truly reform itself until decades later. Those breakdowns had legal consequences, at least in a legal system that looked to the emperor for stability. And for whatever reason, the jurists who wrote during this chaotic period were close to the organs of imperial governance and responsible for administrative activities that had previously been left to others.

This portfolio would have been strange in the context of earlier juristic careers. We sometimes think of jurists as ancient lawyers, as in Honoré's *Emperors and Lawyers* or in Syme's description of Ulpian as a "lawyer in government."[36] But the comparison is imperfect. Inasmuch as classical Romans had any set phrases to describe the people we call jurists, they identified them by training and mastery (*peritus iuris* or *iuris consultus*) rather than by anything they did. While legal training was considered important for effectively representing clients,[37] the training and the work were essentially separate[38] and the language used to indicate status as a jurist heavily privileges the former.[39] Being a jurist meant being a scholar, a writer, and – inasmuch as jurists appear to have trained the next generation and elevated protégés – a teacher.

The Severan jurists did all this work within a career trajectory that also included substantial civil service commitments. It is hard to say

[35] On which see Kemezis, "Fall," p. 370; Ando, *Century*, pp. 70–71; Mennen, *Power and Status*, pp. 22–29.

[36] Honoré, *Emperors and Lawyers*, p. vii (justifying the conflation of lawyers and jurists on the grounds that "their functions were basically the same in the ancient as they are in the modern world"); Syme, "Lawyers in Government."

[37] Pomponius describes the jurist Scaevola telling Servius Sulpicius that "it was shameful for a patrician, a *nobilis*, and an advocate to be unaware of the law upon which his cases were contested" (D.1.2.2.43, Enchiridion: *turpe esse patricio et nobili et causas oranti ius in quo uersaretur ignorare*). Quintilian's *Institutes*, a guide to the training of advocates and rhetoricians, suggests that knowledge of the *ius ciuile* was necessary (12.3: *necessaria*) to be an effective orator.

[38] Riggsby, *Legal World*, pp. 47–54.

[39] See Tuori, "Freedom," pp. 305–07.

exactly how these occupations intersected, but the *Digest* preserves several instances of the Severan jurists using their positions to empower (and financially support) favored students. The clearest example of this phenomenon is Ulpian's and Paul's service in Papinian's *consilium*, which Paul describes at D.12.1.40 (Quaestiones).[40]

Similarly, Paul's writing foregrounds his access to the emperor in ways that suggest that that access was seen as a mark in his favor. Several fragments of the *Digest* consist of Paul describing his attempts (and, remarkably, failures) to influence the judgments of Septimius Severus. Daalder has shown how these fragments, and the decisionmaking processes they commemorated, made adjudication into a venue for public representation or display.[41] They present "a clear picture of Septimius Severus as a conscientious and benevolent judge,"[42] while their author appears "as a true, skillful and knowledgeable jurist with great respect for the law and all of its niceties."[43] But Paul's closely observed eyewitness accounts flaunt his access as much as his learning.[44] Daalder notes that Paul's fragments are too specific, and spend too much time on failed arguments and on the emperor's emotional state, to make sense as explanations of the law.[45] Instead, those details support a more descriptive project that emphasizes Paul's proximity to "the imperial ear."[46] Paul's accounts of Severan decisionmaking call attention to his own role in the judicial dialogue and his extensive conversations with Septimius, but shed no light on the normative principle expressed beyond demonstrating that Paul was in the room as it was expressed.

For example, in D.4.4.38pr. (Decreta), after laying out the facts of the case Paul presents the deliberations as a colloquy in which he argues for upholding the lower verdict (*putabam bene iudicatum*), Septimius disagrees on a different ground (*imperator autem motus est*), Paul responds with an alternate solution (*Dicebam posse magis*

[40] The fragment begins, "A *cautio* of this sort was read out in the auditorium of Aemilianus Papinianus, jurist and praetorian prefect ..." (*Lecta est in auditorio Aemilii Papiniani praefecti praetorio iuris consulti cautio huiusmodi*).

[41] Daalder, *Rechtspraakverzamelingen* is her most extensive work on the subject, but see also "Aequum Putavit Imperator"; "Decreta".

[42] *Ibid.*, p. 52. [43] Daalder, "Aequum Putavit Imperator," pp. 190–91.

[44] See Harries, "Iurisperiti," p. 83 ("Paul's authority ... derived from his access to and influence on imperial decision-making.").

[45] Daalder, "Aequum Putavit Imperator," pp. 169–70. [46] *Ibid.*, p. 191.

ea ratione restitui eam, quod...) and only then, after hearing the jurist out twice, does Septimius issue his own pronouncement (*Quia tamen lex commissoria displicebat ei, pronuntiauit in integrum restituendam*).[47] Like Horace in Chapter 1, Paul knew his audience better than we do. We can take his odd choice of emphasis as evidence of what that audience thought made one jurist more trustworthy than another. Modern parallels abound; the contemporary American legal academy highly values incoming professionals who have assisted judges as clerks. We can see something similar among the Severan jurists, who combined their scholarly pursuits with other jobs that required them to think through problems in different ways. The Severan jurists needed to understand what the law was, but also to help decide what it should be, and to do so in an environment of political unrest and imperial instability.

It would be odd if this sea change in juristic employment and professional identity did not affect juristic writing. Unfortunately, that effect is difficult to see; while an enormous amount of juristic literature survives, it does so in a denatured form. Wieacker has shown that the transmission of juristic writing tended to pare down a corpus with substantial philosophical and literary ambitions, and with substantial disagreement and conflict among its authors, into a repository of normative rules.[48] This paring fell especially hard on what Horak called the *rationes decidendi* of the jurists, or the language they used to justify their opinions.[49] Since any juristic opinion included in the *Digest* was authoritative by definition, Justinian's audience did not need to know why its author thought what he thought. Accordingly, large-scale synchronic analysis of juristic reasoning is all but impossible with the sources we have.

[47] See Babusiaux, "Ethos and Pathos," pp. 254–55.

[48] Wieacker, *Textstufen*, pp. 427–57; see also McGinn, "The Sea Common to All," p. 178 (on the "weed[ing] out" of juristic conflict). On juristic writing as a literary corpus Wibier, "Marcus Antistius Labeo"; Mantovani, *Les juristes écrivains*.

[49] Notably Horak focuses on jurists of the Republican period: *Rationes*, p. 77. While Horak claims (p. 78) that ancient jurists were generally unconcerned with "*Praktabilität*" Willems (*Justinian als Ökonom*, pp. 49–51) isolates economic reasoning and logic in the constitutions of Justinian (which survive in comparatively unabridged form, for obvious reasons). Cf. Harries, "Iurisperiti," p. 99, viewing this lack of justification as inherent to the juristic form ("In juristic writing, authority was often substituted for detailed justification of a preferred option.").

Luckily, a proportional analysis of the kind I discussed in Chapter 4[50] can isolate changes in juristic rhetoric and argumentation within the *Digest*. While the compilers did not treat every jurist identically, those different jurists served similar functions within the *Digest* and accordingly underwent similar redactive pressure.[51] Furthermore, while the texts contained within the *Digest* were altered substantially during the long period between the Severans and Justinian, that transmission process looks roughly the same for all of them. Monographs of the pre-Severan jurists were clearly in circulation under the Severans, and all faced the more chaotic and selective transmissions of the late-antique period. Accordingly differences between different juristic corpora that survive in the *Digest* ought to reflect differences in the texts as they were written, even if none of these texts particularly resemble their originals.

The remainder of this chapter will discuss subtle changes in juristic rhetoric that mark the Severan period. I first discuss the increasing prevalence of rule-consequentialist argumentation among the Severan jurists. These jurists increasingly presented themselves as responsible for public welfare, and their interpretations of existing law as tools to further public welfare. Having emerged from a novel training system and career track deeply intertwined with the imperial bureaucracy, and working in the absence of a widely accepted legitimate sovereign, jurists stepped in to provide the goods for which emperors had historically been responsible. Similarly, these same jurists came to cite imperial documents as sources of authority in their own right as opposed to evidence of the authoritative beliefs of a given imperial speaker. This change – from "the deified So-and-So claimed in a rescript" to "the sacred constitutions claim" – called into question the most basic assumptions of post-Hadrianic sovereignty, and lay the groundwork for the technocratic, impersonal legal order for which "Roman law" would later come to stand.

[50] *Supra* pp. 162–66.

[51] There are some obvious exceptions to this claim – for example, the greater amount of Ulpian that survives than say, Saturninus does not reflect Ulpian's greater productivity but his greater importance to the compilers. That said, my analysis here focuses on variables that I believe to be robust against compiler preference and other similar biases within the dataset.

A Severan Notion of Goodness

Romans liked to throw things out of windows. As in many premodern societies,[52] Roman apartment dwellers sometimes emptied their wastebasket or chamber pot onto the street, much to the consternation of pedestrians below.[53] When Ulpian explains how Roman law ought to deal with the problem, though, he reveals some surprising assumptions about the role of law in the Roman world. Specifically, he assumes that law will be often-enough followed, or should be imagined as often-enough followed, that one can evaluate the desirability of a legal rule based on how widespread compliance would affect the world.

The praetor says of those who throw down or pour out refuse: "When something should be thrown or poured into a place where there is public traffic or in which people mill about, I will give double damages for any harm done or caused by that thing against whoever lives in the place from which it was thrown."

...

No one can deny that the praetor's inclusion of this clause redounds to the highest good: for it is in the public interest to wander through roads without danger or fear. But it should matter little whether the harm might occur in a private or public place, so long as the public makes way through it; since attention is paid to those travelling and not aimed at public streets, and since those places through which people are accustomed to travel ought always to have the same security.

(D.9.3.1pr.–2: Ulpian, ad Edictum) Praetor ait de his, qui deiecerint uel effuderint: "unde in eum locum, quo uolgo iter fiet uel in quo consistetur, deiectum uel effusum quid erit, quantum ex ea re damnum datum factumue erit, in eum, qui ibi habitauerit, in duplum iudicium dabo."

...

Summa cum utilitate id praetorem edixisse nemo est qui neget: publice enim utile est sine metu et periculo per itinera commeari. Parui autem interesse debet, utrum publicus locus sit an uero priuatus, dummodo per eum uolgo iter fiat, quia iter facientibus prospicitur, non publicis uiis studetur: semper enim ea loca, per quae uolgo iter solet fieri, eandem securitatem debent habere.[54]

The praetor's solution is an elegant one. A Roman who was injured by falling crockery or soaked in human waste would rarely see their

[52] For my favorite example of this cross-cultural tendency, see Schopen,"Chamber Pots" (describing early Indian monastic codes forbidding nuns from emptying chamber pots without first checking the street below).

[53] Most famously attested at Iuv. 3.276–77. [54] See also *BTRL* p. 360.

attacker, making a traditional suit for damages difficult to sustain.[55] The praetor here offered a remedy against whoever occupied the apartment that had generated the missile, generally an easier defendant to identify.[56] More notable for our purposes is Ulpian's gloss on the praetorian remedy. Ulpian describes this legal innovation as good because of its beneficial effects, and then interprets its provisions in a specific way that is designed to magnify those effects and justified on that basis.

These moves are unusual within the *Digest*. While the *Digest* often quotes jurists saying what the law is or should be, it rarely preserves very much explicit argumentation in support of those claims. This lack of argument partially results from the *Digest*'s formal oddity. Its compilers excerpted jurisprudential treatises to make something like a law-code, and statements of law were more useful for that purpose than were the arguments that supported them. But even those arguments that do survive rarely focus on the real-world effects of laws and their interpretations. Compare Ulpian's reasoning with the following passage of Neratius: "Women cannot be appointed as tutors, since that is a job for men" (D.26.1.18, Regulae: *Feminae tutores dari non possunt, quia id munus masculorum est*). Neratius here bases his reading on a simple deontic claim, and expects the law to reflect (or describes it as reflecting) abstract notions about the proper roles of men and women. The job of law, in this analytic framework, is not so much to alter the world as it is to embody broader logical principles.

This abstraction frequently manifests in the *Digest* as an interest in elegance or coherence. Much of the argumentation that survives in that text takes the form of logical extension: "Circumstance A resembles Circumstance B, and existing law mandates Outcome C

[55] The usual legal remedy for negligent property damage or injury was laid out by the *Lex Aquilia*, an ancient statute (likely promulgated in 287 BCE) whose third section read: "in matters that go beyond the killing of men or herd animals, if someone has inflicted loss upon another through wrongfully burning, breaking, or despoiling his goods, he shall be forced to pay a penalty of the owner of however much the matter should come to be worth in the next thirty days." On the history of the *lex* see *ibid.*, pp. 327–30.

[56] One presumes (although our surviving sources do not state it explicitly) that if the occupant had not in fact been the one to cause the damages they could then sue whoever had, since that occupant would presumably be in a better position to know what had happened than the victim at street level.

in Circumstance B; ergo, Outcome C is appropriate in Circumstance A."[57] Julianus states this preference most explicitly: "The decisionmaker should look to similar cases and rule accordingly" (D.1.3.12, Digesta: *is qui iurisdictioni praeest ad similia procedere atque ita ius dicere debet*). Julianus here identifies an important principle in any casuistic system, which relies on analogic reasoning to generate predictability.[58]

But it is not a coincidence that this principle is stated most forcefully in Julianus, rather than in a Severan text. Julianus was educated before the time of the *edictum perpetuum*, after all; he wrote the thing. Later jurists not only interpreted the law but also helped produce constitutions that could improve the law, and that were the primary instruments through which such improvements might occur. That kind of work necessarily involves a broad range of considerations, many of which would have lain outside of traditional legal education. Put differently, a decisionmaker who attempts to pronounce existing law (*ius dicere*) applies broad principles to particular facts, and therefore needs above all else access to encyclopedic knowledge of those principles. A decisionmaker who is empowered to make law does different kinds of work and applies different kinds of scrutiny.

That decisionmaker might look more like Ulpian, whose famous account of the juristic profession describes it in almost sacred terms.

> *One might justly call us priests of the law; for we cherish justice and profess the news of the good and the fair, separating what is fair from what is not, separating the licit from the illicit, and hoping to make men good not only by fear of penalties, but also through the exhortation of rewards, striving towards a true (if I am not deceived) philosophy, and not a feigned one.*

[57] A useful example of this reasoning can be found in Paul's discussion of praedial servitudes at D.8.1.14pr. (ad Sabinum): "Although servitudes on rustic estates attach to corporeal objects, they are nevertheless incorporeal and thus cannot be created via habitual use; alternately, this is the case because they are the sort of servitude that do not result in fixed and continuous possession, for no one can go on the permitted path so continually or fixedly that their possession never seems to be interrupted." (*Seruitutes praediorum rusticorum etiamsi corporibus accedunt, incorporales tamen sunt et ideo usu non capiuntur: uel ideo, quia tales sunt seruitutes, ut non habeant certam continuamque possessionem: nemo enim tam perpetuo, tam continenter ire potest, ut nullo momento possessio eius interpellari uideatur.*).

[58] See Waldron, "Stare Decisis," pp. 9–12; Duxbury, *Precedent*, pp. 160–62; Frier, *Rise*, pp. 263–64.

(D.1.1.1.1, Institutiones) Cuius [iuris][59] merito quis nos sacerdotes appellet: iustitiam namque colimus et boni et aequi notitiam profitemur, aequum ab iniquo separantes, licitum ab illicito discernentes, bonos non solum metu poenarum, uerum etiam praemiorum quoque exhortatione efficere cupientes, ueram nisi fallor philosophiam, non simulatam affectantes.

This passage functions as a kind of proem to the *Digest*, and is a well-known example of the moral charge Romans attached to law.[60] But it also shows how juristic and imperial portfolios had commingled by Ulpian's time. Using law to make people better had previously been a job for emperors, and for legislators.[61] Ulpian claims this responsibility for himself and his colleagues, the "priests of the law" who try to make men good. For Ulpian, the work of *ius* is the work of jurists.

We can see that perfectionist vision in Ulpian's treatment of falling chamber pots at D.9.3.1. There, Ulpian makes two distinct claims about how actors can use law to shape public life. When Ulpian describes the praetor's liability regime as a good one because of its effects on the world, he suggests that the job of a praetor is to improve the world; that claim is not particularly innovative. But when Ulpian glosses the language of the praetor's edict in such a way as to induce prosocial behavior, he heads into comparatively uncharted territory.

Ulpian here does not evaluate someone else's legal maneuver, but makes and justifies a legal maneuver of his own. The language of the fragment makes clear that Ulpian, himself, is endorsing a specific interpretation of the provision. He does not say that it "matters little" where the harm occurs (which could be a neutral description of a decision made by other actors to enforce the provision in both private and public spaces), but that it "ought to matter little" (*parui autem interesse debet*). Ulpian supports this claim about the proper

[59] This insertion is logical – I promise. The Latin of D.1.1.1.1 uses a bare connective, and literally translates as "of which one might justly call us priests." That said, it immediately follows a fragment (D.1.1.1pr., Institutiones) in which law (*ius*) is defined as "the art of the good and the fair" (*ars boni et aequi*). Given the reference to *boni et aequi* later in the passage, *ius* is the clear antecedent of *cuius*.

[60] See Gallo, "Ars boni et aequi"; "Diritto e giustizia"; Riccobono, *Ius et ars boni et aequi*.

[61] Most explicitly at *RGDA* 8, discussed *supra* pp. 73–74; "With laws passed on my authority (*legibus . . . latis*) I restored many *exempla* of our elders that were falling out of fashion, and myself handed down *exempla* of many things for imitation by our descendants."

state of the law with a claim about the proper state of the world, using the same terminology of moral obligation. He says that the law should ignore the public/private distinction because both places "ought to have the same security" (*eandem securitatem debent habere*). The parallel forms of *debeo* are striking – Ulpian understands his command of legal interpretation and that interpretation's command of social life to be intrinsically linked. The impersonal passives *prospicitur* and *studetur* might suggest that Ulpian is claiming to interpret the provision in accord with its promulgator's intent, and using consequentialism to determine how a person who might care about consequences would intend their provisions to be read;[62] however, the claim about preferred social outcomes is so clearly Ulpianic that we should assume the similar language of *parui interesse debet* to reflect his moral imagination as well.

This style of reasoning, which evaluates rules on the basis of how compliance with those rules would affect the world, is often called "policy argument" in modern discussions of law.[63] I worry that bringing that phrase wholesale into the *Digest* risks implying more rigor than can be attributed to any jurist in this chapter. If Ulpian engaged in a scientific inquiry about the potential policy effects of legal rules, that inquiry is present nowhere in our text. His language remains in the realm of ethical notions, but those notions take as a given that rules will be followed and that they should be designed in such a way that that compliance would improve public welfare. This idea of the proper function of rules is explicitly consequentialist, and in fact forms one of the core commitments of rule-consequentialism as an ethical theory.[64] What Ulpian is doing is not quite what an ethicist does, since rule-consequentialist ethics involve the formation of moral codes rather than laws and those neither do nor should

[62] For a modern example, see *King* v. *Burwell*, 576 U.S. 473, 487 (2015): "Here, the statutory scheme compels us to reject petitioners' interpretation because it would destabilize the individual insurance market in any State with a Federal Exchange, and likely create the very 'death spirals' *that Congress designed the [Affordable Care] Act to avoid*." (emphasis added).

[63] See e.g. Shapiro, *Legality*, p. 246 ("Indeed, as comparative lawyers have long argued, the formalist self-presentation of civil law judges can only be a façade, hiding the extensive policy argumentation that is the true basis for many of these decisions.").

[64] See Hooker, *Ideal Code, Real World*, p. 2 ("Rule-consequentialism holds that the code whose collective internalization has the best consequences is the ideal code.").

perfectly overlap.[65] But Ulpian's rhetoric is nakedly ethical, and the ethic it most closely approaches is rule consequentialism; therefore, I will use that term to describe this style of legal argumentation hereinafter.

While this sort of argumentation[66] is not unique to Ulpian and the other Severan jurists, it does become markedly more common in the period. In total, 114 such instances survive within the *Digest*, of which 84 date from the Severan period and only 27 from before.[67] The disparity is striking. While the *Digest* does consist of mostly Severan texts, those authors frequently engage with their predecessors in detail and as a result the *Digest* is full of complex arguments from jurists predating the Severan period, in both text and paraphrase. Lenel's *Palingenesia* isolates 5,838 fragments of the pre-Severan jurists in the *Digest* as against 6,813 Severan; while the latter make up the majority of the text, they do so in nowhere near the proportion by which they dominate this corpus of rule-consequentialist arguments. One way to put it is that the Severans argue on rule-consequentialist grounds in one of every 81 fragments, while earlier jurists do so in every one out of every 216. Figure 5.1 shows the ratios somewhat more precisely, with the light bar representing each subgroup's prevalence within the *Digest* as a whole and the darker their prevalence within the specific subset of rule-consequentialist arguments. If the darker bar is lower, that suggests the group is underrepresented within that subset: higher, overrepresented.

65 *Ibid.*, p. 179.

66 The reference to argumentation, rather than logic, is intentional. Jurists frequently offer interpretations of the law that seem to rest on consequentialist principles; see e.g. D.9.4.4 (Paul, ad Edictum). That said, because so many of the arguments in the *Digest* are extremely summary – in the example above Paul claims that a *scienter* standard should not apply to principals who know their agent is about to act badly but cannot prevent it, but only justifies that reading as "more correct" or *rectius* – trying to isolate unstated rule-consequentialism becomes something of a guessing game. I focus on the increase in explicitly consequentialist *language* because that is less ambiguous and easier to track.

67 A full list is collected at Appendix 3. One of those 84, it should be noted, explicitly ascribes its rule-consequentialist reasoning to the emperor Trajan: see D.29.1.1pr. (Ulpian, ad Edictum). Another three of these sorts of arguments survive from the *Sentences of Paul* (*Pauli Sententiae*), a later compilation that purports to epitomize Paul. Since it is not entirely clear whether the reasoning provided in the *Sententiae* comes from lost Pauline texts or the later epitomator, I have included them in the sample without providing a firm dating.

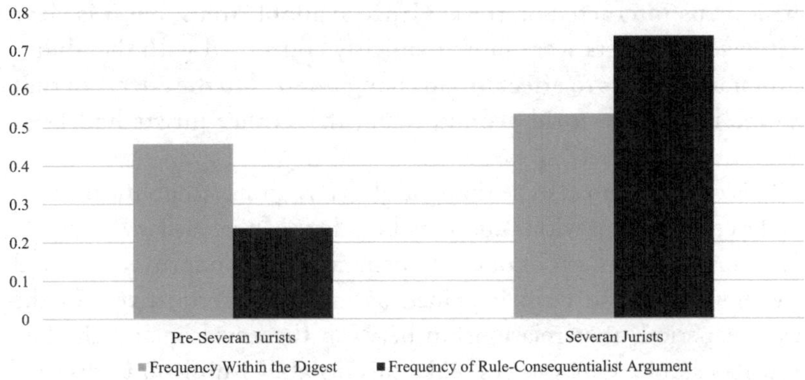

FIGURE 5.1 Comparative frequency of rule-consequentialism in the *Digest*.

On the evidence of this dataset, Severan jurists were about two-and-a-half times more likely to justify their interpretations on rule-consequentialist grounds than were their predecessors. That shift is too large (and over too large a sample) to be a coincidence,[68] but instead seems to reflect broader changes in jurists' roles and self-conceptions over the period. On the one hand, the Severan jurists were more closely and publicly involved in imperial administration than their forebears. As juristic careers came to include positions with greater control over and responsibility for public life, it should not be surprising that jurists considered public welfare more explicitly.[69] This consideration could result from the greater salience of public welfare in other aspects of juristic work: for example, from Ulpian and Papinian contemplating jobs for themselves that would make them responsible for Roman public welfare. The causal arrow might run the other way, though, and the successful jurists of the Severan period might have been the ones who were otherwise inclined to speak in the language of policy outcomes and goals. It is impossible to determine how these two

[68] The correlation between Severan authorship and rule-consequentialist argumentation is highly statistically significant. To use statistical terminology: χ^2 (1, N = 12,772) = 21.46, $p < .00001$. In layman's – or perhaps ancient historian's – terms, the odds of this disparity coming about through random chance are less than one in a million.

[69] See Coriat, "L'empereur juge," p. 61 (on the role of "raison pratique" in imperial decisionmaking and how it caused that decisionmaking to diverge from the sort traditionally practiced by jurists).

phenomena interacted on the evidence available to us, but it is clear that Severan jurists were more explicitly concerned with the ability of their arguments to effect broad change, and with the effects of that change upon the world around them, than other jurists had been before.

This concern can also be thought of as a response to political crisis. We have seen in previous chapters how law of the earlier Principate was represented as a tool of euergetism and moral improvement, and how both of those were imagined as imperial prerogatives. In the Severan period, that relationship between the emperor and the law grew less stable. Our sources make this instability difficult to discern, since the Severan emperors are well represented in the *Corpus Iuris Ciuilis*. But Severan legal order only became dominant and obvious in retrospect, and those living through it would not have known its rules would last. Instead, the jurists of the Severan period saw themselves as part of an imperial chancery that was willing to erase, restore, or redact prior imperial law to an extent not seen in a century. That chancery was headed by emperors whose authority rested on unfamiliar religious claims[70] or naked dynasticism, rather than the personal qualities that had previously underlain this particular vision of imperial competence. The Severans could not necessarily be trusted to make law wisely or well; this period lacked the elite consensus of second-century legitimacy politics, and without that authority it is not clear how imperial legislation could serve the euergetic or educational function that it had for Augustus or Hadrian.

Ulpian's perfectionist bombast makes more sense in this context. Ulpian is not strange for seeing law as serving a purpose, but for talking about law the way that emperors historically had. The relationship between imperial and legal authority had become strained in Ulpian's time, and the legal communications of Severus Alexander (which I discussed in Chapter 4) show a court that was aware of and reacting to the same problem. Roman law of this period was built around a vision of imperial sovereignty that was falling out of date,

[70] In addition to Elagabalus (discussed *supra* pp. 147–48) one thinks in particular of Caracalla, whose coinage and official communications emphasized his personal relationship with the gods and who publicly claimed to be "the most pious of all men" (Dio Cass. 78[77].16.1 [Xiph.]: εὐσεβέστατος πάντων ἀνθρώπων); Calomino, "Caracalla and the Divine"; Rowan, *Under Divine Auspices*, pp. 110–63.

and as a result the men who had previously helped law fulfill its historical role in improving the world were no longer doing so. Ulpian and his contemporaries stepped in.

By treating interpretation, rather than legislation, as the moment of broader-scale change to public life, the Severan jurists took power over that change for themselves. A political scientist might compare this hermeneutical shift to the changing roles of courts in American-style political systems; in the face of legislative sclerosis political blocs might seek to accomplish desired outcomes through changes in the interpretation of existing law.[71] Jurists taking on this role is especially striking, however, since they did not claim to speak on behalf of the state. These were private scholars, taking on responsibilities that the emperors of their time could not or would not perform. From outside, it is difficult to tell whether these shifts represented a greater tendency on the part of decisionmakers to interpret ambiguous provisions on consequentialist grounds, or a stylistic change that made those interpretations more explicit. But either way we see subtle aggrandizement of jurists as the parties responsible for providing public goods, as earlier arrangements for doing so were falling under new pressure.

That aggrandizement may also have something to do with the reception of Severan juristic work. A major theme of Part III of this book will be the impact of distinctly Severan political maneuvering on later understandings of Roman law. The Severan jurists were more explicit than their forebears in justifying their arguments on consequentialist grounds, and later readers who were responsible for the consequences of their decisions might naturally have found such a style to be agreeable. A juristic argumentation that was more explicitly bureaucratic and outcome-oriented was eventually recognized as the zenith of the genre by the bureaucrats of a later era. That recognition was not random, but neither was it driven by the sheer brilliance of Papinian or Ulpian or Paul. They wrote differently because they wrote under different conditions. The rules of Roman

[71] Cf. Siegel, "De Facto ERA," describing a parallel case in American "constitutional culture." The United States Constitution's formal amendment procedure is nearly impossible to complete, and as a result major constitutional changes like the reinterpretation of the Equal Protection Clause as forbidding sex discrimination have come about through judicial review.

legal science were always downstream from the rules of Roman political culture, and the two evolved in tandem.

Citation, Anonymity, and Regicide

Some of those rules were more awkward than others. For example, Macer's treatment of the *Senatusconsultum Turpillianum* brings us face to face with one of the most vexing questions a jurist might encounter: how to cite an on-point constitution whose author has been erased from memory?

> *The* senatusconsultum Turpillianum *applies to those who have suborned accusers; to those who, having been suborned, begin a prosecution and fail to complete it; and to those who cease an action without it being formally concluded. It also applies to those who have given promissory notes on account of a prosecution or made any other sort of agreement. And the language* nec peregissent *ought to be taken as applying to all those described above.*
>
> *It is asked whether the* senatusconsultum *applies to those who investigate in modern criminal courts* extra ordinem; *we apply the law in this way on the basis of the sacred constitutions, namely that it should apply in such a way as to permit the determination of individual punishments in individual circumstances.*
>
> (D.48.16.15.1: Macer, de Iudiciis Publicis) In senatusconsultum Turpillianum incidunt, qui subiecissent accusatores, aut subiecti postulassent nec peregissent reos, aut aliter quam abolitione facta destitissent: quique chirographum ob accusandum dedissent pactionemue aliquam interposuissent. hoc autem uerbum "nec peregissent" ad uniuersos supra scriptos pertinere dicendum est.
>
> An ad eos, qui hodie de iudiciis publicis extra ordinem cognoscunt, senatusconsultum pertineat, quaeritur: sed iam hoc iure ex sacris constitutionibus utimur, ut pertineat ita ex singulis causis singulae poenae irrogentur.

Macer's topic is important. The *SC Turpillianum* (which Tacitus mentions as being issued in 61 CE) penalized plaintiffs who abandoned lawsuits before their formal conclusion.[72] By Macer's time, however, the *SC* was nearly two centuries old and contemplated a different court system than the one about which he wrote. The somewhat more formal praetorian courts of the Republic and early Principate were now largely

[72] Tac. *Ann.* 14.41; Levy, "Anklägervergehen," pp. 421–24.

sidelined in place of imperial *cognitiones*, with state prosecutions in particular now proceeding exclusively through that channel.[73] So if – as Macer states and as authorities appear to have presumed – the *SC* applied to those who induced others to sue, how would its remedies work when the induced pressed charges on behalf of the state?

Macer dodges the question, in several senses. His proposed solution is too flexible to mean much, but that flexibility would be useful in cases as political and delicate as those he describes.[74] That solution, however, interests me less than the authority Macer relies upon to justify it. Macer invokes *sacrae constitutiones* in support of his claim, but does not say whose. While *sacer* clearly indicates imperial authorship, the norm for juristic writing is to cite emperors by name.[75] For example:

Someone who has promised that he will undertake a project in a city for their own or another's honor can be forced to perform, as can their heirs, according to a constitution of the deified Trajan.

(D.50.12.14: Pomponius, Epistulae et Variae Lectiones) Si quis sui alieniue honoris causa opus facturum se in aliqua ciuitate promiserit, ad perficiendum tam ipse quam heres eius ex constitutione diui Traiani obligatus est.

[73] See Palazzolo, "Dalle cognitiones alla cognitio"; Harries, *Law and Crime*, pp. 21–22.

[74] I should be clear here that the specific solution proposed might not reflect Macer's own reasoning. The language of this portion of the fragment is extremely laconic, and Classical jurists rarely leave matters to a judge's discretion without at least setting forth preferred decisional criteria (as at D.47.2.52.20 (Ulpian, ad Edictum), referenced *supra* p. 191, which directs a judge to establish "theftuous intent" (*animo furandi*) before determining which *actio* should lie). This fragment may be interpolated. I would not be surprised if a jurist were unusually circumspect on this of all topics, but neither would I be shocked if *singulis causis singulae poenae* reflected Justinianic intervention.

[75] *Sacer*-forms would come to denote institutions linked with the imperial court over the course of the late-antique period (most obviously in the *quaestor Sacri Palatii*), but they began to indicate imperial authorship of documents in the Severan period. See D.19.1.43 (Paul, Quaestiones), D.23.2.60 (Paul, ad Orationem Diui Antonini et Commodi), D.26.7.5.5 (Ulpian, ad Edictum), D.40.1.5 (Marcianus, Institutiones), D.42.1.27 (Modestinus, Responsa), D.49.5.4 (Macer, de Appellationibus), D.49.8.1 (Marcianus, de Appellationibus), D.49.14.18 (Marcianus, de Delatoribus); also, and importantly, θεῖαι διατάξεις at D.27.1.15.5 (Modestinus, Excusationes). The first references to *sacrae constitutiones* in "official" communications, to my knowledge, come much later; the phrase appears in Diocletianic rescripts at C.2.42.3 (293), 7.43.11 [n.d.] and 10.47.2 [n.d.]. While this somewhat proleptic terminology can indicate interpolation, its appearance in Greek-language juristic writing strikes me as strong evidence for at least partial use during the third century.

Unlike Macer Pomponius here clearly links the legal claim to an identifiable authority, and one most readers would understand as superior to the jurist himself. While Roman jurisprudence might imply that *responsa prudentium* stood on equal footing with imperial constitutions, in practice this was obviously not the case; imperial communication was the final word on an issue, at least as long as that emperor was in power or in favor.

This tendency becomes apparent when we examine the *Corpus* as a whole. As Appendix 1 shows, jurists cite emperors some 1,255 times in the *Digest*; while many of these citations are neutral (as for example in D.1.12.1 (Ulpian, de Officio Praefecti Urbi), which describes the jurisdiction of the urban prefect and thus begins with an *epistula* of Septimius Severus setting that jurisdiction out), not once does a surviving juristic fragment contradict imperial opinion. The one circumstance I am aware of where a jurist explicitly disagrees with an existing imperial constitution[76] is Ulpianic:

But let us see whether only an acknowledged debt can be taken, or also one from a debtor who denies that he owes it. It is superior that only debt that is confessed can be seized: On the other hand if a debt should be denied, it will be fairest to leave it be unless someone should follow the analogy with corporalia pignora *and pursue it as far as to say that judges themselves should investigate the debt, as they do for ownership. But a rescript says otherwise.*

(D.42.1.15.9: Ulpian, de Officio Consulis) Sed utrum confessum nomen tantum capi possit an etiam si neget quis se debere, uideamus. et magis est, ut id dumtaxat capiatur, quod confitetur: ceterum si negetur, aequissimum erit discedi a nomine, nisi forte quis exemplum secutus corporalium pignerum ultra processerit dixeritque ipsos debere iudices de nomine cognoscere, ut cognoscunt de proprietate: sed contra rescriptum est.

Ulpian here makes clear what he thinks the law should be, but never claims the rescript is wrong or invalid. Elsewhere Ulpian describes a disagreement between jurists and emperors in a way that makes clear his sympathy with the former, but he still acknowledges the latter's supremacy.

[76] I exclude from this claim cases where a jurist describes themselves in colloquy with an emperor, like the disagreement between Paul and Septimius Severus mentioned *supra* pp. 194–95.

Nor will one hesitate to appoint a son as his father's curator; *although it was held otherwise in the writings of Celsus and of many others besides, and although it might be unseemly for a father to be ruled by his son, nevertheless the deified Pius said in a rescript to Instius Celer (with the Deified Brothers holding similarly) that a son, if he lives soberly, ought to be appointed as his father's* curator *before one is selected from outside the family.*

(D.26.5.12.1, de Officio Proconsulis) Nec dubitabit filium quoque patri curatorem dare: quamuis enim contra sit apud Celsum et apud alios plerosque relatum, quasi indecorum sit patrem a filio regi, attamen diuus Pius Instio Celeri, item Diui Fratres rescripserunt filium, si sobrie uiuat, patri curatorem dandum magis quam extraneum.

Ulpian's language makes clear that juristic argument cannot, no matter how persuasive, outweigh the *rescriptum*. Ulpian presents the standard authorities of juristic reasoning (a prior juristic claim of Celsus', his own moral intuition about what counts as *indecorum*) within the concessive *quamuis*-clause, balances them against the bare fact of imperial rescripts in the *attamen*-clause, and then says that there is no ambiguity or doubt (*nec dubitabit*) that the rescripts win. The *Digest* also records jurists offering complex theoretical justifications for a given legal point before adding, as an aside, that it has been settled by the emperor. For example, Ulpian concludes a long argument based primarily on analogic reasoning with "The deified Marcus has also followed our reasoning in a rescript" (D.29.1.3, ad Edictum: *secundum nostram sententiam etiam diuus Marcus rescripsit*), and Papinian appeals to "the logic of the law and the words of the constitution [of the Deified Brothers]" (D.48.19.33, Quaestiones: *ratio iuris et uerba constitutionis*) with the *ratio iuris* placed in the emphatic position. This ranking of authorities should not surprise us, given how jurists had traditionally worked. Juristic writing began as an aristocratic pursuit, and approached law as a philosophical discipline that was more interesting than it was straightforward.[77] Simply quoting an on-point rescript would not be any fun.[78]

But that rescript still mattered, and jurists who cited it provided an important good to their readers. These citations might direct a savvy

[77] Peachin, "Jurists and the Law," pp. 119–20.

[78] See Bretone, *Ius controversum*, pp. 768–69, 800–08.

litigant towards records of an emperor's rescripts in order to find a valuable authority, or they might alert that litigant to the potential instability of a given legal claim by indicating that it rested on the authority of someone who was currently on the outs. Notably, both of these goods depend on the emperor being mentioned by name. A reference to *sacrae constitutiones*, or to any other anonymous imperial claim, gives the reader no tools to find the *constitutio* for themselves, or to evaluate its utility under their present political conditions.

So why reference *sacrae constitutiones* like this? In the case of D.48.16.15.1, an answer immediately suggests itself. The *SC Turpillianum* was put forward in 61 CE: i.e. under Nero. If Nero's court was the first to clarify how the *SC* applied to *cognitiones extra ordinem* then Macer might not have wanted to cite him by name. But too many of these citations survive, and with too great a concentration among Macer and his peers, for us to blame it all on Nero.

So what is happening instead? Quantitative analysis shows that this citational practice becomes dramatically (and significantly) more common in the Severan period. Showing that disparity begins with the 1,255 citations to imperial lawmaking that I mentioned above. These citations come overwhelmingly from the Severan jurists: Earlier juristic fragments cite emperors 94 times (about 8% of the total), while the Severans cite emperors 1,150 times (over 91%). Of the remaining, one cannot be dated with confidence;[79] the other ten come from the Diocletianic jurists Arcadius Charisius and Hermogenianus, and will be discussed in a bit.

That difference is massive, but not necessarily interesting. As I mentioned above, most pre-Severan juristic work in the *Digest* survives in quotation – it is easy to imagine that Severan authors might not cite their predecessors for the existence of an imperial constitution and might instead cite the constitution directly themselves. In fact, only once (at D.39.6.15: Julianus, Digesta, quoted in Paul, Notatio ad Digestum Iuliani) does a quoted fragment

[79] D.28.2.26 is a fragment of the *Pauli Sententiae*, which cites an Augustan edict. It is impossible to know if this citation was from Paul and should be considered Severan, or is instead one of the many late-antique emendations to the *Sententiae*.

include a mention of imperial legal writing.[80] Accordingly we cannot simply track the *number* of citations, even anonymous ones; instead, we can productively track the *rate* of anonymous citation and see how it changes in the Severan jurists.

Now we can get somewhere. Pre-Severan jurists only employ anonymous citation-forms seven times, out of the ninety-four total; in other words, they only cite anonymously 7.4% of the time or roughly once out of every thirteen-and-a-half citations.[81] That rate more than doubles in the Severan period. Severan jurists provide 219 anonymous citations of 1,150 total; that is a rate of 19.0%, or one out of every five-and-a-quarter. The difference is statistically significant at a 99% confidence level.[82]

Some other intriguing tendencies can be seen in the data, even if they require carving the sample too finely for *chi*-squared analysis. For example, those ten post-Severan citations I mentioned above carry this citational tendency to a far greater extreme. Six of the ten are anonymous, making up an absolute majority (60.0%) of the post-Severan sample.[83] That said, once the sample is cut down that severely I lose statistical confidence in my findings: the significant

[80] This also occurs twice in summary, at D.8.3.35 (Paul, ad Plautium) (*Atilicinus ait Caesarem Statilio Tauro rescripsisse in haec uerba*) and D.30.49pr (Ulpian, ad Sabinum) (*ita imperatorem decreuisse Marcellus scripsit*). In the latter case Ulpian's summary excludes authorship information that was likely clear in context, since Marcellus elsewhere uses this language to refer to *cognitiones* under Marcus. See Daalder, *Rechtspraakverzamelingen*, p. 415.

[81] D.12.2.31 (Gaius, ad Edictum Prouinciale), D.29.1.2 (same); D.29.1.25 (Marcellus, Responsa), D.34.9.6 (Marcellus, Digesta) D.39.6.15 (Julianus, Digesta, as quoted by Paul, Notatio ad Digestum Iuliani), D.41.3.40 (Nerva, Regulae), and D.50.1.24 (Scaevola, Digesta).

[82] For the full list of jurists citing emperors, see Appendix 1. The hypothesis that Severan jurists were more likely than their predecessors to cite unnamed imperial authorities is statistically significant at $p < .01$: $\chi 2$ (2, N = 1,244) = 7.861, $p = .005052$. In lay terms, the odds of this disparity arising through random chance are around one in 200.

[83] The six anonymous late antique citations are: D.22.5.1.2 (Arcadius Charisius, de Testibus), D.22.5.25 (Arcadius Charisius, de Testibus), D.40.1.24 (Hermogenianus, Epitome Iuris), D.48.18.10.2 (Arcadius Charisius, de Testibus), D.49.14.46.5 (Hermogenianus, Epitome Iuris), and D.50.4.18.23 (Arcadius Charisius, de Muneribus Ciuilibus). The four which cite emperors by name are D.37.5.23 (Hermogenianus, Epitome Iuris), D.48.4.9 (Hermogenianus, Epitome Iuris), D.48.18.10pr. (Arcadius Charisius, de Testibus), and D.50.4.18.30 (Arcadius Charisius, de Muneribus Ciuilibus). I discuss institutionalizing trends of the late-antique period in Chapter 6.

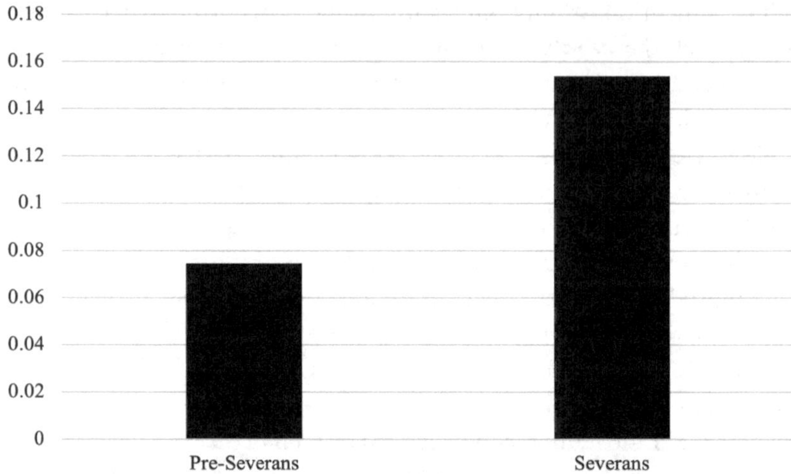

FIGURE 5.2 Proportion of citations to imperial lawmaking that employ anonymous naming forms, among the pre–Severan and Severan jurists.

conclusion is that anonymous citation increases in jurists of the Severan period (Figure 5.2).

The question remains: why? Why would the Severan jurists simultaneously take on for themselves some of the prerogatives of imperial lawmaking, and elide the identities of those imperial lawmakers themselves? The nature of Roman juristic transmission, which privileged first-order rules (like the reach of the *SC Turpillianum* or of *effodere uel deicere* liability) over second-order argument norms like the subject of this chapter, makes this question impossible to answer with confidence. But some reasons present themselves that bridge the gap between the Severan jurists' novel/dangerous institutional position and their novel/transformational argumentative style.

One answer is straightforward – the Severan jurists had more to work with. The political upheaval of the period masks some administrative continuities, and emperors kept on answering questions and writing constitutions. Accordingly, the sheer volume of imperial authority that jurists could cite grew as time went on. Some of the anonymous citations we have appear to respond to that profusion; for example, when Ulpian cites "the divine Pius and all of the emperors after him" (D.43.24.15.6, ad Edictum: *et ita diuus Pius et deinceps omnes principes rescripserunt*) he might simply not have wanted to list rescripts of Marcus and

Septimius Severus et cetera. Furthermore, folding all of these different authorities into a nameless *omnes principes* could make rescripts easier to think with. These citations elide differences and contradictions between rescripts (which might reflect small variations in emperors' or their *consilia*'s understanding of law, or which might reflect differences in facts)[84] by focusing instead on the commonalities behind an emergent body of "rescript law." Finding law in many different specific rescripts would be annoying, and confusing; looking to "rescripts" as a synthetic authority was simpler.

That said, the story of anonymous citation is not just a story of simplifying law. For one thing, certain emperors seem to have been anonymized more than others. The most extreme example of this tendency is Commodus, who – despite being redeified by Septimius Severus[85] – is almost never cited in the *Digest* by name.[86] Jurists cite Commodus only seven times in the *Digest* as sole emperor, and another fifteen times as a joint authority with Marcus Aurelius. By contrast, Marcus *solus* is cited 110 times in the *Digest*, the Deified Brothers 133, and Septimius Severus 108. Figure 5.3 shows the disparity.

Jurists of the Severan period avoided citing one particular disfavored ruler, while simultaneously adopting a rhetorical strategy that made it impossible to tell who exactly was being cited at any given time. Coincidence seems unlikely; these anonymous citations allowed

FIGURE 5.3 Citations to imperial lawmaking in the *Digest* by emperor, 99–217 CE

[84] See Babusiaux, *Quaestiones*, pp. 33–36. [85] See *supra* p. 174.
[86] See Hekster, *Commodus*, p. 75 n. 195.

Severan jurists to refer to Commodan legal activity without having to say so out loud, and thus to avoid explicitly linking themselves to a controversial authority.

In other words, we can see this new citation practice as a form of self-preservation. A jurist who wanted to remain in favor during the political shifts of the Severan period could benefit from being circumspect in their argumentation. This explanation is perhaps the most boring, but also makes a great deal of sense. The Severan jurists were savvy political operators because they had to be. The conventions of second-century legal culture had been built upon a politic no longer in force, and the third century was a dangerous time for making pronouncements about which imperial authorities were still valid and which were not.

On the other hand, the *sacrae constitutiones* of the Severan *Digest* can also be taken as a kind of jurisprudential fantasy. Imperial writing settled the law; it located legal authority in a fixed place outside of the jurists' traditional ambit, which was more useful to litigants than even the cleverest juristic argument. Macer and his contemporaries knew that, and knew how they were being read. Citing a rescript from a particular emperor would presumably direct one's reader towards the cited authority and thus obviate the delicate alchemies of confidence, erudition, and expertise that underlay juristic work. Instead, that citational practice would send readers on a quest for the definitive answer contained within a different archive; anyone who has used law review articles to research a doctrinal question is familiar with the transition from scholarship to case law and the greater utility of the latter. Citing unnamed emperors, or unlabeled documents, permitted no such thing. These citational practices contain the reader within the closed universe of the juristic treatise. The reader might trust the jurist and probably should, but is primed to argue from the treatise's own reasoning and not from the authority to which it gestures. The *sacrae constitutiones* construct a legality that proceeds along the scholarly, technical lines of jurisprudence and that empowers the jurist in producing legal truth.[87]

That empowerment could also explain the practical turn in Severan juristic work. Macer had been trained to write laws of general

[87] For a more literary account of how anonymity can function to alter the reading and meaning of Roman texts see Geue, *Anonymity*.

applicability, which could be widely promulgated without catastrophic effect; any Severan jurist we have heard of was successful in a bureaucracy that specialized in that sort of work. Some of the Severans' comfort with consequence can be ascribed to that bureaucratic orientation, since jurists with hammers might see things as nails. But these arguments also subtly aggrandize the jurist-as-policymaker, in ways that could have appealed to a frightened semi-professional class. The Severan jurists were the first generation to hold major public offices as a result of their scholarly reputations, and had been trained to see themselves as part of the grand project of the Roman state – "making men better" in Ulpian's words. A man with that training, and the understanding of his own calling that that training would impart, might develop certain ideas about his place in the world that his predecessors did not.

Even here, though, we see traces of the fantastic. Juristic writing was necessarily an imaginative endeavor, in the sense that it offered guidance to subsequent disputes and thus constructed a later context in which it might be useful. Imagination of this sort will always be a part of the history of law, because law is prospective and aims at fixing or rendering predictable an unbounded future.[88] But law can imagine a present as well, and the *Digest* constructs decisional practices that only make sense as a dream of order.

That dream was understandable. Severan historiographers describe the politics of their time in apocalyptic terms, most famously in Cassius Dio's dismissal of the era after Marcus Aurelius as an age of "iron and rust" (72[71].36.4 [Xiph.]: σιδηρᾶν καὶ κατιωμένην).[89] Living through unrest is a frightening thing, and legal experts might look to law as a source of political goodness when that virtue was otherwise scarce. It must have been tempting for the Severan jurists to see themselves and their art as something that could save a world that needed saving. Severan juristic work elevates the jurist, as both a source of authority and a world-changing agent, when traditional forms of authority and governance were collapsing. This aggrandizement looks like a power grab, but could just as easily be a comforting daydream: a vision of

88 See Constable, *Bond*, pp. 73–74.

89 See Scott, "Cassius Dio and the Age of Iron and Rust"; "Historiographic Method"; Noe, "The 'Age of Iron and Rust.'"

bureaucratic governance, of power in the hands of trained and competent interpreters rather than the child dynasts history records.

* * * * *

To be clear, these last few paragraphs are speculation. I know that Severan juristic writing looks different than its forebears, and can only guess as to why. But these speculations about motive are common in other genres – such reasoning is common, and often unspoken, in discussions of literary writing. Juristic writing discourages us from asking those questions, but the fantasies I have described are deeply bound up with the history of Roman law. We have seen them in Augustus' stories of law and moral revival, in Vespasian's imagined license to rule, in Trajan's and Septimius' pretense of legal subjecthood, and – most importantly for the moment – in Severus Alexander's precedential and dynastic project. We all agree that these stories are relevant for the historiography of imperial politics, which has long understood itself as bound up in unreality and doublespeak.[90] Juristic writing is closer to this historiography than it appears. The Severan jurists wrote scholarly treatises on private law that did not discuss imperial power out loud, but that represented themselves as operating within a political system that did not really exist. This construction is hortatory in the same way as something like Pliny's *Panegyricus*, and calls its reader to imagine a state governed by law. Authors like Ulpian come down to us through a centuries-long tradition that presents them as authorities, but reading outside of that tradition lets us ask different questions, and gain new insight in how some elite Romans of the third century reconciled themselves to political unrest.

At a time when the emperor was no longer a plausible source of moral authority, two intertwined communities reimagined that authority in different ways. Alexander's court sited law's authority in a dynasty, the Severan jurists in a technocracy. Both of these stories – desperate, hopeful, and only tangentially related to a messier reality – are obscured in our sources, since Severan legal communications survive mostly as evidence of disembodied rules. But those disembodied rules postdate the documents in which they claim to reside; the jurists who wrote them down lived in a very different world. Part III of this book, which discusses late-antique legal culture up to Justinian, shows how their dreams came true.

[90] See Bartsch, *Actors*, pp. 10–31.

PART III

NEW RULES

6

Towards Late-Antique Legalities

The stories I have discussed in this book have a vexed relationship with time. From the nostalgic innovations of Augustus or Titus, to the more subtle rewritings of history that we see in the Severan jurists or in the rescripts of Severus Alexander, we have seen Roman legal actors mix past and future in order to better negotiate the challenges of their present. This tendency partly arises from the generic expectations of law talk; law is an inherently prospective mode of speaking, which instructs its listener to reason from the past. But it also reflects the particular ways in which Roman legal rhetoric worked. These texts purport to intervene in the legal operations of a world that never existed, and condition savvy readers to imagine that world as they try to think with Roman law. I have referred to that representational process as "construction," and it gives Roman legal stories a persuasive force that more blatant misdescription cannot attain.

Later readers would take those stories as true. After Severus Alexander was killed in 235 Roman governance entered a period of dynastic instability and border unrest, commonly known as the "Third Century Crisis," which only ended when Diocletian took the throne in 284.[1] Diocletian instituted a system known as the tetrarchy or "rule by

[1] See e.g. Hose, "Historiographie in der Krise," p. 38 ("Bis zu Diokletian, 'scheiterten' Kaiser und Dynastien nach jeweils so kurzer Zeit, dass heute nur noch Spezialisten unter den Althistorikern deren genaue Abfolge und Regierungsdaten auswendig kennen."). Other historians have pushed back and suggested greater continuity between the mid

four," but retired in 305 to raise cabbages in Split;[2] shortly afterwards Constantine won a complicated civil war and reformed the government along more frankly autocratic lines.[3] Roman rulers throughout this time looked to the past for legitimating narrative, and they found that past in law.

More specifically, they found it in jurists. As discussed in the last chapter, Severan jurists and Severan emperors told different stories about how Roman sovereignty worked. Severus Alexander used law to represent himself as a kind of Severan caretaker, but the *Soldatenkaisers* (soldier-emperors) of the mid third century did not have the same kinds of dynastic claims as Alexander did, and thus could not follow Alexander's strategy of using law to connect himself to legitimate forebears.

By contrast, the Severan jurists constructed legal authority in more institutional terms. Authors like Ulpian and Macer described emperors as supreme bureaucrats, as sources for the development of a fixed, sovereign law that could command legitimacy even when individual rulers could not. This story worked better in the mid third century, and offered more appealing rhetorical options. As time went on, Diocletian and his successors came to imagine law as the jurists did even while applying it to a very different state. This period sees very little juristic writing as we would now understand it, but the Severan treatises remained in circulation and exercised extraordinary influence on the legal system of the Dominate.[4]

third century and earlier periods, while still acknowledging meaningful changes in imperial selection and accession. See de Blois, *Image and Reality*; Witschel, *Krise, Rezession, Stagnation?*. Cultural historians of the third century have made the related point that high-level unrest could mask deep continuities within Roman social life. See e.g. Poulter, "Moesia and Thrace"; Borg, *Crisis and Ambition*. Further bibliography contained in Sommer, "A Vast Scene of Confusion."

[2] Retirement: Lact., *de mort. pers.* 19. Cabbage: Aur. Vict. *Caes.* 39.6; Cheung, "Born Roman," pp. 672–73. Split: Wilkes, *Diocletian's Palace*.

[3] For a more detailed historical narrative see Bowman, "Diocletian."

[4] On the rather sudden stoppage in juristic production during the mid third century, see de Blois, "Influence," pp. 226–31; "Roman Jurists," pp. 147–50 (attributing the decline in juristic careers to much broader shifts in administration and appointment procedures over the course of the third century). On the changing role of jurists in third and fourth century Roman legal culture see also Piacente, "Giurisprudenza," pp. 288–89; Honoré, *Crisis*, pp. 6–11.

I here consider this imaginative process, and the peculiar legality that emerged from it. Historians of late-antique governance[5] have noted features of that governance (centralization, hierarchy, expertise) that organized it along the lines we see in the *Digest*. Men like Diocletian – or his courtiers – looked to the jurists to understand how Classical law worked, and accordingly developed a legal regime unlike anything we see in Classical Rome. They wrote rescripts that described their own power in the terms set out by Ulpian and his contemporaries, they codified those rescripts in forms that more closely resembled the juristic treatise than they did earlier ways of collecting imperial constitutions, and they supervised a bureaucracy that was better able to apply the teachings of the jurists than anything those jurists themselves had encountered.[6] In so doing emperors and bureaucrats of the late-antique period created the world that the jurists imagined, a world which looks to us now to have been governed by a comparatively neutral law on the books.

This story helps us understand why Roman law looks the way it does, since so many of the background features of that law date to the later empire. But it also helps us see why construction, as a rhetorical device, is so powerful. Severan juristic treatises seem to simply describe law's operations in the late Principate; following their instructions, however, meant transforming the Roman state.

This chapter studies three major developments in late-antique legality, and shows how they reorganized Roman legal life into something like the law of the jurists. First I consider the rhetoric of imperial legal writing from the mid third century up to Constantine, which describes law as earlier jurists had and which treats those jurists as an authoritative guide to how Roman law ought to work. I next

[5] I will be engaging with this scholarship throughout the chapter, so a full literature review feels somewhat redundant; a brief one, however, can't hurt. On changes to the form of late-antique imperial legal writing see Dillon, *Justice*; Schmidt-Hofner, *Reagieren*; Eich and Eich, "Verlautbarungsstil." On innovation by actors outside of the imperial system see Connolly, *Lives*; Humfress, *Orthodoxy*. On imperial codificatory movements as themselves reflecting shifting attitudes towards legal authority see Letteney, *Christianization*; Liebs, "The Code System"; Corcoran, "Assembled and Shattered"; Matthews, *Laying Down the Law*; Harries and Wood (eds.), *The Theodosian Code*.

[6] See Schulz, *Roman Legal Science*, p. 262 ("We shall call the period from Diocletian to Justinian the bureaucratic period of Roman jurisprudence.").

trace how that writing was codified, and show how our modern understanding of that codification (multiauthor collections, organized into titles on the basis of subject) was a tetrarchic innovation based on earlier juristic writing. I then discuss how the massive expansion of Roman bureaucracy that took place in the fourth century CE made Roman *Reichsrecht* into something that could govern a world – it allowed parties to put questions before legally trained adjudicators, operating within a regularized system of appealable judgments by experts. I end with a particularly clear vision of late-antique legal order, the *Codex Theodosianus*. That compilation shows how the charismatic lawgivers of the second century had receded, in favor of close evaluation and consideration of long-dead jurists.

Settled Law in Unsettled Times

Many things changed in the mid third century. The fifty years after the Severans were marked by near-constant civil war and border crisis; accordingly, the short-lived emperors of this period tended to come from military rather than aristocratic backgrounds. That said many existing features of imperial sovereignty lasted into this period and beyond, as these new kinds of rulers faced old kinds of problems.

Some of those problems were legal. The rescript system, by which imperial correspondence could settle questions of law, survived the fall of the Severans and provides some of our best records of administration after Alexander. Like earlier rulers the *Soldatenkaisers* used rescripts as a tool of self-fashioning, through which they could tell stories about themselves and the kind of authority they held. Unlike in the Principate, however, the rescripts of these men purport to explain rather than make the law. These documents describe settled legal precepts as if those precepts themselves govern the matter at hand; they do not so much decline to intervene as construct a paradigm in which the emperor cannot intervene. Emperors here appear as guides to the law, who interpret its commands rather than making them.

In other words, emperors of this period sound like jurists. Their impersonal, bureaucratic language matches that of the juristic treatise; rather than effecting positive legal change rescripts of this period purport to guide questioners through the law as it already exists and already governs any given dispute. This isagogic tendency represents the emperor as wise but oddly powerless, since he describes the commands of *leges* as sovereign rather than his own choices. That descriptive maneuver comes from jurists, who could not unilaterally alter the law; in imperial constitutions, by contrast, it represents a paradigm shift. These constitutions construct a Roman law that works the way it would in the *Digest*, rather than the way it did in earlier imperial courts.

I begin with the rescripts of Decius (r. 249–251). Decius is a relatively typical emperor of the period, not least because he was not emperor for very long. Shortly after defeating his predecessor Philip the Arab (r. 244–249) in battle, Decius was himself killed fighting Goths. In between, however, Decius appears to have maintained a legal program and several of his rescripts survive in the *Codex Justinianus*. These rescripts show how emperors of this time talked about legal problems; Decius explains how the law applies to a given legal question, rather than creating new law in order to settle that question himself. For example:

If, after an inheritance had descended to a son-in-power, his father acted as an heir with his son's consent, it has often been held in rescripts that [the requirements for proper inheritance] are satisfied in terms of legal formality.

(C.6.30.4: Decius, 250) Filio familias delata hereditate si pater pro herede uoluntate filii gessit, sollemnitati iuris satisfactum uideri saepe rescriptum est.

This passage represents Decius as explaining a settled point of law, and I have no reason to doubt it, but the language he uses to explain that point is striking. Like Severus Alexander, Decius presents himself as operating within a system that exists outside of him. The question posed has been answered before, and while Decius does not portray himself as bound to respect that precedent he certainly describes it as a source of authority.[7] The difference is in how Alexander and Decius describe that authority. Alexander cited people like his putative father and grandfather, and even the anonymous *constitutum est* of C.6.23.3

[7] A chance remains that Decius is describing the rule in order to transcend it: we only have an excerpt, and I cannot dismiss the possibility that Decius went on to break with tradition in a later portion of the rescript that does not survive. That said, it would be surprising for Decius to explain a rule in this much detail were he not intending to enforce it.

is followed by a probable quote from the same.[8] Decius cites documents. *Saepe rescriptum est* refers to prior imperial authority without actually naming any authorities, and sites the power of imperial legal communication in the act of *rescriptio*. Decius sounds more like the Severan jurists than he does the Severan emperors, despite being an emperor himself.[9]

This style of anonymous, institutionalizing citation reflects a different approach not just to Roman legal authority but also to the writing and giving of rescripts. The document is short, which is to be expected; rescripts were generally brief.[10] But even within this somewhat summary genre of legal speech Decius stands out. Specifically, Decius does not claim to decide the case himself, or even to decide the point of law on which he was consulted. He instead refers to and participates in a suprapersonal tradition of *rescripta*, which C.6.30.4 joins without dramatically altering. This vision of imperial authority privileges continuity, looks to the past as a source of instruction, and imagines correct answers as residing within a tradition rather than a person.

Similarly, Decius' reply to a woman named Asclepiodota claims that "it is a matter of settled law (C.6.58.3pr., 250: *explorati iuris*) that women can also be admitted to the intestate succession by their rights of consanguinity." Decius is not lying; this is another very straightforward point of law, and while Roman inheritance law disadvantaged women in all sorts of ways[11] intestate succession

[8] The language and reasoning of C.6.23.3 (Severus Alexander, 232) is discussed *supra* pp. 179–82.

[9] In fact this formulation (with *saepe* or *saepissime* and a verb of legal decision in the passive) appears sixteen times in the *Digest*: thirteen times in Ulpian (D.12.3.4pr., ad Edictum; D.13.7.36pr., ad Edictum; D.14.6.3.1, ad Edictum; D.27.1.5, de Officio Praetoris Tutelaris; D.29.2.25.2, ad Sabinum; D.29.7.1, Disputationes; D.34.3.9, ad Sabinum; D.40.5.24.21, Fideicommissa; D.42.8.10.13, ad Edictum; D.42.8.10.14, ad Edictum; D.47.10.13.7, ad Edictum; D.48.18.1.7, de Officio Proconsulis; and D.50.15.4.10, de Censibus); twice in Hermogenianus (D.40.1.24, Iuris Epitome; D.49.14.46.5, Iuris Epitome); and once in Macer (D.42.1.63, de Appellationibus).

[10] Corcoran, *Tetrarchs*, pp. 46–47 ("rescripts tend not to be long"); Honoré, *Emperors and Lawyers*, pp. 187–89.

[11] Probably the best known is the *lex Voconia*, a Republican statute that forbade women from inheriting large estates. This law was substantially weakened over time, particularly with the increased use of trusts or *fideicommissa* to sidestep some of the rituals of Roman testation. See Köstner, "Geschlechterrollen"; Crook, "Women in Roman Succession"; Dixon, "Infirmitas"; Vigneron, "L'antiféministe loi."

was formally neutral regarding the sex of potential inheritors.[12] But Decius invokes *ius* as binding. The emperor here acts as a guide to the law, and the remainder of C.6.58.3 applies existing principles to a reasonably simple inheritance dispute between Asclepiodota and her nephews. But the rescript assumes, as a matter of course, that existing law should govern these sorts of problems.

These shifts in rhetoric were not unique to Decius. We can see similar maneuvers in the more numerous (>250) surviving rescripts of Gordian III, who was acclaimed emperor in 238 at the age of thirteen and ruled for six years.[13] Take the following, preserved at *Cons.* 9.10:[14] "The logic of the law does not protect pacts which are entered into contrary to good morals" (*Pacta, quae contra bonos mores interponuntur, iuris ratio non tuetur*). Once again, we see the emperor positioned as explaining or enforcing the judgments of a *ius* that exists above him. Gordian cites *ius* (specifically the ancient *ius ciuile*) more directly at C.8.47.1 (239): "Those who are in another's power cannot be adopted, according to the *ius ciuile*, except in a proceeding before someone with full jurisdiction." (*Hi, qui in aliena sunt potestate, iuxta ius ciuile non nisi apud eum, apud quem plena legis actio est, adoptari possunt.*).[15] Rather than presenting himself as giving – or even as following – the law, Gordian constructs legal authority as straightforwardly binding and himself as merely

[12] See *BTRL* pp. 222–23; Crook, "Women in Roman Succession," pp. 61–63. Early Roman inheritance law was sharply patrilineal and thus did not permit women to serve as links in a testamentary chain, but women could inherit from an intestate relative even if their children could not. A later succession procedure generally called "praetorian succession" removed even this boundary and treated agnatic consanguinity (consanguinity running only through male relatives) and cognatic consanguinity (consanguinity running through both male and female relatives) identically.

[13] On the reign of Gordian III see Aur. Vict. *Caes.* 27; Drinkwater, "Maximinus to Diocletian," pp. 33–36.

[14] Since my analysis here is not quantitative, using material from corpora other than the *Codex* does not risk introducing endogeneity into my claims.

[15] The phrase *apud quem plena legis actio est* is not entirely clear. Blume translates it as referring to "plenary jurisdiction," followed by Frier et al. That phrase has no exact parallel in surviving legal writing, but certain texts in the *Corpus Iuris Ciuilis* refer to adoptions needing to occur before officials with broad jurisdictional authority. See *J. Inst.* 1.11 (referring to adoptions occurring *siue apud praetorem uel apud praesidem prouinciae*); D.1.7.4 (Modestinus, Regulae) (citing an opinion of Neratius that magistrates *apud quem legis actio est* could ratify adoptions). For my purposes, fortunately, an exact gloss on *plena legis actio* is unnecessary.

explaining it. The power relations that put Gordian in this position and that govern his relationship with law are shifted to the background, in favor of law as a decisional agent in its own right. While the emperor is on some level *choosing* to follow the law, he does not appear in these documents to be making that choice. Gordian is similarly deferential when referring to prior imperial judgments, citing "the judgments of prior emperors" (C. 1.50.1 (240): *scita diuorum principum*) and "the shape of the constitutions" (C.5.53.4.1 (238), C.5.62.14.1 (239): *formam constitutionum*). This rhetorical posture somewhat resembles that of the last child to hold the throne; the quantitative analysis of the *Codex Justinianus* that I first referenced in Chapter 4 (Figure 6.1) shows that Gordian, like Severus Alexander, was unusually likely to cite prior emperors by name. But these citations to earlier emperors coexist with invocations of law as an authority that governs the world through the emperor – rather than the other way around.

These arguments continue into the tetrarchy. As I discuss later in this chapter Diocletian kept extensive records of his replies to legal queries, and accordingly our archive of imperial legal communication vastly expands once we reach the 290s.[16] Those records have helped historians reconstruct the world of the Roman litigant at the turn of the fourth century; one thinks in particular of Connolly's social history of petitioners in Sirmium and Heraclea[17] and Corcoran's more institutional exploration of Diocletian's chancery.[18] But as Babusiaux notes these records also help us to fill out the discursive environment within which Roman legality was dialogically constituted, or better understand how people talked about law and what kind of law they talked into being.[19] We can see in the Diocletianic *rescripta* what Diocletian (and his courtiers) thought people expected of him, or what it meant to be a tetrarch.

What it meant, once again, seems to have been following the law. While Diocletian's position was comparatively secure, his writing shows many of the same rhetorical features as that of his third-century predecessors.

[16] See *infra* p. 243.
[17] Connolly describes her subjects as "the middling sort" (*Lives*, p. 21) following Coriat, *Le prince législateur*, p. 317.
[18] Corcoran, *Tetrarchs*, pp. 75–95. [19] Babusiaux, "Zitate," especially pp. 263–65.

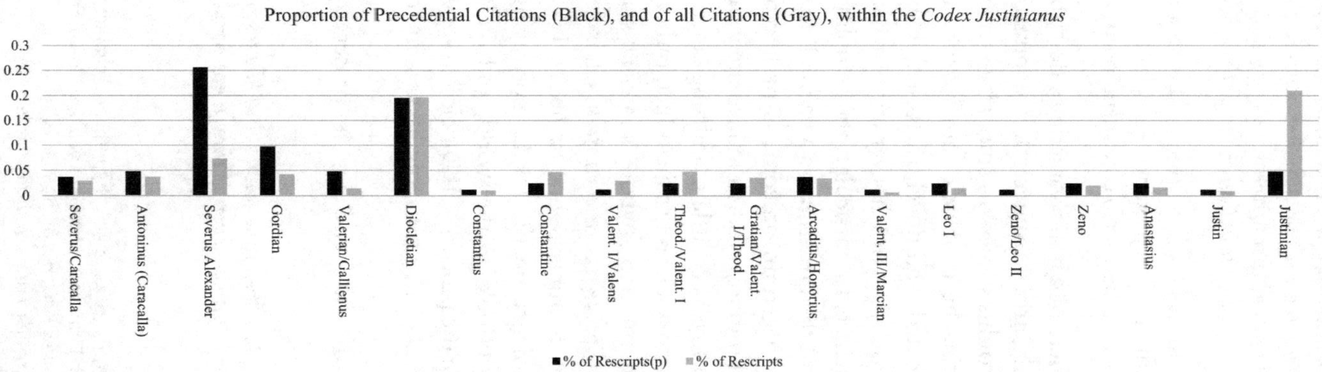

FIGURE 6.1 Precedential citation in the *Codex Justinianus*, again.

If a freedman has either not attained equestrian status [lit. *has not gained the right to wear gold rings*] *or has not been restored to their natal status, the governor of the province shall not only forbid them from serving on their local council, but will exact an appropriate punishment in keeping with the severity of the law.*

(C.10.33.1 [n.d.]) Si libertus uel ius aureorum anulorum adeptus non est uel natalibus suis non restitutus, praeses prouinciae non tantum curiae participare non permittet, sed iuxta legis seueritatem congruenti poena ulciscetur.

This document and others like it are sometimes described as "terse."[20] That judgment partially arises from readers contrasting Diocletianic legal writing with that of his successor, since if we see Diocletian as the precursor to Constantine he can look rather gruff. But Diocletian's brevity masks sophisticated, and novel, rhetorical maneuvers. In some ways the rescripts of Diocletian, or whoever wrote in his name, maintain traditional drafting practice. In particular, they employ the conditional form that had always marked rescripts as a genre. If the facts are as the petitioner claims, then a certain outcome is preferred.[21] Within that form, though, Diocletian innovates. An immediately striking feature of C.10.33.1 is that it employs very little moralizing language. Every word in the constitution describes a legally salient fact, rather than evaluating it; we are given no real guide to anybody's internal state or reasoning. The one exception is *legis seueritatem*. Diocletian attributes a personality trait not to himself but to *lex*.[22] The dryness of the writing focuses its audience on the *lex* by portraying it as the only agent with a specific outlook on the world, and the syntax obscures Diocletian's own role in the process.[23] If Diocletian sounds like a jurist[24] it is because he describes law as a jurist might: as something to interpret, understand, and apply.

Another example of this tendency is preserved at C.8.50.16 (Diocletian, 293):

The sons of a woman who has been ransomed should be restored based on their mother's original freeborn status – even if they were conceived with a slave

[20] Dillon, *Justice*, p. 71.

[21] See Harries, *Law and Empire*, p. 29 on the "hypothetical character" of legal decisions rendered via rescript; also Humfress, *Orthodoxy*, p. 42; Corcoran, *Tetrarchs*, pp. 61–62; Simon, *Konstantinisches Kaiserrecht*, p. 6.

[22] Cf. Cic. *Sull.* 33.92 (referring to the *seueritatem iudicorum*).

[23] See Eich and Eich, "Verlautbarungsstil," pp. 77–78.

[24] Dillon, *Justice*, p. 68.

during her period of captivity – according to those judgments which have benignly pleased [i.e. according to benign imperial judgments].

Commercio redemptae filios, licet ex seruo medio susceptos tempore, origini ingenuitatis matris iuxta ea quae benigne placuerunt reddi conuenit.

Diocletian once more explains how a lower official should resolve a specific fact pattern, with the conditional nature of the judgment implicit in *redemptae* but the structure otherwise unchanged. Again, the language is utilitarian and dry despite the strong emotional charge of C.8.50.16's facts. The rescript's laconic participial phrases suggest that the *redempta* in question has been kidnapped, enslaved, and sexually exploited, and freeborn people (*ingenui*) who "unjustly" suffered the depredations of Roman slavery appear in other sources as figures of pity.[25] Not so here. Diocletian rules the way a sympathetic listener might, but he does not describe himself as sympathetic; compare C.4.55.4 (224), in which Severus Alexander begins his reply to a petitioner alleging that he was kidnapped and sold into slavery with "I am moved" (*moueor*).[26] Once again only one word in Diocletian's rescript bears any ethical charge: *benigne*. The goodness inherent in the designation *benignus*[27] is attributed to the unnamed judgments (*ea*) of unnamed emperors (implied by the use of *placuerunt* as a verb of decision). The emotional valence of C.10.33.1 and C.8.50.16 differs, but they are identical in how they represent Diocletian's reasoning and the broader universe of legal authorities within which – not above which – he works.

Another striking feature of these paired *rescripta* is that they represent imperial decisionmaking as effectively coterminous with law. Diocletian treats an unnamed *lex* identically to an unnamed *id quod placuit*, not only in how they affect the world but in how they affect him. This treatment is one more way in which imperial writing came to resemble that of the Severan jurists. Rather than treating imperial citation as an opportunity to commemorate an earlier emperor or to rhetorically connect past and present, Diocletian folds

25 Richlin, *Slave Theater*, pp. 357–66; Stewart, *Plautus and Roman Slavery*, pp. 132–55; McCarthy, *Art of Authority*, p. 14.

26 Garrido, "Curious Case," pp. 358–60; also Evans-Grubbs, "Between Slavery and Freedom," pp. 53–55.

27 *TLL* 2.1901.57–1904.81.

earlier imperial judgment into an overarching, determinative, and knowable law.

This tendency might explain another puzzling feature of Diocletianic rescripts. As Babusiaux notes, Diocletian's legal program engages closely with juristic writing.[28] For example, C.9.22.11 (Diocletian, 287) cites the opinion of Paul as dispositive.

If a suit for money has been delegated to petty judges, hearings about the reliability of documents should be held before those same judges according to a response of Paul, a most prudent man.

Si lis pecuniaria apud pedaneos iudices remissa est, etiam de fide instrumenti ciuiliter apud eos iuxta responsum uiri prudentissimi Pauli requiretur.

We can likely attribute some of this engagement to particular features of Diocletian's *consilium*, since two major jurists from that time (Hermogenianus and Arcadius Charisius) worked for Diocletian and probably helped compose his replies.[29] But it also reflects a broader shift in how the emperor worked within Roman legality. These clarifying, isagogic statements participate in a juristic tradition; they do what juristic texts had historically done, which may explain why they treat jurists like their generic forebears.[30] If unidentified *ea quae benigne placuerunt* operate as a sovereign law, jurists like the *uir prudentissimus* Paul operate as the authorities which help Diocletian interpret that law.

Of course, Diocletian did more than simply interpret the law. Diocletianic "legislation" (by which I mean explicit changes to the legal system, issued autonomously and not in a response to a particular query) adopted a different rhetorical strategy while maintaining some of the tendencies already discussed. Consider the single best-known piece of Diocletianic legislation, the Edict of Maximum Prices. Lactantius describes the edict as a miserable failure (*de. mort. pers.* 7), and Corcoran rightly notes the lack of evidence for active compliance.[31] But the edict – particularly its preface – is nevertheless an example of what MacMullen has called "hortatory legislation"; it imagines the empire it governs as a "single, indivisible

[28] Babusiaux, "Zitate," pp. 255–58. [29] Liebs, *Hofjuristen*, pp. 83–86.

[30] See Corcoran, *Tetrarchs*, p. 49 ("[rescripts] are, in effect, part of the system of *responsa prudentium* carried to its extreme.").

[31] *Ibid.*, p. 233 ("[T]he measure was rescinded (or simply ignored), and … the epigraphic record was left as a testimony of its failure.").

whole" and entreats it to virtue.[32] The edict's elevated language calls its audience to participate in a shared endeavor, while defining and justifying that endeavor with reference to law. Diocletian and his fellow tetrarchs claim that

We felt a limit had to be set in order that, when some shortage occurred – may the gods prevent it! – greed, which previously could not be constrained from raging with its peculiar intensity as if across scattered fields, might be held in check by the limits of our statute and the boundaries of a moderative law.

(para. 8) sed modum statuendum esse censuimus, ut, cum uis aliqua caritatis emergeret – quod dii omen auerterent – auaritia, quae uelut campis quadam inmensitate diffusis teneri non poter<at>, statuti nostri finibus et moderaturae legis terminis stringeretur.

Later in the same document, Diocletian justifies the harshness of the edict by referencing past law.

Since it is clear that our ancestors considered it a basis for legislation that audacity be constrained by the imposition of fear ... we decree that if anyone should set their daring against the form of this statute they should undergo capital sanction.

(para. 9) quia igitur et apud maiores nostros hanc ferendarum legum constat fuisse rationem, ut praescripto metu conpesceretur audacia ... placet, ut, si quis contra formam statuti huius conixus fuerit audentia, capitali periculo subiugetur.

No one would call this terse. The language of the edict is rhetorical and emotionally charged, but the obedience it demands is an obedience to law: to *nostri statutum* and *moderatura lex*, not to *nos*. In practical terms the difference is meaningless, but we can see in the Edict of Prices how the more charged rhetoric of late-antique legislation still imagined law as a distinctive and ethically freighted genre of imperial speech. The edict foregrounds its status as law and demands obedience on that basis. The tetrarchs are not portrayed as legal subjects like Vespasian was, but neither are they lawgiving tyrants; instead, the boundary between emperor and law vanishes entirely. Submitting to the emperor means obeying the law, and vice versa. If Diocletian's rescripts portray the emperor as a guide to the sovereign law, the Edict of Prices shows what it meant for that law to be sovereign over the world.

32 MacMullen, *Response to Crisis*, p. 30; also Eich and Eich, "Verlautbarungsstil," pp. 82–85.

I admit some caution about identifying these texts as "Diocletianic," however. On the one hand they were produced in a collaborative process, and we should understand the "Diocletian" who appears in them as a ceremonial public figure whom the texts themselves help constitute, rather than an actual person whose thinking they serve to commemorate.[33] Collaboration, however, meant something very different in the early fourth century. These texts date from a period in which the Roman empire was at least nominally run by multiple men acting in concert, and that collaboration fit awkwardly with existing rhetorics of imperial legitimation.[34] The most famous example of this collaborative tendency is a tetrarchic sculpture group (Figure 6.2) originally displayed in Byzantium and later removed to Venice. This porphyry tableau shows the tetrarchs literally embracing each other, presenting tetrarchic rule as a joint endeavor rather than control by a single, enlightened sovereign.

It is perhaps not a coincidence, then, that Diocletian described Roman law in such elevated terms. A man who could not easily claim to govern the whole empire instead interpreted a law that did. While earlier emperors like Decius invoked law in a context of dynastic crisis, Diocletian here responds to a more complex challenge of legitimation: an ascendant tetrarchy that was incompatible with earlier traditions of singular, inspired judgment. Even something as florid as the Edict of Prices is impersonal, in ways that fit both the reality of rescript production and the fantasy of collaborative rule.

That florid style outlasted its author. The legalistic bombast of the edict is generally associated with Diocletian's successors, and particularly with Constantine. There are good reasons for that; our Constantinian evidence inclines more strongly towards general law than does that of Diocletian, and Constantine may also have preferred to describe himself in more grandiose terms.[35] That

[33] For this dichotomy see Kantorowicz, *Bodies*, pp. 259–72.

[34] On the tetrarchy as a period of ideological innovation see Carlà-Uhink and Rollinger (eds.), *The Tetrarchy as Ideology*; on collaboration as a cornerstone of emergent tetrarchic political representation see Carlà-Uhink, "Families and Family Relationships."

[35] *Contra* Vernay's early argument ("Changement") that the stylistic evolution of late-antique legal writing was an accident of sourcing (also adopted by Turpin, "Law Codes"), scholars now generally accept a meaningfully new "late-antique style" and

FIGURE 6.2 Tetrarchic statue group. Venice: San Marco Square.[36]

latter trait is not unusual in imperial history but is hard to ignore in Constantinian biography. Ancient biographers like Eusebius highlight Constantine's transformation of the

generally date it to the accession of Constantine. Eich and Eich attribute these stylistic changes to greater centralization of the late-antique state: "Verlautbarungsstil," pp. 98–103. Dillon (*Justice*, pp. 81–89), by contrast, reads the change as primarily aesthetic but dates it to the final years of Diocletian's reign (p. 81: "around 300") rather than the first years of Constantine's.

[36] On this statue group see Kampen, *Family Fictions*, pp. 104–22.

empire,[37] and modern historians take Constantine's extremely idiosyncratic representational program as motivated at least in part by his extremely idiosyncratic self-perception.[38] Even a ruler as strange as Constantine, however, describes himself and his governance in legal terms. The section of the *Codex Theodosianus* that describes the legal function of rescripts – *CTh* 1.2 – preserves several opinions from Constantine on the subject, which describe law in more deferential terms than we might expect from such a transformational figure.[39] For example:

When we are entreated to calm or lessen the rigor of the law in a specific instance it should be noted that rescripts obtained before the edict was posted shall maintain their force, and the former are not invalidated by a later rescript. However, those which are sought after the posting ought to have no precedential force unless they agree with the public laws; for it is right and proper that we alone consider an interpretation that is placed between fairness and law.

(*CTh.* 1.2.3) Vbi rigorem iuris placare aut lenire specialiter exoramur, id obseruetur, ut rescripta ante edictum propositum impetrata suam habeant firmitatem, nec rescripto posteriore derogetur priori. Quae uero postea sunt elicita, nullum robur habeant, nisi consentanea sint legibus publicis; maxime cum inter aequitatem iusque interpositam interpretationem, nobis solis et oporteat et liceat inspicere.[40]

CTh 1.2.3 is not easy to understand, since it balances two different legal principles: a preference for general over specific imperial pronouncements, and a preference for later over earlier documents. It asserts that a specific grant at time X is not superseded by a specific grant at a later date, but is by a general pronouncement issued at that same time. The reason given is that only the emperor is capable of negotiating with law, and even his space for negotiation is limited. While the emperor can carve out a small space within the legal regime

[37] See Barnes, *Constantine and Eusebius*, pp. 265–71. In general, both modern and ancient historians have fit Constantine within existing paradigms of imperial evaluation, while still treating him as an unusual – and rather egoistic – figure. See e.g. *Amm. Marc.* 16.8.12; van Dam, *Revolution of Constantine*, p. 11. For more extensive bibliography on Constantine and his historians see Flower, "Visions of Constantine."

[38] E.g. Lenski, *Cities*, p. 27.

[39] I discuss this section of the *CTh* in more detail *infra* p. 254.

[40] The consular dating for *CTh* 1.2.3 is unclear, but the document was published on December 3 of either 316, 317, or 318. See also Massei, "Citazioni," pp. 443–47.

for other ethical considerations that regime exists regardless, carries its own normative force, and serves as an equal pole with *aequitas* in Constantine's moral universe.

Constantine's pronouncements were not always so modest, and many of his edicts describe him as responsible for his subjects in more messianic and less circumscribed terms. Consider, for example, an *edictum* Constantine issued to "all those in the provinces" (*uniuersos prouinciales*):

If there is anyone, of any place or social station, who believes that they can prove something clearly and convincingly against any of my judges, counts, friends, or palace retainers, specifically that said person seems to have behaved unfairly or unjustly, let them come to me without fear or insecurity, let them appeal to me: I myself will hear everything, I will investigate and if the matter should be proved I will avenge myself. Let him speak safely and with knowledge: if he proves it, as I said, I will avenge myself upon that one who has deceived me up until that point with his feigned integrity. However, that other man, who has proved the matter, I will reward in both goods and rank. Thus may the highest divinity always favor me and keep me unharmed, I hope, with a glorious and flourishing state.

(*CTh* 9.1.4) Si quis est cuiuscumque loci ordinis dignitatis, qui se in quemcumque iudicum comitum amicorum uel palatinorum meorum aliquid ueraciter et manifeste probare posse confidit, quod non integre adque iuste gessisse uideatur, intrepidus et securus accedat, interpellet me: ipse audiam omnia, ipse cognoscam et si fuerit comprobatum, ipse me uindicabo. Dicat, securus et bene sibi conscius dicat: si probauerit, ut dixi, ipse me uindicabo de eo, qui me usque ad hoc tempus simulata integritate deceperit, illum autem, qui hoc prodiderit et comprobauerit, et dignitatibus et rebus augebo. Ita mihi summa diuinitas semper propitia sit et me incolumem praestet, ut cupio, felicissima et florente re publica.

As Dillon rightly notes, *CTh* 9.1.4's elevated language transmutes administrative practices into the realms of apostasy and treason.[41] But Constantine was not the first emperor to issue grandiose legislation, and even this somewhat bathetic example shows Constantine's turn to law. We can see the turn more clearly by comparing *CTh.* 9.1.4 with another piece of "ostentatious legislation"[42] from an earlier period, the *CA*. In the *CA*, Caracalla

[41] Dillon, *Justice*, pp. 165–66.
[42] Schmidt-Hofner, "Ostentatious Legislation," p. 90.

extends citizenship to all free inhabitants of the empire in order to thank the gods for letting him kill his brother Geta.

[Imperator Caesar] Marcus Aurelius Augustus Antoninus [Pius] says: —— rather —— the causes and considerations ——— to [the] immortal gods I may give thanks that [when] the so frightful [ambush occurred] they preserved me. Therefore, thinking that I should be able [on a grand scale and with piety] to make the return which would correspond to their majesty, [if] I were to lead [to the sanctuaries] of our gods [all those presently my people and others too] as often as they enter the ranks of my people, I grant to all those [who throughout] the world [are under my rule] Roman citizenship without the [extras], with [the claim of communities] (on the services of their members) remaining unimpaired. For the [whole population?] ought [———] already to have been included also in the victory. [——my] edict would expand the majesty of the Roman [People . . . .[43]

——— Μᾶ]ρκο̣ς Α̣ὐρήλι[ος . . . .] Ἀ̣ντωνῖνο̣[ς] Ε[ὐσεβὴ]ς v λ̣έγει.
————]Η̣̇ μᾶλλο̣ν ΑΝ[————— τὰ]ς αἰ̣τ̣ὶα̣ς κ[α]ὶ τ̣ο̣[ὺς] λ̣[ογι]σμοὺς̣
——— θ]εοῖς̣ [τοῖ]ς ἀθ̣[αν]άτοις ε̣ὐχ̣α̣ριστήσιαμι, ὅτι τῆ[ς] τ̣οιαύτη[ς]
————]η̣ς̣ με συν[ετ]ή̣ρησαν / Τοιγ̣α̣ρ̣ο̣ῦν ν̣ομ̣ίζω[ν ο]ὕτω με
————]ω̣ς δύ[ν]α̣σθαι τ̣ῇ μεγ̣α̣λ̣ειό̣τητι αὐτῶν τὸ ἱκ̣α̣νὸν ποι
——— ὁσ]άκις ἐ̣ὰν ὑ̣[π]ε̣ι̣σέλ̣θ̣[ωσ]ι̣ν εἰς τοὺς ἐ̣μ̣οὺ̣ς̣ ἀν[θ]ρ̣ώπους
——— τῶ]ν̣ θεῶν συνε̣ι̣σ̣ενέγ[κοι]μι vvv δίδωμι τοῖ[ς σ]υναπα
——— τ]ὴ̣ν ο̣ἰκουμέν̣η̣ν π[ολειτ]είαν Ῥωμαίων, μένοντος
—————]άτων̣ χωρ[ὶς] τῶν [. . .]ειτ̣ικίων vvv Ὀ[φ]είλει [γ]ὰρ τὸ
————————]ν̣ε̣ι̣ν πάντα Α[. . .]Α ἤδη κ[α]ὶ τῇ νίκ̣η ἐνπεριει
———— διάτ]α̣γμα ἐ̣[ξα]π̣λώσ̣ει[ε τὴν] μεγαλειότητα [το]ῦ Ῥωμα[ι]
————————] π̣ε̣ρ̣ὶ τοὺ̣ς [. . . ο]υς γ̣εγεν̣ῆσ̣θαι ἧ̣περ δ[—]
————————]ταλειφ[————]ων τῶ[ν ἐ]κάστης

Like Caracalla, Constantine uses his administrative control over the empire to express his personal relationship to the divine.[44] And like Caracalla, Constantine reframes the Roman world and its workings in terms of his personal welfare. But where Caracalla paints his subjects' engagement with the state in religious terms (referring to them as potential worshippers of the gods whom Caracalla wishes to thank)[45] Constantine's language highlights the administrative and

[43] Reconstruction and translation Oliver's: *Greek Constitutions*, pp. 498–500. See also, however, van Minnen, "Three Edicts?" for a more recent reconstruction.

[44] De Blois, "Taxes or Religion?"; Rowan, *Under Divine Auspices*, pp. 110–63.

[45] See Besson, *L'universalisation*; Imrie, *Caracallan Empire*; Corbo, *Ius philosophia religio*; Ando (ed.), *Citizenship and Empire*; Buraselis, *Θεῖα Δωρεά*.

judicial. His subjects are drawn into his state as litigants and petitioners, and Constantine grants them, literally, a hearing (*ipse audiam omnia*) in order to ensure that their business is handled fairly (*iuste*). Constantine describes his own interests in the stark language of revenge or *uindicatio*, but upon a bureaucracy and not his brother.[46]

That bureaucracy was new. On the one hand we can understand this language as reflecting shifts in the nature of imperial administration, and I discuss those shifts later in this chapter. But the shift in rhetoric is meaningful in its own right. Constantine confronts a state that stands in both subservience and opposition to his rule, composed of unruly subordinates who do something more than merely carry out his will. In *CTh* 9.1.4 Constantine imagines the government as standing outside of him, even as he claims to bring it to heel, and in doing so he shows how charismatic rulers might adapt their speech to a new administrative landscape.

Those changes did not begin with Constantine, or even with the tetrarchy. We have already seen how the Severan jurists told stories of a world in which state power was governed by something other than an emperor acting on his own. That imaginary became reality in the turbulent third century, and even as Constantine inaugurated a radically new account of imperial sovereignty he did not put the genie back in the bottle. Roman legal writing had come to describe state power as residing in institutional frameworks outside of the emperor's mind, and in Constantine's rhetoric those frameworks continued to operate according to their own logic.

Constantine portrays himself as taming and regularizing these unruly institutions, with new techniques of supervision and control. Some of these techniques have obvious implications – Constantine created a vastly more regularized[47] and predictable mechanism for appeal, which helped to "legalize" lower-level decisionmaking.[48] But other changes were more subtle. Constantine's administrative project

[46] Eich and Eich, "Verlautbarungsstil," p. 88 ("Der neue Stil löste sich von der Fixierung auf die Herrscherperson und thematisierte die Inhalte der kaiserlichen Regierungstätigkeit.").

[47] On the increasing regularization of legal rulings at this time see MacMullen, "Savagery."

[48] Dillon, *Justice*, pp. 214–50; Humfress, *Orthodoxy*, pp. 50–51; Harries, *Law and Empire*, pp. 110–13.

presumed that officials would have access to the materials they needed in order to make correct decisions. Those materials might include not only general laws – issued rarely and issued widely – but also statements of legal principle that were expressed in the more voluminous imperial correspondence. This supervisory project relied upon different strategies for recording and organizing legal decisions, but those strategies were not new; codifiers in this period took old techniques for collecting and indexing juristic writing and adapted them to imperial letters. In doing so, they showed how late-antique legality had formed itself along juristic lines.

Codification: Indexing Sovereignty

Law arises from, and changes with, technology. The storytelling inherent to Roman legal writing, both the tales of woe that mark its petitions and the tales of reason and mercy that mark its responses, relied on mechanisms for transmitting information. Bryen's history of Egyptian petitions reminds us that these mechanisms evolve; the shift from *subscriptiones* – short responses attached to the original petition – to more formal *rescripta* allowed for greater commemoration of imperial thinking at the expense of recording subjects' complaints.[49] As a result of that change, the archive of *rescripta* that goes roughly from Hadrian to Diocletian helps us track shifts in how emperors represented themselves as they solved legal problems.

That archive was not only meant for historians. Other actors within the Roman legal system – litigants, advocates, and adjudicators – needed to know the law and thus needed access to records of imperial decisionmaking. It is nightmarishly difficult to reconstruct those records and how they changed over the course of the empire, but we can see some important shifts in archival practice. I here discuss the rise of subject-matter organization in archives of imperial correspondence over the third century, and how that organizational technique facilitated bureaucratic approaches to imperial legal writing. Subject-matter organization began as a feature of juristic treatises, and was thus already to hand for compilers who wished to reimagine the imperial archive; the resulting *codices* present imperial rescripts in

[49] Bryen, *Violence*, p. 207.

forms that were already familiar to readers of jurists, and thus subtly elide differences between the two sources of legal authority.

While no surviving ancient source explicitly discusses the organization of imperial archives, there is strong circumstantial evidence suggesting a chronological schema. Four different ancient legal sources refer to imperial responses, and particularly responses from Marcus Aurelius, being preserved in *semestribus* or *semenstribus*. Tryphoninus claims that a "constitution of the deified Marcus is recorded in the *semestribus*" (D.2.14.46, Disputationes: *in semestribus relata est constitutio diui Marci*), Scaevola summarizes what "the deified Marcus held in the *semenstribus*" (D.18.7.10, Digesta: *diuus Marcus ... in semenstribus constituit*), and Ulpian cites "a rescript in the *semenstribus* addressed to the Vibii Victorinus and Soter" (D.29.2.12, ad Edictum: *est in semenstribus Vibiis Soteri et Victorino rescriptum*). The *Institutes* of Justinian also reference a rescript of Marcus preserved in the *semestribus*: "The deified Marcus wrote in the *semestribus* that ministers of the fisc can be excused from guardianship duties during the period of their administration" (25.1: *Item diuus Marcus in semestribus rescripsit eum, qui res fisci administrat, a tutela uel cura quamdiu administrat excusari posse*).

These are our only surviving explicit references to official collections of Classical rescripts. While the term they use, *seme(n)stria*, is never defined it clearly means something like "six-monthers": compare Suetonius referencing Nero's "six-month consulships" or *consulatus ... semenstres* at *Nero* 14.[50] This naming convention suggests that imperial legal writing was stored in collections covering specific spans of time: namely, six months. A researcher looking for a specific document in those collections might need to check all *seme(n)stria* from the regnal period of a particular authority, unless they knew the date of issuance.[51]

It is not explicit in these texts how long the *seme(n)stria* system lasted. While writers as late as Justinian contemplate access to the

[50] The context makes even clearer that *semenstres* denotes a span of time. *Consulatus quattuor gessit: primum bimenstrem, secundum et novissimum semenstres, tertium quadrimenstrem*.

[51] Circumstantial evidence suggests that the individual responses contained with any given *seme(n)ster* were organized nonchronologically, and likely by name; I plan to argue this at greater length elsewhere, but that organizational scheme would make the *seme(n)stria* dramatically more "user-friendly" than they would initially appear.

seme(n)stria, they go there to get rescripts of Marcus Aurelius. No later emperor can be placed in these particular compilations. That said, we can see clues to the organization of rescripts in Severan archival practice, and those clues suggest that chronological ordering persisted. As I mentioned in Chapter 4, rescripts survive under the name of Severus Alexander that were almost certainly issued under Elagabalus. The first of these (C.9.1.3, promulgated on February 3 of 222) predates Alexander's accession by over a month. It is striking that all of these relabeled rescripts date to 222; Alexander was named *Caesar* in June of 221 according to the *Feriale Duranum*, but rescripts only begin to be attributed to him in the calendar year in which he became sole ruler.[52]

We can thus presume that calendar years still mattered. Some kind of sharp break separates June of 221 (in which Alexander took on a visible role in government) from March of 222 (in which that role became the one customarily commemorated in rescript headings), but does not separate February and March of 222. The likeliest explanation is that rescripts from late 221 were stored in an entirely Elagabalic collection of correspondence, which was suppressed; those from early 222 were included in a collection attributed to Severus Alexander. I remain agnostic as to whether this collection remained biannual and accordingly whether the *seme(n)stria* system outlived Marcus, but in either case rescripts would have been organized within imperial archives based on their date of issuance or promulgation.

These archives were not the only ones that existed. We know of various concurrent archival practices, which followed their own logics and served different scholarly or practical ends. Individual petitioners kept responses that they had received or that might be particularly helpful for their own engagements with Roman authority,[53] towns might archive favorable responses via inscription,[54] and rescripts were collated on papyri for use in court or in legal training.[55] It

[52] A translation of the *Feriale*, which is catalogued at *P. Dura* 54, is available at Hekster and Zair, *Rome and its Empire*, pp. 127–29; the only long-form treatment of the papyrus remains Reeves, "The 'Feriale Duranum.'"

[53] On this archival practice see Kelly, *Social Control*, pp. 20–21.

[54] There are too many examples of this phenomenon to count, but consider *SEG* 12.759, on which see Williams, "Rhetoricians."

[55] See Ando, *Ideology*, pp. 377–78; Katzoff, "Precedents," pp. 282–89.

would not be quite fair to call this collation "subject-matter organization," if that term refers to the schemata we see in juristic texts or later compilations. But these archives let their users see (and perhaps more importantly demonstrate) at a glance what emperors had said over a long span of time about a particular place or person, rather than what they had said on a wide range of topics over a particular period of time. It is hardly surprising that litigants and advocates would organize imperial rescripts differently than a central archivist, but the difference shows us the implications of different methods of organizing, and the plurality of organizational practices to which imperial writing might be subjected.

Our first example of "subject-matter organization" of imperial rescripts, at least in the sense I use it here, dates from the late second century CE. Around the year 170, the jurist Papirius Iustus published *On the Constitutions* (*de constitutionibus*), which collected writings of the Deified Brothers and of Marcus Aurelius and summarized them without commentary.[56] Relatively little of *de constitutionibus* survives. Only eighteen fragments of it appear in the *Digest*,[57] perhaps because the compilers of the *Corpus Iuris Ciuilis* found it a strange generic fit with the more jurisprudential commentaries that make up the bulk of that work. But *de constitutionibus* now appears as a remarkable experiment, not least because of its structure. The twenty books of Iustus were organized like a juristic commentary,[58] with different rescripts grouped together according to the area of law they addressed.[59]

[56] *EDRL* 617.

[57] Following Lenel's order (*PG*, *Papirius Iustus* 1–18), as well as that of Licandro and Palazzolo (*Libri XX de constitutionibus*, pp. 110–23), the fragments survive at D.8.2.14, D.8.3.17, D.18.1.71, D.48.12.3, D.42.5.30, D.42.7.4, D.48.16.18, D.49.1.21, D.39.4.7, D.42.1.35, D.50.1.38, D.50.2.13, D.2.14.37, D.50.8.11, D.50.8.12, D.50.8.13, D.50.12.13, and D.2.14.60.

[58] Licandro and Palazzolo, *Libri XX de constitutionibus*, p. 109.

[59] Because so little of *de constitutionibus* survives, there have been debates for some time about its internal organization. Earlier historians, particularly Berger (PWRE XVIII.3.1061) and Scarlata Fazio ("Osservazioni," p. 418), argued that the text had to have been chronologically organized given the nature of archives at the time. Huschke ("Codex," p. 328) went so far as to claim that *de constitutionibus* was simply another term for the *seme(n)stria*; Wenger (*Quellen*, p. 440 n. 144) dismisses the possibility but acknowledges that Papirius likely relied upon chancery publications like the *seme(n)stria* in his own work. Volterra ("L'ouvrage," pp. 219–22) convincingly falsifies Huschke's hypothesis and shows that different books of the *de*

The implications of this organizational shift are hard to overstate. *De constitutionibus* imagines a wholly different sort of reader, engaged in a wholly different sort of project. It groups together documents that might have been produced years apart, so that a reader can easily see what Marcus and Verus had said on a particular legal topic. For example, it is clear from surviving quotations that the second book of *de constiutionibus* contained a variety of constitutions on the administration of cities outside Rome.[60] This kind of reading had long been possible for consumers of scholarly commentaries about law, and the first "systematic" commentary on Roman law is traditionally attributed to the Republican jurist Quintus Mucius Scaevola.[61] But imperial replies had previously existed outside of that system, as singular interventions from above. The only framework into which they could be fit was that of a timeline, or an archive of correspondence; the *seme(n)stria* and their organization imagine a vision of imperial rescripts as discrete actions and not contributions to a systematized legal order. *De constitutionibus* imagines rescripts as law.[62]

More precisely, *de constitutionibus* imagines some rescripts as law. Papirius Iustus almost certainly published while Marcus Aurelius was still alive, and only included rescripts from Marcus' reign (including his tenure with Verus as one of the Deified Brothers). This editorial decision is not necessarily surprising; while imperial decisions had outlived their deciders since Titus, the Edict of Titus clearly contemplates those decisions being cited by those directly affected. By contrast Papirius Iustus writes for an audience looking to the *constitutiones* for abstract legal principles, and holding one emperor to another's general claims might seem a little more risky. The impression given by Iustus' caution, however, is that of an imperial

constitutionibus contained rescripts on different subjects. For a more recent overview of the debate see Licandro and Palazzolo, *Libri XX de constitutionibus*, pp. 79–86.

60 *Ibid.*, p. 82. Scarlata Fazio ("Osservazioni," pp. 415–17) is correct to doubt Lenel's equation of this area of law with the *ius municipale*, but overly formalistic in denying Book 2's clear focus on questions of city governance.

61 D.1.2.2.41 (Pomponius, Enchiridion); see also Schulz, *Roman Legal Science*, pp. 62–64; *Principles*, p. 53. On more recent receptions of Scaevola see Tuori, "Myth."

62 See Mantovani, *Les jurists écrivains*, pp. 21–23 on the inherently legal quality of subject-matter organization; see also Wieacker, *Textstufen*, p. 96 (taking Papirius Iustus as part of "die damals beginnende Annäherung des Ius an des Kaiserrecht").

law that still had to reform itself upon the death of any given sovereign. Rome had laws that lasted, but they came from her traditional organs of legal order and not from the more powerful, but less reliable, mechanics of the imperial reply.

Until Diocletian. It is only in the tetrarchy that we see a multiauthorial, subject-matter-organized collection of imperial rescripts: the *Codex Gregorianus*. The *Codex Gregorianus* contained a selection of imperial rescripts dating from the time of Hadrian until the late third century,[63] organized into *tituli* based on subject matter.[64] Little is known about the eponymous codifier. Mommsen suggested that he was a teacher of law in Beirut,[65] but Honoré argued that he served in Diocletian's chancery.[66]

It is clear, however, that the *Codex Gregorianus* was well received. Within a few years of its publication, the *magister libellorum* (Minister of Correspondence) Hermogenianus began collecting rescripts issued by Diocletian's court for publication in the form of the *Codex Hermogenianus*.[67] We know that Gregori(an)us'[68] work was not suppressed, and Diocletian condoning (if not necessarily ordering) Hermogenianus' subsequent project further indicates imperial support.[69]

63 The latest rescripts we can safely assume to come down to us via the *Codex Gregorianus* survive at C.7.43.10 and C.9.41.12, both promulgated on May 13 of 291. However, a few constitutions from late as 302 are also attributed to the work. See Dillon, *Justice*, pp. 27–28; Liebs, *Spätantiken Italien*, p. 37.

64 Sperandio, *Codex Gregorianus*, pp. 307–25; Schulz, *Principles*, p. 55.

65 Mommsen, "Heimath," p. 141.

66 Honoré, *Emperors and Lawyers*, pp. 163–81; see also Liebs, *Hofjuristen*, pp. 85–86; *Hermogenians Iuris epitome*. Sperandio gives a useful overview of the debates at *Codex Gregorianus*, pp. 10–13, but resolves them best at p. 215: "In effete, la 'carriera' di *Gregorianus* è completamente avvolta nel mistero."

67 Corcoran notes that rescripts originally collected in the *Codex Hermogenianus* have unusual headings within the *Codex Justinianus*; *Tetrarchs*, p. 28. These rescripts are often marked as "given" (*D*, for *datum*) or "signed" (*S*, for *subscriptum*) rather than "posted" (*PP*, for *praepositum*) on a specific date. This makes clear that Hermogenianus was collecting these rescripts from the place in which they were composed, rather than the locations in which they were posted.

68 Both *Gregorius* and *Gregorianus* appear in ancient sources to describe the author of the *codex*; see Sperandio, *Codex Gregorianus*, pp. 209–12.

69 Corcoran (*Tetrarchs*, p. 28) and Simon (*Konstantinisches Kaiserrecht*, p. 10 n. 49) both discuss the compiler's close proximity to imperial archives. Harries notes that Hermogenian was "almost certainly one of Diocletian's lawyers"; *Law and Empire*, p. 15. See also Chastagnol, "Un nouveau préfet."

These two *codices*[70] function differently. The *Codex Hermogenianus*, which collects tetrarchic rescripts issued over a specific period of time, could be understood as a newer version of Papirius Iustus' compilatory project.[71] But the *Gregorianus* is something else entirely. Its organization mixes the legal communications of a living sovereign with those of the dead and presents them both as similarly authoritative.[72] As long as the emperor who made a given claim about the law was well remembered, his opinions seem to hold the same weight as any other emperor's. The *Codex Gregorianus* presented its reader with an "imperial law" that outlived a given sovereign the same way that other forms of Roman law did, and organized that law into *tituli* offering a synchronic view of the *sacrae constitutiones* on a given topic. While the *Codex Gregorianus* made its reader aware of individual imperial authors in its headings (which survive in the *Codex Justinianus*), its structure would have been suboptimal for any reader who was particularly concerned with who said what, or when.

The importance of that structure is perhaps best demonstrated by analogy. Modern historians of Roman law have access to two compilations of its constitutive documents, organized according to two different schemata. The ancient compilations (and modern editions of those ancient compilations) generally follow the example of *de constitutionibus* or the *Codex Gregorianus*, or for that matter of juristic treatises; their authorities are organized into titles by subject matter. Thus the *Digest* as edited by Mommsen and Krüger, the Theodosian Code edited by Mommsen and Meyer, or the *Codex Justinianus* edited by Frier et al. make it easy to see all of the different claims made about, say, "farmers of either the appropriate census class or the colonate" (*de agricolis censitis uel colonis*) within a manageable page range.[73] On the

[70] Ancient sources are not unanimous in referring to the Gregorianic compilation as a *codex*: see e.g. *Cons.* 9.8; *AV* 2.7. Nevertheless, scholars have assumed since Krüger ("Verwendung," pp. 81–82) that the text was published in *codex* form (i.e. as something like a recognizable bound book, and not a scroll). I agree, not least because the subject-matter organization of the *Gregorianus* contemplates a reading practice that (as noted by Mantovani, *Les juristes écrivains*, pp. 40–41) would be far more difficult if performed on a scroll. Nevertheless, my argument does not depend on the *CTh*'s understanding of this material as a *codex* being contemporary or widely shared.

[71] On the internal organization of the *Codex Hermogenianus* see Cenderelli, *Ricerche sul codex Hermogenianus*, pp. 137–40.

[72] See Liebs, *Spätantiken Italien*, pp. 134–37.

[73] C.11.48, on pp. 2726–45 of the Frier *Codex*.

other hand, modern compilations known as *palingenesiai* (like Lenel's *Palingenesia iuris ciuilis*, or the "*palingenesia* of third–century imperial rescripts"[74] that accompanies the 1994 edition of Honoré's *Emperors and Lawyers*) rearrange the authorities found in the ancient sources by author and date. Thus the 1960 edition of Lenel's *Palingenesia* collects all surviving juristic material from Papirius Iustus at the page range I.947–51, and Honoré collects the surviving rescripts of Decius at entries 1296–1303 of his own compilation.

Historians use both versions of these texts, for different purposes. If I want to quickly check "the law" of a given topic I turn to Mommsen and Krüger; for example, when researching the first chapter of this book I found Ulpian's treatment of the Augustan marriage legislation in the fifth title of the forty-eighth book of that document. By contrast, if I want to see how Gordian writes, or where Diocletian was in 293–294 CE, or what language Papinian specifically uses to cite imperial rescripts, those corpora exist in the *palingenesiai.* The *palingenesiai* show me what a given person thought and said, and thus render legal texts legible as sources of traditional historical knowledge.[75] By contrast the *codices* juxtapose the thoughts and sayings of different people and thus seem to give instruction themselves, while giving *to* their instructions the generalizing character that we associate with positivistic legal order.[76]

We can thus see in these evolving codification practices an evolving notion of what rescripts were and did. The *seme(n)stria*, like *palingenesiai*, form a chronicle of an emperor's actions; they imagine a reader who wants to know what Marcus Aurelius was doing, or who he was talking with, at a given time. *De constitutionibus* is a guide to an emperor's thinking; it imagines a reader who wants to know what "the constitutions" say about a particular topic, but who takes "the constitutions" as a reflection of Marcus Aurelius' understanding of the Roman state rather than of any essential or transdynastic quality that said state might possess. By contrast, the *Codex Gregorianus* does not aim to archive the ideas of a given emperor, but those of the bureaucracy within which emperors fit and for which they speak.

[74] Honoré, *Emperors and Lawyers*, pp. xiv–xvii.

[75] See Coriat, "Palingénésie," pp. 874–76 on how palingenetic arrangements of Roman legal texts facilitate historical research.

[76] See Hart, *Concept*, pp. 21–22; Johnston, "Interpretation," pp. 152–53.

That impersonality is central to our understanding of what Roman law is. One of the reasons why the Severan jurists seemed to struggle with the rescript system in their work is that it fit poorly with the principled, systematic *ius* they preferred. But the rescript system evolved to match that juristic vision, as its pronouncements came to be collected in anthologies and looked at as evidence of a law that could outlive their lawgivers. This bureaucratic account of Roman legality was not quite the same as that of Ulpian and his fellow priests, but it shared many of the characteristics we now see as fundamental to both. In particular, both accounts placed their authority in a technical, regularized, *tricky* law. It is only in the fourth century and beyond that we begin to see the broader changes in employment, education, and training that could make Roman law, as we understand it today, actually work.

How to Build a *Rechtsstaat* Without Really Trying

An important thing to understand about Roman law is that it is hard to understand. Even leaving aside the tendency of jurists to home in on edge cases,[77] settled doctrine on common issues like testamentary succession could be monstrously complex.[78] Complexity is not unfamiliar to students or practitioners of modern legal systems, but we sometimes take for granted the infrastructure that accompanies it and that allows citizens to gain the benefits of legal expertise without putting in the effort to acquire it for themselves (i.e. the existence of relatively affordable and easy-to-find legal counsel, or of legally trained adjudicators employed by the state). Without that infrastructure, the relationship between law and society is necessarily more contingent. While legal subjects might resolve their conflicts in ways that are informed by legal norms in a broad sense, those resolutions will not necessarily exhibit the goods that a given legal culture values or that motivate its particular rules.

That infrastructural necessity makes Classical legal texts, and especially juristic texts, difficult to apply in the real world. When Ulpian claims that the "logic of the law" supports a judge ruling in a particular way, he seems to imagine a judge with much more training (or access to much more training) than most adjudicators of his own

[77] See Schulz, *Roman Legal Science*, pp. 223–26. [78] As shown by, e.g. D.28.

time. In the late third and fourth centuries, however, Roman administration caught up to Roman law. The changes in Roman governmental practice that marked this period not only changed the face of Roman power but also allowed the technical legality of the jurists to map more closely onto potential legal outcomes.

Those changes themselves are well known and often discussed in summary. For example, Jones' *The Later Roman Empire* refers to the late-antique civil service as an "elaborate centralized machine,"[79] and Brown's *The Making of Late Antiquity* describes the period as marking a change from "'soft' to 'hard' government."[80] What they mean is that the state payroll exploded. The number of professional administrators serving within the imperial apparatus expands approximately threefold between the early Principate and the early sixth century.[81] That payroll also took on a more centralized and hierarchical form than it had previously had. The *Notitia Dignitarum* (*ND*), a roster of offices organized by rank and compensation developed sometime around the end of the fourth century, lists an elaborate, ordered procession of officials from supraprovincial *uicarii* and prefects down to thirty-five separate *procuratores* managing individual production sites and linked to particular cities.[82] It is difficult to imagine such a document applying to the whole Roman empire before this time; ground-level administration under the Principate was comparatively light and coexisted with earlier local forms of control.[83]

These changes can be sited with some confidence after the tetrarchic period, and Constantine in particular likely oversaw a massive increase in the number and specialization of imperial officials. For example,

79 Jones, *The Later Roman Empire*, p. I.406. 80 Brown, *Making*, p. 48.

81 Kelly, *Ruling*, pp. 110–11; for numbers Jones, *The Later Roman Empire*, pp. III.341–42.

82 The *ND* was first published at Böcking (ed.), *Notitia dignitatum*, with the now-standard edition being Seeck (ed.), *Notitia dignitatum*. Bury ("The Notitia Dignitatum") notes the *ND*'s fundamentally internal character and argues that the *ND* was meant to help the Roman bureaucracy organize itself and not to represent that bureaucracy for other audiences. For more recent overviews of the *ND*'s contents and structure see Clemente, "L'immagine"; *La Notitia Dignitatum*; Kulikowski, "Historical Source"; Brennan, "The *Notitia Dignitatum*"; "The User's Guide"; Demougeot, "La Notitia dignitatum." On the greater trend towards toward hierarchization and ordering in late-antique social life see Kulikowski, "Ordo."

83 See Saller, *Personal Patronage*; for the persistence of pre-Roman institutions and hierarchies within the empire see Dench, *Cultures*; Woolf, *Becoming Roman*.

Constantine created a new quaestorship which would later be come to known as the *Sacri Palatii* (Quaestorship of the Sacred Palace), intended to oversee the production of legal documents.[84] Comparing the *quaestor Sacri Palatii* to his predecessors shows how this administrative shift could simultaneously reflect and implement a newer understanding of imperial legality. On the one hand, quaestors predated emperors and had historically been understood as holding a senatorial position. By granting that particular name to an imperial appointee, Constantine further appropriated traditional Roman governance into the imperial administrative apparatus.[85] On the other hand, the actual job of the *quaestor Sacri Palatii* combined responsibilities of previous officials and in doing so demonstrated the increasing salience of law as a generic marker for imperial correspondence. The post-Hadrianic rescript system divided these responsibilities among a number of different actors, depending on the audience for any particular document and the language in which it was written; placing all of these different forms of document production under one official, and combining them with other forms of public address, suggests that Constantine understood the normative force of imperial writing to be more important than the particularities of correspondence that had differentiated earlier bureaucrats.[86]

This burgeoning "administrative state" changed what litigants could expect. Under the earlier rescript system, litigants were responsible for delivering petitions to the emperor through his relatively small cadre of officials. Those who lacked the connections to get a document into his hands, or the wherewithal to personally visit the imperial court, could only access imperial adjudication if the emperor happened to be in

84 Zos. 5.32.6. Harries ("The Roman Imperial Quaestor," p. 148) doubts Zosimus and places the development of the quaestorship slightly later, under Constantius II; also *Law and Empire*, pp. 45–47. On selection of *quaestores* Honoré (*Tribonian*, p. 201) emphasizes legal expertise, but see Matthews, *Laying Down the Law*, pp. 74, 176–79 (noting that *quaestores* were more reliably skilled in literary and rhetorical writing than they were in Roman legal rules). Faro, "Il questore imperiale" gives earlier bibliography on the post-Constantinian quaestorship.

85 See Harries, "The Roman Imperial Quaestor," p. 154 ("[T]he main difference between the new-style imperial quaestorian communicators and their senatorial predecessors was that the new quaestors were based at court and their careers were not tied to the senatorial cursus of the Roman senators at Rome."); Faro, "Il questore imperiale," pp. 133–34.

86 See Harries, "The Roman Imperial Quaestor," p. 149.

town.[87] By contrast, by the time of the emperor Julian (r. 361–363) access to the imperial chancery was determined less by connections than by price. A Julianic inscription, found in modern Thamugadi, lays out an elaborate fee schedule for judicial services, promising a hearing to anyone who could manage the fees.[88] Those fees were substantial; serving a defendant, for example, cost the equivalent of anywhere between ten and two hundred gallons of wheat depending on their proximity to the city center. Accordingly, the Thamugadi inscription describes a legal system that was no paragon of "access to justice."[89] But the greater volume of hierarchized officials administering the late-antique state, and the greater regularization of procedures for bringing problems to their attention, made it easier for litigants to get their cases heard and – importantly – to get those verdicts reviewed than had previously been the case.

The officials hearing these cases and appeals, moreover, had access to more regularized legal training. This period likely saw a dramatic expansion in the number and size of elite law schools.[90] The best-known school of Roman law existed in Beirut; Diocletian and Maximian formally exempted Beirut law students from civic obligations, and the local rhetorician Libanius complained in the 380s that his best students were abandoning oratory for law.[91] But other schools enter the record over the course of this period, most prominently at Constantinople and Rome.[92] Similarly, a school-text

87 Millar, *Emperor*, pp. 36–38. The authoritative treatment of the mechanics of the rescript system remains Williams, "Procedure."

88 On the impact of this shift see Kelly, *Ruling*, p. 108 ("The proclamation of a carefully graded schedule of fees for administrative services represents a shift in the pattern of power within an ancient Mediterranean society in which access to government and its advantages was traditionally determined by the personal influence exercised by friends, family, and their connections."). On the Thamugadi inscription itself see Chastagnol, *Timgad*, pp. 75–78.

89 This term is most closely associated with the work of Rhode: e.g. *Access*, pp. 34–35.

90 Harries, "Legal Education," pp. 160–62; Riggsby, "Roman Legal Education," pp. 449–50.

91 First attested in the 230s CE, when Gregory Thaumaturgus studied law there before becoming a bishop: see *Panegyricus in Originem* 5. Diocletian's recognition of the students at Beirut survives at C.10.50.1 [n.d.]. Libanius' complaint: *ep.* 652. For scholarly surveys of the literature for legal education in Beirut see Schuol, "Rechtsschule"; Hall, *Roman Berytus*, pp. 195–220.

92 Our best evidence for the importance of the Constantinopolitan law school is Justinianic (*Omnem* 9), but *CTh* 14.9.3pr. shows that one was in business (and

based on Gaius' *Institutes*, known as the *Fragments of Autun* and dated to around 300 by Wibier, suggests that legal education was also available in the late-antique west.[93]

This evidence differs from our sources for earlier forms of legal education (sketchy as they are), which imply a more informal process of apprenticeship and mentoring.[94] In contrast to the *Digest* and its implicit narrative of post-Severan collapse, these educational innovations suggest vastly increased demand for legal training among late-antique Romans and show how that demand might have been met. The more professionalized bureaucracy that late-antique sources contemplate could apply complicated legal concepts better, and more regularly. For example, the late fourth-century historian Ammianus Marcellinus describes (and attacks) the legal profession of his own time as able to procure desired outcomes for paying clients due to practitioners' mastery of arcane legal doctrine.

But now are plain to see, in all of the eastern lands, violent and rapacious sorts of men who fly through every forum and ambush wealthy houses; like the dogs of Crete or Sparta, by cleverly tracing footprints they come to the very bedrooms of their lawsuits.

...

Second [after forensic orators] *is the type of men who profess knowledge of the law, which the disagreements of statutes, fighting amongst themselves, have destroyed; these men, silent as if from chains at the mouth, rival their own shadows for eternal silence. Like readers of horoscopes, or interpreters of the Sybilline Oracles, they set their solemn faces to a gloomy expression and offer up their yawns for sale. They speak of Trebatius and Cascellius and Alfenus in order to seem more experienced in law, and of the long-lost laws of the Aurunci and Sicani, buried long ago with Evander's mother. Even if you tell them you've*

large enough to require dedicated lecturing space) in 425. Rome's law school was important enough to require a copy of the *Corpus Iuris Ciuilis*: *Omnem* 7; Harries, "Legal Education," p. 161. Other law schools are attested in the eastern empire, even if they were somewhat less prominent. *Omnem* 9 itself mentions schools at Caesarea and Alexandria, and Libanius briefly refers to a chair of Roman law at Antioch (*ep.* 209; see also Liebeschuetz, *Antioch*, pp. 242–43).

[93] Wibier, "Legal Culture in Gaul," pp. 473–75; "Realpolitik," pp. 89–93. The *Fragments* were first published at Chatelain, "Fragments de Droit Antéjustinien"; for more recent treatments see, in addition to Wibier, Liebs, *Gallien*, p. 123; Martín, *Fragmenta augustodunensia*; Nelson, "Fragment."

[94] E.g. Plin. *ep.* 7.24.8; Harries, "Legal Education," pp. 153–56.

murdered your own mother, they promise that their many clever readings of the law will urge your acquittal – if they think you're rich.

(30.4.8–12) At nunc uidere est per eos omnes tractus uiolenta et rapacissima genera hominum, per fora omnia uolitantium, et subsidentium diuites ut Spartanos canes aut Cretas, uestigia sagacius colligendo, ad ipsa cubilia peruenire causarum.

...

Secundum est genus eorum, qui iuris professi scientiam, quam repugnantium sibi legum aboleuere discidia, uelut uinculis ori impositis reticentes, iugi silentio umbrarum sunt similes propriarum. Hi uelut fata natalicia praemonstrantes, aut Sibyllae oraculorum interpretes, uultus grauitate ad habitum composita tristiorem, ipsum quoque uenditant, quod oscitantur. Hi ut altius uideantur iura callere, Trebatium loquuntur et Cascellium et Alfenum, et Auruncorum Sicanorumque iam diu leges ignotas, cum Euandri matre abhinc saeculis obrutas multis. Et si uoluntate matrem tuam finxeris occidisse, multas tibi suffragari absolutionem lectiones reconditas pollicentur, si te senserint esse nummatum.[95]

Marcellinus describes a system of laws that is contradictory but also all-important. His lawyers tell a story to clients in which their mastery of law is a tool to change legal outcomes, and even to defend the indefensible. In doing so, they imply that law governed legal outcomes, and that that those in charge of legal outcomes would be impressed by *scientia iuris*. Instead of relying on the judgment of the sovereign who had stood astride Roman decisionmaking for centuries, Marcellinus' jurists and clients relied on a system of technocratic rules. All of the changes I have discussed in this section – from emperors describing their adjudicative processes as applying settled law, to rescripts being rearranged to emphasize doctrinal continuity between different sovereigns, to an administrative state applying specialized legal training to individual cases – contribute to this new image of late-antique legality. They tell the story of a legal culture folding imperial decisionmaking into an existing and knowable law, whose holdings could be predicted by litigants and manipulated by specialists.

Perhaps the most striking development in late-antique legal culture, though, is Constantine's establishment of permanent

[95] See Riedlberger, *Prolegomena*, pp. 24–25; Humfress, *Orthodoxy*, pp. 16–17.

iudices uice sacra: imperial functionaries whose decisions could not be appealed, even to the emperor himself.[96] We have already seen Constantine using the language of law to describe himself waging war on an unaccountable bureaucracy, and it might be surprising that he oversaw so great a delegation to that bureaucracy. But the *iudices uice sacra* operated within a new kind of legal culture, and made sense within that culture. On the one hand, given the vast expansion of imperial business that took place under Diocletian and Constantine the *iudices* would be a necessary timesaver.[97] On the other, more formalized law schools like those in Beirut or Autun were generating the kinds of experts who could staff multiple courts of last resort. But maybe most importantly the early fourth century saw a new account of how Roman law worked, which I have described throughout this chapter, and which looked to trained legal experts as more obvious or appropriate decisionmakers than the emperor himself.

For all of the majestic pomp of late-antique court culture, and its rhetorical focus on a single extraordinary ruler, this same period sees a more visible and more elevated administrative apparatus than the Principate ever did.[98] That apparatus could operate on its own, and issue legitimate commands even in the absence of imperial supervision. Whether we describe that legitimating impulse in Canepa's language of "institutional sanctity"[99] or Ando's/Foucault's "governmentality" matters little, since both approaches situate late-antique legal culture within a broader paradigm of administrative spectacle.[100] That spectacle focused its audience on different actors providing different goods than did the euergetic judging of earlier periods. It prepared that audience to accept the precise, impersonal judgments for which Roman law now appears to stand.

[96] Peachin discusses the evidence for regular, permanent *iudices uice sacra*, and dates their establishment to sometime between 313 and 315 CE; *Iudex Vice Caesaris*, pp. 188–200.

[97] See Dillon, *Justice*, pp. 215, 249.

[98] Harries, *Law and Empire*, pp. 46–47.

[99] Canepa, "Emperor," p. 160.

[100] This spectacle extended, strikingly, to a built landscape increasingly defined by monuments of lower-level bureaucrats. For an excellent recent treatment of this phenomenon and its implications for evolving notions of the late-antique state, see Hellström, "Monumental Bureaucracy," pp. 154–58.

The Afterlife of the Severan Jurists

The story I have told in this chapter is long and somewhat messy. I have described major changes in how different actors approached and imagined the law, but the moments in which those changes happened are hard to pin down. It is easier to see the world that late-antique legal culture produced than the moment at which that culture emerged. In that spirit, it seems best to conclude my argument by examining a text from the early fifth century, to see what it understood Roman law to be and how it understood jurists to lie at the center of that law.

I refer to the *Codex Theodosianus*. I discuss the *CTh* more thoroughly in Chapter 7, but it is an extraordinary document: a compilation published in 438, under the emperor Theodosius II (r. 408–450), that collected imperial constitutions from Constantine on.[101] The *CTh* aimed not only to generate a coherent set of legal authorities for use by legal subjects but also to provide a kind of history of normative thought and to reconcile Roman with Christian legal traditions.[102] These goals make the *CTh* a helpful chronicle of legal culture, and while its vision of the law could be fairly considered idiosyncratic[103] it makes presumptions about its audience that the modern reader might find informative. I here focus on three introductory titles: 1.1 (*On the Constitutions and Edicts of the Emperors*), 1.2 (*On Various Rescripts*), and 1.4 (*On the Responses of the Learned*). All three lay out second-order rules, of the sort with which I am particularly concerned: what counts as authority, whose writings can be taken to establish a legal norm and why. But they engage in vastly different kinds of reasoning.

[101] *CTh* 1.1.5. On initial public reception of the *CTh* Matthews, *Laying Down the Law*, pp. 31–54; on the relationship between the *CTh* and earlier late-antique legal writing Riedlberger, *Prolegomena*, pp. 19–252.

[102] This "strong account" of the *CTh*'s role within late-antique legal culture is perhaps most strongly associated with Archi, who argued that the *CTh* was intended to reconcile *ius et rescripta*: *Teodosio II*, pp. 6–24; I discuss this tension in more detail *infra* pp. 203–203. Dillon argues that the *CTh* reflects a historiographic as well as a codificatory impulse; *Justice*, pp. 16–17. Letteney suggests that the *CTh's* internal organization and preference for *leges generales* reflects the "'Christianization' of structures of knowledge and governance in the later Roman Empire": *Christianization*, p. 232. Sirks provides an excellent overview of the earlier historiography at *Study*, pp. 36–53.

[103] Harries, *Law and Empire*, pp. 59–64.

The titles that concern imperial writing focus on that writing's formal characteristics. They constrain imperial writing's applicability to prior wrongdoing (1.1.3), instruct judges to evaluate imperial legal writing by its generality (1.1.3; 1.2.1; 1.2.2) or by the validity of its claim to imperial authorship (1.1.1), and explain that the *CTh* itself simply compiles and sorts all the "edicts and general constitutions" (*edictales generalesque constitutiones*: 1.1.6.1) of Constantine and his successors (*diuus Constantinus posterioresque principes ac nos*: 1.1.6.1) as if they were a new law-code. While individual promulgators are named in the headings, it is unimportant who wrote what; anyone who ruled after Constantine gets put in the Code the same as anyone else, and the *CTh* instructs readers to resolve contradiction not by considering the goodness of individual rules or authors but by robotically favoring the newest constitution (1.1.5). In practice, editorial judgments were clearly being made. For example, Barnes has argued that constitutions of Licinius were reattributed to Constantine in the *CTh*, much like the rescripts of Elagabalus I discussed in Chapter 4.[104] But those judgments are unexplained and invisible. The *CTh* never evaluates emperors, and never suggests that the particular skills or qualities of an emperor might affect his authority. Similarly, it follows the *Codex Gregorianus* in organizing its imperial writing by topic. Every emperor after Constantine plays the same role in contributing to a synchronic body of positive law. That role is assigned on the basis of the institutional position of "emperor" rather than any individual emperor's individual qualities.

CTh 1.4, by contrast, treats jurists as individuals. *CTh* 1.4.1 begins by quoting Constantine for the claim that Ulpian and Paul's notes on Papinian "aimed at praising his genius, but preferred to corrupt than to correct it" (*dum ingenii laudem sectantur, non tam corrigere eum, quam deprauare maluerunt*). In *CTh* 1.4.2 Constantine deems the *Pauli Sententiae* worthy of celebration (*omni ueneratione celebranda*) on the basis of their "luminosity, flawless elocution, and most just legal reasoning" (*plenissima luce et perfectissima elocutione et iustissima*

[104] Barnes, "Three Imperial Edicts"; see also Corcoran, *Tetrarchs*, pp. 288–91; "Hidden." For a more skeptical view see Matthews, *Laying Down the Law*, pp. 165–66.

iuris ratione), and the final fragment in the title is Valentinian III's (r. 425–455) famous Law of Citations.

We affirm in their entirety the writings of Papinian, Paulus, Gaius, Ulpian, and Modestinus, with the effect that the same authority should attend Gaius that currently attends Paul, Ulpian, and others, and that readings should be admitted from the whole body of their work. We also certify as valid the wisdom of those whose treatises and arguments those aforementioned jurists have included in their own work, such as the wisdom of Scaevola, Sabinus, Julianus, and Marcellus, as well as all those others whom they cite, provided that (owing to the uncertainty of antiquity [i.e. the textual difficulties arising from their long circulation]) *their texts are confirmed by collating the codices. When different opinions are offered, let the greater number of jurists prevail, or alternately in case of a tie let the authority of the side containing Papinian (a man of extraordinary genius) carry the day; nevertheless, as Papinian conquers any one opponent let him cede to two.*

(*CTh* 1.4.3) Papiniani, Pauli, Gai, Vlpiani atque Modestini scripta uniuersa firmamus ita, ut Gaium quae Paulum, Vlpianum et ceteros comitetur auctoritas lectionesque ex omni eius corpore recitentur. Eorum quoque scientiam, quorum tractatus atque sententias praedicti omnes suis operibus miscuerunt, ratam esse censemus, ut Scaeuolae, Sabini, Iuliani atque Marcelli omniumque, quos illi celebrarunt, si tamen eorum libri propter antiquitatis incertum codicum collatione firmentur. Vbi autem diuersae sententias proferuntur, potior numerus uincat auctorum, uel, si numerus aequalis sit, eius partis praecedat auctoritas, in qua excellentis ingenii uir Papinianus emineat, qui ut singulos uincit, ita cedit duobus.[105]

[105] The Law of Citations is an object of controversy in late-antique legal historiography. Jones (*The Later Roman Empire*, p. I.471) calls it "the low-water mark of Roman jurisprudence" following Schulz's own withering judgment at *Principles*, pp. 281–82; both men accuse the law of excessive and robotic simplicity. Later historians have defended the law, but often by arguing that it was not as simple as it seemed (e.g. Matthews, *Laying Down the Law*, pp. 24–26; Watson, *Spirit*, pp. 82–83). Harries makes a somewhat different point, that the law "would have come as a relief to hard-pressed judges" (*Law and Empire*, p. 19; also "Sacra Generalitas," pp. 34–35). We see here a broader disagreement about the different goods Roman legal order ought to provide. I tend to agree with Harries; most legal subjects do not look to a legal order to provide opportunities for brilliance or erudition, so much as to clearly define obligations in advance. It is nevertheless striking how many legal scholars see the Law of Citations as interfering in a scholarly, rather than as a legal, endeavor. Getzler, "The Snake Oven Revisited" p. 292 ("It may be glib to condemn the *lex* ... for it is chiefly a rule for permissible citation, strange though it seems to modern eyes to then substitute 'head counting' for reasoned argument in weighting admissible authorities.").

All of these texts evaluate individual jurists and do so in bombastic terms. Constantine and Valentinian pick out specific authors on the basis of their intellectual gifts, and justify their reasoning with the hyperbolic praise one might expect from panegyric. Papinian merits respect not because he is a jurist, but because he is a brilliant jurist.

That difference between *CTh* 1.1–2 and 1.4 speaks to how thoroughly Roman legal order had transformed itself over the intervening century-plus. The *Codex Theodosianus* addresses itself to an audience that has been primed on the one hand to treat imperial laws as somewhat impersonal and fixed,[106] and on the other to debate the intelligence and equity of precepts drawn from individual jurists. As hard as it is for us to reconstruct the theory and practice of the late-antique courtroom, we can see both of these impulses in earlier Severan juristic writing. While emperors of the Severan period framed their legal work as a medium for religious revival or familial piety, the bureaucrats who worked for them wrote as if imperial constitutions were an institutional backdrop for the euergetic, world-improving task of jurisprudence. Imperial administration evolved into something more like what the jurists envisioned.

It is impossible to isolate any specific reason for this evolution, but a few trends may help explain it. The mid third century saw weak, contested rulers who could not exercise broadly legitimated authority. Those rulers spoke in a different language, one that invoked institutional continuity rather than individual charisma, and in doing so began to describe imperial rulings as something like laws. These rhetorical tendencies continued into the tetrarchy and beyond. At the same time, the broader administrative projects of Diocletian and Constantine both facilitated and necessitated more coherent accounts of imperial lawmaking.

This story of law, which relied on trained lawyers consulting texts like the *Codex Gregorianus* to understand the rules, rendered imperial pronouncements subject to the kind of scrutiny jurists were historically understood to provide. As the imperial author receded into the headings of a *codex* named after someone else, the juristic interpreter took on a more central and scrutinized role. We cannot know how

[106] In fact, *CTh* 1.1.6 explicitly models the *Codex*'s project on the *Codices Gregorianus et Hermogenianus*.

perfectly the *CTh* mapped onto the society to which it was addressed. For example, it seems likely that the men who taught and learned from the *Fragments of Autun* were more interested in the living emperor than the readers contemplated by the *CTh*.[107] But the idea of the *CTh* – let alone its contents – would have shocked legal subjects of an earlier period. Its positivistic vision of law emerged from Severan juristic treatises, but by the fifth century it underlay legal projects that emerged from the imperial court. This change was downstream of much more consequential shifts in imperial sovereignty and administration, but transformed our vision of Roman law just the same.

[107] Wibier, "Realpolitik," pp. 96–98.

7

The Embodiment of the Civil Law

The story of Classical Roman law, of course, does not end with Theodosius' compilation in 438. Instead, it goes to (at least) 534, when Justinian promulgated the *Corpus Iuris Ciuilis*. The *Corpus* collected authorities from the last four centuries of Roman legal writing into large collections (such as the *Codex Justinianus*, containing imperial constitutions, and the *Digest* containing juristic writing), which were themselves organized into *tituli* addressing different legal concepts.[1] The *Corpus* remained a source of law in one form or another for centuries, and as a result fixed in place the intellectual structures by which we organize Roman law as a field of knowledge.[2] It has a relatively clear manuscript tradition – we know mostly what it contained, and where – and arranges its authorities in a way that lends itself to legal study. A reader who wants to know what the jurists thought about *infamia* between the mid second and mid third centuries CE, or how emperors from Pius to Justinian handled interest-bearing loans, will not only consult the collections of juristic and imperial writing that the *Corpus* provides but will describe the information found there in terms that foreground the Justinianic schema (for jurists on *infamia* D.3.2; for imperial constitutions on interest C.4.32) over the organizational structures within which the quoted authorities

[1] Thus Humfress, "Law and Legal Practice," pp. 161–62 ("Justinian's new law books contained old wine in new skins.").

[2] See, for example, Stolte, "Codification in Byzantium"; Stein, *Roman Law in European History*, pp. 45–54 (on the centrality of the *Corpus Iuris Ciuilis* to the first modern European law school at Bologna); Müller, "Recovery."

were produced. We go so far as to label the few non-Justinianic sources of Classical law – including the *Fragmenta Vaticana,* the *Consultation of a Certain Old Jurist*, and fragments of the Diocletianic *codices* that survive in Visigothic texts – the *Sources of Roman Law from Before Justinian* (*Fontes Iuris Romani Anteiustiniani*).[3]

Justinian's centrality in the history of Roman law poses some problems. The most obvious – and most thoroughly explored – is that of Justinianic alteration. As discussed in Chapter 4 the broader context of the *Corpus Iuris Ciuilis*, by which I mean the evaluative paradigm its compilers used in selecting material and the internal logics of the documents constructed out of that material, exercises its own gravitational pull.[4] The *Corpus* affects how we understand the documents we go to the *Corpus* to find. Untangling that influence requires the Classical legal historian to reckon, at least somewhat, with what Justinian and his compilers were trying to do.

That is my goal in this final chapter. Justinian's distinctive approach to rulership inflected Justinianic legality, and thus transformed the Roman legal tradition for which the *Corpus Iuris Ciuilis* constitutes our best evidence. I discuss the particular political circumstances in which the *Corpus Iuris Ciuilis* was compiled, before considering how Justinian's unusual role within the *Codex Justinianus* affected the representation of pre-existing legal rules within the *Corpus*. Justinian is represented in the *Corpus* as improving the law, which required flattening the other authors contained within the *Corpus* – emperors and jurists – into a law for him to improve.

"The Whole of the Ancient Law:" The *Corpus Iuris Ciuilis* in Justinian's Words

The *Corpus Iuris Ciuilis* did not come out of nowhere, and it did not come out quickly. To modern readers the *Corpus Iuris Ciuilis* appears as a roughly tripartite document, promulgated over the course of 533–534 CE, which includes both imperial legal communication (in the

[3] The most recent edition of which is Riccobono, *Fontes*.

[4] The best discussion of this gravitational pull, or of how Justinianic compilation changes our understanding of texts without necessarily altering their language, remains Johnston, "Interpretation."

Codex Justinianus) and juristic commentaries on the law (in the *Digest*) as well as an educational treatise known as the *Institutiones*. However, we can piece together a longer and more complicated story. The *Codex* precedes its neighbors by four years and originally stood alone. Justinian gave a speech to the Senate of Constantinople in February of 528, in which he announced his intention to combine existing collections of imperial law into a single, authoritative document:

These things, which struck many earlier emperors as urgently requiring correction but which none of them dared to fully correct, we have now resolved with God's help to grant for the common welfare: first, to shorten the length of trials by curtailing the multiplicity of constitutions which were previously contained in the three Gregorian, Hermogenian, and Theodosian codices, and also of those promulgated by Theodosius (of divine memory) and other subsequent emperors after the aforementioned codices, as well as those promulgated by my own mercy; and further by composing a single book under the blessed designation of our own name, in which should be collected not only the constitutions of those three books but also those newer ones (novellas) put forward after.

(*Haec* pr.) Haec, quae necessario corrigenda esse multis retro principibus uisa sunt, interea tamen nullus eorum hoc ad effectum ducere ausus est, in praesenti rebus donare communibus auxilio Dei omnipotentis censuimus et prolixitatem litium amputare, multitudine quidem constitutionum, quae tribus codicibus Gregoriano et Hermogeniano atque Theodosiano continebantur, illarum etiam, quae post eosdem codices a Theodosio diuinae recordationis aliisque post eum retro principibus, a nostra etiam clementia positae sunt, resecanda, uno autem codice sub felici nostri nominis uocabulo componendo, in quem colligi tam memoratorum trium codicum quam nouellas post eos positas constitutiones oportet.

Haec (*constitutio Haec*, conventionally known as such because of its first word) is our earliest evidence for the logic of the *Corpus Iuris Ciuilis*. While the document is not a reliable guide to Justinian's interiority, it can tell us how Justinian wanted the audience for his collection to understand it.

In *Haec*, codification is spectacular. The document fits well into Justinian's image of (as Sarris puts it) "active, triumphant, and pious rulership"; Justinian describes the work of governance in language that highlights his own transformative role in Roman/Byzantine history.[5] In particular, Justinian describes his codification as unique. Instead of highlighting continuities with earlier administrative practices – continuities which would seem immediately apparent, given the three imperial *codices* then extant – Justinian begins the address by claiming to do what no emperor before him had dared to do (*nullus ... ausus est*). Furthermore, *Haec* presents codification as euergetic. While the *CTh* aimed to satisfy "lawyerly pursuit" (*Gesta* 4: *scholastica intentio*),[6] Justinian portrays codification as a tool with which he can grant his public the gift (*donare*) of shortening trials (*prolixitatem litium amputare*).[7] Justinian connects law and society more firmly than Theodosius did, and portrays solving a somewhat abstract problem as providing concrete and longed-for help.

Specifically, Justinian solves the problem by charging professionals with making the law coherent. *Haec* appoints a committee of ten legal experts who had previously held very different jobs (practitioners, professors, and salaried members of Justinian's administration)[8] and instructs them "to compose fixed and succinct laws out of the three aforementioned *codices* and new constitutions" (2: *certas et breui sermone conscriptas ex isdem tribus codicibus, nouellis etiam constitutionibus leges componere*). In doing so, it offers an unusually explicit account of what codification was supposed to do. It is clear enough why fixity might be desirable in a legal system, and predictable laws have functioned as an important public good throughout the period covered by this book. But that desire for predictability has generally been latent. By contrast, Justinian links fixed laws (*certas ... leges*) to the

[5] Sarris, *Economy and Society*, p. 1. Also Cameron, *Procopius*, pp. 255–57; Honoré, *Tribonian*, p. 16 ("Justinian is conscious of living in the age of Justinian."). Image was not reality, of course. Sarris (*Economy and Society*, pp. 200–27) tracks a much more complicated relationship between Justinian and the aristocratic stakeholders he claimed to be bringing to heel, and Meier (*Zeitalter*, pp. 104–05) notes the contrast (*Gegensatz*) between Justinian's "active, energetic, and markedly optimistic" self-representation and the apocalyptic tone of other depictions of that same period.

[6] On the *Gesta* see Matthews, *Laying Down the Law*, pp. 31–54.

[7] Literally "shortening the *prolixitas* of trials." *Prolixitas* is a difficult word to define, especially in such a rhetorical passage. The term can refer both to length of time (as at e.g. D.36.1.23.3 [Ulpian, Disputationes]; *prolixitate temporis*) and to loquaciousness in writing and speech (e.g. Symm. *ep.* 2.8., contrasted with *litteras ... breues*). Justinian's similarly rhetorical conclusion to *Haec* suggests that the codification process will lead to "quicker judicial outcomes" (3: *citiores litium decisiones*).

[8] *Haec* 1; *Summa* 2: Iohannes, Leontius, Phocas, Basilides, Thomas, Tribonianus (Tribonian), Constantinus, Theophilus, Dioscurus, and Praesentinus.

pruning of contradictory legal material on the one hand, and to efficient litigation on the other. Codification can make laws more predictable and secure, and in doing so serve the public interest (3: *rerum communium utilitate*) by making trials faster. This is not the only reason why someone might produce a *codex* of constitutions, but it was Justinian's; nearly every piece of Classical (pre-Constantine) imperial lawmaking that survives does so because it fit this purpose. The *Codex Justinianus* is more complicated than this account makes it sound, but the idea of a coherent and "fixed" law was present from its earliest stages and influences what comes down to us today.

That said, what comes down to us today is not quite what *Haec* describes. Fourteen months after *Haec* Justinian issued *Summa* (also named for its first word), which celebrated Justinian's success in rendering law "most secure" (pr.: *firmissima*) and announced that the new *Codex* would come into force as a definitive legal compilation on April 16 of 529 (5). This *Codex* – now commonly called the *Nouus Codex* – was in force for several years but has not come down to us as part of the *Corpus*; our only firm evidence for its existence and circulation is papyrological.[9]

Justinian followed the *Nouus Codex* with an even more ambitious – and even more self-consciously ambitious – course of legal reforms. In December of 530 Justinian issued the constitution *Deo Auctore*, which authorized the *quaestor Sacri Palatii* Tribonian to compile extant juristic commentaries into what is now the *Digest*.[10] Like the other authorizing constitutions, *Deo Auctore* includes a highly rhetorical account of Justinian's divine calling, but that calling has evolved from helping subjects to ordering the universe.

Although there is nothing so eagerly desired in the whole world as the authority of the laws, which benignly govern both heaven and earth and banish all wickedness, we found that the whole path of the laws – running from Rome's founding and the times of Romulus – was so confused as to stretch out to infinity and beyond the bound of human comprehension: Our first goal was to go back to the most sacred emperors of the past, and to edit their

[9] Specifically *P. Oxy* 1814, which excerpts *Nouus Codex* 1. The first major treatment of the implications of *P. Oxy* 1814 for the *Nouus Codex* is de Francisci, "Frammento"; for more recent discussion Corcoran, "Justinian and His Two Codes."

[10] Honoré, *Tribonian*, pp. 139–86; for the quaestorship *Sacri Palatii* see *supra* pp. 247–48.

constitutions and to put them into a clear plan through which they might, once collected into a single codex and stripped of all redundancy and most vicious contradiction, offer the protection of their clarity on display to all mankind.

When this work was finished, and put together into one volume adorned by our glorious name, although just raised from few and trifling matters we hastened to accomplish the highest and fullest emendation of the law and to collect all Roman authority and to edit it and to display the scattered volumes of so many commentators brought together into one, a task which no one else dared to wish or hope for, indeed a task most difficult even for us, which seemed closer to impossible.

(*Deo Auctore* 1–2) Cum itaque nihil tam studiosum in omnibus rebus inuenitur quam legum auctoritas, quae et diuinas et humanas res bene disponit et omnem iniquitatem expellit, repperimus autem omnem legum tramitem, qui ab urbe condita et Romuleis descendit temporibus, ita esse confusum, ut in infinitum extendatur et nullius humanae naturae capacitate concludatur: primum nobis fuit studium a sacratissimis retro principibus initium sumere et eorum constitutiones emendare et uiae dilucidae tradere, quatenus in unum codicem congregatae et omni superuacua similitudine et iniquissima discordia absolutae uniuersis hominibus promptum suae sinceritatis praebeant praesidium.

Hocque opere consummato et in imo uolumine nostro nomine praefulgente coadunato, cum ex paucis et tenuioribus releuati ad summam et plenissimam iuris emendationem peruenire properaremus et omnem Romanam sanctionem et colligere et emendare et tot auctorum dispersa uolumina uno codice indita ostendere, quod nemo alius neque sperare neque optare ausus est, res quidem nobis difficillima, immo magis impossibilis uidebatur.

Deo Auctore remains recognizably Justinianic. Justinian still portrays his legal work as part of a transformational project, which sets him apart from and above a grateful public composed of everybody on Earth (*uniuersis hominibus*).[11] Justinian also sets himself apart in time, echoing *Haec* and emphasizing how no one else in history (*nemo alius*) ever did what he proposes to do now.[12] But his aims have become – if anything – grander since 529. Whereas Justinian then described the *Nouus Codex* in terms of its practical effects on the world, here both it and the *Digest* appear as tools to render the world comprehensible. This more metaphysical project, extending from the courtroom to

[11] See Humfress, "Law and Legal Practice," p. 165; Meier, *Zeitalter*, pp. 104–14.

[12] See Harries, *Law and Empire*, pp. 9–10. While it was never completed, *CTh* 1.1.5 appears to contemplate a juristic codification much like the *Digest*: Humfress, *Orthodoxy*, pp. 65–66; Matthews, *Laying Down the Law*, pp. 55–71.

heaven itself (*et diuinas et humanas res*), could never be satisfied by modernizing the Gregorian/Hermogenian/Theodosian *codices*.

Justinian's new project led to the *Digest*, which unlike the *Nouus Codex* really was unprecedented. The juristic literature circulating at this time likely did so in monographic or epitomated forms. As to the first, it is clear enough that the compilers of the *Digest* worked by reading and excerpting single-author commentaries like Ulpian's *ad Edictum* or Papinian's *Quaestiones*.[13] We also know of epitomes like the *Pauli Sententiae*, whose anonymous authors claimed to summarize or explain the work of a particular jurist.[14] But it was rare for collections to include opinions by more than one jurist, even though constitutions from different emperors shared space in widely circulated texts.[15]

The *Digest*, which combined snippets from different juristic treatises into subject-matter-focused *tituli*, was a new way to collect and present juristic authority. Even though the juristic literature of the *Digest* was generally older than the constitutions contained in *codices*, in terms of its structure the *Digest* should be understood as a descendant of and innovation upon the *codex* form. *Codices* of constitutions borrowed their overarching scheme from juristic treatises, but the *Digest* transformed those treatises into something like a *codex* of constitutions.

[13] This is the core assumption of what is now called the Bluhme-Krüger or BK *Ordo*, a reconstruction of the *Digest*'s compilation that focuses on how individual monographs were allocated among and excerpted by subcommittees of compilers. The details of the *Ordo* remain very much in dispute, but Bluhme and Krüger's claim that the works of the *Digest* could be broken up by book and author – and thus that the compilers had access to and worked from monographs – is taken as fact. For modern reconstructions of the *Ordo* see Honoré, *Character and Compilation*, pp. 151–61; Mantovani, *Digesto e masse bluhmiane*, pp. 90–103. For further bibliography on the *Ordo* see Honoré, *Character and Compilation*, pp. 46–78; Pugsley, "Numbers Game."

[14] On the *Sententiae* see Licandro, "Pauli Sententiae"; Ruggiero, *Ricerche sulle Pauli Sententiae*.

[15] The two exceptions, both unusual, are the *lex Dei / collatio legum Mosaicarum et Romanarum* and the *Fragmenta Vaticana*. The former attempts to demonstrate the superiority of Judeo-Christian to Roman jurisprudence, and thus renders Roman jurisprudence as something of a mass; the latter is a loosely organized collection of juristic and imperial authorities whose purpose is unknown and which has no equivalent in extant Latin legal writing. On the *collatio*'s unusual rhetorical project see Pilipow, "The Jeweled Jurist"; Lucrezi and Rocca, *Studi sulla Collatio*; Frakes, *Compiling*, pp. 129–51; Jacobs, "Roman Christians and Jewish Law." On the *Fragmenta Vaticana* see Sirks, *Study*, pp. 8–9; Wieacker, *Römische Rechtsgeschichte*, p. 117 ("nur einmal durch einen *codex unicus* … überliefert").

Importantly, the *Digest* is not a kind of document with which any of its major constitutive authors would have been familiar at the time they wrote, let alone that they expected to populate. It is distinctly Justinianic, and its attempt to render jurisprudence – as opposed to individual jurists – coherent and univocal only makes sense in the context of Justinian's towering ambition and appetite for novelty.

That ambition soon proved incompatible with the *Nouus Codex* itself. In November of 534 Justinian announced that the *Nouus Codex* would itself be changed to accommodate his successfully perfecting the law.

In the beginning of our reign, we resolved to collect the most sacred constitutions, which had been scattered into diverse volumes and which tottered under their redundancy and contradiction, into one corpus and to purge them of all vice; and this was done by excellent and eloquent men and confirmed by us afterwards. Our twin constitutions, promulgated earlier, confirm this.

Later, when we took the ancient law under consideration, we put out the fifty decisions and promulgated many other constitutions which aimed at the improvement of the work in question, and through these the greatest part of the old laws was edited and condensed and we presented the whole of the ancient law, free of unnecessary verbiage and laid out in our Institutiones *and* Digest.

But because our new laws – both decisions and constitutions – which had been issued after the completion of our Codex *were roaming outside of the bounds of that same* codex *and seemed to demand our providence and counsel, and indeed because some of them required, as a result of newer information, some alteration or editing in accordance with wiser counsel, it struck us as necessary . . . to trim down our constitutions and sort them into individual chapters and to place them under appropriate titles with an eye towards the structure of the ones already sorted, and then to combine them with those prior constitutions.*

(*Cordi* pr.–2) [I]n primordio nostri imperii sacratissimas constitutiones, quae in diuersa uolumina fuerant dispersae et quam plurima similitudine nec non diuersitate uacillabant, in unum corpus colligere omnique uitio purgare proposuimus, et hoc iam per uiros excelsos et facundissimos perfectum est et a nobis postea confirmatum: quod geminae constitutiones nostrae quae ante positae sunt ostendunt.

Postea uero cum uetus ius considerandum recepimus, tam quinquaginta decisiones fecimus quam alias ad commodum propositi operis pertinentes plurimas constitutiones promulgauimus, quibus maximus antiquarum rerum articulus emendatus et coartatus est omneque ius antiquum superuacua prolixitate liberum atque enucleatum in nostris institutionibus et digestis reddidimus.

Sed cum nouellae nostrae tam decisiones quam constitutiones, quae post nostri codicis confectionem latae sunt, extra corpus eiusdem codicis diuagabantur et nostrum prouidentiam nostrumque consilium exigere uidebantur, quippe cum earum quaedam ex emersis postea factis aliquam meliore consilio permutationem uel emendationem desiderabant, necessarium nobis uisum est . . . easdem constitutiones nostras decerpere et in singula discretas capitula ad perfectarum constitutionum soliditatem competentibus supponere titulis et prioribus constitutionibus eas adgregare.

The remainder of the constitution goes on to celebrate the edited compilation, which comes down to us as the *Codex Justinianus*. The passage quoted above is our best source for understanding how the *Nouus Codex* changed between 529 and 534, and also – more importantly for my purposes – for understanding why.

On the one hand the difference in material does not appear to have been enormous. Justinian followed the *Nouus Codex* with a series of constitutions known as the Fifty Decisions, which aimed to resolve ambiguities in existing law that had survived codification,[16] and with other laws to the same effect. In order to preserve the central conceit of the *Codex* (namely that it contained all relevant imperial law), the *Codex* needed to include Justinian's explanations and was edited until it did.

On the other hand, Justinian links this update to the much more ambitious ordering project represented by the *Digest*. The *Nouus Codex*, like its generic forebears, fit into a broader ecosystem that included commentaries, teaching curricula, and other documents produced outside of the imperial court. Justinian took that ecosystem for himself. *Constitutio Omnem* rearranged legal education throughout the Justinianic empire,[17] Justinian's *Institutes* provided a new imperially authorized text for those educators to use (*Tanta* 11), and both *Deo Auctore* 4 and *Tanta* 19 forbid litigants from using pre-Justinianic material found outside the *Corpus*.

[16] Justinian describes them as such at *Cordi* 1; see Haarer, *Empire and Society*, p. 96; Corcoran, "Justinian and His Two Codes," p. 85; Russo Ruggeri, *Quinquaginta decisiones*.

[17] Corcoran, "Two Languages," p. 101; Harries, "Legal Education," pp. 161–62.

Any documents that survived the purge, no matter how old and no matter who wrote them, were now part of Justinian's legal revival. *Deo Auctore* 6 boasts that Justinian "properly makes all [juristic writing] ours, since the whole of its authority derives from us" (*omnia enim merito nostra facimus, quia ex nobis omnis eis impertietur auctoritas*), *Tanta* (issued upon the completion of the *Digest*) claims that "whatever is written [in the *Digest*] should appear as ours and as arranged according to our will" (10: *quidquid ibi scriptum est, hoc nostrum appareat et ex nostra uoluntate compositum*) and *Cordi* that "the full radiance of the constitutions of our *codex* should shine upon all" (3: *constitutionum nostri codicis plenum iubar omnibus clareat*). All law was now Justinianic. While *Cordi* recognizes (4) that new facts might arise and require the publication of new constitutions or *nouellae*,[18] the promulgation of the *Codex Justinianus* marked a watershed moment in the history of "Roman law." For the first time, that law was a closed universe. Every authority was approved by the emperor, every argument was vetted in advance and organized according to subject matter in one of three very large books. I argued in Chapter 6 that the vision of the law that survives in the *Digest* and *Codex* has its roots in a late-antique project of centralization and regularization. The *Corpus Iuris Ciuilis* is that project's ultimate, fleeting success.

It is also propaganda. Like all of the law described in this book the *Corpus Iuris Ciuilis* changes the world – setting out rules for it, structuring Byzantine economic and social life – but also tells a story about the world, and twists each of those projects into the service of the other. The *Corpus*, in particular, tells a story about Justinian. Its introductory constitutions celebrate a transformational leader, chosen by God to reorder both human and divine society.[19] That story makes the *Corpus*' rules easier to swallow; any good Weberian can explain how narratives of transformation, exceptionality, and superhuman virtue might legitimate the exercise of authority. But the chain of inference runs both ways. The *Corpus Iuris Ciuilis* really did

[18] As, in fact, occurred; see *infra* pp. 289–90.

[19] On law as a medium of Justinianic representation see Sarris, *Justinian*, pp. 122–32; Haarer, *Empire and Society*, pp. 98–100; Bell, *Social Conflict*, pp. 310–16; Maas, "Roman History and Christian Ideology," p. 18 (describing Justinan's post-*Corpus* legislation as "intact specimens of imperial propaganda, presenting Justinian and his reforms precisely as he wished.").

transform Roman legal life and that transformation really did prove Justinian's extraordinary power. The *Corpus* makes claims about Justinian's sovereignty over the Roman world, which it then backs up; it symbolically arranges the world, and then assigns real benefits and punishments based on the symbology. The charisma justifies the authority, which demonstrates the charisma.

This slantwise, hortatory relationship between law and the world is not unique to Justinian. As Merry puts it, law's "power to shape consciousness depends both on its capacity to generate symbols and categories which persuasively constitute the social world and on its capacity to exert force beyond those symbols and categories."[20] But it poses problems for historians that it does not for sociologists, and particularly for historians who try to use law to understand the world. Roman legal writing appears in the *Corpus* as staid, impersonal, and rulebound because Justinian (and his compilers) wanted it that way. The *Corpus Iuris Ciuilis* stages an encounter between Justinian and the law; that representational paradigm affects the image of Justinian that inheres in its text, but also that of the hundred-odd other authors whose writing it portrays as, or portrays into, law.

The remainder of this chapter thinks through how classical Roman law might have been affected by the Justinianic logics of the *Corpus*. That question resembles one which is hardly new. Legal historians have worried for years about how Justinian's compilers altered the texts they excerpted and how the language of the *Corpus* might differ from that of Classical emperors and (especially) jurists.[21] My concern is slightly different but builds off of these centuries of work, particularly Kaser's observation that Justinian's compilers were far more likely to remove language from Classical texts than to add it in.[22] A historian trying to figure out the nature of, say, *fideicommissa* as imagined by Ulpian might find this observation a relief. Given my project, I do not. By carving out extraneous language – and by only

20 Merry, *Getting Justice*, p. 10.

21 Lokin, "Epilegomena," p. 261 ("This procedure [interpolation criticism] was supposed to bring to the surface the pure Roman law as it was in its hey-day. This was generally felt to show the immense distance between the high level of classical law and the level of the 'Byzantine' vandals.").

22 See especially Kaser, "Glaubwürdigkeit," p. 303.

including fragments or constitutions that might be useful to a sixth-century audience trying to understand the law, and by then arranging those fragments and constitutions around the needs of such a reader – Justinian and his compilers made a law-code out of texts that were not written to be part of a law-code.[23]

In doing so, these men created a Roman law that has been enormously influential. But they also made that law appear older than it was. Both the jurists and – as discussed in the next section – the emperors we find in the *Corpus* used legal writing to engage in their own imaginative or storytelling projects. It is impossible to reconstruct those projects, but important to try.

Why Imperial Constitutions Look Nicer in Retrospect

Changing law, like changing rulers, is an awkward business. To revise a rule is to acknowledge the unfitness of the prior rule and potentially call into question the processes by which it came to be. It is striking, for example, that Justinian describes new law made after the *Corpus Iuris Ciuilis* as responding to new facts, and not as correcting errors in existing law.[24] Justinian is less diplomatic, however, when discussing other people's work.

Since the edict of the deified Hadrian, which was issued on the topic of the inheritance tax [Literally 'the twentieth of the inheritances,' referring to a 5% estate tax],[25] *has fallen into utter desuetude with its many ambiguities and difficulties and incoherent narratives, and since all other ancient laws that were promulgated about the revitalization or interpretation of that edict have done similarly (since the tax has receded from our governance), we rule that should anyone . . .*

(C.6.33.3pr.: 531) Edicto diui Hadriani, quod sub occasione uicesimae hereditatum introductum est, cum multis ambagibus et difficultatibus et indiscretis narrationibus penitus quiescente, quia et uicesima hereditatis a nostra recessit re publica, antiquatis nihilo minus et aliis omnibus, quae circa repletionem uel interpretationem eiusdem edicti promulgata sunt, sancimus, ut, si quis . . .

[23] See Ando, *Ideology*, p. 144; Johnston, "Interpretation," p. 155.

[24] As, for example, at *Tanta* 18: "We are sure that certain matters shall arise at a later date, which have not yet been ensnared within the traps of the law" (*non desperamus quaedam postea emergi negotia, quae adhuc legum laqueis non sunt innodata*).

[25] Dio Cass. 59.28; Plin. *Pan.* 37. See also Álvarez, "Vicesima."

Justinian goes on to clarify how courts should handle property disputes in the context of a challenged will. The connection between Hadrian's tax edict and Justinian's procedural innovations is not obvious, but Hadrian's tax clearly required judges to determine the value of inherited property and that valuation procedure could be useful in other sorts of suits. Justinian establishes a new procedure that can be initiated at any time, by a plaintiff who feels they have been deprived of inheritance through a forged or otherwise invalid will.

More interesting for present purposes is the rhetoric accompanying the constitution. Justinian describes Hadrian's law as obsolete, both in the sense that other rulers before him seem to have stopped enforcing it (*penitus quiescente*) and in the sense that other changes in administrative practice have removed its key reason to exist (*quia et uicesima hereditatis a nostra recessit re publica*). But Justinian goes further. He attacks Hadrian's law – attacks really being the right word – as confusing, poorly drafted, and (ironically) long-winded. These criticisms go beyond mere obsolescence and seem to implicate the competence of Hadrian's drafters, or of Hadrian himself. Furthermore, they serve no obvious "legal" purpose. Justinian's actual innovation is presented in C.6.33.3 as simply an updated inheritance procedure that reflects other Justinianic changes in the taxation of estates. C.6.33.3 is not necessitated by Hadrian's poor legal writing, which makes Justinian's swipe even more marked.

C.6.33.3 is unique in its vitriol, but similar – and similarly odd – rhetorical flourishes persist in the Justinianic portions of the *Codex*. A more representative example of this tendency presents itself as clarifying a *senatusconsultum* passed under Marcus Aurelius:

> *Since we are obliged to reinforce, as well as to praise, the* Senatusconsultum Silanianum *and the oration of the deified Marcus that accompanied it, although we have found there no mention of liberty [i.e. of freed people], and a question regarding freed people left in the will of a murdered testator moved earlier [jurists], it struck us as necessary to settle these matters.*
>
> (C. 6.35.11pr.: 531) Cum Silanianum senatus consultum et a nobis tam laudandum quam corroborandum est nec non diui Marci oratio, quae circa id facta est, inuenimus autem in ea nullam mentionem libertatis factam et ueteres mouit quaedam de libertatibus relictis in testamento necati testatoris quaestio, necessarium nobis uisum est etiam haec dirimere.

Justinian here begins with effusive praise before identifying the error that requires his intervention (anyone who has graded student work can relate). He also puts his criticisms in the mouths of earlier legal professionals, claiming that the question C.6.35.11 seeks to answer (what should happen to people who are freed in a will when that will's effectuation is delayed because of possible murder?) has vexed commentators for years. These rhetorical maneuvers let Justinian paint his innovation as extending (C.6.35.11.2: *producere*) and perfecting (3: *replere*) Marcus' legislative logic.

As a general rule, when Justinian criticizes his predecessors' laws he does so with these sorts of arguments. At C.7.2.15 [n.d.] Justinian prefaces a constitution regarding the satisfaction of postmortem creditors by stating that "many questions have emerged about a constitution of the deified Marcus" (*uariae dubitationes ex hac constitutione emerserunt*),[26] and at C.7.6.1.1a (531) Justinian claims that "the greatest difficulties arose" (*difficultates maximae emergebant*) from a tangle of citizenship laws that included a Trajanic edict. Justinian then solves these problems, often by creating certainty in circumstances where existing constitutions have failed to provide it.[27]

Within the closed legal-historiographic world of the *Codex Justinianus*, these asides are remarkable. We have already seen emperors using legal writing to make themselves look powerful, moral, or generous; that sort of representational work is common in the *Codex*. But when other emperors describe a pre-existing legal order – and especially the imperial constitutions that made up that order – they are far more circumspect than Justinian appears to be. When a pre-Justinianic constitution preserved in the *Codex Justinianus* evaluates a prior imperial decision, it does so positively and usually in the context of a citation. Not so here; Justinian almost never cites prior imperial constitutions as authority in justifying the decisions preserved in the *Codex* (Figure 7.1).

[26] To be clear, Justinian is probably discussing the same constitution as at C.6.35.11; both interventions focus specifically on people manumitted via a dubious or contested will.

[27] As, for example, at C.7.71.8pr. [n.d.]: "there used to be doubts every day" (*cotidie dubitabatur*) about the mechanics of existing procedures for default on debt.

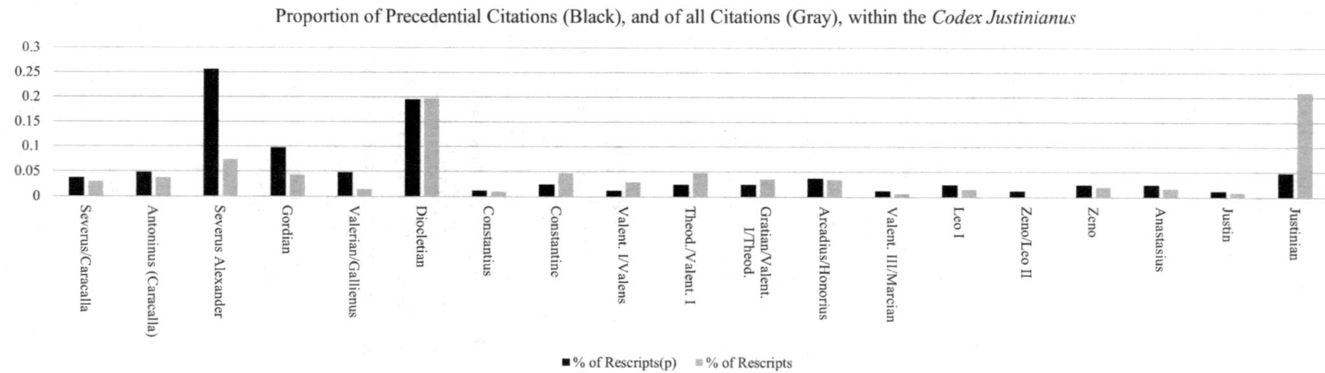

FIGURE 7.1 Precedential citation in the *Codex Justinianus*. Last one, I promise.

Justinian is vastly – and significantly – less likely to represent himself as following precedent than his neighbors in the *Codex*.[28] Ironically, one of Justinian's few approving citations – using the *secundum* form familiar from the rescripts of Severus Alexander – cites his own work; at C.1.2.23.4 (530) Justinian allows real and hypothecated actions in cases involving testamentary donation "according to the logic of our constitution" (*secundum nostrae tenorem constitutionis*).[29] Justinian is less deferential to his imperial predecessors than is anyone else whose rescripts survive in the *Codex Justinianus*.[30]

On the one hand, nothing about this stylistic quirk should surprise us. We have already seen how the *Corpus*' authorizing constitutions paint Justinian as an unprecedented figure, and how they describe codification as making all prior legal thought into Justinian's own. The lawmaker who appears in those texts is not one who has to justify his legal arguments by referencing earlier emperors. On the other hand, such a stark disparity should raise questions for Roman legal historians about the collection within which Justinian's constitutions are preserved and from which they stand out. It is easy to see how the *Codex Justinianus* tells a story about Justinian: both in explicitly narrative constitutions like *Cordi*, and in documents like C.6.33.3 that represent Justinian's place in history while making legal changes in their own right. But when the *Codex* constructs Justinian as transcending a staid legal order, it necessarily constructs centuries of complex legal politicking as a staid legal order for Justinian to transcend.

That ought to worry us. When we treat the *Codex Justinianus* as an archive of imperial constitutions, we risk reading those constitutions

28 For the statisticians: Justinianic authorship is negatively correlated with precedential reasoning. The correlation is significant at 99% certainty: χ^2 (1, N = 7,448) = -13.32, p = .000262. In layman's terms, the odds of this correlation appearing in the dataset via random chance are a little more than one in ten thousand.

29 This constitution is itself preserved at C.6.43.1 (Justinian, 529), as noted by Frier et al., *Codex*, p. 63 n. 58.

30 Cf. Puliatti, "La politica legislativa" p. 142; Massei, "Citazioni," p. 450 (both noting Justinian's idiosyncratic tendency to reference jurisprudential authority). These two citational tendencies, taken together, suggest that Justinian was perhaps less concerned with portraying his own reasoning as unique than with portraying it as transformative; as already discussed, jurisprudence had generally existed parallel to imperial lawmaking, but Justinian merges the two within his own constitutions and his own compilation.

the way they appear in that same archive: as a synchronic morass of rules that Justinian organized and clarified. There are techniques that the historian can use to isolate diachronic change in this odd compilation, and I have used them in this book. But they require reading against the grain of the *Codex*, and they cannot tell us how any emperor before Justinian actually wrote. I know that Severus Alexander was more likely than other emperors to cite his predecessors and to cite them in a certain way. I do not know, however, how often he actually did so. These moments of citation and conflict are particularly sensitive to Justinianic redaction, because they run counter to functionalist readings of the *Codex*. If everything in the *Codex Justinianus* operates as a unitary authority, that operation is not helped when the authority overrules or disagrees with itself. The archival logic of the *Codex Justinianus* has caused its constitutive documents to be stripped of their rhetoric and context, and especially of any interplay between the authorities Justinian paints as a single tradition.

This redactive tendency is not so apparent in other *codices*. While the *Gregorianus* and *Hermogenianus* do not survive except in other documents, the *CTh* clearly has a more historiographical aim[31] and preserves numerous constitutions that were no longer in force.[32] In fact, its introductory titles set forth a procedure for how adjudicators should resolve conflicts between constitutions included in the document.[33] Even in the *CTh*, however, constitutions do not *explicitly* overrule each other the way that Justinian's sometimes do in the *Codex Justinianus*. One constitution might supersede another but never criticize it, let alone as harshly as Justinian can. Justinian appears in the *Codex Justinianus* as altering laws for a variety of explicitly stated reasons, and occasionally as evaluating prior emperors' legal regimes. These sorts of asides are absent from the *CTh*, even as that document acknowledges the reality of legal change.

There are a few different ways to think about that absence. The *CTh* describes itself as comprehensive; if we take that claim at face value (at

[31] See Matthews, *Laying Down the Law*, pp. 57–58. [32] *CTh* 1.1.5.

[33] Per *CTh* 1.1.5, disputes are settled by reference to "the order of readings" (*lectionum probetur ordine*); the constitution then clarifies that, since the *CTh*'s titles are arranged in chronological order, whichever constitution was promulgated most recently should govern (*ualidiora esse, quae sunt posteriora*). See also *supra* p. 254.

least as to the project's intention; in other words, if we assume *CTh* included everything of which the compilers were aware) then we can assume that prior law did not include the kinds of asides we see in Justinianic constitutions. Such a claim would certainly be plausible, and Justinianic messaging is certainly idiosyncratic. On the other hand, the *CTh* probably misrepresents itself. As Harries notes, the *CTh* is nowhere near the size it would need to be to justify Theodosius II's claims.[34] Accordingly the *CTh* includes only a selection of legal material produced by Christian emperors, and even if Matthews is right that the compilers included everything they could find[35] we should not assume that all constitutions were equally easy to find or that they all made it into the compilers' hands in unabridged form.[36] Rescripts that criticized prevailing legal order might not have aged as well, or survived to codification.

Furthermore, the *CTh* explicitly authorizes some redaction and empowers its compilers to remove extraneous material (like commentary on earlier legal regimes) from the text.[37] For both of these reasons, it seems likely (not certain, but likely) that pre-Justinianic rescripts broke with existing law more often than codified sources suggest. Specifically, Justinian's criticism survives because he

[34] Harries, *Law and Empire*, pp. 22–23.

[35] Matthews, *Laying Down the Law*, p. 290 ("If some law meeting the formal criterion of *generalitas* cannot be found in the Theodosian Code, it is because the editors did not find it, not because they found but rejected it.").

[36] Like Justinian, Theodosius explicitly empowered his compilers to alter the law; *ibid.*, p. 63.

[37] 1.1.6: *circumcisis ex qua[que] constitutione ad uim sanctionis non pertinentibus solum iu[s] relinquatur*. The exact scope of this command has been questioned. Sirks ("Obsolete Constitutions?"; *Study*, pp. 147–54; "Sources," pp. 57–58) argues that *ad uim sanctionis non pertinentibus* empowered compilers to remove any constitution not then in force, as Justinian's compilers were later empowered to do. Honoré (*Crisis*, pp. 142–46) and Matthews (*Laying Down the Law*, p. 65) take the phrase as essentially synonymous with an earlier reference to compilers removing unnecessary verbiage (*inanem uerborum copiam*) in 1.1.5. I find the latter reading more plausible, particularly given Dillon's (*Justice*, pp. 20–23) account of parallel references to legal *uis* in extant Latin, and nearly all recent historiography rejects Sirks' account. See e.g. Riedlberger, *Prolegomena*, p. 147 n. 217; Huck, "Compilateurs," pp. 84–91. All agree, however, that Theodosius' compilers could and did remove extraneous material from constitutions that were included in their text. Parallel transmissions like the Sirmondian Constitutions (Matthews, *Laying Down the Law*, pp. 121–67) show the abridgement clearly, and this kind of material could easily have been abridged.

was in the unusual position of having his legal rhetoric enter the *Codex* unaltered; only one other emperor has a similar relationship to a surviving *codex* (Theodosius II). In other words, imperial constitutions may have looked much more like Justinian's than we realize.

This feature of imperial constitutions could explain an otherwise puzzling tendency in later Roman law. From Ulpian on, we can see a long tradition of writing explaining the superiority of "general laws" to "specific rescripts."[38] This tendency is most clearly visible in Christian authors and Letteney locates it in a theological tradition,[39] but it appears in pagans as well. Leaving Ulpian aside, the *Historia Augusta*'s *uita Macrini* includes an odd digression about how Macrinus "resolved to erase all of the rescripts of prior emperors, in order that affairs be governed by law and not by rescripts" (13.1: *statuisset omnia rescripta ueterum principum tollere, ut iure non rescriptis ageretur*).[40] Most scholarship on this material has treated the preference for (borrowing Macrinus' terminology) laws over rescripts as a settled rule,[41] but settled rules do not need to be stated as often or over as long a period as this one is. It is clear from these sources that the people who produced and enumerated Roman law were worried that rescripts could make their law worse: less elegant, less predictable, or even less fair.

That worry is hard to understand if imperial rescripts looked like those that survive in the *codices*. The rescripts we find there, even when addressed to and concerned with specific petitioners, state general legal principles. But if more emperors wrote like Justinian did, and used the forms of imperial legal writing to cast doubt on their predecessors and affirm their unique wisdom and power, we can see why Ulpian might get nervous. Roman law comes down to us as a coherent, systematic set of rules that could be altered at will by an absolute monarch. That

38 See D.1.4.1.2 (Ulpian, Institutiones): "Clearly, some constitutions are personal (*personales*) and have no precedential force (*nec ad exemplum trahuntur*)."

39 Letteney, *Christianization*, pp. 245–49.

40 Notably Macrinus is described in the same *uita* as legally trained (4.3). Cameron argues against the standard "pro-pagan" account of the *HA*, suggesting that the text predates the major persecution of Roman pagans to which it had previously been thought to respond; *Last Pagans*, pp. 743–82. The *HA* remains, however, clearly non-Christian.

41 E.g. Sirks, "Making a Request," pp. 133–35.

contradiction is easy to miss in our sources, and particularly in codified law, because constitutions that clashed with that law's positivistic rules do not survive. But Justinian shows us what that writing might have looked like, and offers a glimpse into lost and troubling legal histories. I cannot be certain that these two phenomena (Justinian's unusual willingness to criticize prior rulings, and the consistent preference for general over specific constitutions) are connected; I feel confident that the *Codex* selected against criticism, but less so that that criticism was the object of Ulpian *et al.*'s anxiety. Either way, however, later Romans' repeated preference for *lex generalis* responds to a legality that has dropped out of the *Codex Justinianus*. We do not know what imperial constitutions looked like, outside of a particular subset that was collected in order to represent "imperial constitutions" in a particular way. That subset allows for certain kinds of analysis, if we are careful, but must not be mistaken for the whole.

* * * * *

I end with one intriguing example of the chaos at the margins of codified law. Philostratus (a Greek author and rhetorician writing in the third century CE) preserves several examples of Caracalla hearing legal disputes. Caracalla appears in Philostratus as arbitrary and almost whimsical; he rules based on his annoyance with the petitioner,[42] or admiration of that petitioner's oratorical endurance.[43] Other sources bear this image out. An inscription from Dmeir describes Caracalla abruptly ending a hearing after becoming bored,[44] and another from Ephesus suggests that Caracalla had appointed his mother to hear and respond to petitions.[45] Similarly, Dio records at 78[77].8 [Xiph.] an instance of Caracalla dismissing a criminal case against a man named

42 As for example in his dismissal of Philiscus of Thessaly: *V S* II.30 [621–23].

43 Heliodorus: *V S* II.32 [626]. See also Scott, "Cassius Dio, Caracalla, and the Senate," p. 168 ("[T]his anecdote strengthens the notion that Caracalla was capricious and distrustful of precedents when making appointments."); Eshleman, "Defining the Circle," p. 405.

44 *SEG* 12.759 The most sustained treatment of this feature of the Dmeir inscription is Williams, "Rhetoricians," but see also Wankerl, *Appello ad principem*, pp. 203–26; Crook, *Advocacy*, pp. 91–95; Kunkel, "Prozess"; Wenger, "Ein Prozess"; Arangio-Ruiz, "Una cognitio"; Roussel and de Visscher, "Dmeir," pp. 173–94.

45 *SEG* 51.1579; Peachin, *Iudex Vice Caesaris*, pp. 160–61. On representations of Julia Domna under Caracalla see Temporini, *Kaiserinnen*, pp. 265–79.

Alexander, because the accusations sounded to him like slander of Alexander the Great.

None of this idiosyncrasy is visible in the *codices*. At most, the roughly 200 Caracallan constitutions that survive might contain some novel rhetorical flourishes;[46] Caracalla appears in the *Codex Justinianus*, and in those excerpts from the *Codex Gregorianus* that survive in the Visigothic corpus,[47] as another source of rules.[48] It is impossible to know whether something like C.12.35.1 [n.d.], which tells its petitioner that he is wrong to request (*non iure desideras*) back pay upon returning from enemy custody, represents normal Caracallan legal production or an outlier that was useful for codifiers seeking legal rules in imperial speech. The more idiosyncratic documents at which Caracallan epigraphy hints stay out of the *codices* and remain tantalizing glimpses. Codification meant breaking down the messy business of imperial judgments into something more reliable and impersonal, but Justinian's own constitutions show us other ways that Roman law could work.

The Death of a Crossdresser and the Life of a Treatise

The juristic texts that survive within the *Corpus Iuris Ciuilis* raise their own problems.[49] On the one hand, they resemble the constitutions in that both are imperfect copies; as I mentioned above Justinian's

[46] See Williams, "Authorship."

[47] For example, at *AV* 1.5: "If you removed yourself from your father's estate and are approached by his creditors, you can defend yourself against their claims according to the structure of the law" (*Si paterna hereditate te abstinuisti et a paternis creditoribus conueniris, secundum iuris formam tueri te potes*).

[48] As Daalder notes, Caracalla's legal regime as represented in the *Codex* is remarkably conventional. Daalder, "Tradition and Innovation."

[49] The subject of this section is a juristic account of someone who basically conforms with Roman ideas of maleness, but who enjoys wearing women's clothing without otherwise being addressed as, or treated like, a woman. As such, I refer to him as a crossdressing man or transvestite, rather than as a trans woman or transgender woman. I am not certain that this is the right approach, to be honest, if we imagine this story as a historical reality; the legal problem posed by the cross-dressing senator, however, literally depends upon the senator understanding the clothes he wears as men's clothes. This is a *trans story*, in Heyam's (*Before We Were Trans*, p. 28) account of the term, inasmuch as it is a story about someone who "approached gender disruptively or messily." But it is a story told in the context of a categorical sex binary that relies upon its subject occupying a specific position within that binary.

introductory constitutions explicitly authorized his compilers to alter the texts they compiled, and Roman legal historians have accordingly viewed both juristic and imperial material preserved in the *Corpus* with some suspicion.[50] But like with the constitutions, most Romanists now believe that compilers altered juristic treatises by cutting them down, rather than by adding new material. As a result we are reasonably confident that the snippets of juristic writing that survive – like the constitutions that survive – closely resemble those in the lost books from which the compilers worked.

In other ways, however, the *Digest* and *Codex* are very different. For one thing, juristic writing was an outdated genre well before it crossed Tribonian's desk. The *Codex Justinianus* includes constitutions from Hadrian to Justinian, but the *Digest* has a much narrower temporal scope. The compilation includes almost no juristic writing from after the mid third century and its latest authors, Hermogenianus and Arcadius Charisius, worked under Diocletian.[51] Juristic commentary seems to have reached its peak in the early third century, and fallen off the map soon after.[52] While demand for skilled legal professionals increased over the fourth and fifth centuries, those professionals had different jobs; the jurists of this era were teachers, advisers, and compilers rather than authors in their own right.[53]

Furthermore, Justinian's jurists could not excerpt their predecessors' writing without radically altering the structure of that writing. Unlike imperial constitutions, which were written as self-contained documents, juristic literature survives in short quotes from long books. Historical accounts of juristic practice suggest that jurists originally wrote short answers to queries,[54] and it seems plausible that some of the Classical texts excerpted in the *Digest* might have taken that form (e.g. Papinian's *Quaestiones* or Paul's *Responsa*). But the books whence come the vast majority of the *Digest* would have had

[50] See *supra* p. 163.

[51] Lenel records 110 fragments from two jurists working in the late third and early fourth centuries: six from Arcadius Charisius and 104 from Hermogenianus. *PG Arcadius Charisius* 1–6; *Hermogenianus* 1–104.

[52] De Blois, "Influence"; Piacente, "Giurisprudenza."

[53] See among others Ruggiero, *Ricerche sulle Pauli Sententiae*, pp. 148–49; Honoré, *Crisis*, pp. 6–10; *Tribonian*, p. 39.

[54] Harries, *Cicero and the Jurists*, pp. 32–35; Tuori, "Myth," p. 245; Frier, *Rise*, pp. 142–43.

a very different generic character. Commentaries on civil or edictal law were likely written in continuous prose, at least if we go by the evidence of those sections of the *Digest* which quote a given work at length. School-texts would have looked similar, by analogy with the *Institutes* of Gaius.[55] The *Digest* transmits these texts in pieces, organized according to a Justinianic (or Tribonianic) schema.

In doing so, the *Digest* builds off a long tradition of late-antique excerpting. While Gaius' *Institutes* is the only juristic monograph to survive, smatterings of juristic writing survive in compilations like the *Fragmenta Vaticana* or the *Law of God/Comparison of the Mosaic and Roman Laws* (*lex Dei/collatio legum Mosaicarum et Romanarum*). These texts – which predate the *Corpus Iuris Ciuilis* by centuries in some cases – cut down their source material in a similar fashion. Another, far more common form of excerpting was single-author compilations like the *Pauli Sententiae*, which circulated widely enough to merit discussion in the *Codex Theodosianus* and which provided short statements attributed to the jurist Paul.[56] While the *Digest*'s compilers had access to original copies of texts like Ulpian's *ad Edictum*, the *Digest*'s audience was already reading denatured collections of juristic quotes and could understand juristic writing in those terms.

So, then, the *Digest* hands down third-century legal principles collected in a sixth-century structure for a sixth-century audience. Even if we think those principles are accurately transmitted – and I do, for the most part – they come to us devoid of larger context. The last few decades have seen an explosion of scholarship dedicated to restoring this lost scholarly milieu. One thinks of the *Scriptores Iuris Romani* project, which collects fragments from the same work and organizes them into "monographs" with commentary; this work is invaluable but can only put together the fragments we already have.[57] Another strand of scholarship looks at individual fragments to see (sometimes latent) indicators of a broader artistic program

[55] On Gaian style see Wibier, "Transmitting Legal Knowledge"; Nelson, *Gai Institutiones*, pp. 395–423.

[56] As mentioned briefly *supra* p. 187, *CTh* 1.4.2 singles out the *Pauli Sententiae* for discussion and thus implies that questions regarding their usage had crossed Constantine's desk.

[57] Schiavone, "Singularity and Impersonality," pp. 3–4.

amidst the rules. For example, Daube has explored juristic arguments about Homer that are only preserved in *Digest* 18 because of their relevance to the law of sale,[58] Candy has isolated complex rhetorical maneuvers such as chiastic ring-composition in a fragment of Pauline epitome,[59] Christol links Ulpian's discussion of Tyre in *de censibus* to a broader tradition of municipal panegyric,[60] and Nasti has explored the connections between the jurist Pomponius (a particularly good test case, for reasons I explain later) and Greek literary forebears from Aristotle to Polybius.[61] Mantovani's account of the capaciousness (*épaisseur*) of juristic writing within Roman literary thought now seems incontrovertible, but the exact nature of that *épaisseur* is mostly lost.[62] In order to think through how juristic texts might have functioned in their natural habitat – and how their idiosyncratic transmission affects our understanding of juristic writing as a genre – I now discuss one of the most famous surviving examples of juristic whimsy.

There is no distinction between a man's garment and men's clothing: but the mind of the legator can cause difficulty, if he was in the habit of wearing clothes which were also meant for women. In such a case we must say before all else that that thing was legated which the testator had intended, not that one which is, in reality, either a men's or a women's garment. For Quintus Titius [Scaevola] said that he knew a certain senator who was accustomed to wearing women's dining-clothes who, if he were to make a legacy of "women's clothing," would not seem to have been thinking of that garment which he used as if it were a men's dining gown.

(D 34.2.33: Pomponius, ad Quintum Mucium) Inter uestem uirilem et uestimenta uirilia nihil interest: sed difficultatem facit mens legantis, si et ipse solitus fuerit uti quadam ueste, quae etiam mulieribus conueniens est. itaque ante omnia dicendum est eam legatam esse, de qua senserit testator, non quae re uera aut muliebris aut uirilis sit. nam et Quintus Titius ait scire se quendam senatorem muliebribus cenatoriis uti solitum, qui si legaret muliebrem uestem, non uideretur de ea sensisse, qua ipse quasi uirili utebatur.

58 Daube, "Three Quotations"; see also Watson, *Spirit*, pp. 66–67.

59 Candy, "Sandal," pp. 316–20, 329–33, 336 ("[The *responsum*] is composed in the intermediate style with a view to instruct as well as delight.").

60 Christol, "Entre la cité et l'empereur"; see also Ferrary, Marotta, and Schiavone, *Ulpianus: Institutiones, de censibus*, pp. 7–9.

61 Nasti, "Greek Thought and Roman Jurists"; *L'Enchiridion*, pp. 25–33.

62 Mantovani, *Les juristes écrivains*, p. 237.

This story comes from a strange fragment of a strange text in a strange title of the *Digest*. Working backwards through that trilogy: D.34.2, titled "On Silver and Gold and Ornaments and Unguents and Dress or Clothing and Statues that Have Been Handed down Via Legacy" (*de auro argento mundo ornamentis unguentis ueste uel uestimentis et statuis legatis*) does not work like other portions of the *Digest* might lead one to expect. As the name suggests, D.34.2 is more like a dictionary than it is an internally coherent set of logical principles; it tells its reader how to interpret different provisions they might encounter in a will. As a result, the fragments contained therein are unstructured and picaresque. Instead of laying out coherent principles of testamentary interpretation, or even exploring edge cases at the limits of a principle, they interpret hyperspecific and increasingly strange bequests.[63]

It is easy enough to imagine why this particular area of Roman law might lend itself to such a style of argumentation. By Justinian's time Roman wills were generally interpreted according to the testator's intent,[64] which can be difficult to discern without the help of a necromancer. As a result, the *Digest* seemingly aims to address as many kinds of ambiguous provisions as possible, with the effect that a testator could be assumed to be familiar with existing interpretive practice and intended their language to be read through its lens.[65]

D.34.2 thus highlights the difference between a juristic treatise, produced as part of a broader corpus of persuasive authorities who were under no obligation to agree, and codified law. When the jurists debated the proper meaning of *uestimenta muliebria*, they were trying to answer an open question with resort to broader testamentary principles.[66] Any given juristic interpretation would sway a judge by convincing them of the principles on which the interpretation rested,

[63] For example, D.34.2.25 (Ulpian, ad Sabinum) suggests that a legacy of clothing includes pieces of felt (*coactilia*) and seatcovers (*tegimenta supselliorum*), but not horse blankets (*stragulas ... quae equis insterni solent*).

[64] See Meyer, *Legitimacy and Law*, pp. 265–76.

[65] Notably, as Meyer explains at *ibid.*, pp. 270–76, intent becomes more important in later Roman testamentary law. These sorts of ambiguous provisions would pose different problems for Justinianic audiences than for Pomponius or his contemporary readers. The clarity-forcing mechanism of D.34.2 gets at a question – what did the testator want? – that would become more central in the late-antique courts.

[66] On this process see Ando, "Analogy," pp. 113–16.

and which distinguished it from that of other jurists urging different results. By contrast, in the *Digest* the exact same piece of writing served a necessarily different function. The guidelines of the *Digest* function more like conventions in a game of bridge[67] than proper arguments. In other words, because those guidelines are universal and uncontested (per *Deo Auctore*) they become a language in which an adjudicator could presume testators to be fluent. Fuller describes this as a "channeling function" of law; laws like D.34.2 "force the raw material of meaning into defined and recognizable channels" and thus give the testator a more thoroughly articulated language with which to speak.[68]

Juristic writing did not, and could not, do this kind of work. D.34.2 only makes sense as a set of universally held canons, because once a court admits the possibility that other interpretations might be plausible it is forced to inquire about the testator's preferred interpretation and to confront the epistemic void D.34.2 evades.[69] Fuller imagines this channeling as "one of the most important functions" of legal formality,[70] but it requires a universal agreement on the validity (if not prudence) of a given legal rule. There is no channeling without unanimity, and juristic writing was never universal in the way the *Digest* was.[71] The *Corpus Iuris Ciuilis* trains us to expect this clarity and coherence, and includes *tituli* like D.34.2

[67] A bridge convention is a universally understood metonymic device in which a particular bid is understood to convey a particular piece of information about the partner's hand; conventions are publicized in advance so that all possible parties can understand a given piece of information equally well. For example, under the Blackwood Convention a bid of four no-trumps is understood as a request for information from one's bidding partner rather than as a commitment to win ten tricks in a game without trump cards.

[68] Fuller, "Consideration and Form," p. 802; see also Crawford, "Wills Formalities," pp. 275–79; Langbein, "Substantial Compliance," p. 494.

[69] On the *Digest* minimizing – without completely excising – indeterminacy, see Bretone, *Ius controversum*, p. 770.

[70] Fuller, "Consideration and Form," p. 801.

[71] For the difficulties attendant clarity/fixity in different legal systems, Shapiro, *Legality*, p. 258. Shapiro follows Fuller in taking clarity to be an important feature of law (pp. 394–97) while framing this clarity not as a moral good but as a necessary component of law's ability to engage in social planning. This planning resembles Fuller's channeling, except perhaps in its level of scope and abstraction; Shapiro accepts that a workable legal regime can allow for some adjudicative discretion even at the risk of legal uncertainty, as long as the general contours of legal behavior are well enough understood for a society to organize itself around them.

that rely on those properties in ordering the world. We should not assume, however, that the fragments contained therein were written for that same purpose or played that same role.

That assumption is particularly dangerous in the case of D.34.2.33, a fragment of Pomponius' *ad Quintum Mucium*. The second-century jurist Pomponius plays an unusual role in the *Digest*. While Paul and (especially) Ulpian quote him frequently on traditional doctrinal questions, the compilers rely heavily upon Pomponius' *Enchiridion* (presumably an instructional text) for their account of the legal profession.[72] D.1.2, "On the Origin of the Law, and of All of the Magistracies, and the Succession of the Jurists" (*de origine iuris et omnium magistratuum et successione prudentium*) consists of one fragment of Gaius followed by fifty-three of the *Enchiridion*.[73] D.1.2 is explicitly historical and explicitly distinct from the work of the rest of the compilation, as that opening bit from Gaius makes clear.

As I was preparing to write an interpretation of the ancient laws, I thought that I should first necessarily go back to the origins of the city of Rome, not because I wanted to write a verbose commentary but because I realize that in all matters that thing is only complete which arises from all of its individual parts.

(D.1.2.1: ad Leges XII Tabularum) Facturus legum uetustarum interpretationem necessario prius ab urbis initiis repetendum existimaui, non quia uelim uerbosos commentarios facere, sed quod in omnibus rebus animaduerto id perfectum esse, quod ex omnibus suis partibus constaret.

This excerpt, from the first book of Gaius' commentary on the Twelve Tables, served as a preface for his own historical narrative and explains why that narrative might belong in his own text. It is clear that Gaius – and the compilers as well – contemplate a reader who needs to be convinced of the value of history, and who sees that history as a different kind of work than even the *interpretatio* of a historical law. It makes sense, then, that D.1.2 excerpts different authors than does the legal analysis that follows it. But it is equally clear that jurists like Ulpian and Paul, whose writing makes up such a large proportion of the *Digest*, saw Pomponius as a fellow traveler; they quote him

[72] See Nasti, *L'Enchiridion*.

[73] I assume that Pomponius and Gaius are different. This assumption is not universal in the discipline – see Pugsley, "Gaius or Sextus Pomponius" – but neither is it necessary for my argument.

frequently. Gaius predicts criticism from readers who want their legal writing divorced from other kinds of literary work, and the *Digest* serves that writing up on a platter.[74] But that separation was not a given in juristic writing, and authors like Pomponius straddled the line.[75]

D.34.2.33 shows us what that kind of literary/legal hybrid literature might look like, and gives us tools with which to think critically – if speculatively – about how and why it was lost. For one thing, the fragment has a very different structure than the *Digest* trains us to expect. By way of comparison, another famous story from juristic writing (the "Barber Case") presents its absurd facts as the staging-ground for a legal dispute.

Indeed Mela wrote that, if when some people are playing with a ball one of them strikes it rather forcefully against a barber's hand, thus jolting that hand and causing the throat of a slave whom the barber was shaving to be slit by his razor, whoever acted negligently [with *culpa*] *is subject to the* lex Aquilia.

(D.9.2.11pr.: Ulpian, ad Edictum) Item Mela scribit, si, cum pila quidam luderent, uehementius quis pila percussa in tonsoris manus eam deiecerit et sic serui, quem tonsor habebat, gula sit praecisa adiecto cultello: in quocumque eorum culpa sit, eum lege Aquilia teneri.

The Barber Case is an outstanding example of a kind of argument that appears frequently in the *Digest*. An odd situation arises, leading to a legal problem that different jurists think should be solved differently. Sometimes these situations purport to be real, sometimes not. While Ulpian, Mela, and Proculus address a fact pattern that is clearly invented, Paul's claim that "if a father should be captured by the enemy while his son stays in Roman territory, his will remains valid upon his return" (D.28.3.9, ad Sabinum: *si pater ab hostibus capiatur filio manente in ciuitate, reuerso eo non rumpitur testamentum*) bears

[74] On Gaius' argument for the necessity of historical sophistication in legal analysis see Mantovani, *Les juristes écrivains*, pp. 145–47.

[75] While he has not yet published it, Graeme Cunningham's 2018 doctoral dissertation ("Law, Rhetoric, and Science") makes a similar argument for the role of rhetorical instruction in informing the juristic treatise. Similarly, Humfress (*Orthodoxy*) argues for broad interplay between "legal" and "nonlegal" genres of writing and structures of knowledge in constructing late-antique juridical culture. The most thorough treatments of Pomponius' assimilation of nonlegal traditions are made by Nasti: "Greek Thought and Roman Jurists"; *L'Enchiridion*, pp. 25–60;

a more ambiguous relationship to real-life problems. What survives in the *Digest* is not necessarily a chronicle of jurists responding to actual legal queries; jurists often used hypothetical disputes to illuminate more general legal concepts.[76] D.34.2.33 works differently than either of these. Instead of using specific cases or hypotheticals to develop a principle, Pomponius states outright what decisional rule one should follow when interpreting a will (*omnia dicendum est eam legatam esse, de qua senserit testator, non quae re uera ... sit*) and applies it to the question at hand.

More strikingly, in D.34.2.33 Pomponius uses the form of juristic quotation to a very different end than do other authors in the *Digest.* After providing the rule and applying it to a hypothetical crossdressing decedent, Pomponius adds that Quintus Titius [probably the jurist Scaevola][77] "said that he knew a certain senator who was accustomed to wearing women's dining clothes" (*ait scire se quendam senatorem muliebribus cenatoriis uti solitum*) and who would have confused his heirs if he had referred to bequests of gendered clothing in his will. If Scaevola has an opinion on how the crossdressing senator's legacy should be interpreted, Pomponius does not supply it. He cites Scaevola for the mere fact of the senator's existence, and not for any legal reasoning or principle. Scaevola *ait se scire*, rather than *ait cenatorias legatas esse*; Pomponius focuses his reader's attention on the strangeness of the fact pattern, not on any legal questions it might pose.

That choice of emphasis has impacted how D.34.2.33 appears in scholarship. While some early work takes Pomponius' legal claims at face value[78] D.34.2.33 appears more frequently in historiographies of sexuality, as evidence that the facts reported by Scaevola were both attested and unremarkable.[79] Watson is a holdout, and takes Pomponius to be hostile to the reported practice: "[i]t is not difficult

[76] Harries, *Cicero and the Jurists*, p. 105. [77] Tuori, "Return," p. 103.

[78] As, for example, in a 1970s debate regarding the possibility of a latent distinction in D.34.2.33 between legacies and stipulations; see Astolfi, "Abiti"; Martini, "Legato di vesti"; Guarino, "Sul legato di vesti."

[79] Ferri ("What the Text Wants to Say," p. 293) takes the fragment to demonstrate the importance of close reading in juristic law, and Gardner ("Gender-Role Assumptions," p. 381) to demonstrate the sexing of clothes within the Roman imaginary. An older strand of scholarship tries to read transvestitism out of the text, most notably at Albanese, "Volontà," pp. 157–58 and Wacke, "Potentiores," p. 568, but more recent authors use it as evidence of crossdressing more specifically,

to detect a hint of malice."[80] Who is right? Does the *Digest* record Pomponius describing an unmarked practice, or gossiping about an oddball who happens to pose an interesting legal problem?

The truth lies somewhere in the middle, and reveals the transfigurations of genre lurking within Justinian's law-code. On the one hand, the structure of the fragment makes it impossible to read as a neutral description of a social practice. Pomponius and Scaevola emphasize the existence of the crossdressing senator over his legal ramifications, and thus suggest that they viewed his existence as in some way fascinating. On the other hand, that fascination is not scornful, and Watson's malice is rather difficult for this reader to detect.[81] We can instead take Scaevola's and Pomponius' interest at face value, as evidence that they found the idea of a crossdressing senator remarkable and strange. There is ample evidence that Romans found crossdressing worthy of comment – they commented on it quite a lot – and elsewhere in the title Ulpian defines women's clothing (D.34.2.23.2, ad Sabinum: *uestimenta muliebria*) as "those clothes which men cannot easily wear without censure" (*sine uituperatione*). That censure is easy enough to find in our sources. For just a few examples, Cicero accuses Mark Antony of crossdressing at *Phil.* 2.44, Juvenal describes *cinaedi* participating in a mock *Bona Dea* festival at 2.86–90, and the *Historia Augusta* describes philosophers wearing their hair in women's style (*caput reticulo componerent*) at *Elag.* 11. These cases are likely fiction, but paint male transvestitism as pathetic and horrifying.

and often as evidence that Pomponius and Scaevola considered crossdressing to be normal. The most sustained treatment is Tuori, "Return," which sees the case as a neutral example of a legal problem (p. 199), but other examples abound. Carlà-Uhink ("'Between'," p. 11) takes Pomponius to claim that there was "no censorship" of crossdressing in imperial Rome; Kondratuk ("Travestissement," p. 56) simply states that the crossdressing senator "interpelle" Pomponius; Raggi ("Cross-Dressing," p. 41) claims that Pomponius attempts to resolve the case "without social, moral or sexual considerations"; Perry ("Defining Gender," p. 438) notes the passage's lack of "vitriol or moral undertones"; and Richlin ("Not Before Homosexuality," p. 540) assumes the case is real and takes its "bland[]" discussion of crossdressing as evidence for the existence of *cinaedi* in Roman society.

80 Watson, *Succession*, p. 88 n. 2.

81 Tuori ("Return," pp. 197–98) notes that the dinners at which a *cenatoria* might be worn were highly social affairs, and thus that the senator in question was hardly acting in secret; see also Gowers, *The Loaded Table*, pp. 255–56.

Pomponius drafts off of this discursive tendency without participating in it. He instead speaks in a different register, one common in Pomponius' intellectual milieu of the second century but otherwise largely absent from the *Digest*. I refer to the description of *mirabilia*, sometimes called "paradoxes": remarkable events of which the writer claims first- or secondhand knowledge and which he describes in order to entertain his audience.[82] Gender roles and inversions are a major theme in Pomponius' rough contemporaries Phlegon of Tralles (see *Mir.* 4.3. on Tireisias) and Lucian of Samosata (see *Ver. Hist.* 2.17, describing male marriage and pregnancy). Both paradoxographers describe gender inversion in less abusive terms than do Cicero, Juvenal, and the *HA*.[83]

Pomponius' attitude towards the crossdressing senator is difficult to understand on its own terms, as part of a discussion of testamentary law. Instead, it belongs in a literary universe that was familiar to Pomponius' original readers but that the *Digest* excludes and to some extent obscures.[84] The *Corpus Iuris Ciuilis* trains us to see descriptions of events as fact patterns, and to read them as bases for legal argumentation. But other genres of ancient literature marshal facts for their own purposes, and Pomponius' writing here makes much more sense when we read it as in dialogue with those genres, and not just with its neighbors in D.34.2.

* * * * *

The meaning of D.34.2.33 depends upon its context. We do not have very much of Pomponius' *ad Quintum Mucium*,[85] but the fragment invites a different kind of reading practice than the one at which the rest of the *Digest* is aimed. Pomponius' most extensive appearance in the *Digest*, the enormous quotation from his *Enchiridion* that makes up D.1.2, suggests that Pomponius was no stranger to more literary forms of writing. Furthermore, Pomponius' popularity among the Severan jurists suggests that they understood him to be a core part of their own history. So why does his writing look so strange to us today?

[82] On paradoxography in general see Geus and King, "Paradoxography"; on gender inversion as a paradoxographical trope see Doroszewska, "Hermaphrodites."

[83] For a good Latin comparand, albeit quite a bit earlier, see *NH* 7.1 on *hermaphroditi*.

[84] On this conflictual, ludic quality in juristic writing Bryen, "Aggadah," pp. 14–22.

[85] Lenel isolates 107 fragments, all preserved within the *Digest: PG Pomponius* 219–325.

One answer is that juristic writing was preserved not for its traditionally literary qualities, but for its value in argumentation and research. Pomponius imagined one sort of reader, with one sort of interests, but the *Digest* imagines another.

The clearest example of this tendency is, again, Justinian. *Deo Auctore* makes clear that the "stuff" (4: *materia*) Justinian's compilers excerpted from the classical jurists was the material best suited for explaining legal precepts, and *Deo Auctore* 5 orders that the "ancient law" (*ius antiquum*) be separated from its context within the juristic treatises as if by a wall (*quasi quodam muro uallatum*). But this kind of practice-oriented excerpting predates the sixth century. Juristic epitomes like the *Pauli Sententiae*, or broader compendia of authority like the *Fragmenta Vaticana*, sliced and diced juristic writing for usable statements of legal principle. Monographs presumably survived in some great libraries, but in few enough numbers that judges could not reasonably be expected to consult them.[86] Instructional texts were a different story, but were meant to be used in a specific pedagogical context rather than to be read as literature. Juristic texts became more important over this period than they had ever been before but were reimagined to fit the framework within which they were so valued. The law that comes down to us today in the *Corpus Iuris Ciuilis* subsumed its authors – both emperors and jurists – within a legal science that was more isolated than its predecessors and less "Classical" than it pretended to be.

The Law, Ensouled

The *Corpus Iuris Ciuilis* was not the end of Justinian's legal project. Justinian kept on hearing new questions and issuing new constitutions in response; these constitutions, which have been preserved as Justinian's *Novels*,[87] fit uneasily with the universalizing ambitions of

[86] This is the unavoidable implication of the *CTh* treating the *Sententiae* and certain other anonymous epitomes as equivalent to the original work; those constitutions presume that judges have been and will be unable to check citations to the corpus of the epitomated author.

[87] The *Novels* are collected at Miller and Sarris, *Novels*. Kearley and Kroll, *Justinian's Novels*, pp. 9–18 provides a useful layman's explanation of the mechanics by which *constitutiones* were requested and promulgated in the Justinianic period.

the earlier compendium.[88] Nevertheless, the *Novels* give us further insight into Justinian's approach to the law, and can help us better understand why the *Corpus Iuris Ciuilis* looks the way it does. Towards that end, I conclude this chapter with a remarkable claim that survives from Novel 105, issued in December of 537. Three years after claiming a divine prerogative to organize the laws of heaven and earth, Justinian went one step further and claimed to be the law made flesh.

Let the fortune of the king be exempted from all that said above, a fortune beneath which god has put the laws themselves, sending it down to mankind as a law made flesh; on account of this the king shall possess a consulate for life, since he daily decides what is best in every city and among all the cities and clans and peoples, and since the robe of office is granted at his assent; for all these reasons the consulship of the kingdom should accompany the scepter of kingship.

Πάντων δὲ δὴ τῶν εἰρημένων ἡμῖν ἡ βασιλέως ἐξηρήσθω τύχη, ᾗ γε καὶ αὐτοὺς ὁ θεὸς τοὺς νόμους ὑπέθηκε νόμον αὐτὴν ἔμψυχον καταπέμψας ἀνθρώποις· διότι τῷ μὲν βασιλεῖ διηνεκὴς ὕπεστιν ὑπατεία πᾶσι πόλεσί τε καὶ δήμοις καὶ ἔθνεσι καὶ ἐφ' ἑκάστης τὰ δοκοῦντα διανέμοντι, προσέρχεται δὲ ἡνίκα αὐτὸς νεύσειεν ἡ στολή, ὡς καὶ ἡ τῆς βασιλείας ὑπατεία διὰ πάντων ἔσται ἀκολουθοῦσα τοῖς σκήπτροις.

Justinian presents himself as the νόμος ἔμψυχος, literally the "law with a soul in it" or the Law Incarnate, sent by God to give justice to his subjects. Justinian thus exempts himself from the restrictions on consular behavior that take up the majority of Novel 105 – since the law cannot be bound by law – and also erases any distinction between himself and the majesty of the sixth-century Byzantine state. This concept of the sovereign as "living law" has clear precedents in late-antique political culture, at the intersection of the doctrine of the Incarnation and nascent ideas of divine kingship, and Justinian certainly did not invent it.[89] But as used here, it strikingly recalls

[88] For example, the Byzantine emperor Leo VI argued that in promulgating his *nouellae* Justinian had unknowingly (*Nov. L.* 1.6: ἔλαθεν) corrupted (1.7: λυμηνάμενος) the *Corpus Iuris Ciuilis*. Noailles and Dain (eds.), *Novelles*, p. 13; also Humfress, "Law and Legal Practice," p. 175; Lokin, "The Novels of Leo," p. 138. On the Leonine novels more broadly Chitwood, "Byzantine Legal Culture," pp. 35–42; Wenger, *Quellen*, pp. 705–07.

[89] Pazdernik, "Justinianic Ideology," pp. 198–202; Steinwenter, "Νόμος ἔμψυχος"; Enßlin, *Gottkaiser*, pp. 91–93. Miller and Sarris refer to the phrase as "epitomis[ing]

Cicero's account of the ideal magistrate as a *lex loquens*. The difference is that Cicero and Justinian imagine different law-codes.

Whereas Cicero imagines his talking law as general and evenhanded, Justinian's is unquestioned and omnipotent. The distinction is easy enough to understand, in light of the legal culture within which each man wrote. In the fraying aristocracy of the late Republic law, with its archaisms and arcana, could be safer and fairer than the world – for Justinian law had a reach, and a connection to the divine, that befit imperial glory.[90] But both understood law and men to be different kinds of rulers, and the gulf between them to be something worth trying to bridge. Law appears in both texts as a perfect sovereign for perfect humans to become.

Nobody, however, is perfect. Cicero's ideal types are no more real than Justinian's aggrandizing rhetoric, even if both choose law as the device with which to weld fantasy and reality. These maneuvers are inseparable from the hortatory tradition this book has mapped out. Emperors like Vespasian and Severus Alexander – accompanied by subjects like Ulpian, "Samosata," and Horace – used the language and institutions of law to tell stories about Roman power. Law does that everywhere, and legal texts make claims about the world that are not quite as true as they appear.[91] But Roman law, and particularly the law of the Classical period, has enthralled audiences for over a thousand years. Its stories of a rulebound society have been taken as fact and inspiration, while its specific doctrines and precepts came to exercise more control over later societies than the Severan jurists imagined when they wrote them down. The *Corpus Iuris Ciuilis* is a corpus of accidents, rhetoric, and dreams, compiled on the orders of a megalomaniac. That such a book forms the basis of entire legalities today should astound us, and the miracle of Roman law is that it does not. The law spoke, and Europe listened.

Justinian's view of the person of the emperor as the one and only legitimate source of law" (*Novels*, p. 695 n. 26). Earlier references to the emperor (here Theodosius I) as νόμος ἔμψυχος survive at e.g. Them. *or.* 5.2.64 B; also de Giovanni, "Il principe e la legge," pp. 227–28.

90 See Dagron, *Emperor and Priest*, pp. 20–21.

91 See Fitzpatrick, *Mythology*, pp. 51–63.

Conclusion: What We Talk About When We Talk About Roman Law

This book has traced the emergence of an idea. I have argued that over the course of Rome's imperial period, different participants in legal culture iteratively developed a story about how law could work in an autocracy. That story adapted very old features of Roman thinking – in particular, a vision of law as sacred, impersonal, and Republican, as well as nostalgic attachments to the past – to a dynamic paradigm of imperial sovereignty. It is a story that suffuses our compendia of Classical Roman law without necessarily having penetrated as deeply into Classical courts, and it primes its reader to imagine a world that never existed, or perhaps to build it anew.

What was that story? Roman codifications treat law as suprapersonal, technocratic, and supreme. The law that survives in these texts is suprapersonal, in the sense that its authority does not depend on the identity of its promulgator; it is technocratic, in the sense that it can only be applied by experts who merit some level of deference; and it is supreme, in the sense that it sets out both the necessary and sufficient conditions for the deployment of legitimate violence in enforcement.[1] None of these claims were universally accepted at any point in Rome's legal history, but that is hardly unusual for a law-code's representations of itself and its world. What makes Roman law extraordinary is how those claims operated in later

[1] See Schmidt-Hofner, *Reagieren*, pp. 17–18.

contexts, and how readily they have been taken as straightforward depictions of the world in which they were made.

I have made this argument in three parts. First, I have considered how "imperial legality" developed over the course of the first two centuries CE. This legality encompassed several competing discursive tendencies. On the one hand, emperors of this period were often represented as conforming to what Noreña has called an "ethic[] of autocracy"[2] and engaged with law as a potent signifier within that ethical system: as a set of unjust rules to abrogate or as a guide to archaic virtues that someone might seek to restore. On the other hand, emperors of the Principate often sought to appear as private citizens, and submitting to legal order helped them in that representational work. This odd tension between emperor-as-legal-subject and emperor-as-enlightened-paragon did not resolve itself during the Principate but eventually found a kind of synthesis in the newer figure of the imperial legislator. Hadrianic administrative innovations led to the gradual development of a new system in which the emperor headed a broader administrative apparatus that developed and refined the law. This apparatus could accommodate Roman ideas of legal sovereignty while also responding to the demands of a broader empire and bringing imperial will into harmony with the nominal supremacy of *ius*. This novel vision of Roman legality built off the political stability of the second century and grounded legal order in a broadly accepted, legitimate sovereign.

I next discussed how Roman legality responded to the loss of that broad acceptance. The Severan period was, simultaneously, the zenith of the jurists and the death knell of the Principate. Earlier paradigms of imperial legitimacy struggled to adapt to the military coups, child rulers, and murderous regents of the 220s. Accordingly, this period saw the development of new ideas for reconciling emperors and law. Rather than the enlightened lawgiver of earlier periods, Severan legal writing constructs the emperor as something like a caretaker: a man who ought to be listened to because he speaks for an institutional order that merits respect in its own right. That construction works differently in the two kinds of legal writing that emerge from the Severan period. The constitutions of Severus Alexander looked to the Severan dynasty

[2] Noreña, "Ethics of Autocracy."

for legitimacy and not to Alexander's own judgment; Alexander himself appears so unimportant that his name could be usefully attached to documents issued under before he took the throne. By contrast, jurists of the Severan period aggrandized their own role in improving Roman social life. These scholars-*cum*-administrators described their work as providing the public goods that had previously been understood as imperial prerogatives. Similarly, these jurists took up a citation practice that grounded legal order not in individual emperors' individual virtues, but in an anonymous bureaucracy that produced empowered documents like the *sacrae constitutiones*. One genre of writing handles an unfit ruler by looking to his dynastic predecessors, the other by looking to the institution of imperial law itself.

As it happened, Roman law lasted longer than the Severan dynasty. Accordingly, it was the jurists' vision of legal sovereignty that took root in the late-antique period. The last part of this book tracked how Roman law caught up to the impersonal, positivistic account of the Severan jurists. Late-antique constitutions began to construct a legality in which emperors served as guides to a disembodied and determinative *ius*; those constitutions were collected in *codices* that juxtaposed the writing of different emperors and presented them all as equally legitimate; and those *codices* were read by a newly expanded and newly trained corps of legal bureaucrats. This new legal world approached imperial constitutions as a depersonalized, codified law to be understood through the writings of brilliant long-dead jurists. Finally, both emperors and jurists were caught up in the grand codificatory project of Justinian, which rendered both imperial and juristic law into the disembodied rules that now seem to make up Classical Roman legal order.

All told, I have argued that Classical Roman law should be understood not as a record of Classical Romans actually handling their legal business, but instead as a record of Romans using the structures of law to tell stories about their world and in particular about their state. If you find that argument interesting in its own right – for reasons of disciplinary situation or personal pathology – then I salute you. But Roman law does not only matter to Romanists. Later societies have often looked to Rome as a political exemplar, and law is perhaps the field of study that is most inclined to draw inspiration from a normatively charged past. Roman law is thus very important to later legal histories, and the vision of Roman law that influenced those periods is the fictive, positivistic account whose emergence I have here tracked. Accordingly, I end this book with some particularly vivid examples of how later legal actors used a rules-based Roman legality to think about their own world. Roman law is a dream of order, which appealed to people who needed to dream.

The Lawyer in the Maelstrom

The most forceful exponent of this legality is probably the mid twentieth-century jurist Fritz Schulz. Per Schulz' principle of "isolation" (*Isolierung*) the commands of Roman law were supreme within legal fora and trumped other historical or political considerations.[3] This positivistic legal order would decay during the "general cultural decline in post-classical times," but until that happened Roman law was autonomously powerful and stood above other normative orders.[4] This vision of Roman law now seems like a somewhat cabined account of what that law was. Roman legal developments were always inseparable from broader political shifts, even if the law itself elides those connections.

Schulz' historiography, though, is inseparable from the circumstances in which it was written. Schulz was a German Protestant of Jewish descent[5] who attained the highest post in German legal history (a chair in Roman law at Berlin) in 1931;[6] one sees the problem rather quickly. Schulz was classified as Jewish under Nazi law and, in the wake of the 1933 "Law for the Restoration of the Professional Civil Service" (*Gesetz zur Wiederherstellung des Berufsbeamtentums*), faced increasing marginalization within the German academy before fleeing to Oxford.[7] This was the intellectual context of Schulz' most famous works. *The Principles of Roman Law*

[3] Schulz, *Principles*, pp. 19–39; while Schulz acknowledges (p. 247) that legal rules provided enormous discretion to magistrates and that this discretion could easily lead to the consideration of extralegal factors, he claims that "Roman feeling for tradition and *constantia*, however, created in actual fact the legal security unprovided by the law itself."

[4] *Ibid.*, p. 242. [5] Ernst, "Fritz Schulz," p. 107. [6] *Ibid.*, pp. 121–22.

[7] Tuori, *Empire of Law*, p. 45; Kmak, "Impact of Exile," pp. 18–19; Ernst, "Fritz Schulz," pp. 122–71.

was originally delivered as a lecture series at Berlin[8] before eventual publication in 1934, and Schulz' *History of Roman Legal Science* was written during his time in England. While Schulz' earlier work was traditionally doctrinalist[9] these books are historical in nature and argue forcefully for a legal order based on binding and authoritative rules.

Whether that argument is normative or descriptive is hard to say. As Tuori's recent treatment of Schulz' historical context makes clear, *Principles* works as a clear rebuke to Nazi legal science and its Schmittian antiformalism.[10] Schulz paints Roman law as both a monument of legal positivism and an indispensable piece of Europe's legal heritage. But *Principles* and *Legal Science* are primarily books about the past, and their most obvious and most influential claims are about the imagined legal order of Classical and postclassical Rome.

Schulz' interlocutors understood Roman law similarly, as a binding set of rules; the difference is that the Nazis saw this as a bad thing. One of the earliest statements of principle to come from the Nazi Party, a 25-point program presented by Adolf Hitler in February of 1920, had as its nineteenth point a demand for "replacing Roman law, which serves the interests of a materialistic world order, with a German common law" (*Ersatz für das der materialistischen Weltordnung dienende römische Recht durch ein deutsches Gemein-Recht*).[11] Nazi scholarship was in many cases similarly dismissive of Roman legal writing, and focused particularly on the dominant role played by "Semitic" jurists in the *Corpus Iuris Ciuilis*. For example, Wagemann criticized the "Jewish lawless spirit" (*jüdische Unrechtsgeist*) inherent in Roman property law and Nicolai's *Racial Theory of Law* (*rassegesetzliche Rechtslehre*) pointedly dismissed Rome's legal legacy as a foreign importation or "*Fremdgut*."[12]

[8] Tuori, *Empire of Law*, p. 45; Giltaij, "Reinventing," pp. 11–12; Ernst, "Fritz Schulz," pp. 123–24.

[9] Tuori (*Empire of Law*, pp. 46–47 n. 8) lists Schulz' best-known writings from 1926 and earlier; outside of a comparative piece on the law of purchase (Schulz, "System") they focus almost exclusively on fragmentary remnants of juristic texts.

[10] Tuori, *Empire of Law*, pp. 46–47.

[11] *Ibid.*, p. 14; Zatloukal, "Regime," p. 18; Kohlhepp, "NS-Zeit," p. 203.

[12] Nicolai, *Die rassegesetzliche Rechtslehre*, p. 6; Wagemann, *Rechtsvergangenheit*, p. 110; see also Gamauf, "Kritik," pp. 53–55.

To state the obvious, none of these people are really talking about Ulpian. The legal tradition that the Nazis attacked as degenerate and sclerotic, and that Schulz viewed as Rome's primary legacy, was a metonym for liberal legal order as it was understood in the early twentieth century.[13] But we can see why this imagined legality was so appealing when *Principles* and *Legal Science* were written. Nazis had destroyed the Weimar *Rechtsstaat*, explicitly suspending normal political order under the *Reichstagsbrandverordnung*, and replaced it with a genocidal horror that Schulz only barely escaped.[14] The exiles who fled this nightmare transformed several different fields, having been transformed themselves.[15] It is clear enough why *Isolierung* might appear to Schulz as an urgent desideratum, and why he might take the Justinianic sources – who themselves wrote about law as if it governed a violent world – as evidence for it.

That said, Schulz' distinctive understanding of Roman law does not only animate his writing on Roman topics. During his time at Oxford[16] Schulz published a series of articles on the thirteenth-century English legal treatise known as *Bracton*.[17] *Bracton* is itself an important monument in the reception of the *Corpus Iuris Ciuilis*, offering a guide to English law in the manner (and often using the exact language) of Classical jurists and reformulating the monarchy along romanistic lines. As McSweeney has recently shown, *Bracton* is a more complicated work than it seems. Far from neutrally describing existing practice *Bracton* carves out a new and central place for judges and jurisprudence in a system that had not cast them – at least in the eyes of the disgruntled men who wrote the thing – in sufficiently important roles.[18]

[13] See Osler, "The Fantasy Men," pp. 191–92.

[14] See Honig, *Emergency Politics*, pp. 66–67; Dyzenhaus, *The Constitution of Law*, pp. 58–59 (on the "black hole" inherent in regimes that embrace unlimited emergency powers).

[15] See e.g. Benhabib, *Exile, Statelessness, and Migration*; Burke, *Exiles and Expatriates*; Camurri, "The Exile Experience Reconsidered"; Ash and Söllner (eds.), *Forced Migration and Scientific Change*; Fermi, *Illustrious Immigrants*.

[16] Schulz arrived at Oxford in late 1939 as an impoverished refugee and remained there until his death in 1957.

[17] Schulz, "Bracton as a Computist"; "Bracton and Raymond de Peñafort"; "Bracton on Kingship"; "A New Approach to Bracton"; "Critical Studies on Bracton's Treatise."

[18] McSweeney, *Priests*, pp. 199–204.

It is obvious why *Bracton* featured in Schulz' Oxonian work. Like many other scholars-in-exile produced by the Second World War, Schulz needed a new research topic that better fit the interests of his new colleagues (and potential employers).[19] *Bracton*, specifically, let Schulz apply the skills he had brought from Berlin – careful reconstruction of damaged or fragmentary Latin texts – to an English legal tradition.[20] But Schulz' writings on *Bracton* also show the close connection between Roman law and legal supremacy, and why the former might have been so appealing to those who cared about the latter. Schulz addresses these themes most directly in "Bracton on Kingship," which focuses on Henry de Bracton's account of regal sovereignty, excerpted below. Bracton (and *Bracton*) present a vision of the rule of law that was plausible in the thirteenth century but that is hard to square with the Roman sources.

The king, on account of his being a minister of God and his representative on earth, may do nothing except what is permitted to him by law.

*It does not matter the saying "what pleases the emperor (*princeps*) has the force of law," since it is followed at the end of the law by: "because of a kingly law which has been brought regarding his sovereignty."*

(2.305) Nihil enim aliud potest rex, cum sit Dei minister et uicarius in terris, nisi id solum, quod de iure potest.

Nec obstat quod dicitur: "Quod principi placet, legis habet uigorem," quia sequitur in fine legis: "cum lege regia, quae de imperio eius lata est."[21]

Schulz notes that the first part of the claim is entirely unique to *Bracton*; no Roman jurist would state limits on imperial power as baldly as the text does here.[22] But Schulz nevertheless reads that state of affairs back into the Classical period, and claims that the *lex de imperio Vespasiani* shows that Ulpian would not have been able to

19 A useful comparison is the legal philosopher Hans Kelsen, who was only able to find work in the United States as a political scientist; the American common-law tradition made jurisprudence more easily intelligible as a branch of political theory than as a necessary component of legal education. See Tuori, *Empire of Law*, p. 27; Kmak, "Impact of Exile," pp. 25–26; Burke, *Exiles and Expatriates*, pp. 165–66; Ladavac, "Philosophy of Law and Theory of Law," p. 230; Dreier, "Hans Kelsen," pp. 716–17. On Kelsen's work more broadly and its central European context Wheatley, *Life and Death*, pp.162–78.

20 Ernst, "Fritz Schulz," pp. 185–86.

21 See McSweeney, *Priests*, pp. 64–66.

22 Schulz, "Bracton on Kingship," p. 139.

conceive of unlimited imperial power.[23] This is a very strange claim to make. The *lex* explicitly grants Vespasian unlimited power in its sixth paragraph[24] and also predates Ulpian's writing by 150 years. Furthermore, Ulpian lived in a world that – as Schulz well knew – did not feature practical constraints on imperial power besides the threat of assassination. Schulz acknowledges this practical omnipotence but treats it as a distraction, referring to the emperor's freedom from legal constraint as "merely a political theory" that "obviously contradicted the legal principles of the Augustan principate" but was "nevertheless[] adopted by Roman political writers" and as a "Greek doctrine" rather than "Roman constitutional law."[25] Schulz thus positions legal sovereignty as a uniquely Roman idea, while simultaneously cabining it off from Roman political practice. When Schulz claims that "the *princeps* is not entitled to do whatever he likes, as a non-professional reader might assume"[26] he forces the Roman lawyer in his audience to choose their profession; historians of the empire understand imperial sovereignty as far broader than Schulz' account, even if a jurist might take the constitutionalizing story of the *Digest* at face value and find a rule more honored in the breach than the observance.

Bracton stood on firmer ground than Schulz in delimiting regal power. England in the mid thirteenth century – decades after the issuance of the *Magna Carta* – had a strong aristocratic class whose members understood themselves as possessing certain privileges against the king, understood those privileges as something like bargained-for legal rights, and could make real trouble if those rights were abrogated. Their king – who, notably, had taken the throne as a child – operated under a set of constraints that could be described with the language of *ius*.[27] But even so, the project of *Bracton* was an ideal one. *Bracton* constructed a world in which the royal justices who wrote it are not so much functionaries as "living oracles":[28] "The work

[23] *Ibid.*, p. 154 ("Ulpian cannot have said that by the classical *lex de imperio* an unlimited power was conveyed to the emperor. We know by the *lex de imperio Vespasiani* that only a strictly limited power was given to him, though this *lex* contained a clause by which the emperor was authorized to create law.").

[24] See *supra* p. 86. [25] Schulz, "Bracton on Kingship," pp. 157–58.

[26] *Ibid.*, p. 154.

[27] This is a vast oversimplification – for a more granular account of the development of English constitutionalism in the thirteenth century see Carpenter, *Minority*.

[28] McSweeney, *Priests*, p. 244.

they did was not simply that of a judge or of a royal servant. It was the work of a *iuris prudens*, a jurist."[29] *Bracton* used the structures and texts of Roman law to construct a world slightly different than the one in which it was written, and to present that world as real. In other words, *Bracton* told a story.

* * * * *

So have I, and the story of Roman law that I have told in this book is the story of a world that never quite existed. It is the history of a world that proceeded according to prospective, sovereign rules, as opposed to real worlds which do not work that way. This slantwise relationship to reality is not unique to Roman legal history, or historiography; Schulz and *Bracton* show us that. That said, because Roman law has been so wildly influential on later legalities its stories are sometimes taken to be true.[30] They are not, at least in the predictive sense that we sometimes use to evaluate the truth of a legal system's claims. They do not tell us how a Classical courtroom would have necessarily worked, but they still mattered then and still matter today.

What Law Does Instead

Law can break your heart. The disjunct between "law on the books" and "law on the ground" is often quite depressing, and both Roman and modern law trains us to look for an order that real life rarely provides. What we get instead is violent and unpredictable – the legally unmediated states of being that Agamben termed "bare life" are unsettling, especially to the kind of person who writes legal history.[31] We want the rules and general statements contained with the law-code to have something to do with reality, especially when reality is so often less just.

Accordingly, legal historians sometimes end their work in strange places. The classic example of this problem is Thompson's *Whigs and Hunters*, which describes a sinister encroachment of the industrial state upon premodern subsistence practices and the subordination of law to class oppression before ending with an almost fantastical account of law's civilizing force. In Thompson's telling, England's "culture of constitutionalism"[32] caused its wealthy to mediate their power through

[29] *Ibid.*, p. 240. [30] Tuori, *Ideals*, p. 186. [31] Agamben, *Homo Sacer*, pp. 6–10.
[32] Thompson, *Whigs and Hunters*, p. 259.

legal forms, and those forms inherently rendered that power more evenhanded and fair.[33] Ironically, Thompson views this feature of law as a legacy of Roman jurisprudence, not of statute law or practice; the intellectual exercise of the jurists produced a "universal value" to the benefit of Europe's ruled.[34] Law is not as powerful as Thompson here claims: not even for the Romans.[35] The procedures contained within the English law-code or the *Corpus Iuris Ciuilis* are more evenhanded and orderly than what other sources preserve, and we should not assume that codified law will always bring readers up to its level.

In fact, the polarity often runs the other way. For example, I write as a citizen of a country that has a real problem with lawless state violence. America has all kinds of rules about when its police are authorized to use deadly force, and those rules are often ignored in arbitrary and racialized ways.[36] The web of regulations that purports to govern police killing often has a perverse legitimating effect – people assume that, since it is illegal for cops to shoot someone without a good reason, they probably had a good reason.[37] A state can have all kinds of legal protections on their books while still tolerating different conditions on the ground, and may in fact use those protections as prophylactics against social change.

That said, those legal protections may in time take on a different character. This book has described a legality that was largely fiction as it was written, but that (much) later readers looked to for guidance in making their own rules. Juristic texts played a different role in sixth-century Constantinople than they did in Severan Rome, and a different one still in thirteenth-century England. If law is, as Gordon says, where a society distills and collects its vision for an ideal polity, that vision may outlive the conditions of its drafting.[38] Ulpian's story of the legally authorized king inspired *Bracton*, and the United States Constitution's guarantee of "equal protection of the laws" coexisted with race- and sex-

[33] *Ibid.*, p. 266 ("The forms and rhetoric of law acquire a distinct identity which may, on occasion, inhibit power and afford some protection to the powerless.").

[34] *Ibid.*, p. 267. Thompson distinguishes between the common and civil laws, with Roman jurisprudence only influencing the latter, but takes them both as means to the same social end.

[35] Horwitz, "Unqualified?"; see also Levinson and Balkin, "Wrestles."

[36] See, for scattered and grim examples, Hirschfield, "Exceptionally Lethal"; Starr, "Testing Racial Profiling."

[37] This mechanism is laid out in Lerner and Simmons, "Observer's Reaction."

[38] Gordon, "Histories," pp. 120–22; also Tushnet, *Humanity and Interest*, pp. 27–30.

based subordinations at the time it was written but still informs efforts to stamp those out. Later political formations have often taken legal rhetoric more seriously than those in which the rhetoric was first composed.

This hortatory effect arises from the distinctive generic qualities of law, which constructs an ideal world in the process of governing a real one.[39] That duplicative register helps law misrepresent its own reality – as it has for much of this book – but also lets subsequent actors use legalizing rhetoric to minimize the revolutionary nature of their own projects. For example, theories of "living constitutionalism" position social change as in line with pre-existing (and perhaps unfulfilled) constitutional commitments;[40] Rosenberg's theory of American constitutional development holds that courts reinterpret existing provisions as a way to accommodate political shifts without appearing to change codified law;[41] and (most importantly for the present project) advocates for liberal legal order can subsume that order within a millennia-old tradition by reading historical texts as neutral descriptions of premodern legal practice.[42] Roman law is not the only Classical corpus to be read as a guide to modernity,[43] but law is unique in its ability to bridge past and present. Law trains its reader to look to prior decisions as authoritative, and to see those decisions as more authoritative than they were or are. Whether this representation is idealistic or misleading depends on your point of view, but either way Roman law is a remarkable and extreme case.

I cannot tell you how to feel about law, but this feature of legal storytelling makes it a bit easier for me to take. I live in a society that I want to be fairer and safer than it is, but I am hardly the first – the laws that govern my imperfect world do not order it in the way that I would like but they might, later, help structure something better. That is not the rule of law, to be sure. But neither is it nothing.

[39] See Constable, *Bond*, p. 10 (describing legal claims as "social acts that appeal implicitly to justice and that occur within the horizon of a world that is shown and yet not exhausted by our saying").

[40] E.g. Balkin, *Living Originalism*, pp. 277–319; Strauss, *The Living Constitution*.

[41] Rosenberg, *The Hollow Hope*; for a less pessimistic account Siegel, "De Facto ERA."

[42] For example, when Reinhart Zimmermann describes the increasingly transnational private law of Europe as a "new *ius commune*" he portrays European integration as the renovation of ancient Roman practice. Zimmermann, *Roman Law, Contemporary Law, European Law*, p. 109.

[43] See Herz, "Epistemology of the Courthouse," pp. 30–34; Butler (ed.), *Deep Classics*; Tziovas (ed.), *Re-Imagining the Past*; Winterer, *Classicism*.

APPENDIX I

Juristic Citations of Imperial Lawmaking in the *Digest*

Please find below the 1,255 fragments preserved withi n the *Digest* in which jurists cite imperially made law. When fragments cite multiple imperial authorities they are separated by commas and arranged in chronological order; when a fragment cites an authority written by multiple emperors those emperors are separated by a slash. Thus, a fragment that cites an edict of the emperor Pius and a rescript jointly authored by Septimius Severus and Caracalla will be coded as 'Pius, Severus/Caracalla'.

Location	Author	Text	Authority
1.2.2.32	Pomponius	Enchiridion	Augustus, Claudius, Titus, Nerva
1.2.2.49	Pomponius	Enchiridion	Augustus, Hadrian
1.3.38	Callistratus	Quaestiones	Severus
1.5.8	Papinian	Quaestiones	Pius
1.5.17	Ulpian	Ad Edictum	Caracalla
1.5.18	Ulpian	Ad Sabinum	Hadrian
1.6.1.2	Gaius	Institutiones	Pius
1.6.2	Ulpian	De Officio Proconsulis	Hadrian, Pius
1.7.8	Modestinus	Regulae	Claudius
1.7.32.1	Papinian	Quaestiones	Pius
1.7.39	Ulpian	De Officio Consulis	Marcus
1.8.4	Marcianus	Institutiones	Pius

(*continued*)

Location	Author	Text	Authority
1.8.6.1	Marcianus	Institutiones	Diui Fratres
1.8.7	Ulpian	Ad Edictum	Diui Fratres
1.9.3	Modestinus	Regulae	Severus/Caracalla
1.9.12pr.	Ulpian	De Censibus	Caracalla
1.12.1pr.	Ulpian	De Officio Praefecti Urbi	Severus
1.12.1.4	Ulpian	De Officio Praefecti Urbi	Severus
1.12.1.8	Ulpian	De Officio Praefecti Urbi	Severus
1.12.1.14	Ulpian	De Officio Praefecti Urbi	Severus
1.12.2	Paul	De Officio Praefecti Urbi	Hadrian
1.15.1	Paul	De Officio Praefecti Vigilum	Augustus
1.15.3.2	Paul	De Officio Praefecti Vigilum	Caracalla
1.15.4	Ulpian	De Officio Praefecti Urbi	Severus/Caracalla
1.16.4pr.	Ulpian	De Officio Proconsulis	Severus/Caracalla
1.16.4.5	Ulpian	De Officio Proconsulis	Caracalla
1.16.6.3	Ulpian	De Officio Proconsulis	Severus/Caracalla
1.16.10.1	Ulpian	De Officio Proconsulis	Hadrian
1.18.13.1	Ulpian	De Officio Proconsulis	Pius, Diui Fratres
1.18.14	Macer	De Iudiciis Publicis	Marcus/Commodus
1.19.3.1	Callistratus	De Cognitionibus	Pius
1.19.3.2	Callistratus	De Cognitionibus	Severus/Caracalla
1.20.2	Ulpian	Ad Sabinum	Marcus
1.21.4pr.	Macer	De Officio Praesidis	Severus/Caracalla
1.22.2	Marcianus	De Iudiciis Publicis	*aliquo … decreto principali*
2.1.11pr	Gaius	Ad Edictum Prouinciale	Pius
2.4.3	Callistratus	De Cognitionibus	Diui Fratres

(*continued*)

Location	Author	Text	Authority
2.4.10pr.	Ulpian	Ad Edictum	Marcus
2.8.7pr.	Ulpian	Ad Edictum	Pius
2.12.1pr.	Ulpian	De Omnibus Tribunalibus	Marcus
2.12.2	Ulpian	Ad Edictum	Marcus
2.12.7	Ulpian	De Officio Consulis	Marcus
2.12.9	Ulpian	De Officio Proconsulis	Trajan
2.13.4.5	Ulpian	Ad Edictum	*hoc est constitutum*
2.14.8	Papinian	Responsa	Marcus
2.14.10pr.	Ulpian	Ad Edictum	Pius, Marcus
2.14.16pr.	Ulpian	Ad Edictum	Pius
2.14.37	Papirius Iustus	De Constitutionibus	Diui Fratres
2.14.46	Tryphoninus	Disputationes	Marcus
2.14.52.3	Ulpian	Opiniones	*rescriptum est*
2.14.60	Papirius Iustus	De Constitutionibus	Marcus
2.15.3pr.	Scaevola	Digesta	Diui Fratres
2.15.7.2	Ulpian	Disputationes	*sit et dictum et rescriptum*
2.15.8pr.	Ulpian	De Omnibus Tribunalibus	Marcus
2.15.8.12	Ulpian	De Omnibus Tribunalibus	Marcus
3.1.8	Papinian	Quaestiones	Hadrian, Pius
3.1.11pr.	Tryphoninus	Disputationes	Severus
3.2.13.7	Ulpian	Ad Edictum	*ut est constitutum est et responsum*
3.2.24	Ulpian	Ad Edictum	Severus
3.3.33.2	Ulpian	Ad Edictum	Caracalla
3.5.3.4	Ulpian	Ad Edictum	Pius
3.5.5.14(12)	Ulpian	Ad Edictum	Pius
3.5.33(34)	Paul	Quaestiones	Pius
3.5.37	Tryphoninus	Disputationes	*est constitutum a diuis principibus*
3.5.43(44)	Ulpian	Disputationes	Severus
3.6.1.3	Ulpian	Ad Edictum	Caracalla
3.6.5pr.	Ulpian	Ad Edictum	*nam est constitutum*
4.1.6	Ulpian	Ad Edictum	*saepissime constitutum*

(*continued*)

Location	Author	Text	Authority
4.1.7pr.	Marcellus	Digesta	Pius
4.2.9.3	Ulpian	Ad Edictum	Caracalla
4.2.13	Callistratus	De Cognitionibus	Marcus
4.2.16.2	Ulpian	Ad Edictum	*ut est et rescriptum*
4.2.18	Julianus	Digesta	Pius
4.4.2	Ulpian	Ad Legem Iuliam et Papiam	Severus
4.4.3pr.	Ulpian	Ad Edictum	Severus/Caracalla
4.4.3.1	Ulpian	Ad Edictum	*est et constitutum*
4.4.3.4	Ulpian	Ad Edictum	Claudius
4.4.7.2	Ulpian	Ad Edictum	*constitutione principum*
4.4.7.9	Ulpian	Ad Edictum	*et hoc et rescriptum et responsum est*
4.4.7.10	Ulpian	Ad Edictum	Pius, Caracalla
4.4.11pr	Ulpian	Ad Edictum	Severus
4.4.11.1	Ulpian	Ad Edictum	Marcus
4.4.11.2	Ulpian	Ad Edictum	Severus
4.4.18.1	Ulpian	Ad Edictum	Severus/Caracalla
4.4.18.2	Ulpian	Ad Edictum	Severus/Caracalla
4.4.18.3	Ulpian	Ad Edictum	Caracalla
4.4.20.1	Ulpian	Ad Edictum	*ut est saepissime rescriptum*
4.4.22	Ulpian	Ad Edictum	Severus/Caracalla
4.4.38pr	Paul	Decreta	Severus
4.4.45.1	Callistratus	Edictum Monitorium	Pius
4.6.8	Paul	Breuia	Marcus/Commodus
4.6.26.9	Ulpian	Ad Edictum	*et saepissime constitutum est*
4.6.35.4	Paul	Ad Legem Iuliam et Papiam	Pius
4.8.27.2	Ulpian	Ad Edictum	Pius
4.8.32.14	Paul	Ad Edictum	Caracalla
5.1.2.3	Ulpian	Ad Edictum	Pius
5.1.2.4	Ulpian	Ad Edictum	Pius
5.1.36pr	Callistratus	De Cognitionibus	Diui Fratres
5.1.37	Callistratus	De Cognitionibus	Hadrian
5.1.47	Callistratus	Quaestiones	Hadrian

(*continued*)

Location	Author	Text	Authority
5.1.48	Paul	Responsa	Hadrian
5.1.50pr.	Ulpian	Fideicommissa	*multis constitutionibus cauetur*
5.1.50.2	Ulpian	Fideicommissa	*Sed et rescriptum est*
5.1.51	Marcianus	Institutiones	Severus/Caracalla
5.1.67	Ulpian	Disputationes	*constitutio . . . praecipit*
5.2.6.2	Ulpian	Ad Edictum	*et quibusdam rescriptis significatur*
5.2.7	Paul	De Septemuiralibus Iudiciis	Pius
5.2.8.2	Ulpian	Ad Edictum	*saepissime rescriptum est*
5.2.8.15	Ulpian	Ad Edictum	Pius
5.2.8.16	Ulpian	Ad Edictum	Hadrian, Pius
5.2.18	Paul	De Inofficioso Testamento	Diui Fratres
5.2.28	Paul	De Septemuiralibus Iudiciis	Hadrian
5.2.29pr.	Ulpian	Opiniones	*constitutum est*
5.2.30.1	Marcianus	Institutiones	Severus/Caracalla
5.3.5pr	Ulpian	Ad Edictum	Pius
5.3.5.1	Ulpian	Ad Edictum	Hadrian
5.3.7pr	Ulpian	Ad Edictum	Trajan
5.3.7.1	Ulpian	Ad Edictum	Pius
5.3.7.2	Ulpian	Ad Edictum	Pius
5.3.20.12	Ulpian	Ad Edictum	Severus
5.3.22	Paul	Ad Edictum	Hadrian
5.3.25.16	Ulpian	Ad Edictum	Marcus
5.3.40pr	Paul	Ad Edictum	Hadrian
5.3.43	Paul	Ad Plautium	Caracalla
6.2.11pr.	Ulpian	Ad Edictum	Severus
6.2.12pr.	Paul	Ad Edictum	Pius
7.5.12	Marcianus	Institutiones	Severus/Caracalla
7.8.22pr.	Pomponius	Ad Quintum Mucium	Hadrian
8.2.14	Papirius Iustus	De Constitutionibus	Diui Fratres

(*continued*)

Location	Author	Text	Authority
8.3.16	Callistratus	De Cognitionibus	Pius
8.3.17	Papirius Iustus	De Constitutionibus	Diui Fratres
8.3.35	Atilicinus	Ad Plautium (Paul)	Caesar
8.4.2	Ulpian	Ad Edictum	Caracalla
9.2.29.1	Ulpian	Ad Edictum	Severus
10.1.7	Modestinus	Pandectae	*idque ita rescriptum est*
10.2.2.1	Ulpian	Ad Edictum	Pius
10.2.18.3	Ulpian	Ad Edictum	Severus/Caracalla
10.2.20.1	Ulpian	Ad Edictum	Caracalla
10.2.25	Paul	Ad Edictum	*constitutiones*
10.2.41	Paul	Decreta	Severus
11.1.6.1	Ulpian	Ad Edictum	Hadrian
11.2.2	Papinian	Quaestiones	*rescriptis principum continetur*
11.4.1.2	Ulpian	Ad Edictum	Marcus/Commodus
11.4.3	Ulpian	De Officio Proconsulis	Pius, Marcus
11.4.5	Tryphoninus	Disputationes	Pius
11.6.7.3	Ulpian	Ad Edictum	Severus
11.7.6pr.	Ulpian	Ad Edictum	*et saepissime idem constitutum est*
11.7.6.1	Ulpian	Ad Edictum	Diui Fratres
11.7.12pr.	Ulpian	Ad Edictum	Severus/Caracalla
11.7.14.7	Ulpian	Ad Edictum	Caracalla
11.7.14.14	Ulpian	Ad Edictum	Marcus
11.7.37.1	Macer	Ad Legem Vicensimam Hereditatium	Hadrian
11.7.39	Marcianus	Institutiones	Diui Fratres
12.1.33	Modestinus	Pandectae	*principalibus constitutionibus cauetur*
12.2.5.1	Ulpian	Ad Edictum	Pius
12.2.13.6	Ulpian	Ad Edictum	Severus/Caracalla
12.2.31	Gaius	Ad Edictum Prouinciale	*constitutionibus principum*
12.3.4pr.	Ulpian	Ad Edictum	Diui Fratres, Severus/Caracalla, *hoc enim saepissime rescriptum est*

(*continued*)

Location	Author	Text	Authority
12.3.4.1	Ulpian	Ad Edictum	Severus/Caracalla
12.3.10	Callistratus	Quaestiones	Commodus
12.4.5.1	Ulpian	Disputationes	*constitutio succedit*
12.5.2.2	Ulpian	Ad Edictum	Caracalla
12.6.2.1	Ulpian	Ad Sabinum	Hadrian
12.6.3	Papinian	Quaestiones	Pius
12.6.4	Paul	Ad Sabinum	Hadrian
12.6.5	Ulpian	Ad Sabinum	*rescriptum est*
12.6.23.1	Ulpian	Ad Sabinum	Severus/Caracalla
12.6.26pr.	Ulpian	Ad Sabinum	Severus
12.6.39	Marcianus	Institutiones	Severus/Caracalla
13.6.3pr.	Ulpian	Ad Edictum	Pius
13.6.5.2	Ulpian	Ad Edictum	*ut est et constitutum*
13.7.11.6	Ulpian	Ad Edictum	Caracalla
13.7.13.pr	Ulpian	Ad Edictum	*scripsit Julianus et est rescriptum*
13.7.17	Marcianus	Ad Formulam Hypothecariam	Severus/Caracalla
13.7.26pr.	Ulpian	Disputationes	Severus/Caracalla
13.7.36pr.	Ulpian	Ad Edictum	*est saepissime rescriptum*
14.2.9	Volusius Maecianus	Ex Lege Rhodia	Augustus, Pius
14.5.8	Paul	Decreta	Severus
14.6.3.1	Ulpian	Ad Edictum	*et est saepe constitutum*
14.6.9.4	Ulpian	Ad Edictum	Hadrian
14.6.15	Marcianus	Institutiones	Severus/Caracalla
15.1.52	Paul	Quaestiones	*id rescriptum est*
16.1.2pr	Ulpian	Ad Edictum	Claudius
16.1.2.3	Ulpian	Ad Edictum	Pius, Severus
16.1.4pr.	Ulpian	Ad Edictum	Pius, Caracalla
16.2.11	Ulpian	Ad Edictum	Severus
16.2.12	Ulpian	ad Edictum	*constitutum*
16.2.24	Paul	Decreta	Severus
16.3.7.3	Ulpian	Ad Edictum	*rescripto principali significatur*
16.3.24	Papinian	Quaestiones	*et est quidem constitutum*

(*continued*)

Location	Author	Text	Authority
17.1.6.7	Ulpian	Ad Edictum	Diui Fratres
17.1.8.8	Ulpian	Ad Edictum	Diui Fratres
17.1.12.9	Ulpian	Ad Edictum	*ut est constitutum*
17.1.12.10	Ulpian	Ad Edictum	Severus
17.2.23.1	Ulpian	Ad Sabinum	Marcus
17.2.25	Paul	Ad Sabinum	Severus
17.2.52.5	Ulpian	Ad Edictum	Severus
17.2.52.10	Ulpian	Ad Edictum	Marcus
18.1.42	Marcianus	Institutiones	Diui Fratres
18.1.46	Marcianus	De Delatoribus	Severus/Caracalla
18.1.71	Papirius Iustus	De Constitutionibus	Diui Fratres
18.2.16	Ulpian	Ad Edictum	Severus
18.3.4pr.	Ulpian	Ad Edictum	Severus/Caracalla
18.7.5	Papinian	Quaestiones	*principum mandatis praeciperetur*
18.7.10	Scaevola	Digesta	Hadrian, Marcus
19.1.11.16	Ulpian	Ad Edictum	*multis constitutionibus effectum est*
19.1.13.26*	Papinian	Responsa	*in fraudem constiutionum uideri*
19.1.43	Paul	Quaestiones	*quo continebatur Arescusam pertinere ad rescriptum sacrarum constitutionum*
19.2.9.1	Ulpian	Ad Edictum	Severus/Caracalla
19.2.9.4	Ulpian	Ad Edictum	Severus/Caracalla
19.2.15.3	Ulpian	Ad Edictum	*rescriptum est*
19.2.15.5	Ulpian	Ad Edictum	Caracalla
19.2.15.6	Ulpian	Ad Edictum	Caracalla
19.2.19.9	Ulpian	Ad Edictum	Severus/Caracalla
19.2.49pr.	Modestinus	Excusationes	Severus
19.2.54pr	Paul	Responsa	*constitutiones, quibus cauetur*
20.1.16.9	Marcianus	Ad Formulam Hypothecariam	Severus/Caracalla

(*continued*)

Location	Author	Text	Authority
20.3.1.2	Marcianus	Ad Formulam Hypothecariam	Pius
20.5.12pr.	Tryphoninus	Disputationes	Severus
22.1.3pr.	Papinian	Quaestiones	Marcus
22.1.6.pr	Papinian	Quaestiones	Caracalla
22.1.6.1	Papinian	Quaestiones	Severus
22.1.16.1	Paul	Decreta	Severus
22.1.17pr.	Paul	De Usuris	Marcus
22.1.17.1	Paul	De Usuris	Pius
22.1.17.2	Paul	De Usuris	Pius
22.1.17.3	Paul	De Usuris	Pius
22.1.32pr.	Marcianus	Regulae	Pius
22.3.13	Celsus	Digesta	Hadrian
22.3.26	Papinian	Quaestiones	Commodus
22.3.29pr.	Scaevola	Digesta	Diui Fratres
22.5.1.2	Arcadius Charisius	De Testibus	*ex constitutionibus principum*
22.5.3.1	Callistratus	De Cognitionibus	Hadrian
22.5.3.2	Callistratus	De Cognitionibus	Hadrian
22.5.3.3	Callistratus	De Cognitionibus	Hadrian
22.5.3.4	Callistratus	De Cognitionibus	Hadrian
22.5.3.6	Callistratus	De Cognitionibus	Hadrian, Diui Fratres
22.5.25	Arcadius Charisius	De Testibus	*Mandatis cauetur*
22.6.9.1	Paul	De Iuris et Facti Ignorantia	*constitutiones principales*
22.6.9.5	Paul	De Iuris et Facti Ignorantia	Pius, Severus/ Caracalla
23.1.16	Ulpian	Ad Legem Iuliam et Papiam	Marcus/Commodus
23.2.14.4	Paul	Ad Edictum	Augustus
23.2.16pr.	Paul	Ad Edictum	Marcus
23.2.19	Marcianus	Institutiones	Severus/Caracalla
23.2.20	Paul	Ad Orationem Diui Antonini et Commodi	Severus/Caracalla
23.2.45pr.	Ulpian	Ad Legem Iuliam et Papiam	Severus/Caracalla
23.2.45.3	Ulpian	Ad Legem Iuliam et Papiam	*secundum constitutiones*

(*continued*)

Location	Author	Text	Authority
23.2.57a	Marcianus	De Adulteriis (Papinian)	Diui Fratres
23.2.58	Marcianus	Regulae	Pius
23.2.60pr.	Paul	Ad Orationem Diui Antonini et Commodi	*sacris constitutionibus*
23.2.60.3	Paul	Ad Orationem Diui Antonini et Commodi	*sacris constitutionibus*
23.2.65pr.	Paul	Responsa	*idque etiam quibusdam mandatis contineri*
23.2.67.3	Tryphoninus	Disputationes	Marcus
23.3.9.3	Ulpian	Ad Sabinum	Marcus, Severus/ Caracalla
23.3.33	Ulpian	Ad Sabinum	Pius
23.3.40	Ulpian	Ad Edictum	Severus
23.4.11	Ulpian	Ad Edictum	Severus
24.1.3pr.	Ulpian	Ad Sabinum	Caracalla
24.1.3.1	Ulpian	Ad Sabinum	Severus
24.1.7pr.	Ulpian	Ad Sabinum	Severus/Caracalla
24.1.7.2	Ulpian	Ad Sabinum	Hadrian
24.1.7.5	Ulpian	Ad Sabinum	Severus/Caracalla
24.1.7.6	Ulpian	Ad Sabinum	Severus/Caracalla
24.1.7.8	Ulpian	Ad Sabinum	Marcus
24.1.23	Ulpian	Ad Sabinum	Severus
24.1.32pr.	Ulpian	Ad Sabinum	Caracalla
24.1.32.1	Ulpian	Ad Sabinum	Caracalla
24.1.32.14	Ulpian	Ad Sabinum	Caracalla
24.1.32.16	Ulpian	Ad Sabinum	Caracalla
24.1.32.19	Ulpian	Ad Sabinum	Severus/Caracalla
24.1.32.21	Ulpian	Ad Sabinum	Caracalla
24.1.41	Licinius Rufinus	Regulae	Caracalla
24.1.42	Gaius	Ad Edictum Prouinciale	Pius
24.2.8	Papinian	De Adulteriis	Hadrian
24.2.11.2	Ulpian	Ad Legem Iuliam et Papiam	Severus/Caracalla

(*continued*)

Location	Author	Text	Authority
24.3.2.2	Ulpian	Ad Sabinum	Caracalla
25.3.1.15	Ulpian	Ad Edictum	Pius
25.3.5.5	Ulpian	De Officio Consulis	Pius
25.3.5.6	Ulpian	De Officio Consulis	Pius
25.3.5.7	Ulpian	De Officio Consulis	Pius
25.3.5.9	Ulpian	De Officio Consulis	Marcus
25.3.5.11	Ulpian	De Officio Consulis	*rescriptum est*
25.3.5.12	Ulpian	De Officio Consulis	*rescriptis continetur*
25.3.5.14	Ulpian	De Officio Consulis	Marcus
25.3.5.16	Ulpian	De Officio Consulis	*rescriptum est*
25.3.5.17	Ulpian	De Officio Consulis	*rescriptum est*
25.3.6.1	Modestinus	De Manumissionibus	Commodus
25.3.9	Paul	De Iure Patronatus	*plurimis principum constitutionibus*
25.4.1pr.	Ulpian	Ad Edictum	Diui Fratres
26.1.3.1	Ulpian	Ad Sabinum	Caracalla
26.2.2	Ulpian	Ad Sabinum	Diui Fratres
26.2.19.1	Ulpian	Ad Edictum	Diui Fratres
26.3.1.1	Modestinus	Excusationes	ἁι διατάξεις συνεχώρησαν
26.4.1.3	Ulpian	Ad Sabinum	Pius
26.4.3.2	Ulpian	Ad Sabinum	Marcus
26.5.1.1	Ulpian	Ad Sabinum	Marcus
26.5.2	Ulpian	Ad Edictum	Pius
26.5.10	Marcianus	Regulae	Diui Fratres
26.5.12.1	Ulpian	De Officio Proconsulis	Pius, Diui Fratres
26.5.12.2	Ulpian	De Officio Proconsulis	Pius
26.5.13pr.	Papinian	Quaestiones	Hadrian
26.5.18	Ulpian	Ad Edictum	Severus
26.5.21.1	Modestinus	Excusationes	Severus
26.5.24	Paul	Responsa	Diui Fratres
26.5.28	Paul	Decreta	Severus
26.5.29	Paul	De Cognitionibus	Marcus
26.6.2.2	Modestinus	Excusationes	Severus
26.6.2.6	Modestinus	Excusationes	Severus/Caracalla

(*continued*)

Location	Author	Text	Authority
26.6.4.2	Tryphoninus	Disputationes	Severus
26.6.4.4	Tryphoninus	Disputationes	Severus
26.7.1.1	Ulpian	Ad Edictum	Marcus
26.7.2pr.	Ulpian	Ad Edictum	Pius, *et exinde multis rescriptis declaratum est*
26.7.3.4	Ulpian	Ad Edictum	Severus/Caracalla
26.7.5.5	Ulpian	Ad Edictum	*sacris enim constitutionibus*
26.7.7.4	Ulpian	Ad Edictum	Severus
26.7.7.14	Ulpian	Ad Edictum	*multis rescriptis*
26.7.9.6	Ulpian	Ad Edictum	Severus/Caracalla
26.7.11	Ulpian	Ad Edictum	Pius
26.7.12.1	Paul	Ad Edictum	Trajan, Hadrian
26.7.31	Modestinus	Excusationes	Severus/Caracalla
26.7.33.1	Callistratus	De Cognitionibus	Marcus/Commodus
26.7.33.2	Callistratus	De Cognitionibus	*principalibus constitutionibus*
26.7.46.2	Paul	Responsa	*contra constitutiones*
26.7.53	Paul	Decreta	Severus
26.7.55.2	Tryphoninus	Disputationes	*constitutiones, quae iubent*
26.8.1pr.	Ulpian	Ad Sabinum	Pius
26.8.5pr.	Ulpian	Ad Sabinum	Pius
26.8.5.3	Ulpian	Ad Sabinum	Severus/Caracalla
26.10.1.4	Ulpian	Ad Edictum	Severus/Caracalla
26.10.1.7	Ulpian	Ad Edictum	Severus
26.10.3pr.	Ulpian	Ad Edictum	Pius, Severus
26.10.3.13	Ulpian	Ad Edictum	Severus/Caracalla
26.10.7.2	Ulpian	De Omnibus Tribunalibus	Severus/Caracalla
27.1.1.4	Modestinus	Excusationes	Marcus, Severus
27.1.2.4	Modestinus	Excusationes	Severus
27.1.2.6	Modestinus	Excusationes	Severus
27.1.2.7	Modestinus	Excusationes	ταῦτα δὲ καὶ ἐκ διατάξεων
27.1.2.8	Modestinus	Excusationes	Severus/Caracalla
27.1.2.9	Modestinus	Excusationes	Severus/Caracalla
27.1.4pr.	Modestinus	Excusationes	Severus/Caracalla

(*continued*)

Location	Author	Text	Authority
27.1.4.1	Modestinus	Excusationes	Severus/Caracalla
27.1.5	Ulpian	De Officio Praetoris Tutelaris	*saepe rescriptum est*
27.1.6.2	Modestinus	Excusationes	Pius
27.1.6.6	Modestinus	Excusationes	Severus/Caracalla
27.1.6.7	Modestinus	Excusationes	Pius
27.1.6.8*	Modestinus	Excusationes	Pius, Commodus
27.1.6.9	Modestinus	Excusationes	Severus/Caracalla
27.1.6.10	Modestinus	Excusationes	Pius
27.1.6.11	Modestinus	Excusationes	Severus/Caracalla
27.1.6.17	Modestinus	Excusationes	Severus
27.1.6.18	Modestinus	Excusationes	Diui Fratres
27.1.6.19	Modestinus	Excusationes	Hadrian, Caracalla
27.1.7	Ulpian	Excusationes	Diui Fratres
27.1.8.8	Modestinus	Excusationes	καὶ τούτοις ἅπασιν διατάξεις μαρτυροῦσιν
27.1.8.10	Modestinus	Excusationes	Severus/Caracalla
27.1.8.12	Modestinus	Excusationes	ἐκ διατάξεων βασιλικῶν
27.1.9	Ulpian	De Officio Praetoris Tutelaris	Severus/Caracalla
27.1.10.4	Modestinus	Excusationes	Severus/Caracalla
27.1.10.6	Modestinus	Excusationes	Severus
27.1.10.8	Modestinus	Excusationes	Severus/Caracalla
27.1.12pr.	Ulpian	Excusationes (Modestinus)	Severus/Caracalla
27.1.13pr.	Modestinus	Excusationes	Severus/Caracalla
27.1.13.2	Modestinus	Excusationes	Marcus
27.1.13.5	Modestinus	Excusationes	Severus/Caracalla
27.1.13.6	Modestinus	Excusationes	Severus/Caracalla
27.1.13.7	Modestinus	Excusationes	Severus/Caracalla
27.1.13.10	Modestinus	Excusationes	Severus/Caracalla
27.1.13.12	Modestinus	Excusationes	Severus/Caracalla
27.1.14.2	Modestinus	Excusationes	Caracalla
27.1.15pr.	Modestinus	Excusationes	Severus/Caracalla
27.1.15.2	Modestinus	Excusationes	Marcus/Commodus
27.1.15.5	Modestinus	Excusationes	αἱ θεῖαι διατάξεις

(*continued*)

Location	Author	Text	Authority
27.1.15.16	Ulpian	de Excusationibus (Modestinus)	*invenio rescriptum*
27.1.15.17	Modestinus	Excusationes	Hadrian
27.1.16	Modestinus	Responsa	Marcus
27.1.17pr.	Callistratus	De Cognitionibus	*principalibus constitutiones*
27.1.17.1	Callistratus	De Cognitionibus	Pius
27.1.17.2	Callistratus	De Cognitionibus	*principalibus constitutiones*
27.1.17.4	Callistratus	De Cognitionibus	Marcus
27.1.17.6	Callistratus	De Cognitionibus	Trajan
27.1.26	Paul	Excusationes	Marcus/Commodus
27.1.30pr.	Papinian	Responsa	Severus/Caracalla
27.1.44pr.	Tryphoninus	Disputationes	Marcus, Severus/ Caracalla
27.1.44.2	Tryphoninus	Disputationes	*exemplo eo, quo placuit et rescriptum est*
27.1.46.2	Paul	De Cognitionibus	Severus/Caracalla
27.2.1.1	Ulpian	Ad Edictum	Severus
27.2.1.3	Ulpian	Ad Edictum	Severus
27.3.1.3	Ulpian	Ad Edictum	Severus
27.3.1.13	Ulpian	Ad Edictum	Pius, Severus/ Caracalla
27.3.1.15	Ulpian	Ad Edictum	Caracalla, *saepissime rescriptum est*
27.3.4.3	Paul	Ad Sabinum	*constitutum est*
27.3.17	Ulpian	De Officio Consulis	Severus/Caracalla
27.5.1.2	Ulpian	Ad Edictum	Severus
27.7.8.1	Paul	Responsa	*constitutionibus*
27.8.1.2	Ulpian	Ad Edictum	Marcus
27.8.1.8	Ulpian	Ad Edictum	Hadrian
27.8.1.9	Ulpian	Ad Edictum	Hadrian
27.8.6	Ulpian	Ad Edictum	Pius
27.8.9	Modestinus	Pandectae	Severus/Caracalla
27.9.1pr.	Ulpian	Ad Edictum	Severus
27.9.3pr.	Ulpian	Ad Edictum	Severus/Caracalla
27.9.8.1	Ulpian	De Omnibus Tribunalis	Severus

(*continued*)

Location	Author	Text	Authority
27.9.13pr.	Paul	Ad Orationem Diui Severi	Severus/Caracalla
27.9.14[1]	Paul	Responsa	*orationem diuorum principum*
27.10.1.1	Ulpian	Ad Sabinum	Pius
27.10.16pr.	Tryphoninus	Disputationes	Marcus
28.1.15	Ulpian	Ad Edictum	Pius
28.1.20.9	Ulpian	Ad Sabinum	Marcus
28.2.26	Pauli Sententiae		Augustus
28.3.3.2	Ulpian	Ad Sabinum	Marcus
28.3.6.6	Ulpian	Ad Sabinum	Hadrian
28.3.6.7	Ulpian	Ad Sabinum	Hadrian, *constitutiones*
28.3.6.8	Ulpian	Ad Sabinum	*saepissime est constitutum*
28.3.6.9	Ulpian	Ad Sabinum	Marcus
28.3.6.10	Ulpian	Ad Sabinum	*quemadmodum est constitutum*
28.3.12pr.	Ulpian	Disputationes	Hadrian, Caracalla
28.4.3	Marcellus	Digesta	Marcus
28.5.1pr.	Ulpian	Ad Sabinum	Trajan
28.5.1.5	Ulpian	Ad Sabinum	Pius
28.5.1.6	Ulpian	Ad Sabinum	Pius
28.5.9.2	Ulpian	Ad Sabinum	*rescriptis . . . generalibus*
28.5.30	Ulpian	Ad Edictum	Severus
28.5.42(41)	Pomponius	Ex Variis Lectionibus	Tiberius
28.5.49(48).2	Marcianus	Institutiones	Severus/Caracalla
28.5.52(51)pr.	Marcianus	Regulae	Marcus
28.5.85(84).1	Paul	Quaestiones	Marcus
28.5.93(92).1	Paul	Decreta	Severus/Caracalla
28.6.2.4	Ulpian	Ad Sabinum	Caracalla
28.6.4pr.	Modestinus	De Heurematicis	Diui Fratres

[1] In the context of the *Digest*, Paul's claim is linked to an *oratio* of Severus delivered in 195, but the plural genitive – and the lack of any equivalent oratio delivered during Severus and Caracalla's period of joint rule – suggest that Paul's original reference was generic.

(*continued*)

Location	Author	Text	Authority
28.6.4.1	Modestinus	De Heurematicis	Pius
28.6.4.2	Modestinus	De Heurematicis	Severus/Caracalla
28.6.10.6	Ulpian	Ad Sabinum	Pius
28.7.14	Marcianus	Institutiones	*contra edicta imperatorum aut contra leges*
28.7.18pr.	Marcianus	Institutiones	Pius
29.1.1pr.	Ulpian	Ad Edictum	Titus, Domitian, Nerva, Trajan
29.1.2	Gaius	Ad Edictum Prouinciale	*constitutionibus principales*
29.1.3	Ulpian	Ad Sabinum	Marcus
29.1.9.1	Ulpian	Ad Sabinum	Pius
29.1.13.4	Ulpian	Ad Edictum	Severus/Caracalla
29.1.15.2	Ulpian	Ad Edictum	Pius
29.1.21	Africanus	Quaestiones	*quod constitutum est*
29.1.24	Florentinus	Institutiones	Trajan
29.1.25	Marcellus	Responsa	*constitutionibus principum*
29.1.28	Ulpian	Ad Sabinum	Diui Fratres
29.1.30	Paul	Quaestiones	Pius
29.1.34pr.	Papinian	Quaestiones	Hadrian
29.1.41.1	Tryphoninus	Disputationes	Hadrian
29.1.44	Ulpian	Ad Edictum	*rescripta principum*
29.2.6.3	Ulpian	Ad Sabinum	Pius, Caracalla
29.2.12	Ulpian	Ad Edictum	*est in semenstribus rescriptum*
29.2.25.2	Ulpian	Ad Sabinum	*est saepe rescriptum*
29.2.25.3	Ulpian	Ad Sabinum	Pius
29.2.30pr.	Ulpian	Ad Sabinum	Pius
29.2.52pr.	Marcianus	Institutiones	Pius
29.2.61	Macer	De Officio Praesidis	Severus
29.2.86pr.	Papinian	Responsa	Pius
29.4.2pr.	Ulpian	Ad Sabinum	Hadrian
29.4.10.1	Ulpian	Ad Edictum	Pius
29.5.1.5	Ulpian	Ad Edictum	Pius
29.5.1.28	Ulpian	Ad Edictum	Hadrian
29.5.1.29	Ulpian	Ad Edictum	Hadrian

(*continued*)

Location	Author	Text	Authority
29.5.2	Callistratus	De Cognitionibus	Marcus/Commodus
29.5.10.1	Paul	Ad Senatusconsultum Silanianum	Trajan
29.5.15.1	Marcianus	De Delatoribus	Severus/Caracalla
29.6.1pr.	Ulpian	Ad Edictum	Hadrian
29.7.1	Ulpian	Disputationes	*saepissime rescriptum et constitutum est*
29.7.6pr.	Marcianus	Institutiones	Severus/Caracalla
30.34.3	Ulpian	Ad Sabinum	Pius
30.37pr.	Ulpian	Ad Sabinum	Severus/Caracalla
30.41.3	Ulpian	Ad Sabinum	Severus/Caracalla, *ex senatusconsulto et constitutionibus*
30.41.5	Ulpian	Ad Sabinum	Severus/Caracalla
30.41.7	Ulpian	Ad Sabinum	Diui Fratres
30.49pr.[2]	Ulpian	Ad Sabinum	*ita imperatorem decrevisse Marcellus scripsit*
30.73.1[3]	Gaius	De Legatis ad Edictum Praetoris	*rescripto imperatoris nostri significatur*
30.74	Ulpian	Disputationes	Severus/Caracalla
30.77	Ulpian	Disputationes	Pius
30.111	Marcianus	Institutiones	Severus/Caracalla
30.112pr.	Marcianus	Institutiones	Marcus/Commodus
30.112.4	Marcianus	Institutiones	Severus/Caracalla
30.113.1	Marcianus	Institutiones	Severus/Caracalla
30.114.11	Marcianus	Institutiones	Severus/Caracalla
30.114.12	Marcianus	Institutiones	Severus/Caracalla
30.114.14	Marcianus	Institutiones	Severus/Caracalla
30.114.15	Marcianus	Institutiones	Severus/Caracalla
31.1.14.1	Ulpian	Fideicommissa	Hadrian, Caracalla

[2] Ulpian cites Marcellus for the fact of this decree but does not identify the promulgator; because Marcellus frequently describes his own personal interactions with Marcus, the latter is the likely authority here, but Ulpian simply refers to an unnamed imperial author.

[3] The author of this rescript is unknown to us, given our poor knowledge of Gaian chronology. However, it would not have been unknown to Gaius' reader.

(*continued*)

Location	Author	Text	Authority
31.8.5	Paul	Ad Plautium	Hadrian
31.56	Gaius	Ad Legem Iuliam et Papiam	Pius
31.57	Junius Mauricianus	Ad Legem Iuliam et Papiam	Hadrian, Pius
31.61.1	Ulpian	Ad Legem Iuliam et Papiam	Severus
31.64	Papinian	Quaestiones	Marcus/Commodus
31.66pr.	Papinian	Quaestiones	*constitutio principis*
31.67.8	Papinian	Quaestiones	*constitutioni, qua cauetur*
31.67.9	Papinian	Quaestiones	Severus
31.67.10	Papinian	Quaestiones	Marcus
31.69pr.	Papinian	Quaestiones	*idque rescriptum est*
31.70pr.	Papinian	Quaestiones	Caracalla
31.78.1	Papinian	Responsa	Severus
31.87.1	Paul	Responsa	*quamuis enim constitutum sit*
31.87.3	Paul	Responsa	Severus Alexander
31.87.4	Paul	Responsa	Severus Alexander
32.1.4	Ulpian	Fideicommissa	Severus/Caracalla
32.1.9	Ulpian	Fideicommissa	Caracalla
32.8.2	Paul	Fideicommissa	Pius
32.11.1	Maecianus	Unknown (quoted in Ulpian)	Pius
32.11.2	Ulpian	Fideicommissa	Pius
32.11.14	Ulpian	Fideicommissa	*diui constitutiones*
32.11.18	Ulpian	Fideicommissa	Pius
32.11.19	Ulpian	Fideicommissa	Caracalla
32.11.23	Ulpian	Fideicommissa	Diui Fratres
32.11.24	Ulpian	Fideicommissa	Marcus
32.11.25	Ulpian	Fideicommissa	Marcus
32.27pr.	Paul	Decreta	Severus
32.27.1	Paul	Decreta	Severus
32.27.2	Paul	Decreta	Severus
32.37.3	Scaevola	Digesta	Pius
32.39pr.	Scaevola	Digesta	Marcus
32.58	Ulpian	Disputationes	*rescriptum est*

(*continued*)

Location	Author	Text	Authority
32.85[4]	Pomponius	Ad Quintum Mucium	*nuper constitutum est a principe*
32.96	Gaius	Fideicommissa	Pius
32.97	Paul	Decreta	Severus
33.1.23	Marcianus	Institutiones	Severus/Caracalla
33.1.24	Marcianus	Institutiones	Severus/Caracalla
33.2.23	Junius Mauricianus	Ad Legem Iuliam et Papiam	Pius
33.5.1	Ulpian	Ad Sabinum	Pius
33.8.6.4	Ulpian	Ad Sabinum	Severus/Caracalla
33.8.8.7	Ulpian	Ad Sabinum	Severus/Caracalla
34.1.2pr.	Marcianus	Institutiones	Severus/Caracalla
34.1.3	Ulpian	De Officio Consulis	Pius, *rescripta subiecta*
34.1.13.1	Scaevola	Responsa	Pius
34.1.14.1	Ulpian	Fideicommissa	Hadrian, Caracalla
34.3.9	Ulpian	Ad Sabinum	*est saepissime rescriptum*
34.3.25	Paul	Quaestiones	Pius
34.4.13	Marcianus	Institutiones	Severus/Caracalla
34.5.9(10).1	Tryphoninus	Disputationes	Hadrian
34.5.16(17)pr.	Marcianus	Regulae	Pius
34.6.2	Marcianus	Institutiones	Severus/Caracalla
34.8.3pr.	Marcianus	Institutiones	Pius
34.9.1	Marcianus	Institutiones	Severus/Caracalla
34.9.2.1	Marcianus	Institutiones	Severus/Caracalla
34.9.3	Marcianus	Regulae	Pius
34.9.5.1	Paul	De Iure Fisci	Pius
34.9.5.9	Paul	De Iure Fisci	Severus/Caracalla
34.9.5.10	Paul	De Iure Fisci	Severus
34.9.5.15	Paul	De Iure Fisci	Pius
34.9.5.19	Paul	De Iure Fisci	Pius, Marcus
34.9.5.20	Paul	De Iure Fisci	Trajan

[4] *Nuper* suggests that the identity of the promulgator would have been known to readers with a more exact grasp of the commentary's date of publication.

(*continued*)

Location	Author	Text	Authority
34.9.6	Marcellus	Digesta	*rescriptum est*
34.9.12	Papinian	Quaestiones	Marcus
34.9.16.1	Papinian	Responsa	Severus/Caracalla
34.9.16.2	Papinian	Responsa	Marcus
34.9.18pr.	Papinian	Responsa	Severus
35.1.7pr.	Ulpian	Ad Sabinum	Pius
35.1.33pr.	Marcianus	Institutiones	Severus/Caracalla
35.1.33.2	Marcianus	Institutiones	Severus/Caracalla
35.1.48	Marcellus	Digesta	Pius
35.1.50	Ulpian	De Officio Consulis	Pius
35.1.72.1[5]	Papinian	Quaestiones	*imperator permisit*
35.1.72.3	Papinian	Quaestiones	*rescriptum est*
35.1.77pr.	Papinian	Responsa	Pius
35.1.90	Gaius	Fideicommissa	Pius
35.1.92	Ulpian	Fideicommissa	Severus
35.1.113	Paul	Imperiales Sententiae in Cognitionibus Prolatae	*rescriptum est*
35.2.1.14	Paul	Ad Legem Falcidiam	Caracalla
35.2.11.2	Papinian	Quaestiones	Marcus
35.2.13	Papinian	Quaestiones	*constitutum est*
35.2.18pr.	Paul	Quaestiones	Pius
35.2.49pr.	Paul	Ad Plautium	Pius
35.2.59.1	Modestinus	Pandectae	Pius
35.2.89pr.	Marcianus	Institutiones	Severus/Caracalla
35.2.89.1	Marcianus	Institutiones	Severus/Caracalla
35.2.91	Marcianus	Institutiones	Pius
35.2.93	Papinian	Quaestiones	Hadrian
35.3.3.4	Ulpian	Ad Edictum	Diui Fratres
35.3.3.5	Ulpian	Ad Edictum	Pius
35.3.6	Callistratus	De Cognitionibus	Commodus

[5] In the context of the *Quaestiones*, this likely refers to a proceeding held under either Severus or Caracalla; that context has been lost but this does not appear to be a generic citation.

(*continued*)

Location	Author	Text	Authority
35.3.7	Paul	Ad Legem Iuliam et Papiam	Pius
36.1.1.13	Ulpian	Fideicommissa	Severus
36.1.1.17	Ulpian	Fideicommissa	Pius
36.1.3.4	Ulpian	Fideicommissa	Caracalla
36.1.11.2	Ulpian	Fideicommissa	Pius
36.1.12	Papinian	Quaestiones	Pius
36.1.15.2	Ulpian	Fideicommissa	Pius
36.1.15.4	Ulpian	Fideicommissa	Severus/Caracalla
36.1.17(16).17	Ulpian	Fideicommissa	Pius
36.1.18(17).8	Ulpian	Fideicommissa	Pius
36.1.19(18).1	Ulpian	Ad Sabinum	*est et rescriptum*
36.1.19(18).3	Ulpian	Ad Sabinum	Marcus
36.1.20(19)pr.	Paul	Ad Sabinum	*rescriptum est*
36.1.23(22)pr.	Ulpian	Disputationes	Marcus
36.1.25(24)	Papinian	Quaestiones	*uarie rescriptum et iudicatum est*
36.1.30(29)	Marcianus	Institutiones	Severus/Caracalla
36.1.31(30).5	Marcianus	Institutiones	Trajan, Hadrian, Caracalla
36.1.32(31).1	Marcianus	Institutiones	Pius
36.1.36(35)	Ulpian	De Officio Proconsulis	Pius
36.1.38(37).1	Ulpian	Ad Edictum	Severus
36.1.52(50)	Papinian	Quaestiones	Hadrian
36.1.56(54)	Papinian	Quaestiones	Marcus
36.1.57(55).1	Papinian	Quaestiones	Pius
36.1.60(58).3	Papinian	Responsa	Hadrian
36.1.65(63).5	Gaius	Fideicommissa	Pius
36.1.76(74)pr.	Paul	Decreta	Severus
36.1.76(74).1	Paul	Decreta	Severus
36.1.76(74).1	Paul	Decreta	Hadrian, Marcus, Severus
36.1.76(74).1	Paul	Decreta	Marcus
36.3.1.11	Ulpian	Ad Edictum	Pius
36.3.5.1	Papinian	Quaestiones	Marcus
36.3.5.3	Papinian	Quaestiones	Pius
36.3.14.1	Ulpian	Ad Edictum	Pius

(*continued*)

Location	Author	Text	Authority
36.4.1.3	Ulpian	Ad Edictum	Pius
36.4.3.1	Ulpian	Ad Edictum	Pius
36.4.3.3	Ulpian	Ad Edictum	Pius
36.4.5.16	Ulpian	Ad Edictum	Caracalla
36.4.5.21	Ulpian	Ad Edictum	Caracalla
36.4.5.25	Ulpian	Ad Edictum	Caracalla
37.5.5.6	Ulpian	Ad Edictum	Pius
37.5.7	Tryphoninus	Disputationes	Pius
37.5.23	Hermogenianus	Iuris Epitome	Pius
37.6.1.14	Ulpian	Ad Edictum	Diui Fratres
37.6.1.15	Ulpian	Ad Edictum	*multis constitutionibus*
37.6.1.21	Ulpian	Ad Edictum	Pius
37.6.5pr.	Ulpian	Ad Edictum	Diui Fratres
37.7.1pr.	Ulpian	Ad Edictum	Pius
37.7.9	Tryphoninus	Disputationes	Marcus
37.8.3	Marcellus	Digesta	Marcus
37.8.4	Modestinus	Pandectae	Marcus
37.8.7	Tryphoninus	Disputationes	Pius
37.9.1.14	Ulpian	Ad Edictum	Hadrian
37.9.8	Paul	De Adulteriis	Hadrian
37.10.1.5	Ulpian	Ad Edictum	Pius
37.10.3.1	Ulpian	Ad Edictum	Pius
37.10.3.2	Ulpian	Ad Edictum	*constitutionibus*
37.10.3.5	Ulpian	Ad Edictum	Hadrian
37.12.1.4	Ulpian	Ad Edictum	Pius
37.12.5	Papinian	Quaestiones	Trajan
37.13.1pr.	Ulpian	Ad Edictum	*constiutiones principales*
37.14.3	Marcianus	Institutiones	Severus/Caracalla
37.14.4	Marcellus	Institutiones	Severus/Caracalla
37.14.5pr.	Marcellus	Institutiones	Claudius
37.14.5.1	Marcellus	Institutiones	Marcus
37.14.7pr.	Modestinus	De Manumissionibus	Vespasian
37.14.7.1	Modestinus	De Manumissionibus	*mandatis imperatorum*
37.14.8pr.	Modestinus	Regulae	Hadrian

(*continued*)

Location	Author	Text	Authority
37.14.17pr.	Ulpian	Ad Legem Iuliam et Papiam	Diui Fratres
37.14.23.1	Tryphoninus	Disputationes	Hadrian
37.14.24	Paul	Decreta	Severus
37.15.4	Marcianus	De Iudiciis Publicis	Severus/Caracalla
38.1.7.4	Ulpian	Ad Sabinum	Hadrian, *rescriptum est a diuo Hadriano et deinceps*
38.1.13pr.	Ulpian	Ad Edictum	Marcus
38.1.13.1	Ulpian	Ad Edictum	Marcus
38.2.3pr.	Ulpian	Ad Edictum	*multis rescriptis*
38.2.3.8	Ulpian	Ad Edictum	Hadrian
38.2.6.1	Ulpian	Ad Edictum	Marcus
38.2.16.4	Ulpian	Ad Edictum	Diui Fratres
38.2.22	Marcianus	Institutiones	Hadrian
38.2.42.3	Papinian	Quaestiones	Marcus
38.5.13	Papinian	Quaestiones	Pius
38.16.1.1	Ulpian	Ad Sabinum	Diui Fratres, Caracalla
38.16.2.7	Ulpian	Ad Sabinum	Pius
38.16.3.3	Ulpian	Ad Sabinum	Marcus
38.16.3.12	Ulpian	Ad Sabinum	Pius
38.16.15	Papinian	Quaestiones	*per . . . constitutionem*
38.17.1.3	Ulpian	Ad Sabinum	Severus/Caracalla
38.17.2.2	Ulpian	Ad Sabinum	Caracalla
38.17.2.9	Ulpian	Ad Sabinum	Pius
38.17.2.23	Ulpian	Ad Sabinum	*constitutio*
38.17.2.32	Ulpian	Ad Sabinum	*rescripto*
38.17.2.47	Ulpian	Ad Sabinum	Severus/Caracalla
38.17.9[6]	Gaius	Ad Senatusconsultum Orphitianum	*sacratissimi principis nostri oratione cauetur*
39.2.48	Marcianus	De Delatoribus	*constitutum est*
39.4.4.1	Paul	Ad Edictum	Hadrian

6 The author of this rescript is unknown to us, given our poor knowledge of Gaian chronology. However, it would not have been unknown to Gaius' reader.

(*continued*)

Location	Author	Text	Authority
39.4.4.2	Paul	Ad Edictum	*principalibus constitutionibus cauetur*
39.4.6	Modestinus	De Poenis	Severus/Caracalla
39.4.7pr	Papirius Iustus	De Constitutionibus	Diui Fratres
39.4.7.1	Papirius Iustus	De Constitutionibus	Diui Fratres
39.4.16pr.	Marcianus	De Delatoribus	Severus/Caracalla
39.4.16.1	Marcianus	De Delatoribus	Severus/Caracalla
39.4.16.2	Marcianus	De Delatoribus	Severus/Caracalla
39.4.16.4	Marcianus	De Delatoribus	Pius, *ita principalibus constitutionibus*
39.4.16.5	Marcianus	De Delatoribus	Hadrian
39.4.16.6	Marcianus	De Delatoribus	Marcus/Commodus
39.4.16.8	Marcianus	De Delatoribus	Diui Fratres
39.4.16.9	Marcianus	De Delatoribus	Pius
39.4.16.10	Marcianus	De Delatoribus	Diui Fratres
39.4.16.11	Marcianus	De Delatoribus	Caracalla
39.4.16.12	Marcianus	De Delatoribus	Severus/Caracalla
39.4.16.14	Marcianus	De Delatoribus	Severus/Caracalla
39.5.12	Ulpian	Disputationes	Pius
39.5.15	Marcianus	Institutiones	Severus/Caracalla
39.6.15	Paul	Notatio ad Digestum Juliani	*constitutum est*
39.6.42.1	Papinian	Responsa	*ad alia constitutum pertinere*
40.1.4pr.	Ulpian	Disputationes	Diui Fratres
40.1.5pr.	Marcianus	Institutiones	Diui Fratres
40.1.8.2	Marcianus	Institutiones	Pius
40.1.8.3	Marcianus	Institutiones	Hadrian
40.1.10	Paul	Imperiales Sententiae in Cognitionibus Prolatae	Marcus, Severus
40.1.14.1	Paul	Ad Plautium	Augustus
40.1.20pr.	Papinian	Responsa	Marcus
40.1.24	Hermogenianus	Iuris Epitome	*saepe constitutum est*
40.2.9	Marcianus	Institutiones	Pius
40.2.20.1	Ulpian	De Officio Consulis	Marcus

(*continued*)

Location	Author	Text	Authority
40.2.21	Modestinus	Pandectae	Augustus
40.3.1	Ulpian	Ad Sabinum	Marcus
40.4.9.1	Ulpian	Ad Sabinum	*Quod constitutum est*
40.4.26	Marcianus	Regulae	Pius, Diui Fratres
40.4.47[7]	Papinian	Quaestiones	*Princeps constituit*
40.4.50pr.	Papinian	Responsa	Marcus
40.4.52	Paul	Quaestiones	Severus/Caracalla
40.4.56	Paul	Fideicommissa	Marcus
40.5.2	Ulpian	Ad Edictum	Marcus
40.5.4.10	Ulpian	Ad Edictum	Marcus
40.5.4.12	Ulpian	Ad Edictum	Marcus
40.5.4.15	Ulpian	Ad Edictum	Marcus
40.5.12pr.	Modestinus	De Manumissionibus	Caracalla
40.5.12.2	Modestinus	De Manumissionibus	Pertinax, Caracalla
40.5.21[8]	Papinian	Quaestiones	*placuit principi*
40.5.24.5	Ulpian	Fideicommissa	Caracalla
40.5.24.6	Ulpian	Fideicommissa	Pius
40.5.24.9	Ulpian	Fideicommissa	Severus/Caracalla
40.5.24.21	Ulpian	Fideicommissa	Hadrian, Pius, *et ita est saepissime constitutum*
40.5.26pr.	Ulpian	Fideicommissa	*constitutum est*
40.5.26.1	Ulpian	Fideicommissa	Severus
40.5.26.2	Ulpian	Fideicommissa	Pius, Severus/ Caracalla
40.5.26.3	Ulpian	Fideicommissa	Severus/Caracalla
40.5.26.2	Ulpian	Fideicommissa	Pius
40.5.26.8	Ulpian	Fideicommissa	Severus/Caracalla
40.5.30pr.	Ulpian	Fideicommissa	Caracalla
40.5.30.3	Ulpian	Fideicommissa	Diui Fratres
40.5.30.5	Ulpian	Fideicommissa	Pius

7 In the context of the *Quaestiones*, this likely refers to a proceeding held under either Severus or Caracalla; that context has been lost but this does not appear to be a generic citation.

8 In the context of the *Quaestiones*, this likely refers to a proceeding held under either Severus or Caracalla; that context has been lost but this does not appear to be a generic citation.

(*continued*)

Location	Author	Text	Authority
40.5.30.6	Ulpian	Fideicommissa	Pius
40.5.30.7	Ulpian	Fideicommissa	Pius
40.5.30.13	Ulpian	Fideicommissa	Diui Fratres
40.5.30.15	Ulpian	Fideicommissa	Caracalla
40.5.30.16	Ulpian	Fideicommissa	Marcus
40.5.30.17	Ulpian	Fideicommissa	Severus/Caracalla
40.5.31.1	Paul	Fideicommissa	Diui Fratres
40.5.31.4	Paul	Fideicommissa	Caracalla
40.5.37	Ulpian	Fideicommissa	Marcus
40.5.38	Paul	Decreta	Severus
40.5.42	Maecianus	Fideicommissa	Pius
40.5.46.3	Ulpian	Disputationes	Severus
40.5.51.9	Marcianus	Institutiones	Pius
40.5.51.11	Marcianus	Institutiones	Pius
40.5.53pr.	Marcianus	Regulae	*constitutum est*
40.7.20.4	Paul	Ad Plautium	Hadrian
40.7.21.1	Pomponius	Ex Plautio	Pius
40.7.34.1	Papinian	Quaestiones	Caracalla
40.8.1	Paul	Ad Plautium	Marcus
40.8.2	Modestinus	Regulae	Claudius
40.8.3	Callistratus	De Cognitionibus	Marcus/Commodus
40.8.6	Marcianus	Ad Formulam Hypothecariam	Marcus
40.8.7	Paul	De Libertatibus Dandis	Severus/Caracalla
40.8.8	Papinian	Responsa	Marcus
40.8.9	Paul	Quaestiones	*constitutiones*
40.9.11.1	Marcianus	Institutiones	Diui Fratres, *principalibus constitutionibus*
40.9.15pr.	Paul	Ad Legem Iuliam	Caracalla
40.9.17pr.	Paul	De Libertatibus	Marcus
40.9.30pr.	Ulpian	Ad Legem Aeliam Sentiam	Marcus
40.10.3	Marcianus	Institutiones	Commodus
40.10.6	Ulpian	Ad Legem Iuliam et Papiam	Hadrian
40.12.23.2	Paul	Ad Edictum	Hadrian

(*continued*)

Location	Author	Text	Authority
40.12.27pr.	Ulpian	De Officio Consulis	Diui Fratres
40.12.27.1	Ulpian	De Officio Consulis	Hadrian
40.12.34	Ulpian	Pandectae	Caracalla
40.12.43	Pomponius	Senatusconsulta	Hadrian
40.14.2pr.	Saturninus	De Officio Proconsulis	Hadrian
40.15.1.2	Marcianus	De Delatoribus	Hadrian
40.15.1.3	Marcianus	De Delatoribus	Marcus
40.15.4	Callistratus	De Iure Fisci	Nerva, Claudius
40.16.2pr.	Ulpian	De Officio Consulis	Marcus
40.16.2.4	Ulpian	De Officio Consulis	Marcus
40.16.3	Callistratus	De Cognitionibus	*principalibus constitutiones*
41.1.16	Florentinus	Institutiones	Pius
41.3.18	Modestinus	Regulae	*constitutum est*
41.3.40	Neratius	Regulae	*constitutum est*
41.3.44pr.	Papinian	Quaestiones	*non enim constitutum est*
41.4.2.8	Paul	Ad Edictum	Trajan
42.1.15pr.	Ulpian	De Officio Consulis	Pius
42.1.15.1	Ulpian	De Officio Consulis	Severus/Caracalla
42.1.15.3	Ulpian	De Officio Consulis	Severus/Caracalla
42.1.15.4	Ulpian	De Officio Consulis	Caracalla
42.1.15.8	Ulpian	De Officio Consulis	Caracalla
42.1.15.9	Ulpian	De Officio Consulis	*rescriptum est*
42.1.20	Modestinus	Differentiae	Pius
42.1.31	Callistratus	De Cognitionibus	Pius
42.1.33	Callistratus	De Cognitionibus	Hadrian
42.1.35	Papirius Iustus	De Constitutionibus	Diui Fratres
42.1.38pr.	Paul	Ad Edictum	Pius
42.1.56	Ulpian	Ad Edictum	Marcus
42.1.59.1	Ulpian	De Omnibus Tribunalibus	*est rescriptum*
42.1.63	Macer	De Appellationibus	*saepe constitutum est . . . ita rescriptum est . . . ex multis*

(*continued*)

Location	Author	Text	Authority
			constitutionibus intellegenda sunt
42.2.6.2	Ulpian	De Omnibus Tribunalibus	Marcus
42.4.7.16	Ulpian	Ad Edictum	Hadrian
42.4.7.19	Ulpian	Ad Edictum	Pius
42.5.24.1	Ulpian	Ad Edictum	Marcus
42.5.30	Papirius Iustus	De Constitutionibus	Diui Fratres
42.6.1.3	Ulpian	Ad Edictum	Severus/Caracalla
42.6.1.6	Ulpian	Ad Edictum	Pius
42.7.4	Papirius Iustus	De Constitutionibus	Diui Fratres
42.8.7	Paul	Ad Edictum	*rescriptum est*
42.8.10.1	Ulpian	Ad Edictum	Severus/Caracalla
42.8.10.13	Ulpian	Ad Edictum	*est saepissime constitutum*
42.8.10.14	Ulpian	Ad Edictum	*est et saepissime constitutum*
43.4.3.1	Ulpian	Ad Edictum	Caracalla
43.4.3.3	Ulpian	Ad Edictum	Hadrian
43.16.1.2	Ulpian	Ad Edictum	*et constitutionibus principum*
43.24.15.6	Ulpian	Ad Edictum	Pius, *deinceps omnes principes rescripserunt*
43.30.1.3	Ulpian	Ad Edictum	Pius, Marcus, Severus
43.30.3.5	Ulpian	Ad Edictum	Pius
44.1.11	Modestinus	Responsa	*principalibus constitutionibus*
44.3.9	Marcianus	Regulae	Caracalla
44.4.4.14	Ulpian	Ad Edictum	*constitutionibus*
44.7.33	Paul	Decreta	*constitutionibus*
45.1.91.3	Paul	Ad Plautium	*habet constitutio*
46.1.26	Gaius	Ad Edictum Prouinciale	Hadrian
46.1.27.1	Ulpian	Ad Edictum	Hadrian
46.1.49.1	Papinian	Quaestiones	Pius
46.1.68pr.	Paul	Decreta	Severus
46.3.5.2	Ulpian	Ad Sabinum	Severus/Caracalla

(*continued*)

Location	Author	Text	Authority
47.4.1.7	Ulpian	Ad Edictum	Marcus, Severus/ Caracalla, *est autem saepissime . . . rescriptum*
47.9.4.1	Paul	Ad Edictum	Caracalla
47.9.7	Callistratus	Quaestiones	Hadrian
47.9.12	Ulpian	De Officio Proconsulis	Severus/Caracalla
47.10.7.6	Ulpian	Ad Edictum	Caracalla
47.10.13.7	Ulpian	Ad Edictum	*est saepissime rescriptum*
47.10.15.13	Ulpian	Ad Edictum	*constiutiones*
47.10.37pr.	Marcianus	Institutiones	*constiutionibus principalibus*
47.10.40	Macer	De Iudiciis Publicis	Severus
47.11.4	Marcianus	Regulae	Severus/Caracalla
47.11.6.1	Ulpian	De Officio Proconsulis	Trajan
47.11.6.2	Ulpian	De Officio Proconsulis	Hadrian
47.11.8	Ulpian	De Officio Proconsulis	Diui Fratres
47.12.3.3	Ulpian	Ad Edictum	Caracalla
47.12.3.4	Ulpian	Ad Edictum	Marcus, Severus
47.12.3.5	Ulpian	Ad Edictum	Hadrian
47.12.3.7	Ulpian	Ad Edictum	Severus
47.14.1pr.	Ulpian	De Officio Proconsulis	Hadrian
47.14.3.3	Callistratus	De Cognitionibus	Trajan
47.15.6	Paul	De Iudiciis Publicis	Severus/Caracalla
47.18.1pr.	Ulpian	De Officio Proconsulis	Diui Fratres
47.18.1.2	Ulpian	De Officio Proconsulis	Marcus
47.19.1	Marcianus	Institutiones	Marcus
47.19.3	Marcianus	De Iudiciis Publicis	Severus/Caracalla
47.21.2	Callistratus	De Cognitionibus	Hadrian
47.21.3.1	Callistratus	De Cognitionibus	Nerva

(*continued*)

Location	Author	Text	Authority
47.22.1pr.	Marcianus	Institutiones	Severus, *mandatis principalibus*
47.22.1.2	Marcianus	Institutiones	Diui Fratres
47.22.3pr.	Marcianus	De Iudiciis Publicis	*mandatis et constitutionibus*
48.1.5pr.	Ulpian	Disputationes	*constitutionibus*
48.1.5.1	Ulpian	Disputationes	Severus/Caracalla
48.1.12.1	Marcianus	De Poenis	*rescriptum est*
48.2.2.1	Papinian	De Adulteriis	Vespasian
48.2.5	Ulpian	De Adulteriis	Marcus
48.2.7.2	Ulpian	De Officio Proconsulis	Pius
48.2.7.3	Ulpian	De Officio Proconsulis	Pius
48.2.7.4	Ulpian	De Officio Proconsulis	Pius
48.2.7.5	Ulpian	De Officio Proconsulis	Pius
48.2.12.1	Saturninus	De Iudiciis Publicis	Hadrian
48.2.13	Marcianus	De Iudiciis Publicis	Severus/Caracalla
48.2.19pr.	Callistratus	De Cognitionibus	Diui Fratres
48.2.19.1	Callistratus	De Cognitionibus	Hadrian
48.2.20	Modestinus	De Poenis	Severus/Caracalla
48.2.22	Papinian	Responsa	Severus/Caracalla
48.3.2.1	Papinian	De Adulteriis	Domitian
48.3.3	Ulpian	De Officio Proconsulis	Pius
48.3.6pr.	Marcianus	De Iudiciis Publicis	Hadrian
48.3.6.1	Marcianus	De Iudiciis Publicis	Pius, *et alii principes rescripserunt*
48.3.7	Macer	De Officio Praesidis	*quibusdam rescriptis*
48.3.12pr.	Callistratus	De Cognitionibus	Hadrian
48.4.5.1	Marcianus	Regulae	Severus/Caracalla
48.4.5.2	Marcianus	Regulae	Severus/Caracalla
48.4.9	Hermogenianus	Iuris Epitome	Severus
48.5.1	Ulpian	De Adulteriis	Augustus
48.5.6.2	Papinian	De Adulteriis	Hadrian
48.5.14(13).3	Ulpian	De Adulteriis	Severus/Caracalla

(*continued*)

Location	Author	Text	Authority
48.5.14(13).8	Ulpian	De Adulteriis	Severus
48.5.20(19)pr.	Ulpian	Ad Legem Iuliam de Adulteriis	*constitutum est*
48.5.28(27).6	Ulpian	De Adulteriis	Hadrian
48.5.30(29).5	Ulpian	De Adulteriis	*rescripto*
48.5.33(32)pr.	Macer	De Iudiciis Publicis	Marcus/Commodus
48.5.34(33)pr.	Marcianus	De Iudiciis Publicis	Pius
48.5.38(37)	Papinian	Quaestiones	*constitutum est*
48.5.39(38).4	Papinian	Quaestiones	Diui Fratres
48.5.39(38).5	Papinian	Quaestiones	Diui Fratres
48.5.39(38).8	Papinian	Quaestiones	Pius, Marcus/ Commodus
48.5.39(38).10	Papinian	Quaestiones	Tiberius
48.6.5.1	Marcianus	Institutiones	Pius
48.6.6	Ulpian	De Officio Proconsulis	Pius
48.7.1.2	Marcianus	Institutiones	Pius, *constitutionibus principum*
48.7.7	Callistratus	De Cognitionibus	Marcus
48.8.1.3	Marcianus	Institutiones	Hadrian
48.8.1.4	Marcianus	Institutiones	Hadrian
48.8.1.5	Marcianus	Institutiones	Pius
48.8.4.1	Ulpian	De Officio Proconsulis	Hadrian
48.8.4.2	Ulpian	De Officio Proconsulis	Hadrian
48.8.5	Paul	De Officio Proconsulis	Hadrian
48.8.11pr.	Modestinus	Regulae	Pius
48.8.14	Callistratus	De Cognitionibus	Hadrian
48.9.5	Marcianus	Institutiones	Hadrian
48.9.9pr.	Modestinus	Pandectae	Hadrian
48.9.9.2	Modestinus	Pandectae	Diui Fratres
48.10.1.4	Marcianus	Institutiones	Severus
48.10.1.9	Marcianus	Institutiones	Severus/Caracalla
48.10.1.10	Marcianus	Institutiones	Severus/Caracalla
48.10.1.11	Marcianus	Institutiones	Severus/Caracalla
48.10.4	Ulpian	Disputationes	Marcus

(*continued*)

Location	Author	Text	Authority
48.10.7	Marcianus	Institutiones	Marcus/Commodus
48.10.11	Marcianus	De Iudiciis Publicis	Diui Fratres
48.10.14.2	Paul	Quaestiones	Claudius
48.10.15pr.	Callistratus	Quaestiones	Claudius
48.10.15.1	Callistratus	Quaestiones	*constitutionibus principalibus*
48.10.15.3	Callistratus	Quaestiones	Pius
48.10.21	Paul	Ad Senatusconsultum Turpillianum	Hadrian
48.10.29	Modestinus	De Enucleatis Casibus	Severus Alexander, *sunt enim rescripta de ea re*
48.10.31	Callistratus	De Cognitionibus	Pius, Diui Fratres
48.10.32.1	Modestinus	De Poenis	Hadrian
48.12.3pr.	Papirius Iustus	De Constitutionibus	Diui Fratres
48.12.3.1	Papirius Iustus	De Constitutionibus	Diui Fratres
48.13.4.2	Marcianus	Institutiones	*constitutionibus*
48.13.5.3 (4.6)	Marcianus	Institutiones	*mandatis principalibus*
48.13.5.4 (3.7)	Marcianus	Institutiones	Trajan, Hadrian
48.13.6(5)	Marcianus	Regulae	Severus/Caracalla
48.13.8.1 (6.2)	Ulpian	De Officio Proconsulis	Pius
48.13.12(10).1	Marcianus	De Iudiciis Publicis	Severus/Caracalla
48.15.3pr.	Marcianus	De Iudiciis Publicis	Severus/Caracalla
48.15.3.1	Marcianus	De Iudiciis Publicis	Severus/Caracalla
48.15.6pr.	Callistratus	De Cognitionibus	Hadrian
48.15.6.1	Callistratus	De Cognitionibus	Hadrian
48.16.7pr.	Ulpian	Disputationes	Hadrian
48.16.10.2	Papinian	De Adulteriis	Trajan
48.16.14	Ulpian	De Officio Proconsulis	Hadrian
48.16.15.1	Macer	De Iudiciis Publicis	*sacris constitutionibus*
48.16.15.4	Macer	Iudicia Publica	Severus/Caracalla
48.16.16	Paul	De Adulteriis	Domitian
48.16.18pr.	Papirius Iustus	De Constitutionibus	Diui Fratres
48.16.18.1	Papirius Iustus	De Constitutionibus	Diui Fratres

(*continued*)

Location	Author	Text	Authority
48.16.18.2	Papirius Iustus	De Constitutionibus	Diui Fratres
48.17.1pr.	Marcianus	De Iudiciis Publicis	Severus/Caracalla
48.17.3	Marcianus	De Iudiciis Publicis	*diui principes uoluerunt*
48.17.5pr.	Modestinus	Pandectae	*Mandatis cauetur*
48.17.5.1	Modestinus	Pandectae	Severus/Caracalla
48.17.5.2	Modestinus	Pandectae	Trajan
48.18.1pr.	Ulpian	De Officio Proconsulis	Augustus, Hadrian
48.18.1.2	Ulpian	De Officio Proconsulis	Hadrian
48.18.1.3	Ulpian	De Officio Proconsulis	Diui Fratres
48.18.1.4	Ulpian	De Officio Proconsulis	Diui Fratres
48.18.1.5	Ulpian	De Officio Proconsulis	Hadrian, Pius
48.18.1.6	Ulpian	De Officio Proconsulis	Diui Fratres
48.18.1.7	Ulpian	De Officio Proconsulis	*saepissime rescriptum est*
48.18.1.9	Ulpian	De Officio Proconsulis	*constitutum est*
48.18.1.10	Ulpian	De Officio Proconsulis	Severus/Caracalla
48.18.1.11	Ulpian	De Officio Proconsulis	Trajan
48.18.1.12	Ulpian	De Officio Proconsulis	Trajan
48.18.1.13	Ulpian	De Officio Proconsulis	Pius
48.18.1.14	Ulpian	De Officio Proconsulis	Diui Fratres
48.18.1.15	Ulpian	De Officio Proconsulis	Severus/Caracalla
48.18.1.16	Ulpian	De Officio Proconsulis	Severus
48.18.1.17	Ulpian	De Officio Proconsulis	Severus
48.18.1.18	Ulpian	De Officio Proconsulis	Severus/Caracalla

(*continued*)

Location	Author	Text	Authority
48.18.1.19	Ulpian	De Officio Proconsulis	Trajan, *constitutiones posteriores*
48.18.1.21	Ulpian	De Officio Proconsulis	Trajan
48.18.1.22	Ulpian	De Officio Proconsulis	Hadrian
48.18.1.23	Ulpian	De Officio Proconsulis	*constitutionibus*
48.18.1.26	Ulpian	De Officio Proconsulis	*quibusdam rescriptis*
48.18.1.27	Ulpian	De Officio Proconsulis	Diui Fratres
48.18.3	Ulpian	Ad Edictum	Severus/Caracalla
48.18.4	Ulpian	Disputationes	*est rescriptum*
48.18.8pr.	Paul	De Adulteriis	Augustus
48.18.9pr.	Marcianus	De Iudiciis Publicis	Pius, Severus, *et aliis rescriptis*
48.18.9.2	Marcianus	De Iudiciis Publicis	Pius
48.18.10pr.	Arcadius Charisius	De Testibus	Pius
48.18.10.2	Arcadius Charisius	De Testibus	*constitutum est*
48.18.12	Ulpian	Ad Edictum	Hadrian
48.18.15.1	Callistratus	De Cognitionibus	Pius
48.18.15.2	Callistratus	De Cognitionibus	Pius
48.18.16pr.	Modestinus	De Poenis	Diui Fratres
48.18.16.1	Modestinus	De Poenis	Pius
48.18.17pr.	Papinian	Responsa	Marcus, Caracalla
48.18.17.2	Papinian	Responsa	Hadrian
48.18.20	Paul	Decreta	Severus
48.18.21	Paul	De Poenis Paganorum	Hadrian
48.19.5pr.	Ulpian	De Officio Proconsulis	Trajan
48.19.8.1	Ulpian	De Officio Proconsulis	Diui Fratres
48.19.8.5	Ulpian	De Officio Proconsulis	Severus
48.19.8.12	Ulpian	De Officio Proconsulis	Caracalla
48.19.9.16	Ulpian	De Officio Proconsulis	Pius

(*continued*)

Location	Author	Text	Authority
48.19.10.2	Macer	De Iudiciis Publicis	*constitutum est*
48.19.15	Venuleius Saturninus	De Officio Proconsulis	*mandatis plenissime cautum est*
48.19.22	Modestinus	Differentiae	Pius
48.19.25pr.	Modestinus	Pandectae	*constitutum est*
48.19.26	Callistratus	De Cognitionibus	Diui Fratres
48.19.27pr.	Callistratus	De Cognitionibus	Diui Fratres, *nonnulla exstant principalia rescripta*
48.19.27.1	Callistratus	De Cognitionibus	*mandatis cauetur*
48.19.28.2	Callistratus	De Cognitionibus	*principalibus rescriptis*
48.19.28.6	Callistratus	De Cognitionibus	Hadrian
48.19.28.7	Callistratus	De Cognitionibus	Pius
48.19.28.13	Callistratus	De Cognitionibus	Hadrian
48.19.28.14	Callistratus	De Cognitionibus	Hadrian
48.19.30	Modestinus	De Poenis	Marcus
48.19.31.1	Modestinus	De Poenis	Severus/Caracalla
48.19.33	Papinian	Quaestiones	Diui Fratres
48.19.35	Callistratus	Quaestiones	Hadrian, *mandatis principalibus*
48.19.39	Tryphoninus	Disputationes	Severus/Caracalla
48.19.43pr.	Paul	Responsa	Caracalla
48.20.1.3	Callistratus	De Iure Fisci	Diui Fratres
48.20.2	Callistratus	De Cognitionibus	Hadrian
48.20.6	Ulpian	De Officio Proconsulis	Hadrian
48.20.7.3	Paul	De Portionibus Quae Liberis Damnatorum Conceduntur	Hadrian
48.20.7.4	Paul	De Portionibus Quae Liberis Damnatorum Conceduntur	Pius
48.21.1	Ulpian	Disputationes	*a principibus decretum est*
48.21.2pr.	Macer	De Iudiciis Publicis	Severus/Caracalla
48.21.3.1	Marcianus	De Delatoribus	Pius

(*continued*)

Location	Author	Text	Authority
48.21.3.2	Marcianus	De Delatoribus	Pius
48.21.3.4	Marcianus	De Delatoribus	Caracalla
48.21.3.5	Marcianus	De Delatoribus	Hadrian
48.21.3.7	Marcianus	De Delatoribus	*mandatis cauetur*
48.21.3.8	Marcianus	De Delatoribus	Pius
48.22.1	Pomponius	Ad Sabinum	Trajan
48.22.2	Marcianus	Institutiones	Pius
48.22.6.1	Ulpian	De Officio Proconsulis	Severus
48.22.6.2	Ulpian	De Officio Proconsulis	Diui Fratres
48.22.7.4	Ulpian	De Officio Proconsulis	*rescriptis quibusdam*
48.22.7.10	Ulpian	De Officio Proconsulis	Diui Fratres, Severus/ Caracalla
48.22.7.15	Ulpian	De Officio Proconsulis	*multis constitutionibus continetur*
48.22.7.18	Ulpian	De Officio Proconsulis	Diui Fratres
48.22.16	Marcianus	Unknown	Caracalla
48.24.2	Marcianus	De Iudiciis Publicis	Severus/Caracalla
49.1.1.1	Ulpian	De Appellationibus	Pius
49.1.1.3	Ulpian	De Appellationibus	Diui Fratres, *multis constitutionibus*
49.1.4.1	Macer	De Appellationibus	Caracalla
49.1.4.4	Macer	De Appellationibus	*constitutum est*
49.1.5.1	Marcianus	De Appellationibus	Pius
49.1.5.2	Marcianus	De Appellationibus	Pius
49.1.5.3	Marcianus	De Appellationibus	*rescriptum est*
49.1.7	Marcianus	De Appellationibus	Severus
49.1.8	Ulpian	De Appellationibus	Diui Fratres
49.1.9	Macer	De Appellationibus	*rescriptum est*
49.1.10.4	Ulpian	Disputationes	*est rescriptum*
49.1.14pr.	Ulpian	Ad Edictum	Pius
49.1.14.1	Ulpian	Ad Edictum	Diui Fratres
49.1.21pr.	Papirius Iustus	De Constitutionibus	Diui Fratres
49.1.21.1	Papirius Iustus	De Constitutionibus	Diui Fratres

(*continued*)

Location	Author	Text	Authority
49.1.21.3	Papirius Iustus	De Constitutionibus	Diui Fratres
49.1.25	Paul	Responsa	Severus Alexander
49.2.1.2	Ulpian	De Appellationibus	Hadrian
49.2.1.4	Ulpian	De Appellationibus	Marcus
49.4.1.1	Ulpian	De Appellationibus	Marcus
49.4.1.7	Ulpian	De Appellationibus	Marcus
49.5.4	Macer	De Appellationibus	*sacris constitutionibus*
49.5.5.3	Ulpian	De Appellationibus	Caracalla
49.5.6	Macer	De Appellationibus	*sacris constitutionibus*
49.5.7pr.	Paul	De Appellationibus	Hadrian
49.6.1.2	Marcianus	De Appellationibus	*constitutiones*
49.7.1.4	Ulpian	De Appellationibus	*sit constitutum*
49.8.1.3	Macer	De Appellationibus	*constitutiones*
49.9.1	Ulpian	De Appellationibus	Diui Fratres
49.11.1	Ulpian	De Appellationibus	Diui Fratres
49.13.1pr.	Macer	De Appellationibus	Severus Alexander
49.13.1.1	Macer	De Appellationibus	Severus/Caracalla
49.14.1.2	Callistratus	De Iure Fisci	Pius
49.14.1.3	Callistratus	De Iure Fisci	Titus
49.14.2pr.	Callistratus	De Iure Fisci	*plurifariam principalibus constitutionibus*
49.14.2.1	Callistratus	De Iure Fisci	Hadrian
49.14.2.2	Callistratus	De Iure Fisci	Diui Fratres
49.14.2.4	Callistratus	De Iure Fisci	Hadrian
49.14.2.5	Callistratus	De Iure Fisci	Pius
49.14.2.6	Callistratus	De Iure Fisci	Severus
49.14.2.7	Callistratus	De Iure Fisci	*complura sunt rescripta principalia*
49.14.3.1	Callistratus	De Iure Fisci	Hadrian
49.14.3.4	Callistratus	De Iure Fisci	Pius
49.14.3.5	Callistratus	De Iure Fisci	Diui Fratres
49.14.3.6	Callistratus	De Iure Fisci	Hadrian, *principalibus rescriptis*

(*continued*)

Location	Author	Text	Authority
49.14.3.8	Callistratus	De Iure Fisci	*multa principalia sunt rescripta*
49.14.3.9	Callistratus	De Iure Fisci	Hadrian
49.14.3.10	Callistratus	De Iure Fisci	Diui Fratres
49.14.6pr.	Ulpian	Ad Edictum	*uarie rescriptum est*
49.14.7	Ulpian	Ad Edictum	Marcus
49.14.8	Modestinus	Regulae	*rescriptum est*
49.14.12	Callistratus	De Cognitionibus	Pius
49.14.13pr.	Paul	Ad Legem Iuliam et Papiam	Trajan
49.14.13.4	Paul	Ad Legem Iuliam et Papiam	Hadrian
49.14.13.5	Paul	Ad Legem Iuliam et Papiam	Hadrian
49.14.13.6	Paul	Ad Legem Iuliam et Papiam	Diui Fratres
49.14.13.7	Paul	Ad Legem Iuliam et Papiam	Caracalla
49.14.13.10	Paul	Ad Legem Iuliam et Papiam	Hadrian, Pius, Diui Fratres
49.14.15.2	Junius Mauricianus	Ad Legem Iuliam et Papiam	Hadrian
49.14.16	Ulpian	Ad Legem Iuliam et Papiam	Trajan
49.14.18pr.	Marcianus	De Delatoribus	*sacris constitutionibus*
49.14.18.2	Marcianus	De Delatoribus	Diui Fratres
49.14.18.3	Marcianus	De Delatoribus	*constitutionibus principum*
49.14.18.4	Marcianus	De Delatoribus	*rescriptum est*
49.14.18.5	Marcianus	De Delatoribus	*sacris constitutionibus*
49.14.18.8	Marcianus	De Delatoribus	Severus/Caracalla
49.14.18.9	Marcianus	De Delatoribus	*constitutum esse refertur*
49.14.18.10	Marcianus	De Delatoribus	*quidam principes ... rescripserunt*
49.14.22pr.	Marcianus	De Delatoribus	Severus/Caracalla
49.14.22.1	Marcianus	De Delatoribus	Severus/Caracalla

(*continued*)

Location	Author	Text	Authority
49.14.22.2	Marcianus	De Delatoribus	Pius
49.14.22.3	Marcianus	De Delatoribus	Severus/Caracalla
49.14.23	Callistratus	De Iure Fisci	Diui Fratres
49.14.25	Ulpian	Ad Sabinum	Severus
49.14.26	Ulpian	Ad Sabinum	*rescriptum est*
49.14.27	Ulpian	Ad Edictum	Severus
49.14.28	Ulpian	Disputationes	*constitutum est*
49.14.29pr.	Ulpian	Disputationes	*constitutum est*
49.14.29.2	Ulpian	Disputationes	Severus/Caracalla
49.14.30	Marcianus	Institutiones	Severus/Caracalla
49.14.31	Marcianus	Institutiones	Commodus
49.14.32	Marcianus	Institutiones	Diui Fratres
49.14.34	Macer	De Iudiciis Publicis	Severus/Caracalla
49.14.42pr.	Valens	Fideicommissa	Trajan
49.14.42.1	Valens	Fideicommissa	Trajan
49.14.43	Ulpian	Fideicommissa	Caracalla
49.14.46.5	Hermogenianus	Iuris Epitome	*saepe constitutum est*
49.14.47pr.	Paul	Decreta	Severus
49.14.47.1	Paul	Decreta	Severus
49.14.48pr.	Paul	Decreta	Severus/Caracalla
49.14.48.1	Paul	Decreta	*constitutum est*
49.14.49	Paul	De Tacitis Fideicommissis	Trajan, Caracalla
49.15.9	Ulpian	Ad Legem Iuliam et Papiam	Severus/Caracalla
49.15.12.17	Tryphoninus	Disputationes	Severus/Caracalla
49.15.12.18	Tryphoninus	Disputationes	*constitutio*
49.15.25	Marcianus	Institutiones	Severus/Caracalla
49.16.3pr.	Modestinus	De Poenis	Severus/Caracalla
49.16.4pr.	Arrius Menander	De Re Militari	Trajan
49.16.4.5	Arrius Menander	De Re Militari	Trajan
49.16.4.9	Arrius Menander	De Re Militari	Caracalla
49.16.4.12	Arrius Menander	De Re Militari	Trajan
49.16.5.6	Arrius Menander	De Re Militari	Hadrian
49.16.5.8	Arrius Menander	De Re Militari	Hadrian
49.16.6.7	Arrius Menander	De Re Militari	Hadrian
49.16.9pr.	Marcianus	Institutiones	Severus/Caracalla

(*continued*)

Location	Author	Text	Authority
49.16.13.6	Macer	De Re Militari	Pius, Severus/ Caracalla
49.17.4.2	Tertullian	De Castrensi Peculio	*constitutiones principales*
49.17.13	Papinian	Quaestiones	Hadrian
49.17.16pr.	Papinian	Responsa	Hadrian
49.17.19.3	Tryphoninus	Disputationes	Hadrian
49.18.4pr.	Ulpian	De Officio Proconsulis	*rescriptum est*
49.18.4.1	Ulpian	De Officio Proconsulis	*rescriptum est*
49.18.5pr.	Paul	De Cognitionibus	Severus/Caracalla
50.1.2.5	Ulpian	Disputationes	*hoc enim et relatum et rescriptum est*
50.1.8	Marcianus	De Iudiciis Publicis	Diui Fratres, *constitutionibus principalibus*
50.1.11pr.	Papinian	Quaestiones	Pius
50.1.17.9	Papinian	Responsa	Pius
50.1.18	Paul	Quaestiones	Severus
50.1.21.6	Paul	Responsa	Severus/Caracalla
50.1.24	Scaevola	Digesta	Diui Fratres, *constitutionibus principum*
50.1.37pr.	Callistratus	De Cognitionibus	Hadrian
50.1.37.2	Callistratus	De Cognitionibus	Diui Fratres
50.1.38pr.	Papirius Iustus	De Constitutionibus	Diui Fratres
50.1.38.1	Papirius Iustus	De Constitutionibus	Diui Fratres
50.1.38.2	Papirius Iustus	De Constitutionibus	Diui Fratres
50.1.38.3	Papirius Iustus	De Constitutionibus	Diui Fratres
50.1.38.4	Papirius Iustus	De Constitutionibus	Diui Fratres
50.1.38.5	Papirius Iustus	De Constitutionibus	Diui Fratres
50.1.38.6	Papirius Iustus	De Constitutionibus	Diui Fratres
50.2.2.8	Ulpian	Disputationes	*constitutionibus*
50.2.3.1	Ulpian	De Officio Proconsulis	Caracalla
50.2.3.2	Ulpian	De Officio Proconsulis	Diui Fratres
50.2.3.3	Ulpian	De Officio Proconsulis	Severus/Caracalla

(*continued*)

Location	Author	Text	Authority
50.2.9pr.	Paul	Decreta	Severus
50.2.11	Callistratus	De Cognitionibus	Severus/Caracalla
50.2.13pr.	Papirius Iustus	De Constitutionibus	Diui Fratres
50.2.13.1	Papirius Iustus	De Constitutionibus	Diui Fratres
50.2.13.2	Papirius Iustus	De Constitutionibus	Diui Fratres
50.2.13.3	Papirius Iustus	De Constitutionibus	Diui Fratres
50.2.14	Paul	Quaestiones	Pius
50.4.6pr.	Ulpian	De Officio Proconsulis	Diui Fratres
50.4.6.1	Ulpian	De Officio Proconsulis	Diui Fratres
50.4.6.2	Ulpian	De Officio Proconsulis	Severus/Caracalla
50.4.7pr.	Marcianus	De Iudiciis Publicis	*principalibus constitutionibus*
50.4.7.1	Marcianus	De Iudiciis Publicis	Severus
50.4.8	Ulpian	Ad Edictum	*constitutum est*
50.4.11pr.	Modestinus	Pandectae	Pius
50.4.11.1	Modestinus	Pandectae	Marcus
50.4.11.2	Modestinus	Pandectae	Diui Fratres
50.4.11.3	Modestinus	Pandectae	Severus/Caracalla
50.4.11.4	Modestinus	Pandectae	Caracalla
50.4.14.4	Callistratus	De Cognitionibus	Severus
50.4.14.6	Callistratus	De Cognitionibus	Hadrian, *conplurimis constitutionibus*
50.4.18.23	Arcadius Charisius	De Muneribus Ciuilibus	*rescriptum est*
50.4.18.30	Arcadius Charisius	De Muneribus Ciuilibus	Vespasian, Hadrian
50.5.1.1	Ulpian	Opiniones	*exemplo decretorum principalium*
50.5.4.17	Ulpian	Ad Edictum	Marcus
50.5.7	Papinian	Quaestiones	Severus
50.5.8pr.	Papinian	Responsa	Severus
50.6.3(2.1)	Ulpian	De Officio Proconsulis	*rescripto*
50.6.6(5).1	Callistratus	De Cognitionibus	Pius
50.6.6(5).2	Callistratus	De Cognitionibus	Pertinax

(*continued*)

Location	Author	Text	Authority
50.6.6(5).4	Callistratus	De Cognitionibus	*principalibus constitutionibus*
50.6.6(5).5	Callistratus	De Cognitionibus	Hadrian
50.6.6(5).6	Callistratus	De Cognitionibus	Diui Fratres
50.6.6(5).8	Callistratus	De Cognitionibus	Hadrian
50.6.6(5).9	Callistratus	De Cognitionibus	Pius
50.6.6(5).10	Callistratus	De Cognitionibus	Diui Fratres
50.6.6(5).12	Callistratus	De Cognitionibus	Pius, *plurifariam constitutum est*
50.6.6(5).12	Callistratus	De Cognitionibus	Pius
50.6.6(5).13	Callistratus	De Cognitionibus	Pertinax
50.7.5(4)pr.	Marcianus	Institutiones	Pius
50.7.5(4).1	Marcianus	Institutiones	Severus/Caracalla
50.7.5(4).3	Marcianus	Institutiones	Diui Fratres
50.7.5(4).5	Marcianus	Institutiones	Hadrian
50.7.5(4).6	Marcianus	Institutiones	Vespasian
50.7.7(6)	Ulpian	De Officio Proconsulis	Severus/Caracalla
50.7.9(8).1	Paul	Responsa	Severus/Caracalla
50.7.12(11).1	Paul	De Iure Libellorum	Caracalla
50.8.11(9)pr.	Papirius Iustus	De Constitutionibus	Diui Fratres
50.8.11(9).1	Papirius Iustus	De Constitutionibus	Diui Fratres
50.8.11(9).2	Papirius Iustus	De Constitutionibus	Diui Fratres
50.8.12pr.(9.3)	Papirius Iustus	De Constitutionibus	Diui Fratres
50.8.12.1(9.4)	Papirius Iustus	De Constitutionibus	Diui Fratres
50.8.12.2(9.5)	Papirius Iustus	De Constitutionibus	Diui Fratres
50.8.12.3(9.6)	Papirius Iustus	De Constitutionibus	Hadrian, Diui Fratres
50.8.12.4(9.7)	Papirius Iustus	De Constitutionibus	Diui Fratres
50.8.12.5(9.8)	Papirius Iustus	De Constitutionibus	Diui Fratres
50.8.12.6(9.9)	Papirius Iustus	De Constitutionibus	Diui Fratres
50.8.13(9.10)	Papirius Iustus	De Constitutionibus	Diui Fratres
50.9.5	Callistratus	De Cognitionibus	Hadrian
50.10.3.1	Macer	De Officio Praesidis	*constitutionibus*
50.10.5pr.	Ulpian	De Officio Curatoris Rei Publicae	Pius
50.10.6	Modestinus	Pandectae	Marcus
50.10.7pr.	Callistratus	De Cognitionibus	Pius

(*continued*)

Location	Author	Text	Authority
50.12.1pr.	Ulpian	De Officio Curatoris Rei Publicae	Severus/Caracalla
50.12.1.1	Ulpian	De Officio Curatoris Rei Publicae	*multis constitutionibus et ueteribus et nouis*
50.12.1.5	Ulpian	De Officio Curatoris Rei Publicae	Severus/Caracalla
50.12.1.6	Ulpian	De Officio Curatoris Rei Publicae	Caracalla
50.12.3pr.	Ulpian	Disputationes	*est constitutum*
50.12.6.1	Ulpian	De Officio Proconsulis	Caracalla
50.12.6.2	Ulpian	De Officio Proconsulis	Severus/Caracalla
50.12.6.3	Ulpian	De Officio Proconsulis	Severus/Caracalla
50.12.7	Paul	De Officio Proconsulis	Severus
50.12.8	Ulpian	De Officio Proconsulis	Diui Fratres
50.12.9	Modestinus	Differentiae	Pius, Severus/ Caracalla
50.12.11	Modestinus	Pandectae	*principalibus constitutionibus*
50.12.12pr.	Modestinus	Pandectae	Severus
50.12.12.1	Modestinus	Pandectae	Caracalla
50.12.13pr.	Papirius Iustus	De Constitutionibus	Diui Fratres
50.12.13.1	Papirius Iustus	De Constitutionibus	Diui Fratres
50.12.14	Pomponius	Epistulae et Variae Lectiones	Trajan, Pius
50.12.15	Ulpian	De Officio Curatoris Rei Publicae	Pius
50.13.1.9	Ulpian	De Omnibus Tribunalibus	Diui Fratres
50.13.1.10	Ulpian	De Omnibus Tribunalibus	Severus/Caracalla

(*continued*)

Location	Author	Text	Authority
50.13.1.12	Ulpian	De Omnibus Tribunalibus	Severus/Caracalla
50.13.1.13	Ulpian	De Omnibus Tribunalibus	Severus
50.13.4	Paul	Ad Plautium	Pius
50.15.1.1	Ulpian	De Censibus	Hadrian
50.15.3.1	Ulpian	De Censibus	Caracalla
50.15.4.10	Ulpian	De Censibus	*saepissime rescriptum est*
50.15.5.1	Papinian	Responsa	Pius
50.15.8.7	Paul	De Censibus	Vespasian, Titus
50.16.60pr.	Ulpian	Ad Edictum	*constitutio*
50.16.131.1	Ulpian	Ad Legem Iuliam et Papiam	*mandatis permissum est*
50.16.220.2	Callistratus	Quaestiones	Marcus
50.16.240	Paul	Imperiales Sententiae in Cognitionibus Prolatae	Severus
50.17.28	Ulpian	Ad Sabinum	Pius
50.17.101	Paul	De Cognitionibus	Severus/Caracalla

APPENDIX 2

Precedential Reasoning in the *Codex Justinianus*

Please find below the 82 occasions on which emperors explicitly represent themselves as following prior imperial precedent within the *Codex Justinianus*. These data were published previously at Herz, "Precedential Reasoning," pp. 123–25.

Location	Issuing Authority	Authority Cited or Language Used
1.3.2.1	Constantius	*nostri genitoris*
1.5.6pr.	Theodosius/Valentinian	Constantine
1.5.8.1	Valentinian/Marcian	*diui principes*
1.17.2.18	Justinian	Hadrian
1.50.1	Gordian	*diui principes*
1.51.10	Theodosius/Valentinian	*diui principes*
2.1.8	Severus Alexander	Caracalla
2.7.17.1	Leo II/Zeno	Leo I
2.13.1.2	Diocletian	Claudius
2.40.1	Severus Alexander	*diui parentes*
3.28.29pr.	Zeno	Leo
4.1.2	Severus Alexander	*diui parentes*
4.35.23pr.	Justinian	Anastasius
4.56.1	Severus Alexander	Hadrian
4.57.2	Severus Alexander	Marcus/Commodus
4.57.3pr.	Severus Alexander	Marcus/Commodus

(*continued*)

Location	Issuing Authority	Authority Cited or Language Used
4.65.4.pr	Severus Alexander	Pius
5.16.3.pr	Caracalla	Severus
5.16.10	Gordian	Severus
5.17.5.pr	Diocletian	Marcus
5.27.5pr.	Zeno	Constantine
5.30.3	Leo	Constantine
5.62.5	Severus Alexander	Marcus
5.62.17	Valerian/Gallienus	Marcus
5.70.2pr.	Gordian	Severus
5.71.9pr.	Diocletian	Severus
5.75.5	Diocletian	Trajan, *parente nostro*
6.4.1.1	Severus/Caracalla	Pertinax
6.21.6pr.	Severus Alexander	*diui parentes*
6.23.23	Justin	*Consulta diualia*
6.24.4	Gordian	Severus/Caracalla
6.26.2	Severus/Caracalla	Marcus
6.30.22pr.	Justinian	Gordian
6.45.2pr.	Gordian	Severus
6.49.4	Diocletian	Caracalla
6.50.4	Severus Alexander	Hadrian
6.50.5	Severus Alexander	Severus
6.54.6	Severus Alexander	Caracalla
6.54.7	Severus Alexander	Marcus/Commodus
7.2.6	Gordian	Marcus
7.2.12.2	Diocletian	Pius
7.4.2	Caracalla	Hadrian
7.8.6	Severus Alexander	*diui parentes*
7.11.3	Severus Alexander	Marcus
7.12.1pr.	Severus/Caracalla	*diuus pater meus*[1]
7.12.2.2	Valerian/Gallienus	*diui parentes*

[1] Frier et al. suggest that *diuus pater meus* refers to one of the Diui Fratres, on the basis of a rescript referenced at D.48.19.33 (Papinian, Quaestiones). Frier et al. (eds.), *Codex*, p. 1813 n. 41.

(*continued*)

Location	Issuing Authority	Authority Cited or Language Used
7.20.1	Diocletian	Pius
7.37.3pr.	Justinian	Zeno
7.64.7	Diocletian	*diui principes*
7.71.4pr.	Diocletian	*diui parentes*
8.10.5	Diocletian	Hadrian
8.23.1.2	Gordian	*diui principes*
8.53.32	Anastasius	Leo
8.54.1.1	Valerian/Gallienus	*diui principes*
8.54.3.1	Diocletian	*diui principes*
8.56.2.2	Gordian	Severus
9.8.6pr.	Unknown[2]	
9.9.6.1	Severus Alexander	*diui parentes*
9.9.16.1	Valerian/Gallienus	*diui principes*
9.22.1	Caracalla	Severus
9.22.2	Severus Alexander	*diui parentes*
9.23.3	Severus Alexander	*diui principes*
9.41.11pr.	Diocletian	Marcus
10.32.61pr.	Leo	Julian
10.40.2pr.	Severus Alexander	Hadrian
10.40.7.pr	Diocletian	Hadrian
10.48.15.pr	Arcadius/Honorius	*diui principes*
10.52.5	Diocletian	*diui parentes*
10.53.4	Diocletian	Pius
10.60.1	Severus Alexander	*diui parentes*
11.14.2pr.	Arcadius/Honorius	*diui parens noster*
11.25.1pr.	Arcadius/Honorius	Constantine
11.33.1	Antoninus (unknown)	*diui principes*
11.33.2.2	Constantine	*rescripta diuorum*
11.35.1	Caracalla	Severus
11.43.11	Anastasius	Theodosius
11.59.1	Constantine	Aurelian
11.61.1.1	Valentinian/Valens	Julian

[2] See Frier et al. (eds.), *Codex*, p. 2293 n. 46.

(*continued*)

Location	Issuing Authority	Authority Cited or Language Used
11.62.6pr.	Gratian/Valentinian/ Theodosius	*diui parentes*
11.71.1pr.	Gratian/Valentinian/ Theodosius	*diuus pater*
12.35.4	Severus Alexander	Marcus, *Antoninus, pater meus*
12.62.4	Diocletian	Aurelian

APPENDIX 3

Rule-Consequentialist Reasoning in the *Digest*

Please find below 114 instances of rule-consequentialist reasoning in the *Digest*. I should note that this selection criterion is far more impressionistic than the previous two – I offer this collection not as a definitive or exhaustive list, but as the raw data upon which the quantitative claims made *supra* pp. 202–04 rely.

Location	Author (Quoting Author)	Work
1.18.6.2	Ulpian	Opiniones
2.7.1pr.	Ulpian	Ad Edictum
2.11.5pr.	Paul	Ad Edictum
2.14.27.4	Paul	Ad Edictum
3.1.1pr.	Ulpian	Ad Edictum
3.2.11.1	Ulpian	Ad Edictum
4.4.24.1	Pauli Sententiae	
4.9.1pr.	Ulpian	Ad Edictum
5.3.25.19	Ulpian	Ad Edictum
9.3.1.1	Ulpian	Ad Edictum
9.3.1.2	Ulpian	Ad Edictum
9.4.13	Gaius	Ad Edictum Prouinciale
9.4.26pr.	Paul	Ad Edictum
10.2.19	Gaius	Ad Edictum Prouinciale
11.1.5	Gaius	Ad Edictum Prouinciale
11.1.6pr.	Ulpian	Ad Edictum
11.1.6.1	Ulpian	Ad Edictum

(*continued*)

Location	Author (Quoting Author)	Work
11.6.1pr.	Ulpian	Ad Edictum
11.7.14.1	Ulpian	Ad Edictum
11.7.16	Ulpian	Ad Edictum
12.1.21	Julianus	Digesta
12.2.3pr.	Ulpian	Ad Edictum
13.4.1	Gaius	Ad Edictum Prouinciale
14.1.1pr.	Ulpian	Ad Edictum
14.1.1.5	Julianus (Ulpian)	Ad Edictum
14.2.2.6	Paul	Ad Edictum
14.4.5.4	Ulpian	Ad Edictum
15.1.51	Scaevola	Quaestiones
16.2.8	Gaius	Ad Edictum Prouinciale
21.1.1.2	Ulpian	Ad Edictum Aedilium Curulium
22.1.38.1	Paul	Ad Plautium
23.3.2	Paul	Ad Edictum
24.1.2	Sextus Caecilius (Paul)	Ad Sabinum
26.4.1pr.	Ulpian	Ad Sabinum
27.9.5.13	Ulpian	Ad Edictum
28.7.8pr.	Ulpian	Ad Edictum
29.1.1pr.	Ulpian	Ad Edictum
29.2.42pr.	Marcellus (Ulpian)	Disputationes
34.2.39pr.	Labeo (Javolenus)	Posteriores
35.1.64	Terentius Clemens	Ad Legem Iuliam et Papiam
36.1.1.3	Ulpian	Fideicommissa
36.1.67(65).2	Maecianus	Fideicommissa
37.3.1.1	Papinian	Quaestiones
37.4.20.1	Tryphoninus	Disputationes
37.5.5.6–7	Julianus (Ulpian)	Ad Edictum
37.6.3.2	Julianus	Digesta
37.10.1.5	Julianus (Ulpian)	Ad Edictum
37.10.3.13	Julianus (Ulpian)	Ad Edictum
37.11.2.1	Julianus (Ulpian)	Ad Edictum
37.12.2	Gaius	Ad Edictum Prouinciale
37.13.1pr.	Ulpian	Ad Edictum
37.14.1	Ulpian	De Officio Proconsulis

(*continued*)

Location	Author (Quoting Author)	Work
38.1.2pr.	Ulpian	Ad Edictum
38.1.20	Paul	Ad Edictum
38.2.1pr.	Servius (Ulpian)	Ad Edictum
38.2.14.2	Ulpian	Ad Edictum
38.2.42pr.	Papinian	Quaestiones
38.9.1pr.	Ulpian	Ad Edictum
38.9.1.12	Ulpian	Ad Edictum
39.1.4	Paul	Ad Edictum
39.1.5.4	Ulpian	Ad Edictum
39.1.5.12	Ulpian	Ad Edictum
39.1.5.17	Ulpian	Ad Edictum
39.1.20.10	Ulpian	Ad Edictum
39.2.1	Ulpian	Ad Edictum
39.3.9.1	Paul	Ad Edictum
39.3.11.2	Proculus (Paul)	Ad Edictum
39.4.3pr.	Ulpian	Ad Edictum
39.4.9.3	Pauli Sententiae	
39.4.12pr.	Ulpian	Ad Edictum
39.4.16.4	Marcianus	De Delatoribus
40.5.24.21	Ulpian	Fideicommissa
40.5.25	Valens (Paul)	Fideicommissa
40.5.26pr.	Ulpian	Fideicommissa
40.5.26.4	Ulpian	Fideicommissa
41.1.41	Ulpian	Ad Edictum
41.3.1	Gaius	Ad Edictum Prouinciale
42.1.50	Tryphoninus	Disputationes
42.8.10.24	Ulpian	Ad Edictum
43.3.1.2	Ulpian	Ad Edictum
43.8.2.37	Ulpian	Ad Edictum
43.8.7	Ulpian	Digesta
43.13.1.1	Ulpian	Ad Edictum
43.15.1.1	Ulpian	Ad Edictum
43.16.1.15	Ulpian	Ad Edictum
43.16.3pr.	Ulpian	Ad Edictum
43.19.3.12	Ulpian	Ad Edictum

(*continued*)

Location	Author (Quoting Author)	Work
43.19.3.16	Ulpian	Ad Edictum
43.23.1.2	Ulpian	Ad Edictum
43.24.4	Servius (Saturninus)	Interdicta
44.7.5pr.	Gaius	Aurea
46.2.19	Paul	Ad Edictum
46.7.5.7	Ulpian	Ad Edictum
47.6.1pr.	Ulpian	Ad Edictum
48.1.12.1	Modestinus	De Poenis
48.1.14	Papinian	Responsa
48.2.7pr.	Ulpian	De Officio Proconsulis
48.2.11.1	Macer	De Iudiciis Publicis
48.2.13	Marcianus	De Iudiciis Publicis
48.5.2.8	Ulpian	Disputationes
48.5.12(11).11	Papinian	De Adulteris
48.5.23(22).4	Papinian	De Adulteris
48.5.28(27).11	Ulpian	De Adulteriis
48.18.18.5	Pauli Sententiae	
48.19.16.10	Saturninus	De Poenis Paganorum
49.4.1pr.	Ulpian	De Appellationibus
49.14.18.3	Marcianus	De Delatoribus
49.15.19.5	Paul	Ad Sabinum
49.16.13pr.	Macer	De Re Militari
50.2.2.2	Papinian (Ulpian)	Disputationes
50.2.6pr.	Papinian	Responsa
50.6.6(5).3	Callistratus	De Cognitionibus
50.11.2	Callistratus	De Cognitionibus
50.13.1.4	Ulpian	De Omnibus Tribunalibus

Bibliography

Abdy, Richard, and Nicholas Harling. "Two Important New Roman Coins." *NC* 165 (2005): 175–81.

Adams, Alison. "The Arch of Hadrian at Athens." In *The Greek Renaissance in the Roman Empire*, edited by Susan Walker and Averil Cameron, 10–16. London: Institute of Classical Studies, 1989.

Adams, Wendy. *Popular Culture and Legal Pluralism: Narrative as Law*. London: Routledge, 2016.

Adler, Eric. "Cassius Dio's Livia and the Conspiracy of Cinna Magnus." *GRBS* 51 (2011): 133–54.

Africa, Thomas. "Adam Smith, the Wicked Knight, and the Use of Anecdotes." *G&R* 42 (1995): 70–75.

Agamben, Giorgio. *Homo Sacer: Sovereign Power and Bare Life*. Palo Alto: Stanford University Press, 1998.

Stato di eccezione. Turin: Bollati Boringhieri, 2003.

Albanese, Bernardo. "Volontà negoziale e forma in una testimonianza di Q. Mucio Scevola." In *De iustitia et iure. Festgabe für Ulrich von Lübtow*, edited by Manfred Harder and Georg Thielmann, 155–61. Berlin: Duncker und Humblot, 1980.

Alonso, José Luis. "Customary Law and Legal Pluralism in the Roman Empire: The Status of Peregrine Law in Egypt." *JJP* 43 (2013): 351–404.

Álvarez, Luis Rodríguez. "Algunas notas en torno a la lex de vicesima hereditatum." *RIDA* 28 (1981): 213–46.

Amelotti, Mario. "*Reichsrecht*, *Volksrecht*, *Provinzialrecht*: vecchi problemi e nuovi documenti." *SDHI* 65 (1999): 211–15.

Ando, Clifford. "Exemplum, Analogy, and Precedent in Roman Law." In Lowrie and Lüdemann, eds., *Exemplarity and Singularity*, 111–22. London: Routledge, 2015.

Imperial Ideology and Provincial Loyalty in the Roman Empire. Berkeley: University of California Press, 2000.

Imperial Rome AD 193 to 284: The Critical Century. Edinburgh: Edinburgh University Press, 2012.

"The Ambitions of Government: Territoriality and Infrastructural Power in Ancient Rome." In *Ancient States and Infrastructural Power: Europe, Asia, and America*, edited by Clifford Ando and Seth Richardson, 115–48. Philadelphia: University of Pennsylvania Press, 2017.

"The Origins and Import of Republican Constitutionalism." *Cardozo Law Review* 34 (2013): 917–36.

Ando, Clifford, ed. *Citizenship and Empire in Europe 200–1900: The Antonine Constitution after 1800 Years*. Stuttgart: Steiner, 2016.

de Angelis, Francesco. "The Emperor's Justice and Its Spaces in Rome and Italy." In *Spaces of Justice in the Roman World*, edited by Francesco de Angelis, 127–59. Leiden: Brill, 2010.

Arangio-Ruiz, Vicente. "Testi e documenti I: Una cognitio dell'imperatore Caracalla in Siria." *BIDR* 49 (1948): 46–57.

Arcaria, Francesco. *Referre ad principem: Contributo allo studio delle epistulae imperiali in età classica*. Milan: Giuffrè, 2000.

Archi, Gian. *Teodosio II e la sua codificazione*. Naples: Edizione Scientifiche Italiane, 1976.

Ascheri, Mario. *The Laws of Late Medieval Italy (1000–1500): Foundations for a European Legal System*. Boston: Brill, 2013.

Ash, Mitchell, and Alfons Söllner, eds. *Forced Migration and Scientific Change: Emigre German-Speaking Scientists and Scholars after 1933*. Washington, D.C.; Cambridge: German Historical Institute; Cambridge University Press, 1996.

Astolfi, Riccardo. "Abiti maschili e femminili." *Labeo* 17 (1971): 33–39.

Austin, J. L. *How to Do Things with Words*. Cambridge [MA]: Harvard University Press, 1975.

Bablitz, Leanne. *Actors and Audience in the Roman Courtroom*. London; New York: Routledge, 2007.

Babusiaux, Ulrike. "Les défauts de l'utilisation du 'ius controversum' en tant que concept herméneutique de droit romain." In *La Controverse: Etudes d'histoire de l'argumentation juridique*, edited by Nicolas Cornu Thénard, Anthony Mergey, and Sylvain Soleil, 19–48. Paris: Société de législation comparée, 2020.

Papinians Quaestiones: Zur rhetorischen Methode eines spätklassischen Juristen. Munich: Beck, 2011.

"Rhetoric in Legal Writing: The Ethos and Pathos of the Roman Jurists." In Bubb and Peachin (eds.), *Medicine and the Law*, 249–83. Oxford: Oxford University Press, 2023.

"Zitate klassischer Juristen in den Reskripten der Soldatenkaiser." In Babusiaux and Kolb (eds.), *Das Recht der "Soldatenkaiser,"* 238–69. Berlin: De Gruyter, 2013.

Babusiaux, Ulrike, and Anne Kolb, eds. *Das Recht der "Soldatenkaiser": Rechtliche Stabilität in Zeiten politischen Umbruchs?* Berlin: De Gruyter, 2013.

Baharal, Drora. "The Emperor Macrinus: Imperial Propaganda and the Gens Aurelia." In *Gli Imperatori Severi*, edited by Enrico Dal Covolo and Giancarlo Rinaldi, 47–65. Rome: LAS, 1999.

Balkin, Jack. *Living Originalism*. Cambridge [MA]: Harvard University Press, 2011.

Barchiesi, Alessandro. *The Poet and the Prince: Ovid and Augustan Discourse*. Berkeley: University of California Press, 1997.

Barnes, Timothy. *Constantine and Eusebius*. Cambridge [MA]: Harvard University Press, 1981.

"Three Imperial Edicts." *ZPE* 21 (1976): 275–81.

Bartoli, Alfonso. "Riccordi di Elagabalo nella sede del Senato romano." *MPAA* 27 (1951): 47–54.

Bartsch, Shadi. *Actors in the Audience: Theatricality and Doublespeak from Nero to Hadrian*. Cambridge [MA]: Harvard University Press, 1994.

Persius: A Study in Food, Philosophy, and the Figural. Chicago: University of Chicago Press, 2015.

Bauman, Richard. *Lawyers and Politics in the Early Roman Empire: A Study of Relations between the Roman Jurists and the Emperors from Augustus to Hadrian*. Munich: Beck, 1989.

Lawyers in Roman Transitional Politics: A Study of the Roman Jurists in Their Political Setting in the Late Republic and Triumvirate. Munich: Beck, 1985.

Bell, Catherine. *Ritual Theory, Ritual Practice*. New York: Oxford University Press, 1992.

Bell, Peter. *Social Conflict in the Age of Justinian: Its Nature, Management, and Mediation*. Oxford: Oxford University Press, 2013.

Benhabib, Seyla. *Exile, Statelessness, and Migration: Playing Chess with History from Hannah Arendt to Isaiah Berlin*. Princeton: Princeton University Press, 2018.

Berdowski, Piotr. "Violence as an Interpretive Category in Cassius Dio: The Terror Under Sulla in 82 BCE." In Lange and Scott (eds.), *Impact of Violence*, translated by Aleksander Nowacki, 15–45. Boston: Brill, 2020.

Berger, Adolf. *Encyclopedic Dictionary of Roman Law*. 3rd ed. Philadelphia: American Philosophical Society, 1991.

Bering-Staschewski, Rosemarie. *Römische Zeitgeschichte bei Cassius Dio*. Bochum: Studienverlag Brockmeyer, 1981.

Bertrand, Estelle. "Cassius Dio and the Roman Empire: The Impact of the Severan Wars on Dio's Narrative." In Lange and Scott (eds.), *Impact of Violence*, 120–37. Leiden; Boston: Brill, 2020.
Bertrand-Dagenbach, Cécile. *Alexandre Sévère et l'Histoire Auguste*. Brussels: Éditions Latomus, 1990.
Besson, Arnaud. *Constitutio Antoniniana: l'universalisation de la citoyenneté romaine au 3e siècle*. Basel: Schwabe, 2020.
Betancourt, Roland. *Byzantine Intersectionality: Sexuality, Gender, and Race in the Middle Ages*. Princeton: Princeton University Press, 2020.
Beverley, Eric. "Frontier as Resource: Law, Crime, and Sovereignty on the Margins of Empire." *Comparative Studies in Society and History* 55 (2013): 241–72.
Bexley, Erica. "Saturnalian Lex: Seneca's Apocolocyntosis." In Ziogas and Bexley (eds.), *Roman Law and Latin Literature*, 45–66. London: Bloomsbury, 2022.
Bingham, Sandra, and Alex Imrie. "The Prefect and the Plot: A Reassessment of the Murder of Plautianus." *JAH* 3 (2015): 76–91.
Birley, Anthony. "Hadrian to the Antonines." *CAH*^{2} 11: 132–94.
"Hadrian's Travels." In *The Representation and Perception of Roman Imperial Power*, edited by Lukas de Blois, Paul Erdkamp, and Olivier Hekster, 425–41. Amsterdam: Gieben, 2003.
"Marius Maximus: The Consular Biographer." *ANRW* 2.34 (1997): 2678–2757.
Septimius Severus: The African Emperor. New Haven: Yale University Press, 1989.
de Blois, Lukas. *Image and Reality of Roman Imperial Power in the Third Century AD: The Impact of War*. London: Routledge, 2018.
"Roman Jurists and the Crisis of the Third Century A.D. in the Roman Empire." In de Blois (ed.), *Administration, Prosopography and Appointment Policies*, 136–53. Amsterdam: Gieben, 2001.
"The Constitutio Antoniniana (A.D. 212): Taxes or Religion?" *Mnemosyne* 67 (2014): 1014–21.
"Why Did the Influence of Scholarly Jurists at the Roman Imperial Court Disappear After About A.D. 241?" In Babusiaux and Kolb (eds.), *Das Recht Der "Soldatenkaiser,"* 225–37. Berlin: De Gruyter, 2013.
de Blois, Lukas, ed. *Administration, Prosopography and Appointment Policies in the Roman Empire*. Amsterdam: Gieben, 2001.
Boatwright, Mary. *Hadrian and the Cities of the Roman Empire*. Princeton: Princeton University Press, 2000.
Hadrian and the City of Rome. Princeton: Princeton University Press, 1987.
Böcking, Eduard, ed. *Notitia dignitatum et administrationum omnium tam civilium quam militarium in partibus Orientis et Occidentis*. Bonn: Marci, 1839.

Boissevain, Ursul, ed. *Cassii Dionis Cocceiani Historiarum Romanarum quae supersunt*. Berlin: Weidmann, 1955.

Bond, Sarah. *Trade and Taboo: Disreputable Professions in the Roman Mediterranean*. Ann Arbor: University of Michigan Press, 2016.

Borg, Barbara. *Crisis and Ambition: Tombs and Burial Customs in Third-Century C.E. Rome*. Oxford: Oxford University Press, 2013.

Borkowski, Andrew. *Borkowski's Textbook on Roman Law*. Edited by Paul du Plessis. 2nd ed. Oxford: Oxford University Press, 2010.

Bowman, Alan. "Diocletian and the First Tetrarchy, A.D. 284–305." *CAH*[2] 12: 67–89.

Bradley, Keith. "Roman Slavery and Roman Law." *Historical Reflections* 15 (1988): 477–95.

Brennan, Peter. "The Notitia Dignitatum." In *Les littératures techniques dans l'antiquité romaine: statut, public et destination, tradition*, edited by Claude Nicolet, 147–78. Vandœuvres: Fondation Hardt, 1996.

"The User's Guide to the Notitia Dignitatum: The Case of the Dux Armeniae (ND Or. 38)." *Antichthon* 32 (1998): 34–49.

Brennan, T. Corey. *The Praetorship in the Roman Republic*. 2 vols. New York: Oxford University Press, 2000.

Bretone, Mario. *Ius controversum nella giurisprudenza classica*. Rome: Bardi, 2008.

Broise, Henri, and Yvon Thébert. "Élagabal et le complexe religieux de la Vigna Barberini: Heliogabalium in Palatino monte iuxta aedes imperatorias consecravit eique templum fecit (HA, Ant. Heliog., III, 4)." *MEFRA* 111 (1999): 729–47.

Brooks, Peter, and Paul Gewirtz, eds. *Law's Stories: Narrative and Rhetoric in the Law*. New Haven: Yale University Press, 1996.

Brown, Peter. *The Making of Late Antiquity*. Cambridge [MA]: Harvard University Press, 1978.

The World of Late Antiquity, AD 150–750. New York: Harcourt, 1971.

Brundage, W. Fitzhugh. "The Long Shadow of Torture in the American South." In *The Oxford Handbook of the Literature of the U.S. South*, edited by Fred Hobson and Barbara Ladd, 114–37. New York: Oxford University Press, 2016.

Brunt, Peter. "The Administrators of Roman Egypt." *JRS* 65 (1975): 124–47.

"Lex de Imperio Vespasiani." *JRS* 67 (1977): 95–116.

Brutti, Massimo. *Iulius Paulus: Decretorum libri tres*. Rome: L'Erma di Bretschneider, 2020.

Bruun, Christer. "Riflessioni sulla parte perduta della cd. Lex de Imperio Vespasiani." In Capogrossi Colognesi and Tassi Scandone (eds.), *La Lex*, 23–45. Rome: L'Erma di Bretschneider, 2009.

Bryen, Ari. "Judging Empire: Courts and Culture in Rome's Eastern Provinces." *LHR* 30 (2012): 771–811.

Violence in Roman Egypt: A Study in Legal Interpretation. Philadelphia: University of Pennsylvania Press, 2013.

"When Law Goes off the Rails: Or, Aggadah among the Iurisprudentes." *Critical Analysis of Law* 3 (2016): 9–29.

Bryen, Ari, and Andrzej Wypustek. "Gemellus' Evil Eyes (P.Mich. VI 423–424)." *GRBS* 49 (2009): 535–55.

Bubb, Claire, and Michael Peachin, eds. *Medicine and the Law under the Roman Empire*. Oxford: Oxford University Press, 2023.

Buraselis, Kostas. *Θεῖα Δωρεά: das göttlich-kaiserliche Geschenk: Studien zur Politik der Severer und zur Constitutio Antoniniana*. Vienna: Austrian Academy of Sciences Press, 2007.

Burgersdijk, Diederik, and Alan Ross, eds. *Imagining Emperors in the Later Roman Empire*. Leiden; Boston: Brill, 2018.

Burke, Peter. *Exiles and Expatriates in the History of Knowledge, 1500–2000*. Waltham: Brandeis University Press, 2017.

Burset, Christian. *Empire of Laws: Legal Pluralism in British Colonial Policy*. New Haven: Yale University Press, 2023.

Bury, John. "The Notitia Dignitatum." *JRS* 10 (1920): 131–54.

Butler, Orma. *Studies in the Life of Heliogabalus*. New York; London: Macmillan, 1908.

Butler, Shane, ed. *Deep Classics: Rethinking Classical Reception*. London: Bloomsbury Academic, 2016.

Calomino, Dario. "Caracalla and the Divine: Emperor Worship and Representation in the Visual Language of Roman Asia Minor." *AS* 70 (2020): 153–79.

Cameron, Alan. *The Last Pagans of Rome*. New York: Oxford University Press, 2011.

Cameron, Averil. *Procopius and the Sixth Century*. Berkeley: University of California Press, 1985.

Campanile, Domitilla, Filippo Carlà-Uhink, and Margherita Facella, eds. *TransAntiquity: Cross-Dressing and Transgender Dynamics in the Ancient World*. London: Routledge, 2019.

Camurri, Renato. "The Exile Experience Reconsidered: A Comparative Perspective in European Cultural Migration during the Interwar Period." *Transatlantica* 1 (2014). journals.openedition.org/transatlantica/6920

Cancelli, Filippo. *La codificazione dell'edictum praetoris: dogma romanistico*. Milan: Giuffrè, 2010.

Candy, Peter. "Judging beyond the Sandal: Law and Rhetoric in D. 19, 2, 31 (Alf. 5 Dig. a Paulo Epit.)." *ZRG* 138 (2021): 310–37.

Canepa, Matthew. "Emperor." In Vidas and Chin (eds.), *Late Ancient Knowing*, 155–74. Berkeley: University of California Press, 2015.

Capogrossi Colognesi, Luigi, and Elena Tassi Scandone, eds. *La Lex de Imperio Vespasiani e la Roma dei Flavi*. Rome: L'Erma di Bretschneider, 2009.

Carandini, Andrea, ed. *The Atlas of Ancient Rome: Biography and Portraits of the City*. Translated by Andrew Campbell Halavais. Princeton: Princeton University Press, 2017.

Carbone, Lucia. *Hidden Power: Late Cistophoric Production and the Organization of Provincia Asia 128–89 B.C.* New York: The American Numismatic Society, 2020.

Carboni, Tiziana. *La parola scritta al servizio dell'Imperatore e dell'Impero: l'ab epistulis e l'a libellis nel II secolo d. C.* Bonn: Habelt, 2017.

Carlà-Uhink, Filippo. "'Between the Human and the Divine': Cross-Dressing and Transgender Dynamics in the Graeco-Roman World." In Campanile, Carlà-Uhink, and Facella (eds.), *TransAntiquity*, 3–37. London; New York: Routledge, 2017.

"Quod Omni Consanguinitate Certius Est, Virtutibus Fratres: Families and Family Relationships in 'Tetrarchic' Ideology." In Carlà-Uhink and Rollinger (eds.), *The Tetrarchy as Ideology*, 25–46. Stuttgart: Franz Steiner Verlag, 2023.

Carlà-Uhink, Filippo, and Christian Rollinger, eds. *The Tetrarchy as Ideology: Reconfigurations and Representations of an Imperial Power*. Stuttgart: Franz Steiner Verlag, 2023.

Carpenter, David. *The Minority of Henry III*. Berkeley: University of California Press, 1990.

Cascio, Elio lo. "The Age of the Severans." *CAH*[2] 12: 137–55.

Cenderelli, Aldo. *Ricerche sul codex Hermogenianus*. Milan: Giuffrè, 1966.

Chaplin, Jane. *Livy's Exemplary History*. Oxford; New York: Oxford University Press, 2000.

Chastagnol, André. *Histoire Auguste: les empereurs romains des IIe et IIIe siècles*. 2nd ed. Paris: Laffont, 2014.

L'album municipal de Timgad. Bonn: Habelt, 1978.

"Un nouveau préfet du prétoire de Dioclétien: Aurelius Hermogenianus." *ZPE* 78 (1989): 165–68.

Chatelain, Louis. "Fragments de Droit Antéjustinien." *RPh* 23 (1899): 169–84.

Cheung, Caroline. "Born Roman between a Beet and a Cabbage." *AJP* 142 (2021): 659–97.

Chitwood, Zachary. *Byzantine Legal Culture and the Roman Legal Tradition, 867–1056*. Cambridge: Cambridge University Press, 2017.

Christoforou, Panayiotis. *Imagining the Roman Emperor: Perceptions of Rulers in the High Empire*. Cambridge: Cambridge University Press, 2023.

Christol, Michel. "Entre la cité et l'empereur: Ulpien, Tyr et les empereurs de la dynastie sévérienne." In *Consuetudinis amor: Fragments d'histoire romaine (IIe-VIe siècles) offerts à Jean-Pierre Callu*, edited by François Chausson and Étienne Wolff, 163–88. Rome: L'Erma di Bretschneider, 2003.

"Marius Maximus, Cassius Dio et Ulpien: destins croisés et débats politiques." In *Cassius Dion: nouvelles lectures*, edited by Valérie Fromentin, Estelle Bertrand, Michèle Coltelloni-Trannoy, Michel Molin, and Gianpaolo Urso, 447–67. Bordeaux: Ausonius, 2016.

Chrysanthou, Chrysanthos. "Sex and Power in Cassius Dio's Roman History: The Case of Elagabalus." *Mnemosyne* 74 (2020): 598–625.

Clauss, James. "Allusion and Structure in Horace Satire 2.1: The Callimachean Response." *TAPA* 115 (1985): 197–206.

Clemente, Guido. *La Notitia Dignitatum*. Cagliari: Fossataro, 1968.

"La notitia dignitatum: l'immagine e la realtà dell'impero tra IV e V secolo." In *Istituzioni, carismi ed esercizio del potere (IV–VI secolo d.C.)*, edited by Giorgio Bonamente and Rita Lizzi Testa, 117–32. Bari: Edipuglia, 2010.

Coleman, Kathleen. "Fatal Charades: Roman Executions Staged as Mythological Enactments." *JRS* 80 (1990): 44–73.

"'Informers' on Parade." In *The Art of Ancient Spectacle*, edited by Bettina Bergmann and Christine Kondoleon, 231–45. Washington (D. C.): National Gallery of Art, 1999.

Conlin, Diane. "Assemblages and Appropriation of Augustan Art and Topography in Flavian Rome." In *Domitian's Rome and the Augustan Legacy*, edited by Raymond Marks and Marcello Mogetta, 15–31. Ann Arbor: University of Michigan Press, 2021.

Connolly, Joy. *The Life of Roman Republicanism*. Princeton: Princeton University Press, 2015.

Connolly, Serena. *Lives Behind the Laws: The World of the Codex Hermogenianus*. Bloomington: Indiana University Press, 2010.

Constable, Marianne. *Our Word Is Our Bond: How Legal Speech Acts*. Redwood City: Stanford University Press, 2014.

Cooley, Alison. "From the Augustan Principate to the Invention of the Age of Augustus." *JRS* 109 (2019): 71–87.

Res Gestae Diui Augusti. Cambridge: Cambridge University Press, 2009.

The Senatus Consultum de Cn. Pisone Patre: Text, Translation, and Commentary. Cambridge: Cambridge University Press, 2023.

Corbo, Chiara. *Constitutio Antoniniana: Ius philosophia religio*. Naples: D'Auria, 2013.

Corcoran, Simon. "Hidden from History: The Legislation of Licinius." In Harries and Wood (eds.), *The Theodosian Code*, 97–119. London: Duckworth, 1993.

"Justinian and His Two Codes: Revisiting P. Oxy. 1814." *JJP* 38 (2008): 73–111.

"Roman Law and the Two Languages in Justinian's Empire." *BICS* 60 (2017): 96–116.

The Empire of the Tetrarchs: Imperial Pronouncements and Government, AD 284–324. Oxford: Clarendon Press, 1996.

"The Gregorianus and Hermogenianus Assembled and Shattered." *MEFRA* 125 (2013): 285–304.

Coriat, Jean-Pierre. "La palingénésie des constitutions impériales: Histoire d'un projet et méthode pour le recueil de la législation du Principat." *MEFRA* 101 (1989): 873–923.

"La technique du rescrit à la fin du principat." *SDHI* 51 (1985): 319–48.

"L'empereur juge et son tribunal à la fin du Principat: Un essai de synthèse." In Haensch (ed.), *Recht haben und Recht bekommen*, 41–61. Warsaw: University of Warsaw, 2016.

Le prince législateur: La technique législative des Sévères et les méthodes de création du droit impérial à la fin du principat. Rome: École Française de Rome, 1997.

Les constitutions des Sévères: Règne de Septime Sévère. Rome: École Française de Rome, 2014.

Cover, Robert. "Nomos and Narrative." *Harvard Law Review* 97 (1983): 4–68.

"Violence and the Word." *Yale Law Journal* 95 (1986): 1601–30.

Cowan, Eleanor. "Hopes and Aspirations: Res Publica, Leges et Iura, and Alternatives at Rome." In Morrell, Osgood, and Welch (eds.), *The Alternative Augustan Age*, 27–45. New York: Oxford University Press, 2019.

Crawford, Bridget. "Wills Formalities in the Twenty-First Century." *Wisconsin Law Review*, 2019, 269–94.

Crawford, Michael. *Roman Statutes*. 2 vols. London: Institute of Classical Studies, 1996.

Crook, John. *Consilium Principis: Imperial Councils and Counsellors from Augustus to Diocletian*. Cambridge: Cambridge University Press, 1955.

Legal Advocacy in the Roman World. Ithaca [NY]: Cornell University Press, 1995.

"Women in Roman Succession." In *The Family in Ancient Rome: New Perspectives*, edited by Beryl Rawson, 50–82. Ithaca [NY]: Cornell University Press, 1986.

Cunningham, Graeme. "Law, Rhetoric, and Science: Historical Narratives in Roman Law." Ph.D., University of Glasgow, 2018.

Curran, John. "'Ius Vitae Necisque': The Politics of Killing Children." *JAH* 6 (2018): 111–35.

Czajkowski, Kimberley. *Localized Law: The Babatha and Salome Komaise Archives*. Oxford: Oxford University Press, 2017.

"The Limits of Legal Pluralism in the Roman Empire." *JLH* 40 (2019): 110–29.

Czajkowski, Kimberley, and Benedikt Eckhardt. "Law, Status and Agency in the Roman Provinces." *P&P* 241 (2018): 3–31.

Daalder, Elsemieke. "'Aequum Putavit Imperator': Imperial Representation and Juristic Self-Fashioning in the Decreta and Imperiales Sententiae of Julius Paulus." *ZRG* 139 (2022): 123–91.

De rechtspraakverzamelingen van Julius Paulus: Recht en rechtvaardigheid in de rechterlijke uitspraken van keizer Septimius Severus. The Hague: Boom juridisch, 2018.

"The 'Decreta' and 'Imperiales Sententiae' of Julius Paulus: Law and Justice in the Judicial Decisions of Septimius Severus." In Hekster and Verboven (eds.), *Impact of Justice*, 49–67. Leiden; Boston: Brill, 2019.

"Tradition and Innovation in the Rescript Practice of the Emperor Caracalla." In *Tradition and Power in the Roman Empire*, edited by Sven Betjes, Olivier Hekster, and Erika Manders, 211–18. Leiden; Boston: Brill, 2024.

Dagron, Gilbert. *Emperor and Priest: The Imperial Office in Byzantium*. Cambridge; New York: Cambridge University Press, 2003.

Dam, Raymond van. *The Roman Revolution of Constantine*. Cambridge; New York: Cambridge University Press, 2007.

Damaška, Mirjan. *The Faces of Justice and State Authority: A Comparative Approach to the Legal Process*. New Haven: Yale University Press, 1986.

Damon, Cynthia. "Potior Utroque Vespasianus: Vespasian and His Predecessors in Tacitus's Histories." *Arethusa* 39 (2006): 245–79.

Daube, David. "Princeps Legibus Solutus." In *Collected Studies in Roman Law*, edited by David Daube, David Cohen, and Dieter Simon, 549–51. Frankfurt am Main: Klostermann, 1991.

"The Peregrine Praetor." *JRS* 41 (1951): 66–70.

"The Three Quotations from Homer in Digest 18. 1. 1. 1." In *Collected Studies in Roman Law*, edited by David Daube, David Cohen, and Dieter Simon, 341–43. Frankfurt am Main: Klostermann, 1991.

Davenport, Caillan. *A History of the Roman Equestrian Order*. Cambridge; New York: Cambridge University Press, 2019.

"Cassius Dio and Caracalla." *CQ* 62 (2012): 796–815.

Davenport, Caillan, and Christopher Mallan. "Hadrian's Adoption Speech in Cassius Dio's Roman History and the Problems of Imperial Succession." *AJP* 135 (2014): 637–68.

"Herodian and the Crisis of Emperorship, 235–238 AD." *Mnemosyne*: 73 (2020): 419–40.

Davis, Kenneth Culp. "An Approach to Problems of Evidence in the Administrative Process." *Harvard Law Review* 55 (1942): 364–425.

Demougeot, Émilienne. "La Notitia dignitatum et l'histoire de l'Empire d'Occident au début du Ve siècle." *Latomus* 34 (1975): 1079–1134.

Dench, Emma. *Empire and Political Cultures in the Roman World*. Cambridge: Cambridge University Press, 2018.

Desautels-Stein, Justin, and Samuel Moyn. "On the Domestication of Critical Legal History." *History and Theory* 60 (2021): 296–310.

Dettenhofer, Maria. *Herrschaft und Widerstand im augusteischen Principat: Die Konkurrenz zwischen res publica und domus Augusta*. Stuttgart: Steiner, 2000.

Didion, Joan. "The White Album." In *The White Album*, by Joan Didion, 11–48. New York: Simon and Schuster, 1979.

Dillon, John. *The Justice of Constantine: Law, Communication, and Control*. Ann Arbor: University of Michigan Press, 2012.

Dirven, Lucinda. "The Emperor's New Clothes." In *Der christliche Orient und seine Umwelt*, edited by Jürgen Tubach, Sophia Vashalomidze, and Lutz Greisiger. Wiesbaden: Harrassowitz, 2007.

Dixon, Suzanne. "Infirmitas Sexus: Womanly Weakness in Roman Law." *TvR* 52 (1984): 343–71.

Dolganov, Anna. "Law as Competitive Performance: Performative Aspects of the Legal Process in Roman Imperial Courts." In Bubb and Peachin (eds.), *Medicine and the Law*, 66–123. Oxford: Oxford University Press, 2023.

"*Reichsrecht* and *Volksrecht* in Theory and Practice: Roman Justice in the Province of Egypt (P.Oxy. II 237, P.Oxy. IV 706, SB XII 10929)." *Tyche* 34 (2019): 27–60.

Doroszewska, Julia. "Between the Monstrous and the Divine: Hermaphrodites in Phlegon of Tralles' Mirabilia." *AAntHung* 53 (2013): 379–92.

Dreier, Horst. "Hans Kelsen (1881–1973): 'Jurist des Jahrhunderts'?" In *Deutsche Juristen jüdischer Herkunft*, edited by Helmut Heinrichs, Harald Franzki, Klaus Schmalz, and Michael Stolleis, 705–32. Munich: Beck, 1993.

Drijvers, Jan Willem. "Jovian Between History and Myth." In Burgersdijk and Ross (eds.), *Imagining Emperors*, 234–56. Leiden; Boston: Brill, 2018.

Drinkwater, John. "Maximinus to Diocletian and the 'Crisis.'" *CAH*[2] 12: 28–66.

Duggan, Charles. *Twelfth-Century Decretal Collections and Their Importance in English History*. London: Athlone Press, 1963.

Duxbury, Neil. *The Nature and Authority of Precedent*. Cambridge: Cambridge University Press, 2008.

Dworkin, Ronald. "Hard Cases." *Harvard Law Review* 88 (1975): 1057–1109.

Law's Empire. Cambridge [MA]: Harvard University Press, 1986.

Dyzenhaus, David. *The Constitution of Law: Legality in a Time of Emergency*. Cambridge: Cambridge University Press, 2006.

Eberle, Lisa. "The Edicts of the Praetors: Law, Time, and Revolution in Ancient Rome." *LHR* 42 (2024): 237–61.

Eck, Werner. "At Magnus Caesar, and Yet!: Social Resistance against Augustan Legislation." In Morrell, Osgood, and Welch (eds.), *The*

Alternative Augustan Age, 78–95. New York: Oxford University Press, 2019.

Edelstein, Dan, and Benjamin Straumann. "On the Liberties of the Ancients: Licentiousness, Equal Rights, and the Rule of Law." *History of European Ideas* 49 (2023): 1037–1060.

Eden, P. T. *Apocolocyntosis*. Cambridge; New York: Cambridge University Press, 1984.

Edwards, Catharine. *The Politics of Immorality in Ancient Rome*. Cambridge: Cambridge University Press, 1993.

Eich, Armin, and Peter Eich. "Thesen zur Genese des Verlautbarungsstils der spätantiken kaiserlichen Zentrale." *Tyche* 19 (2004): 75–104.

Eichbauer, Melodie, and James Brundage. *Medieval Canon Law*. 2nd ed. London: Routledge, 2022.

Elliott, Jackie. *Ennius and the Architecture of the Annales*. Cambridge; New York: Cambridge University Press, 2013.

Enßlin, Wilhelm. *Gottkaiser und Kaiser von Gottes Gnaden*. Munich: Beck, 1943.

Ernst, Wolfgang. "Fritz Schulz (1879–1957)." In *Jurists Uprooted: German-Speaking Emigré Lawyers in Twentieth Century Britain*, edited by Jack Beatson and Reinhard Zimmermann, 105–204. Oxford: Oxford University Press, 2004.

Eshleman, Kendra. "Defining the Circle of Sophists: Philostratus and the Construction of the Second Sophistic." *CP* 103 (2008): 395–413.

Evans-Grubbs, Judith. "Between Slavery and Freedom: Disputes over Status and the Codex Justinianus." *Roman Legal Tradition* 9 (2013): 31–93.

"Singles, Sex and Status in the Augustan Marriage Legislation." In *The Single Life in the Roman and Later Roman World*, edited by Christian Laes and Sabine Huebner, 105–24. Cambridge: Cambridge University Press, 2019.

Fantham, Elaine. *Julia Augusti: The Emperor's Daughter*. London; New York: Routledge, 2006.

Faro, Silvano. "Il questore imperiale: Luci ed ombre su natura e funzioni." *Κοινωνία* 8 (1984): 133–59.

Faust, Stephan, and Florian Leitmeir, eds. *Repräsentationsformen in severischer Zeit*. Frankfurt am Main: Verlag Antike, 2011.

Fermi, Laura. *Illustrious Immigrants: The Intellectual Migration from Europe, 1930–41*. Chicago: University of Chicago Press, 1968.

Ferrary, Jean-Louis. "À propos des pouvoirs d'Auguste." *CCG* 12 (2001): 101–54.

Ferrary, Jean-Louis, Valerio Marotta, and Aldo Schiavone. *Ulpianus: Institutiones, de censibus*. Rome: L'Erma di Bretschneider, 2021.

Ferri, Rolando. "What the Text Wants to Say: Communicative Intention and Meaning in Late Antique Latin Exegesis of Literary Works and the Bible." *Incontri di filologia classica* 16 (2017): 283–95.

Fitzpatrick, Peter. *The Mythology of Modern Law*. London: Taylor & Francis Group, 1992.
Flaig, Egon. *Den Kaiser herausfordern: Die Ursurpation im römischen Reich*. Frankfurt; New York: Campus, 1992.
Flory, Marleen. "Sic Exempla Parantur: Livia's Shrine to Concordia and the Porticus Liviae." *Historia* 33 (1984): 309–30.
Flower, Harriet. *Roman Republics*. Princeton: Princeton University Press, 2010.
The Art of Forgetting: Disgrace and Oblivion in Roman Political Culture. Chapel Hill: University of North Carolina Press, 2006.
Flower, Richard. "Visions of Constantine." *JRS* 102 (2012): 287–305.
Foot, Philippa. "The Problem of Abortion and the Doctrine of the Double Effect." *Oxford Review* 5 (1967): 5–15.
Ford, Lisa. *Settler Sovereignty: Jurisdiction and Indigenous People in America and Australia, 1788–1836*. Cambridge [MA]: Harvard University Press, 2010.
Frakes, Robert. *Compiling the Collatio Legum Mosaicarum et Romanarum in Late Antiquity*. Oxford; New York: Oxford University Press, 2011.
Francisci, Pietro de. "Frammento di un indice del primo Codice Giustinianeo." *Aegyptus* 3 (1922): 68–79.
Frankfurter, David. "Fetus Magic and Sorcery Fears in Roman Egypt." *GRBS* 46 (2006): 37–62.
Freudenburg, Kirk. *Horace, Satires: Book II*. Cambridge: Cambridge University Press, 2021.
"Horatius Anceps: Persona and Self-Revelation in Satire and Song." In *A Companion to Horace*, edited by Gregson Davis, 271–90. Chichester: Wiley-Blackwell, 2010.
Satires of Rome: Threatening Poses from Lucilius to Juvenal. Cambridge: Cambridge University Press, 2001.
Frey, Martin. *Untersuchungen zur Religion und zur Religionspolitik des Kaisers Elagabal*. Stuttgart: Franz Steiner Verlag, 1989.
Frier, Bruce. "Juristic Literature and the Law: Competition and Cooperation." In Bubb and Peachin (eds.), *Medicine and the Law*, 177–95. Oxford: Oxford University Press, 2023.
The Rise of the Roman Jurists: Studies in Cicero's Pro Caecina. Princeton: Princeton University Press, 1985.
Frier, Bruce et al., eds. *The Codex of Justinian: A New Annotated Translation, with Parallel Latin and Greek Text Based on a Translation by Justice Fred H. Blume*. Cambridge; New York: Cambridge University Press, 2016.
Fuller, Lon. "Consideration and Form." *Columbia Law Review* 41 (1941): 799–824.
The Morality of Law. New Haven: Yale University Press, 1969.
Gagarin, Michael. *Writing Greek Law*. Cambridge University Press, 2008.

Galinsky, Karl. *Augustan Culture: An Interpretive Introduction*. Princeton: Princeton University Press, 1996.

Gallo, Filippo. "Ars boni et aequi e ius naturale." *SDHI* 75 (2009): 15–42.

"Diritto e giustizia nel titolo primo del Digesto." *SDHI* 54 (1988): 1–36.

Gamauf, Richard. "Die Kritik am römischen Recht im 19. und 20. Jahrhundert." *Orbis Iuris Romani* 2 (1996): 33–61.

Gardner, Jane. "Gender-Role Assumptions in Roman Law." *EMC* 39 (1995): 377–400.

Garrido, Jacobo Rodríguez. "The Curious Case of Aurelius Papia: Slavery, Legislation and Causae Liberales in the Times of Severus Alexander." *Historia* 72 (2023): 343–69.

Gauthier, Philippe. *Les cités grecques et leurs bienfaiteurs (IVe–Ier siècle avant J.C.): Contribution à l'histoire des institutions*. Paris: De Boccard, 1985.

Gebhardt, Ulrich. *Sermo Iuris: Rechtssprache und Recht in der augusteischen Dichtung*. Leiden: Brill, 2009.

Gelbach, Jonah. "The Dynamic Dilemma: Dynamics and Disuniformity in Statutory Interpretation." In *Research Handbook on Law and Time*, edited by Frank Fagan and Saul Levmore, 1–53. Northampton [MA]; Cheltenham and Camberley: Elgar, 2025.

Genette, Gérard. *Paratexts: Thresholds of Interpretation*. Translated by Jane Lewin. Cambridge; New York: Cambridge University Press, 1997.

George, Marie-Amélie. *Family Matters: Queer Households and the Half-Century Struggle for Legal Recognition*. Cambridge; New York: Cambridge University Press, 2024.

Getzler, Joshua. "Citation and the Authority of Opinions in Roman and Jewish Law: The Snake Oven Revisited." In *Inter Cives Necnon Peregrinos: Essays in Honour of Boudewijn Sirks*, edited by Jan Hallebeek, 289–308. Göttingen: V und R Unipress, 2014.

Geue, Tom. *Author Unknown: The Power of Anonymity in Ancient Rome*. Cambridge [MA]; London: Harvard University Press, 2019.

Geus, Klaus, and Colin King. "Paradoxography." In *Oxford Handbook of Science and Medicine in the Classical World*, edited by Paul Keyser and John Scarborough, 431–44. Oxford: Oxford University Press, 2018.

Gibbon, Edward. *Decline and Fall of the Roman Empire*. New York: Everyman, 1993.

Gibson, Bruce. "Contemporary Contexts." In Roche (ed.), *Pliny's Praise*, 104–24. Cambridge; New York: Cambridge University Press, 2011.

"Unending Praise: Pliny and Ending Panegyric." In *Form and Function in Roman Oratory*, edited by Dominic Berry and Andrew Erskine, 122–36. Cambridge; New York: Cambridge University Press, 2010.

Giddens, Anthony. *The Constitution of Society: Outline of the Theory of Structuration*. Berkeley: University of California Press, 1984.

Giltaij, Jacob. "Reinventing the Principles of Roman Law." SSRN Scholarly Paper. Rochester, NY, April 24, 2019. papers.ssrn.com/abstract=3377309.

Giovanni, Lucio de. "Il principe e la legge: Dalla Lex de Imperio Vespasiani al mondo tardoantico." In Capogrossi Colognesi and Tassi Scandone (eds.), *La Lex*, 219–30. Rome: L'Erma di Bretschneider, 2009.

Gleason, Maud. *Making Men: Sophists and Self-Presentation in Ancient Rome*. Princeton: Princeton University Press, 1995.

Goh, Ian. "It All Comes Out: Vomit as a Source of Comedy in Roman Moralizing Texts." *ICS* 43 (2018): 438–58.

González, Julián. "Un nuevo fragmento de la Tabula Hebana." *AEA* 73 (2000): 253–57.

González, Julián, and Michael Crawford. "The Lex Irnitana: A New Copy of the Flavian Municipal Law." *JRS* 76 (1986): 147–243.

Gordon, Robert. "Critical Legal Histories." *Stanford Law Review* 36 (1984): 57–125.

Gowers, Emily. *The Loaded Table: Representations of Food in Roman Literature*. Oxford; New York: Clarendon Press; Oxford University Press, 1993.

Gowing, Alain. *The Triumviral Narratives of Appian and Cassius Dio*. Ann Arbor: University of Michigan Press, 1995.

Gradenwitz, Otto. *Interpolationen in den Pandekten: Kritische studien*. Berlin: Weidmann, 1887.

Griffin, Miriam. "The Flavians." *CAH*^{2} 11: 1–83.

Griffiths, John. "What Is Legal Pluralism?" *Journal of Legal Pluralism and Unofficial Law* 24 (1986): 1–56.

Gross, Ariela. *What Blood Won't Tell: A History of Race on Trial in America*. Cambridge [MA]: Harvard University Press, 2008.

Grugel, Jean, and Enrique Peruzzotti. "The Domestic Politics of International Human Rights Law: Implementing the Convention on the Rights of the Child in Ecuador, Chile, and Argentina." *Human Rights Quarterly* 34 (2012): 178–98.

Gualandi, Giovanni. *Legislazione imperiale e giurisprudenza*. 2nd ed. Milan: Giuffrè, 2012.

Guarino, Antonio. "La leggenda sulla codificazione dell'editto e la sua genesi." In *Pagine di diritto romano*, by Antonio Guarino, 253–66. Naples: Jovene, 1994.

"Sul legato di vesti." *Labeo* 16 (1970): 58–60.

Gulina, Giovanni. "La cognizione straordinaria del princeps nei casi di C. Tettio e dei fratelli Tracali (Val. Max. 7.7.3–4)." *Iuris antiqui historia* 9 (2017): 41–73.

Haarer, Fiona. *Justinian: Empire and Society in the Sixth Century*. Edinburgh: Edinburgh University Press, 2022.

Habinek, Thomas, and Alessandro Schiesaro, eds. *The Roman Cultural Revolution*. Cambridge: Cambridge Philological Society, 1997.

Haensch, Rudolf, ed. *Recht haben und Recht bekommen im Imperium Romanum: das Gerichtswesen der römischen Kaiserzeit und seine dokumentarische Evidenz*. Warsaw: University of Warsaw, 2016.

Hall, Linda. *Roman Berytus: Beirut in Late Antiquity*. London; New York: Routledge, 2004.

Harries, Jill. *Cicero and the Jurists: From Citizens' Law to the Lawful State*. London: Duckworth, 2006.

"Iurisperiti: 'Men Skilled in Law.'" In *Authority and Expertise in Ancient Scientific Culture*, edited by Greg Woolf and Jason König, 83–106. Cambridge: Cambridge University Press, 2017.

Law and Crime in the Roman World. Cambridge: Cambridge University Press, 2007.

Law and Empire in Late Antiquity. Cambridge; New York: Cambridge University Press, 1999.

"Legal Education and Training of Lawyers." In du Plessis, Ando, and Tuori (eds.), *Roman Law and Society*, 151–63. Oxford: Oxford University Press, 2016.

"Sacra Generalitas: The Administrative Background to the Theodosian Code." In *Estudios de historia del derecho europeo: Homenaje al P. G. Martínez Díez*, edited by María Dolores Gutiérrez Calvo and Rogelio Pérez-Bustamante, 31–42. Madrid: Universidad Complutense de Madrid, 1994.

"The Roman Imperial Quaestor from Constantine to Theodosius II." *JRS* 78 (1988): 148–72.

Harries, Jill, and Ian Wood, eds. *The Theodosian Code: Studies in the Imperial Law of Late Antiquity*. Bristol: Bristol Classical Press, 1993.

Harris, William. "A Roman Father's Power of Life and Death." In *Studies in Roman Law in Memory of A. Arthur Schiller*, edited by Roger Bagnall and William Harris, 81–95. Leiden: Brill, 1986.

Harrison, Geoffrey. "The Confessions of Lucilius (Horace 'Sat.' 2.1.30–34): A Defense of Autobiographical Satire?" *ClAnt* 6 (1987): 38–52.

Hart, H. L. A. *The Concept of Law*. Oxford: Oxford University Press, 2012.

Hartog, Hendrik. "Pigs and Positivism." *Wisconsin Law Review* 1985.4 (1985): 899–936.

Hauken, Tor. *Petition and Response: An Epigraphic Study of Petitions to Roman Emperors 181–249*. Athens: The Norwegian Institute at Athens, 1998.

Haynes, Holly. *The History of Make-Believe: Tacitus on Imperial Rome*. Berkeley: University of California Press, 2003.

Hedrick, Charles. *History and Silence: Purge and Rehabilitation of Memory in Late Antiquity*. Austin: University of Texas Press, 2010.

Hekster, Olivier. "All in the Family: The Appointment of Emperors Designate in the Second Century A.D." In de Blois (ed.), *Administration, Prosopography and Appointment Policies*, 35–49. Leiden; Boston: Brill, 2001.

Commodus: An Emperor at the Crossroads. Amsterdam: Gieben, 2002.

Emperors and Ancestors: Roman Rulers and the Constraints of Tradition. Oxford: Oxford University Press, 2015.

"Imperial Justice?: The Absence of Images of Roman Emperors in a Legal Role." *CQ* 70 (2020): 247–60.

Hekster, Olivier, and Ted Kaizer. "An Accidental Tourist?: Caracalla's Fatal Trip to the Temple of the Moon at Carrhae/Harran." *AS* 42 (2012): 89–107.

Hekster, Olivier, and Nicholas Zair. *Rome and its Empire, AD 193–284*. Edinburgh: Edinburgh University Press, 2008.

Hekster, Olivier, and Koenraad Verboven, eds. *The Impact of Justice on the Roman Empire*. Leiden; Boston: Brill, 2019.

Hellström, Monica. "The Monumental Bureaucracy of Diocletian." In Carlà-Uhink and Rollinger (eds.), *The Tetrarchy as Ideology*, 141–60. Stuttgart: Franz Steiner Verlag, 2023.

Herz, Zachary. "How to Do the History of Elagabalus." In *The Routledge Handbook of Classics and Queer Theory*, edited by Ella Haselswerdt, Sara Lindheim, and Kirk Ormand, 408–22. Oxford; New York: Routledge, 2023.

"Precedential Reasoning and Dynastic Self-Fashioning in the Rescripts of Severus Alexander." *Historia* 69 (2020): 103–25.

"The Epistemology of the Courthouse: Classical Antiquity in American LGBT-Rights Litigation." In *Enticements: Queer Legal Studies*, edited by Joseph Fischel and Brenda Cossman, 29–58. New York: NYU Press, 2024.

Heyam, Kit. *Before We Were Trans: A New History of Gender*. New York: Seal Press, 2022.

Hirschfield, Paul. "Exceptionally Lethal: American Police Killings in a Comparative Perspective." *Annual Review of Criminology* 6 (2023): 471–98.

Hoët-Van Cauwenberghe, Christine. "Marius Maximus, gouverneur de la Gaule Belgique, haut fonctionnaire et historien." *RdN* 101 (2019): 243–62.

Honig, Bonnie. *Emergency Politics: Paradox, Law, Democracy*. Princeton: Princeton University Press, 2009.

Honoré, Anthony. *Emperors and Lawyers: With a Palingenesia of Third-Century Imperial Rescripts, 193–305 A.D.* 2nd ed. Oxford: Clarendon Press, 1994.

Gaius. Oxford: Clarendon Press, 1962.

Justinian's Digest: Character and Compilation. New York: Oxford University Press, 2010.

Law in the Crisis of Empire, 379–455 AD: The Theodosian Dynasty and Its Quaestors with a Palingenesia of Laws of the Dynasty. Oxford: Clarendon Press, 1998.

"The Severan Lawyers: A Preliminary Survey." *SDHI* 28 (1962): 162–232.

Tribonian. Ithaca [NY]: Cornell University Press, 1978.

Ulpian: Pioneer of Human Rights. 2nd ed. Oxford: Oxford University Press, 2002.

Hooker, Brad. *Ideal Code, Real World: A Rule-Consequentialist Theory of Morality*. New York: Oxford University Press, 2000.

Horak, Franz. *Rationes decidendi: Entscheidungsbegründungen bei den älteren römischen Juristen bis Labeo*. Aalen: Scientia Verlag, 1969.

Hornblower, Simon, and Elaine Matthews. *Greek Personal Names: Their Value as Evidence*. Oxford: Oxford University Press, 2010.

Horwitz, Morton. "The Rule of Law: An Unqualified Human Good?" *Yale Law Journal* 86 (1977): 561–66.

Hose, Martin. "Historiographie in der Krise: Herausforderungen und Lösungen der Geschichtsschreibung im dritten Jahrhundert n. Chr." In *Empire in Crisis: Gothic Invasions and Roman Historiography*, edited by Fritz Mitthof, Gunther Martin, and Jana Grusková, 35–49. Vienna: Holzhausen, 2020.

Huck, Olivier. "Les compilateurs au travail: dessein et méthode de la codification théodosienne." In *Société, économie, administration dans le Code Théodosien*, edited by Sylvie Crogiez-Pétrequin and Pierre Jaillette, 79–98. Villeneuve-d'Ascq: Presses Universitaires du Septentrion, 2012.

Humfress, Caroline. "Law and Legal Practice in the Age of Justinian." In Maas (ed.), *Age of Justinian*, 161–84. Cambridge: Cambridge University Press, 2005.

"Legal Pluralism's Other: Mythologizing Modern Law." *LHR* 42 (2024): 155–68.

Orthodoxy and the Courts in Late Antiquity. Oxford: Oxford University Press, 2007.

"Thinking through Legal Pluralism: 'Forum Shopping' in the Later Roman Empire." In *Law and Empire*, edited by Jeroen Duindam, Jill Harries, Caroline Humfress, and Nimrod Hurvitz, 223–50. Leiden; Boston: Brill, 2013.

Hunink, Vincent. *Tertullian: De Pallio*. Amsterdam: Gieben, 2005.

Hurlet, Frédéric. "La Lex de imperio Vespasiani et la légitimité augustéenne." *Latomus* 52 (1993): 261–80.

"Les origines de la jurisdiction impériale: Imperator Caesar Augustus iudex." In Haensch (ed.), *Recht haben und Recht bekommen*, 5–39. Warsaw: University of Warsaw, 2016.

"L'idéologie dynastique sous les Julio-Claudiens: Origines, évolution, modes d'expression et modalités de sa diffusion dans les provinces." In *L'Augusteum de Narona*, edited by Giuseppe Zecchini, 117–43. Rome: L'Erma di Bretschneider, 2015.

Huschke, Philipp. "Über den Gregorianus und Hermogenianus Codex." *ZR* 6 (1867): 279–331.

Icks, Martijn. "From Priest to Emperor to Priest-Emperor: The Failed Legitimation of Elagabalus." In *Private and Public Lies: The Discourse of Deception and Deceit in the Graeco-Roman World*, edited by Andrew Turner, James Chong-Gossard, and Frederik Vervaet, 329–41. Brill, 2010.

The Crimes of Elagabalus: The Life and Legacy of Rome's Decadent Boy Emperor. Cambridge [MA]: Harvard University Press, 2012.

Imrie, Alex. *The Antonine Constitution: An Edict for the Caracallan Empire*. Boston: Brill, 2018.

Innes, Doreen. "The Panegyricus and Rhetorical Theory." In Roche (ed.), *Pliny's Praise*, 67–84. Cambridge; New York: Cambridge University Press, 2011.

Isager, Jacob. "Vespasiano e Augusto." In *Studia Romana in Honorem P. Krarup Septuagenarii*, edited by K. Ascani, et al., 64–71. Odense: Odense University Press, 1976.

Jackson, Claire. "Dio Chrysostom." In *The Oxford Handbook of the Second Sophistic*, edited by Daniel Richter and William Johnson, 217–32. New York: Oxford University Press, 2017.

Jacobs, Andrew. "'Papinian Commands One Thing, Our Paul Another': Roman Christians and Jewish Law in the Collatio Legum Mosaicarum et Romanarum." In *Religion and Law in Classical and Christian Rome*, edited by Clifford Ando, et al., 85–99. Stuttgart: Steiner, 2006.

Jasper, Detlev, and Horst Fuhrmann. *Papal Letters in the Early Middle Ages*. Washington, D.C.: Catholic University of America Press, 2001.

Jensen, Laura. "Government, the State, and Governance." *Polity* 40 (2008): 379–85.

Johnston, David. "Justinian's Digest: The Interpretation of Interpolation." *Oxford Journal of Legal Studies* 9 (1989): 149–66.

Roman Law in Context. 2nd ed. Cambridge; New York: Cambridge University Press, 2022.

"Three Thoughts on Roman Private Law and the Lex Irnitana." *JRS* 77 (1987): 62–77.

Jolowicz, Herbert, and John Nicholas. *Historical Introduction to the Study of Roman Law*. 3rd ed. Cambridge: Cambridge University Press, 1972.

Jones, Arnold. *The Later Roman Empire, 284–602*. 3 vols. Oxford: B. Blackwell, 1964.

Jones, Brian. *The Emperor Titus*. New York: St. Martin's Press, 1984.

Jones, Brian, and Robert Milns. *Suetonius: The Flavian Emperors: A Historical Commentary*. Bristol: Bristol Classical Press, 2002.

Kalman, Laura. *Legal Realism at Yale, 1927–1960*. Chapel Hill: University of North Carolina Press, 1986.

Kampen, Natalie. *Family Fictions in Roman Art*. Cambridge; New York: Cambridge University Press, 2009.

Kantorowicz, Ernst. *The King's Two Bodies: A Study in Mediaeval Political Theology*. 3rd ed. Princeton: Princeton University Press, 1997.

Kapust, Daniel. *Republicanism, Rhetoric, and Roman Political Thought: Sallust, Livy, and Tacitus*. Cambridge; New York: Cambridge University Press, 2011.

Kaser, Max. "Zur Glaubwürdigkeit der römischen Rechtsquellen (Über die Grenzen der Interpolationenkritik)." In Paradisi (ed.), *La critica del testo*, 291–370. Florence: Olschki, 1971.

Zur Methodologie der römischen Rechtsquellenforschung. Vienna: Hermann Böhlaus Nachfolger, 1972.

Kaser, Max, and Karl Hackl. *Das römische Zivilprozessrecht*. 2nd ed. Munich: Beck, 1996.

Katzoff, Ranon. "On the Intended Use of P. Col. 123." In *Proceedings of the XVIth International Congress of Papyrology*, edited by Roger Bagnall, 559–73. Atlanta: Scholars Press, 1981.

"Precedents in the Courts of Roman Egypt." *ZRG* 89 (1972): 256–92.

Kearley, Timothy, and Wilhelm Kroll. *A History of Justinian's Novels: With an English Translation of Wilhelm Kroll's Latin Preface*. Translated by David Miller. Fort Collins: Veterrimus Publishing, 2020.

Kehoe, Dennis. *Law And the Rural Economy in the Roman Empire*. Ann Arbor: University of Michigan Press, 2007.

Kelly, Benjamin. *Petitions, Litigation, and Social Control in Roman Egypt*. Oxford: Oxford University Press, 2011.

Kelly, Christopher. *Ruling the Later Roman Empire*. Cambridge [MA]: Harvard University Press, 2004.

Kemezis, Adam. "Augustus the Ironic Paradigm: Cassius Dio's Portrayal of the Lex Julia and Lex Papia Poppaea." *Phoenix* 61 (2007): 270–85.

"Cassius Dio and Senatorial Memory of Civil War in the 190s." In Lange and Scott (eds.), *Impact of Violence*, 257–86. Boston: Brill, 2020.

Greek Narratives of the Roman Empire under the Severans: Cassius Dio, Philostratus and Herodian. Cambridge: Cambridge University Press, 2014.

"The Fall of Elagabalus as Literary Narrative and Political Reality." *Historia* 65 (2016): 348–90.

"Vox Populi, Vox Mea?: Information, Evaluation, and Public Opinion in Dio's Account of the Principate." In *Emperors and Political Culture in Cassius Dio's Roman History*, edited by Caillan Davenport and

Christopher Mallan, 33–51. Cambridge: Cambridge University Press, 2021.

Kemmers, Fleur. "Out of the Shadow: Geta and Caracalla Reconsidered." In Faust and Leitmeir (eds.), *Repräsentationsformen in Severischer Zeit*, 270–90. Frankfurt am Main: Verlag Antike, 2011.

Kennedy, Duncan. *A Critique of Adjudication: Fin de Siècle*. Cambridge [MA]: Harvard University Press, 1997.

Kikuchi, Shigeto. "Authority at a Distance: Popes, Their Media, and Their Presence Felt in the Frankish Kingdom." In *Communicating Papal Authority in the Middle Ages*, edited by Minoru Ozawa, Thomas Smith, and Georg Strack, 13–30. London; New York: Routledge, 2023.

Kmak, Magdalena. "The Impact of Exile on Law and Legal Science 1934-1964." In *Roman Law and The Idea of Europe*, edited by Kaius Tuori and Heta Björklund, 15–34. London: T. and T. Clark, 2018.

Kohlhepp, Ralf. "Franz Wieacker und die NS-Zeit." *ZRG* 122 (2005): 203–23.

Kondratuk, Laurent. "Le travestissement dans les droits romain et judéo-chrétien." In *Genre, famille, vulnérabilité: Mélanges en l'honneur de Catherine Philippe*, edited by Anne Dorsman, Laurent Kondratuk, and Béatrice Lapérou-Scheneider, 51–64. Paris: L'Harmattan, 2017.

Köstner, Elena. "Geschlechterrollen im römischen Erbrecht im Spiegel des zeitgenössischen Gerechtigkeitsverständnisses und am Beispiel der lex Voconia." In Hekster and Verboven (eds.), *Impact of Justice*, 177–95. Leiden; Boston: Brill, 2019.

Kraus, Christina, and Anthony Woodman. *Latin Historians*. Oxford; New York: Oxford University Press, 1997.

Krüger, Paul. "Über die Verwendung von Papyrus und Pergament für die juristische Litteratur der Römer." *ZRG* 8 (1887): 76–85.

Krüger, Paul, Peter Birks, and Grant McLeod, eds. *Justinian's Institutes*. Ithaca [NY]: Cornell University Press, 1987.

Krüpe, Florian. *Die damnatio memoriae: über die Vernichtung von Erinnerung: eine Fallstudie zu Publius Septimius Geta (189–211 n.Chr.)*. Gutenberg: Computus Druck Satz und Verlag, 2011.

"Die damnatio memoriae von Plautianus und Plautilla: Zerstörte Familie, zerstörte Erinnerungen." In *BilderGewalt: Zerstörung, Zensur, Umkodierung, Neuschöpfung*, edited by Birgit Münch and Andreas Tacke, 15–26. Petersberg: Imhof, 2018.

Kulikowski, Michael. "Ordo." In Vidas and Chin (eds.), *Late Ancient Knowing*, 175–96. Berkeley: University of California Press, 2015.

"The 'Notitia Dignitatum' as a Historical Source." *Historia* 49 (2000): 358–77.

Kunkel, Wolfgang. "Das Wesen des ius respondendi." *ZRG* 66 (1948): 423–57.

"Der Prozess der Gohariener vor Caracalla." In *Festschrift für Hans Lewald*, 81–91. Basel: Helbig & Lichtenhahn, 1953.

Die römischen Juristen: Herkunft und soziale Stellung. 2nd ed. Cologne; Vienna: Böhlau, 2001.

"Über Lebenszeit und Laufbahn des Juristen Julians." *Iura* 1 (1950): 192–203.

Künzer, Isabelle. *Kulturen der Konkurrenz: Untersuchungen zu einem senatorischen Interaktionsmodus an der Wende vom ersten zum zweiten Jahrhundert n. Chr*. Bonn: Habelt, 2016.

Ladavac, Nicoletta. "Philosophy of Law and Theory of Law: The Continuity of Kelsen's Years in America." In *Hans Kelsen in America: Selective Affinities and the Mysteries of Academic Influence*, edited by D. A. Jeremy Telman, 229–47. New York: Springer, 2016.

LaFleur, Richard. "Horace and Onomasti Komodein: The Law of Satire." *ANRW* 2.3 (1981): 1790–1826.

Langbein, John. "Substantial Compliance with the Wills Act." *Harvard Law Review* 88 (1975): 489–531.

Lange, Carsten. "Cassius Dio on Perusia: A Study in Human Nature During Civil War." In Madsen and Lange (eds.), *Cassius Dio the Historian*, 336–62. Boston: Brill, 2021.

"The Battle of Actium: A Reconsideration." *CQ* 61 (2011): 608–23.

Lange, Carsten, and Andrew Scott, eds. *Cassius Dio: The Impact of Violence, War, and Civil War*. Boston: Brill, 2020.

Lange, Carsten, and Jesper Madsen, eds. *Cassius Dio: Greek Intellectual and Roman Politician*. Leiden: Brill, 2016.

Langford, Julie. "Cassius Dio and the Dowager Empresses, Part 1: Livia, the Senate, and the Succession Struggle." In Madsen and Lange (eds.), *Cassius Dio the Historian*, 426–57. Boston: Brill, 2021.

Maternal Megalomania: Julia Domna and the Imperial Politics of Motherhood. Baltimore: Johns Hopkins University Press, 2013.

Langlands, Rebecca. *Exemplary Ethics in Ancient Rome*. Cambridge: Cambridge University Press, 2018.

"Roman Exemplarity: Mediating between General and Particular." In Lowrie and Lüdemann (eds.), *Exemplarity and Singularity*, 68–80. London; New York: Routledge, 2015.

Lanni, Adriaan. *Law and Justice in the Courts of Classical Athens*. Cambridge: Cambridge University Press, 2006.

Larson, Atria, and Keith Sisson. "Papal Decretals." In *A Companion to the Medieval Papacy*, edited by Atria Larson and Keith Sisson, 158–73. Leiden; Boston: Brill, 2016.

Lehne-Gstreinthaler, Christine. *Iurisperiti et oratores: eine Studie zu den römischen Juristen der Republik*. Vienna: Böhlau Verlag, 2019.

Lendon, Jon. *Empire of Honour: The Art of Government in the Roman World*. Oxford: Clarendon Press, 1997.

"The Legitimacy of the Roman Emperor: Against Weberian Legitimacy and Imperial 'Strategies of Legitimation.'" In *Herrschaftsstrukturen Und Herrschaftspraxis*, edited by Anne Kolb, 53–63. Berlin: Akademie Verlag, 2006.

Lenel, Otto. "Interpolationenjagd." *ZRG* 45 (1925): 17–38.

Palingenesia iuris civilis. 2nd ed. Graz: Akademische Druck-Universität Verlagsanstalt, 1960.

Lenski, Noel. *Constantine and the Cities: Imperial Authority and Civic Politics*. Philadelphia: University of Pennsylvania Press, 2016.

Lenski, Noel, and Catherine Cameron, eds. *What Is a Slave Society?: The Practice of Slavery in Global Perspective*. Cambridge: Cambridge University Press, 2018.

Lerner, Melvin, and Carolyn Simmons. "Observer's Reaction to the 'Innocent Victim': Compassion or Rejection?" *Journal of Personality and Social Psychology* 4 (1966): 203–10.

Letteney, Mark. *The Christianization of Knowledge in Late Antiquity: Intellectual and Material Transformations*. Cambridge: Cambridge University Press, 2023.

Levick, Barbara. *Augustus: Image and Substance*. London: Routledge, 2010.

"The Lex de Imperio Vespasiani: The Parts and the Whole." In Capogrossi Colognesi and Tassi Scandone (eds.), *La Lex*, 11–22. Rome: L'Erma di Bretschneider, 2009.

Vespasian. New York: Routledge, 1999.

Levinson, Sanford, and Jack Balkin. "Morton Horwitz Wrestles with the Rule of Law." In *Transformations in American Legal History*, edited by Daniel Hamilton and Alfred Brophy, 1–22. Cambridge [MA]: Harvard University Press, 2009.

Levy, Ernst. "Von den römischen Anklägervergehen." In *Gesammelte Schriften*, by Ernst Levy, 379–432. Cologne: Böhlau Verlag, 1967.

Lewis, Andrew. "Slavery, Family, and Status." In *The Cambridge Companion to Roman Law*, edited by David Johnston, 151–74. New York: Cambridge University Press, 2015.

Licandro, Orazio. "Pauli Sententiae: storia controversa di un testo illustre tra autenticità, apocrifia e appunti di scuola." *SDHI* 84 (2018): 355–66.

Licandro, Orazio, and Nicola Palazzolo. *Papirius Iustus: Libri XX de constitutionibus*. Rome: L'Erma di Bretschneider, 2021.

Liebeschuetz, John. *Antioch: City and Imperial Administration in the Later Roman Empire*. Oxford: Clarendon Press, 1972.

Liebs, Detlef. *Die Jurisprudenz im spätantiken Italien (260–640 n. Chr.)*. Berlin: Duncker und Humblot, 1987.

Hermogenians Iuris epitome: Zum Stand der römischen Jurisprudenz im Zeitalter Diokletians. Göttingen: Vandenhoeck und Ruprecht, 1964.

Hofjuristen der römischen Kaiser bis Justinian. Munich: Beck, 2011.

"Jurisprudenz." In *Die Literatur des Umbruchs*, edited by Klaus Sallmann, 4: 83–217. Munich: Beck, 1997.

"Rechtsschulen und Rechtsunterricht im Prinzipat." *ANRW* 2.15 (1976): 197–286.

Römische Jurisprudenz in Gallien (2. Bis 8. Jahrhundert). Berlin: Duncker und Humblot, 2002.

"The Code System: Reorganizing Roman Law and Legal Literature in the Late Antique Period." In Nasti and Schiavone (eds.), *Jurists and Legal Science*, 261–85. London: Routledge, 2021.

Lindholmer, Mads. "Exploiting Conventions: Cassius Dio's Late Republic and the Annalistic Tradition." In Madsen and Lange (eds.), *Cassius Dio the Historian*, 336–62. Boston: Brill, 2021.

Lobur, John. *Consensus, Concordia and the Formation of Roman Imperial Ideology*. New York; Abingdon: Routledge, 2008.

Lokin, Jan. "The End of an Epoch: Epilegomena to a Century of Interpolation Criticism." In *Collatio iuris romani: Études dédiées à Hans Ankum a l'occasion de son 65 anniversaire*, edited by Robert Feenstra, 261–73. Amsterdam: Gieben, 1995.

"The Novels of Leo and the Decisions of Justinian." In *Analecta Atheniensia Ad Ius Byzantinum Spectantia*, edited by Spyros Troianos, 131–40. Athens: Sakkoulas Publishers, 1997.

Lowrie, Michèle. "Roman Law and Latin Literature." In du Plessis, Ando, and Tuori (eds.), *Roman Law and Society*, 70–82. Oxford: Oxford University Press, 2016.

"Slander and Horse Law in Horace, Sermones 2.1." *Law & Literature* 17 (2005): 405–31.

"The Force of Literature." In Ziogas and Bexley (eds.), *Roman Law and Latin Literature*, 25–44. London: Bloomsbury, 2022.

Writing, Performance, and Authority in Augustan Rome. Oxford; New York: Oxford University Press, 2009.

Lowrie, Michèle, and Susanne Lüdemann, eds. *Exemplarity and Singularity: Thinking through Particulars in Philosophy, Literature, and Law*. London; New York: Routledge, 2015.

Lucrezi, Francesco. *Aspetti giuridici del principato di Vespasiano*. Naples: Jovene, 1995.

"Il mito della Lex de Imperio Vespasiani." In Capogrossi Colognesi and Tassi Scandone (eds.), *La Lex*, 157–68. Rome: L'Erma di Bretschneider, 2009.

Leges super principem: La monarchia costituzionale di Vespasiano. Naples: Jovene, 1982.

Lucrezi, Francesco, and Samuele Rocca. *Studi sulla Collatio: Il deposito in diritto ebraico e romano*. Turin: Giappichelli, 2017.

Lusnia, Susann. *Creating Severan Rome*. Brussels: Éditions Latomus, 2014.

Ma, John. *Antiochos III and the Cities of Western Asia Minor*. 2nd ed. Oxford: Oxford University Press, 2005.

Maas, Michael. "Roman History and Christian Ideology in Justinian Reform Legislation." *Dumbarton Oaks Papers* 40 (1986): 17–31.

Maas, Michael, ed. *The Cambridge Companion to the Age of Justinian*. Cambridge: Cambridge University Press, 2005.

MacMullen, Ramsay. "Judicial Savagery in the Roman Empire." *Chiron* 16 (1986): 147–66.

Roman Government's Response to Crisis, A.D. 235–337. New Haven: Yale University Press, 1976.

Madsen, Jesper, and Carsten Lange, eds. *Cassius Dio the Historian: Methods and Approaches*. Boston: Brill, 2021.

Maehle, Ingvar. "Munificence in the Democratic and Oligarchic Systems of the Ancient World: A Comparative Approach." In *Institution of Sponsorship from Ancient to Modern Times*, edited by Georgios Kakavas, 13–27. Athens: Norwegian Institute at Athens, 2019.

Magioncalda, Andreina. "Un giurista al servizio dell'imperatore: La carriera di Emilio Papiniano." *Materiali per una storia della cultura giuridica* 30 (2000): 451–78.

Mann, Michael. "The Autonomous Power of the State: Its Origins, Mechanisms and Results." *European Journal of Sociology* 25 (1984): 185–213.

Mantovani, Dario. *Digesto e masse bluhmiane*. Milan: Giuffrè, 1987.

"'Leges et iura p(opuli) r(omani) restituit': principe e diritto in un aureo di Ottaviano." In *I tribunali dell'Impero*, edited by Francesco Milazzo, 41–105. Milan: Giuffrè, 2008.

"Les clauses 'sans précédents' de la lex de imperio Vespasiani: Une interprétation uuridique." *CCG* 16 (2005): 25–43.

Les juristes écrivains de la Rome antique: Les œuvres des juristes comme littérature. Paris: Les Belles Lettres, 2018.

"Lex Regia de Imperio Vespasiani: Il vagum imperium e la legge constante." In Capogrossi Colognesi and Tassi Scandone (eds.), *La Lex*, 125–55. Rome: L'Erma di Bretschneider, 2009.

Mantovani, Dario, and Antonio Padoa Schioppa, eds. *Interpretare il Digesto: Storia e metodi*. Pavia: IUSS Press, 2014.

Manuwald, Bernd. *Cassius Dio und Augustus: Philologische Untersuchungen zu den Büchern 45–56 des dionischen Geschichtswerkes*. Wiesbaden: Steiner, 1979.

Martini, Remo. "Ancora sul legato di vesti." *Labeo* 17 (1971): 157–68.

Martini, Rodolfo. "Note in calce ad una falsa emissione aurea di Octavianus recentemente apparsa sul mercato antiquario." *Annotazioni Numismatische* 5 (1992): 94–95.

"Nuova nota a conferma della falsifità dell 'aureo' di Octavianus." *Annotazioni Numismatische* 21 (1996): 465–67.

Mason, Hugh. *Greek Terms for Roman Institutions: A Lexicon and Analysis.* Toronto: Hakkert, 1974.

Massei, Massimo. "Le citazioni della giurisprudenza classica nella legislazione imperiale." In *Scritti di diritto romano in onore di Contardo Ferrini*, 403–75. Milan: University of Pavia, 1946.

Matern, Petra. *Helios und Sol: Kulte und Ikonographie des griechischen und römischen Sonnengottes.* Istanbul: Ege Yayınları, 2002.

Matsuda, Mari. "Looking to the Bottom: Critical Legal Studies and Reparations." *Harvard Civil Rights-Civil Liberties Law Review* 22 (1987): 323–400.

Matthews, John. *Laying Down the Law: A Study of the Theodosian Code.* New Haven: Yale University Press, 2000.

Mazurek, Lindsey. *Isis in a Global Empire: Greek Identity Through Egyptian Religion in Roman Greece.* Cambridge: Cambridge University Press, 2022.

McCarthy, Kathleen. *Slaves, Masters, and the Art of Authority in Plautine Comedy.* Princeton: Princeton University Press, 2009.

McEvoy, Meaghan. *Child Emperor Rule in the Late Roman West, A.D. 367–455.* Oxford: Oxford University Press, 2013.

McGinn, Thomas. "Satire and the Law: The Case of Horace." *CCJ* 47 (2001): 81–102.

"The Sea Common to All in Plautus, Rudens: Social Norms and Legal Rules." In Ziogas and Bexley (eds.), *Roman Law and Latin Literature*, 169–88. London: Bloomsbury, 2022.

McSweeney, Thomas. *Priests of the Law: Roman Law and the Making of the Common Law's First Professionals.* Oxford: Oxford University Press, 2019.

Meier, Mischa. *Das andere Zeitalter Justinians: Kontingenzerfahrung und Kontingenzbewältigung im 6. Jahrhundert n. Chr.* Göttingen: Vandenhoeck und Ruprecht, 2003.

Mennen, Inge. *Power and Status in the Roman Empire, AD 193–284.* Boston: Brill, 2011.

Merry, Sally. *Getting Justice and Getting Even: Legal Consciousness among Working-Class Americans.* Chicago: University of Chicago Press, 1990.

"Legal Pluralism." *Law & Society Review* 22 (1988): 869–96.

Metcalf, William. "Whose 'Liberalitas'?: Propaganda and Audience in the Early Roman Empire." *RIN* 95 (1993): 337–46.

Metzger, Ernest. *A New Outline of the Roman Civil Trial.* Oxford: Clarendon Press, 1997.

Meyer, Elizabeth. *Legitimacy and Law in the Roman World: Tabulae in Roman Belief and Practice.* New York: Cambridge University Press, 2004.

Meyer-Zwiffelhoffer, Eckhard. "Ein Visionär auf dem Thron?: Kaiser Commodus, Hercules Romanus." *Klio* 88 (2006): 189–215.

Mignone, Lisa. "Rome's Pomerium and the Aventine Hill: From Auguraculum to Imperium Sine Fine." *Historia* 65 (2016): 427–49.

Millar, Fergus. "A New Approach to the Roman Jurists." *JRS* 76 (1986): 272–80.

"Emperors at Work." *JRS* 57 (1967): 9–19.

"Empire and City, Augustus to Julian: Obligations, Excuses and Status." *JRS* 73 (1983): 76–96.

The Emperor in the Roman World, 31 BC–AD 337. Ithaca [NY]: Cornell University Press, 1977.

Miller, Carolyn. "Genre as Social Action." *Quarterly Journal of Speech* 70 (1984): 151–67.

Miller, David, and Peter Sarris, eds. *The Novels of Justinian: A Complete Annotated English Translation*. Cambridge; New York: Cambridge University Press, 2018.

Milnor, Kristina. *Gender, Domesticity, and the Age of Augustus: Inventing Private Life*. Oxford; New York: Oxford University Press, 2005.

"Augustus, History, and the Landscape of the Law." *Arethusa* 40 (2007): 7–23.

Mineo, Bernard, and Frédéric Hurlet, eds. *Le principat d'Auguste: Réalités et représentations du pouvoir autour de la res publica restituta*. Rennes: Presses universitaires de Rennes, 2009.

van Minnen, Peter. "Three Edicts of Caracalla?: A New Reading of P.*Giss*. 40." *Chiron* 46 (2016): 205–21.

Mitchell, Richard. "Roman History, Roman Law, and Roman Priests: The Common Ground." *University of Illinois Law Review* 1984.3 (1984): 541–60.

Mitteis, Ludwig. *Reichsrecht und Volksrecht in den östlichen Provinzen des Römischen Kaiserreichs: Mit Beiträgen zur Kenntniss des griechischen Rechts und der spätrömischen Rechtsentwicklung*. Leipzig: Teubner, 1891.

Moatti, Claudia. *Res publica: Histoire romaine de la chose publique*. Paris: Fayard, 2018.

Mommsen, Theodor. "Die Heimath des Gregorianus." *ZRG* 22 (1901): 139–44.

Morgan, Gwyn. *69 AD: The Year of Four Emperors*. Oxford; New York: Oxford University Press, 2006.

Morgan, Teresa. *Popular Morality in the Early Roman Empire*. New York: Cambridge University Press, 2007.

Morrell, Kit. "Augustus as Magpie." In Morrell, Osgood, and Welch (eds.), *The Alternative Augustan Age*, 12–26. New York: Oxford University Press, 2019.

Morrell, Kit, Josiah Osgood, and Kathryn Welch, eds. *The Alternative Augustan Age*. New York: Oxford University Press, 2019.

Müller, Wolfgang. "The Recovery of Justinian's Digest in the Middle Ages." *Bulletin of Medieval Canon Law* 20 (1990): 1–30.

Murison, Charles. *Rebellion and Reconstruction: Galba to Domitian: An Historical Commentary on Cassius Dio's Roman History, Books 64–67 (A.D. 68–96)*. Atlanta: Scholars Press, 1999.

Nappa, Christopher. *Making Men Ridiculous: Juvenal and the Anxieties of the Individual*. Ann Arbor: University of Michigan Press, 2018.

Nasti, Fara. "Greek Thought and Roman Jurists: A Preliminary Survey on Pomponius's Enchiridion." In Nasti and Schiavone (eds.), *Jurists and Legal Science*, 137–58. London: Routledge, 2021.

L'attività normativa di Severo Alessandro. Naples: Satura, 2006.

L'Enchiridion di Sesto Pomponio: una ricostruzione. Rome: L'Erma di Bretschneider, 2023.

Nasti, Fara, and Aldo Schiavone, eds. *Jurists and Legal Science in the History of Roman Law*. London: Routledge, 2021.

Nellen, Henk. *Hugo Grotius: A Lifelong Struggle for Peace in Church and State, 1583–1645*. Boston: Brill, 2014.

Nelson, Hein. "Das Fragment über die cretio in der Autuner Gaiusparaphrase." *Subseciva Groningana* 2 (1985): 1–20.

Überlieferung, Aufbau und Stil von Gai Institutiones. Leiden: Brill, 1981.

Nethercut, Jason. "Ennius and the Revaluation of Traditional Historiography in Lucretius' De Rerum Natura." In *Valuing the Past in the Greco-Roman World*, edited by James Ker and Christoph Pieper, 435–61. Leiden; Boston: Brill, 2014.

Newlands, Carole. "Contesting Time and Space: Fasti 6.637–48." In *Ovid's Fasti: Historical Readings at Its Bimillennium*, edited by Geraldine Herbert-Brown, 225–50. Oxford; New York: Oxford University Press, 2002.

Playing with Time: Ovid and the Fasti. Ithaca [NY]: Cornell University Press, 1995.

Statius' Silvae and the Poetics of Empire. Cambridge; New York: Cambridge University Press, 2002.

Nicolai, Helmut. *Die rassegesetzliche Rechtslehre: Grundzüge einer nationalsozialistischen Rechtsphilosophie*. Munich: Nationalsozialisten Bibliothek, 1932.

Noailles, Pierre, and Alphonse Dain, eds. *Les Novelles de Léon VI, Le Sage*. Paris: Les Belles Lettres, 1944.

Noe, Christopher. "The 'Age of Iron and Rust' in Cassius Dio's Roman History: Influences from Stoic Philosophy." In *Cassius Dio and the Principate*, edited by Christopher Burden-Strevens, Jesper Madsen, and Antonio Pistellato, 141–63. Venice: Ca' Foscari, 2020.

Noreña, Carlos. *Imperial Ideals in the Roman West: Representation, Circulation, Power*. Cambridge: Cambridge University Press, 2011.

"Medium and Message in Vespasian's Templum Pacis." *MAAR* 48 (2003): 25–43.

"Self-Fashioning in the Panegyricus." In Roche (ed.), *Pliny's Praise*, 29–44. Cambridge; New York: Cambridge University Press, 2011.

"The Ethics of Autocracy in the Roman World." In *A Companion to Greek and Roman Political Thought*, edited by Ryan Balot, 266–79. Chichester: Wiley-Blackwell, 2009.

Nörr, Dieter. *Rechtskritik in der römischen Antike*. Munich, 1974.

"Zur Rescriptenpraxis in der hohen Prinzipatzeit." *ZRG* 98 (1981): 1–46.

Nutton, Vivian. *Ancient Medicine*. London; New York: Routledge, 2004.

Oliensis, Ellen. "Ut Arte Emendaturus Fortunam: Horace, Nasidienus, and the Art of Satire." In Habinek and Schiesaro (eds.), *The Roman Cultural Revolution*, 90–104. Cambridge: Cambridge Philological Society, 1997.

Oliver, James. *Greek Constitutions of Early Roman Emperors from Inscriptions and Papyri*. Philadelphia: American Philosophical Society, 1989.

"The Athens of Hadrian." In *Les empereurs romains d'Espagne*, edited by André Piganiol, 123–33. Paris: Éditions du CNRS, 1965.

"The Ruling Power: A Study of the Roman Empire in the Second Century after Christ through the Roman Oration of Aelius Aristides." *TAPhS* 43 (1953): 871–1003.

Oliver, James, and Robert Palmer. "Text of the Tabula Hebana." *AJP* 75 (1954): 225–49.

Optendrenk, Theo. *Die Religionspolitik des Kaisers Elagabal im Spiegel der Historia Augusta*. Bonn: Habelt, 1969.

Osborne, Robin. "Euergetism and the Public Economy of Classical Athens: The Initiative of the Deme." In *The Power of Individual and Community in Ancient Athens and Beyond: Essays in Honour of John K. Davies*, edited by Zosia Archibald and Jan Haywood, 147–62. Swansea: Classical Press of Wales, 2019.

Osgood, Josiah. "Cassius Dio's Secret History of Elagabalus." In Lange and Madsen (eds.), *Greek Intellectual*, 177–92. Leiden: Brill, 2016.

"Ending Civil War at Rome: Rhetoric and Reality, 88 BCE–197 C.E." *AHR* 120 (2015): 1683–95.

Turia: A Roman Woman's Civil War. Oxford; New York: Oxford University Press, 2014.

Osler, Douglas. "The Fantasy Men." *Rechtsgeschichte* 10 (2007): 169–92.

Palazzolo, Nicola. "Dalle cognitiones alla cognitio: principe e giuristi verso la costruzione del nuovo sistema processuale." In *I tribunali dell'Impero*, edited by Francesco Milazzo, 217–40. Milan: Giuffrè, 2015.

Palmer, Robert. "The Topography and Social History of Rome's Trastevere." *PAPhS* 125 (1981): 368–97.

Pandey, Nandini. *The Poetics of Power in Augustan Rome: Latin Poetic Responses to Early Imperial Iconography*. Cambridge; New York: Cambridge University Press, 2018.

Pangerl, Andreas. "Zwei feindliche Brüder: Caracalla und Geta." In *Portraits: 500 Years of Roman Coin Portraits*, edited by Andreas Pangerl, 375–81. Munich: Staatliche Münzsammlung München, 2017.

Pani, Mario. "Costituzionalismo antico: la lex de imperio Vespasiani." In *Storia romana e storia moderna: Fasi in prospettiva*, edited by Mario Pani, 101–14. Bari: Edipuglia, 2005.

Paradisi, Bruno, ed. *La critica del testo*. Florence: Olschki, 1971.

Paschalis, Michael. "The Afterlife of Emperor Claudius in Seneca's Apocolocyntosis." *Numen* 56 (2009): 198–216.

Pauly, August Friedrich von, et al., eds. *Paulys Realencyclopädie der classischen Altertumswissenschaft*. Stuttgart: Druckenmüller Verlag, 1893.

Pazdernik, Charles. "Justinianic Ideology and the Power of the Past." In Maas (ed.), *Age of Justinian*, 185–212. Cambridge: Cambridge University Press, 2005.

Peachin, Michael. "Exemplary Government in the Early Roman Empire." In *Crises and the Roman Empire*, edited by Olivier Hekster, Gerda de Kleijn, and Daniëlle Slootjes, 75–93. Boston: Brill, 2007.

Iudex Vice Caesaris: Deputy Emperors and the Administration of Justice During the Principate. Stuttgart: Franz Steiner Verlag, 1996.

"Jurists and the Law in the Early Roman Empire." In de Blois (ed.), *Administration, Prosopography and Appointment Policies*, 109–20. Amsterdam: Gieben, 2001.

"Weitere Gedanken zum Prozess des Verfassens kaiserliche Reskripte." In Babusiaux and Kob (eds.), *Das Recht der "Soldatenkaiser,"* 211–24. Berlin: De Gruyter, 2015.

Peer, Ayelet. "Cassius Dio, Cicero, and the Complexity of Civil War." In Lange and Scott (eds.), *Impact of Violence*, 219–40. Boston: Brill, 2020.

Pernot, Laurent. "Aelius Aristides and Rome." In *Aelius Aristides: Between Greece, Rome, and the Gods*, edited by William Harris and Brooke Holmes, 175–201. Leiden; Boston: Brill, 2008.

Epideictic Rhetoric: Questioning the Stakes of Ancient Praise. Austin: University of Texas Press, 2015.

La rhétorique de l'éloge dans le monde gréco-romain. Paris: Institut d'Études Augustiniennes, 1993.

Perry, Matthew. "Defining Gender." In du Plessis, Ando, and Tuori (eds.), *Roman Law and Society*, 432–42. Oxford University Press, 2016.

Piacente, Daniele. "Giurisprudenza e fonti del diritto romano nella tarda Antiquità." *Classica et Christiana* 8 (2013): 287–98.

Pilipow, Ryan. "The Jeweled Jurist: Late Roman Legal Aesthetics." *SLA* 4 (2020): 185–202.

Pinkster, Harm. *The Oxford Latin Syntax*. 2 vols. Oxford: Oxford University Press, 2015.

Plaza, Maria. "Solventur Risu Tabulae: Saved by Laughter in Horace (S. II. i.80–6) and Apuleius (Met. III.i-Ii)." *C&M* 54 (2003): 353–58.
du Plessis, Paul, Clifford Ando, and Kaius Tuori, eds. *The Oxford Handbook of Roman Law and Society*. Oxford: Oxford University Press, 2016.
Poulter, Andrew. "Why Did Most Cities in Moesia and Thrace Survive During the 3rd-Century 'Crisis'?" In *Empire in Crisis: Gothic Invasions and Roman Historiography*, edited by Fritz Mitthof, Gunther Martin, and Jana Grusková. Vienna: Holzhausen, 2020.
Powell, Jonathan. "Juvenal and the Delatores." In *Ancient Historiography and Its Contexts: Studies in Honour of A. J. Woodman*, edited by Christina Kraus, John Marincola, and Christopher Pelling, 224–44. Oxford; New York: Oxford University Press, 2010.
Pugsley, David. "Gaius or Sextus Pomponius." *RIDA* 41 (1994): 353–67.
"Justinian, Bluhme and the Numbers Game: Or How Precise Is Bluhme's Massentheorie." *Fundamina* 11 (2005): 63–77.
Puliatti, Salvatore. "La politica legislativa di Giustiniano." In Mantovani and Padoa Schioppa (eds.), *Interpretare il Digesto*, 135–73. Pavia: IUSS Press, 2014.
Purpura, Gianfranco. "I papiri e le costituzioni imperiali in Egitto." *Aegyptus* 89 (2009): 155–220.
"Sulla tavola perduta della Lex de Auctoritate Vespasiani." *Minima epigraphica et papyrologica* 2 (1999): 261–95.
Raditsa, Leo. "Augustus' Legislation Concerning Marriage, Procreation, Love Affairs and Adultery." *ANRW* 2.13 (1980): 278–339.
Raggi, Andrea. "Cross-Dressing in Rome between Norm and Practice." In Campanile, Carlà-Uhink, and Facella (eds.), *TransAntiquity*, 38–51. London; New York: Routledge, 2017.
Rantala, Jussi. *The Ludi Saeculares of Septimius Severus: The Ideologies of a New Roman Empire*. New York: Routledge, 2017.
Rebeggiani, Stefano. "From Civil War to Foreign Expansion: Cultural Identity and the Hellenization of the Empire in Statius and Valerius Flaccus." *RCCM* 64 (2022): 41–60.
Reeves, M. Barbara. "The 'Feriale Duranum', Roman Military Religion, and Dura -Europos: A Reassessment." Ph.D., State University of New York at Buffalo, 2005.
Rhode, Deborah. *Access to Justice*. Oxford: Oxford University Press, 2004.
Riccobono, Salvatore, ed. *Fontes iuris romani antejustiniani*. Florence: S.A.G. Barbèra, 1968.
Ius et ars boni et aequi. Naples: Jovene, 1947.
Rich, John. "Consensus Rituals and the Origin of the Principate." In *Il Princeps romano, autocrate o magistrato? Fattori giuridici e fattori sociali del potere imperiale da Augusto a Commodo*, edited by Jean-Louis Ferrary and John Scheid, 101–38. Pavia: IUSS Press, 2015.

"Making the Emergency Permanent: Auctoritas, Potestas and the Evolution of the Principate of Augustus." *CEFRA* 458 (2012): 37–121.

The Augustan Settlement: Roman History (53.1–55.9). Warminster: Aris & Phillips, 1990.

Rich, John, and Jonathan Williams. "Leges et Iura p. r. Restituit: A New Aureus of Octavian and the Settlement of 28–27 B.C." *NC* 159 (1999): 169–213.

Richlin, Amy. "Not Before Homosexuality: The Materiality of the Cinaedus and the Roman Law against Love between Men." *Journal of the History of Sexuality* 3 (1993): 523–73.

Slave Theater in the Roman Republic: Plautus and Popular Comedy. Cambridge; New York: Cambridge University Press, 2017.

Riedlberger, Peter. *Prolegomena zu den spätantiken Konstitutionen: nebst einer Analyse der erbrechtlichen und verwandten Sanktionen gegen Heterodoxe*. Stuttgart-Bad Cannstatt: Frommann-Holzboog, 2020.

Riggsby, Andrew. *Roman Law and the Legal World of the Romans*. New York: Cambridge University Press, 2010.

"Roman Legal Education." In *A Companion to Ancient Education*, edited by W. Martin Bloomer, 444–51. Chichester: Wiley-Blackwell, 2015.

Robinson, Olivia. *The Sources of Roman Law: Problems and Methods for Ancient Historians*. London; New York: Routledge, 1996.

Robinson, Timothy. "In the Court of Time: The Reckoning of a Monster in the Apocolocyntosis." *Arethusa* 38 (2005): 223–57.

Roche, Paul, ed. *Pliny's Praise: The Panegyricus in the Roman World*. Cambridge; New York: Cambridge University Press, 2011.

"Pliny's Thanksgiving: An Introduction to the Panegyricus." In Roche (ed.), *Pliny's Praise*, 1–28. Cambridge; New York: Cambridge University Press, 2011.

Rodríguez Martín, José-Domingo. *Fragmenta augustodunensia*. Granada: Editorial Comares, 1998.

Rohrbacher, David. *The Play of Allusion in the Historia Augusta*. Madison: The University of Wisconsin Press, 2016.

Roller, Matthew. *Constructing Autocracy: Aristocrats and Emperors in Julio-Claudian Rome*. Princeton: Princeton University Press, 2001.

"Demolished Houses, Monumentality, and Memory in Roman Culture." *ClAnt* 29 (2010): 117–80.

"Exemplarity in Roman Culture: The Cases of Horatius Cocles and Cloelia." *CP* 99 (2004): 1–56.

Models from the Past in Roman Culture: A World of Exempla. Cambridge: Cambridge University Press, 2018.

Rosenberg, Gerald. *The Hollow Hope: Can Courts Bring About Social Change?* Chicago: University of Chicago Press, 1991.

Roussel, Pierre, and Fernand De Visscher. "Les Inscriptions du temple de Dmeir." *Syria* 23 (1942): 173–200.

Rowan, Clare. "Becoming Jupiter: Severus Alexander, the Temple of Jupiter Ultor, and Jovian Iconography on Roman Imperial Coinage." *AJN* 21 (2009): 123–50.

"The Procession of Elagabalus and the Problem of the Parasols." *Journal of the Numismatic Association of Australia* 17 (2006): 114–19.

Under Divine Auspices: Divine Ideology and the Visualisation of Imperial Power in the Severan Period. Cambridge: Cambridge University Press, 2012.

Rubin, Zvi. *Civil-War Propaganda and Historiography*. Brussels: Peeters, 1980.

Ruciński, Sebastian. *Praefectus urbi: Le gardien de l'ordre public à Rome sous le Haut-Empire Romain*. Translated by Bernadeta Pyśk. Poznań: Contact, 2009.

Ruggiero, Iolanda. *Ricerche sulle Pauli Sententiae*. Milan: Giuffrè, 2017.

Russell, Amy. *The Politics of Public Space in Republican Rome*. Cambridge: Cambridge University Press, 2016.

"The Populus Romanus as the Source of Public Opinion." In *Communicating Public Opinion in the Roman Republic*, edited by Cristina Rosillo López, 41–56. Stuttgart: Steiner, 2019.

Russo Ruggeri, Carmela. *Studi sulle quinquaginta decisiones*. Milan: Giuffrè, 1999.

Rutledge, Steven. "Delatores and the Tradition of Violence in Roman Oratory." *AJP* 120 (1999): 555–73.

Saïd, Edward. *Orientalism*. New York: Vintage Books, 1978.

Saksena, Priyasha. "Jousting over Jurisdiction: Sovereignty and International Law in Late Nineteenth-Century South Asia." *LHR* 38 (2020): 409–57.

Salas, Luis Alejandro. "Medicine as Competitive Performance: Eristic and Erudition – Galen on Erasistratus and the Arteries." In Bubb and Peachin (eds.), *Medicine and the Law*, 124–76. Oxford: Oxford University Press, 2023.

Saller, Richard. *Personal Patronage Under the Early Empire*. Cambridge: Cambridge University Press, 1982.

Salway, Benet. "A Fragment of Severan History: The Unusual Career of ... atus, Praetorian Prefect of Elagabalus." *Chiron* 27 (1997): 127–53.

Santos, Francisco Andrés. "Brevissima storia della critica interpolazionistica nelle fonti giuridiche romane." *Revista de estudios histórico-jurídicos* 33 (2011): 65–120.

"El interpolacionismo: Auge y decadencia de un método de investigación sobre el Digesto." In Mantovani and Padoa Schioppa (eds.), *Interpretare il Digesto*, 557–95. Pavia: IUSS Press, 2014.

Sapsford, Tom. *Performing the "Kinaidos": Unmanly Men in Ancient Mediterranean Cultures*. Oxford: Oxford University Press, 2022.

Sarris, Peter. *Economy and Society in the Age of Justinian*. Cambridge; New York: Cambridge University Press, 2006.

Justinian: Emperor, Soldier, Saint. New York: Basic Books, 2023.

Sautel, Gérard. "Usurpations du pouvoir impérial dans le monde romain et rescissio actorum." In *Studi in onore di Pietro de Francisci*, edited by Antonino Giuffrè, 461–91. Milan: Giuffrè, 1956.

Scarlata Fazio, Mariano. "Brevi osservazioni sull'opera di Papirio Giusto Constitutionum l. XX." *SDHI* 5 (1939): 414–19.

Scarry, Elaine. *The Body in Pain: The Making and Unmaking of the World*. New York; Oxford: Oxford University Press, 1985.

Schäfer, Thomas. *Imperii insignia: Sella curulis und Fasces. Zur Repräsentation römischer Magistrate*. Mainz: Zabern, 1989.

Scheid, John, Paola Tassini, and Jörg Rüpke. *Recherches archéologiques à la Magliana: Commentarii Fratrum Arvalium qui supersunt: les copies épigraphiques des protocoles annuels de la confrérie arvale: 21 av.-304 ap. J.-C.* Rome: Ecole Française de Rome, 1998.

Schiavone, Aldo. *Ius: L'invenzione del diritto in Occidente*. 2nd ed. Turin: Giulio Einaudi, 2017.

"Singularity and Impersonality in the Thought of Roman Jurists." In Nasti and Schiavone (eds.), *Jurists and Legal Science*, 3–11. London: Routledge, 2021.

Schmidt, Manfred. "Claudius und Vespasian: Eine neue Interpretation des Wortes vae, puto, Deus fio (Suet. Vesp. 23,4)." *Chiron* 18 (1988): 83–89.

Schmidt-Hofner, Sebastian. "Ostentatious Legislation: Law and Dynastic Change, AD 364–365." In *Contested Monarchy: Integrating the Roman Empire in the Fourth Century A.D.*, edited by Johannes Wienand, 67–99. Oxford; New York: Oxford University Press, 2015.

Reagieren und Gestalten: Der Regierungsstil des spätrömischen Kaisers am Beispiel der Gesetzgebung Valentinians I. Munich: Beck, 2008.

Schmitt, Carl. *Political Theology: Four Chapters on the Concept of Sovereignty*. Translated by George Schwab. Cambridge [MA]: MIT Press, 1985.

Schöpe, Björn. *Der römische Kaiserhof in severischer Zeit (193–235 n. Chr)*. Stuttgart: Steiner, 2014.

Schopen, Gregory. "On Emptying Chamber Pots Without Looking and the Urban Location of Buddhist Nunneries in Early India Again." *Journal Asiatique* 296 (2008): 229–56.

Schulz, Fritz. *A History of Roman Legal Science*. Oxford: Clarendon Press, 1946.

"A New Approach to Bracton." *Seminar* 2 (1944): 41–50.

"Bracton and Raymond de Peñafort." *Law Quarterly Review* 61 (1945): 286–92.

"Bracton as a Computist." *Traditio* 3 (1945): 265–305.

"Bracton on Kingship." *The English Historical Review* 60 (1945): 136–76.

"Critical Studies on Bracton's Treatise." *Law Quarterly Review* 59 (1943): 172–80.

Principles of Roman Law. Translated by Marguerite Wolff. 2nd ed. Oxford: Clarendon Press, 1956.

"System der Rechte auf den Eingriffserwerb." *Archiv für die civilistische Praxis* 105 (1909): 1–488.

Schuol, Monika. "Die Rechtsschule in Berytus: römische Jurisprudenz im Vorderen Orient." In *Interkulturalität in der Alten Welt: Vorderasien, Hellas, Ägypten und die vielfältigen Ebenen des Kontakts*, edited by Robert Rollinger, et al., 161–84. Wiesbaden: Harrassowitz, 2010.

Scott, Andrew. "Cassius Dio and the Age of Iron and Rust." In *Brill's Companion to Cassius Dio*, edited by Jesper Madsen and Andrew Scott, 324–47. Leiden: Brill, 2023.

"Cassius Dio, Caracalla, and the Senate." *Klio* 97 (2015): 157–75.

Emperors and Usurpers: An Historical Commentary on Cassius Dio's Roman History Books 79(78)–80(80) (A.D. 217–229). New York: Oxford University Press, 2018.

"Historiographic Method and Self-Presentation in Cassius Dio's Contemporary History." In Madsen and Lange (eds.), *Cassius Dio the Historian*, 223–41. Boston: Brill, 2021.

"The Legitimization of Elagabalus and Cassius Dio's Account of the Reign of Macrinus." *JAH* 1 (2013): 242–53.

Scott, Rebecca, and Carlos Venegas Fornias. "María Coleta and the Capuchin Friar: Slavery, Salvation, and the Adjudication of Status." *William and Mary Quarterly* 76 (2019): 727–62.

Seeck, Otto, ed. *Notitia dignitatum: accedunt Notitia urbis Constantinopolitanae et laterculi prouinciarum*. Berlin: Weidmann, 1876.

Sewell, William. "Three Temporalities: Toward an Eventful Sociology." In *The Historic Turn in the Human Sciences*, edited by Terrence McDonald, 245–80. Ann Arbor: University of Michigan Press, 1996.

Shannon-Henderson, Kelly. "What Makes a Divus? The Prospective Rhetoric of Deification in Pliny's Panegyricus." In *Rhetoric and Religion in Ancient Greece and Rome*, edited by Sophia Papaioannou, Andreas Serafim, and Kyriakos Demetriou, 221–44. De Gruyter, 2021.

Shapiro, Scott. *Legality*. London: Harvard University Press, 2011.

Shaw, Brent. "Raising and Killing Children: Two Roman Myths." *Mnemosyne* 54 (2001): 31–77.

Sickle, Clifton van. "The Headings of Rescripts of the Severi in the Justinian Code." *CP* 23 (1928): 270–77.

Siegel, Reva. "Constitutional Culture, Social Movement Conflict and Constitutional Change: The Case of the de Facto ERA." *California Law Review* 94 (2006): 1323–1420.

Sijpesteijn, Pieter. "Macrinus' Damnatio memoriae und die Papyri." *ZPE* 13 (1974): 219–27.

Simon, Dietrich. *Konstantinisches Kaiserrecht: Studien anhand der Reskriptenpraxis und des Schenkungsrechts*. Frankfurt am Main: Klostermann, 1977.

Sirks, Boudewijn. "Did the Published Theodosian Code Include Obsolete Constitutions?" *TvR* 89 (2021): 70–92.

"Making a Request to the Emperor: Rescripts in the Roman Empire." In de Blois (ed.). *Administration, Prosopography and Appointment Policies*, 121–35. Amsterdam: Gieben, 2001.

"The Sources of the Code." In Harries and Wood (eds.), *The Theodosian Code*, 45–67. London: Duckworth, 1993.

The Theodosian Code: A Study. Friedrichsdorf: Éditions Tortuga, 2007.

Skinner, Marilyn. "Horace, Catullus, and Maecenas." *SyllClass* 24 (2013): 29–45.

Sommer, Michael. "'A Vast Scene of Confusion': Die Krise des 3. Jahrhunderts in der Forschung." In Babusiaux and Kolb (eds.), *Das Recht der "Soldatenkaiser,"* 15–30. Berlin: De Gruyter, 2013.

"Elagabal: Wege zur Konstruktion eines 'schlechten' Kaisers." *SCI* 23 (2004): 95–110.

Sontag, Susan. "Notes on Camp." In *Against Interpretation: And Other Essays*, by Susan Sontag, 275–92. New York: Octagon Books, 1978.

Soraci, Rosario. *L'opera legislativa e amministrativa dell'imperatore Severo Alessandro*. Catania: Muglia, 1974.

Southern, Richard. *The Making of the Middle Ages*. London; New York: Hutchinson's University Library, 1953.

Spagnuolo Vigorita, Tullio. *Casta domus: Un seminario sulla legislazione matrimoniale augustea*. 3rd ed. Naples: Jovene, 2010.

Speidel, Michael. "Maximinus and the Thracians: Herodian on the Coup of 235, and Ethnic Networks in the Roman Army of the Third Century C.E." In *Mobility in Research on the Black Sea Region*, edited by Victor Cojocaru and Alexander Rubel, 339–65. Cluj-Napoca: Mega, 2016.

Sperandio, Marco. *Codex Gregorianus: Origini e vicende*. Naples: Jovene, 2005.

Starr, Sonja. "Testing Racial Profiling: Empirical Assessment of Disparate Treatment by Police Policing the Police." *University of Chicago Legal Forum* (2016): 485–532.

Stein, Peter. *Roman Law in European History*. Cambridge; New York: Cambridge University Press, 1999.

"The Two Schools of Jurists in the Early Roman Principate." *The Cambridge Law Journal* 31 (1972): 8–31.

Steinwenter, Artur. "Νόμος ἔμψυχος: Zur Geschichte einer politischen Theorie." *Anzeiger der Philosophisch-Historischen Klasse* 83 (1946): 250–68.

Stewart, Roberta. *Plautus and Roman Slavery*. Malden [MA]: Wiley-Blackwell, 2012.

Stollberg-Rilinger, Barbara. *The Emperor's Old Clothes: Constitutional History and the Symbolic Language of the Holy Roman Empire*. Translated by Thomas Dunlap. New York: Berghahn Books, 2015.

Stolte, Bernard. "Codification in Byzantium: From Justinian I to Leo VI." In *Diverging Paths? The Shapes of Power and Institutions in Medieval Christendom and Islam*, edited by John Hudson and Ana Rodríguez, 59–74. Leiden: Brill, 2014.

Stone Peters, Julie. *Law as Performance: Theatricality, Spectatorship, and the Making of Law in Ancient, Medieval, and Early Modern Europe*. Oxford: Oxford University Press, 2022.

Straumann, Benjamin. *Crisis and Constitutionalism: Roman Political Thought from the Fall of the Republic to the Age of Revolution*. New York: Oxford University Press, 2016.

Roman Law in the State of Nature: The Classical Foundations of Hugo Grotius' Natural Law. Cambridge: Cambridge University Press, 2015.

Strauss, David. *The Living Constitution*. New York: Oxford University Press, 2010.

Strazdins, Estelle. *Fashioning the Future in Roman Greece: Memory, Monuments, Texts*. Oxford: Oxford University Press, 2023.

Sunstein, Cass. "Switching the Default Rule." *New York University Law Review* 77 (2002): 106–34.

Swan, Peter. *The Augustan Succession: An Historical Commentary on Cassius Dio's Roman History, Books 55–56 (9 B.C.–A.D. 14)*. New York: Oxford University Press, 2004.

Syme, Ronald. *Emperors and Biography: Studies in the Historia Augusta*. Oxford: Clarendon Press, 1971.

"Lawyers in Government: The Case of Ulpian." *PAPhS* 116 (1972): 406–9.

"Who Was Vedius Pollio?" *JRS* 51 (1961): 23–30.

Tait, Allison, and Luke Norris. "Narrative and the Origins of Law." *Law and Humanities* 5 (2011): 11–22.

Talbert, Richard. *The Senate of Imperial Rome*. Princeton: Princeton University Press, 1984.

Tani, Karen. *States of Dependency: Welfare, Rights, and American Governance, 1935–1972*. New York: Cambridge University Press, 2016.

Tarel, Philippe. *Titus*. Paris: Ellipses, 2016.

Tatum, W. Jeffrey. "Ultra Legem: Law and Literature in Horace, 'Satires' II.1." *Mnemosyne* 51 (1998): 688–99.

Temporini, Hildegard. *Die Kaiserinnen Roms: Von Livia bis Theodora*. Munich: Beck, 2002.

Thesaurus linguae latinae. Leipzig: Teubner, 1907.

Thomas, Rosalind. "Writing, Law, and Written Law." In *The Cambridge Companion to Ancient Greek Law*, edited by Michael Gagarin and

David Cohen, 41–60. Cambridge; New York: Cambridge University Press, 2005.

Thomas, Yan. "Vitae Necisque Potestas: The Father, The State, Death." In *Legal Artifices: Ten Essays on Roman Law in the Present Tense*, by Yan Thomas, edited by Thanos Zartaloudis and Cooper Francis, 144–209. Translated by Chantal Schütz and Anton Schütz. Edinburgh: Edinburgh University Press, 2021.

Thompson, Edward. *Whigs and Hunters: The Origin of the Black Act.* London: Allen Lane, 1975.

Thomson, Mark. *Studies in the Historia Augusta*. Brussels: Éditions Latomus, 2012.

Todisco, Elisabetta. "La res publica restituta e i Fasti Praenestini." In *Epigrafia e territorio, politica e società: Temi di antichità romane*, edited by Mario Pani, 341–58. Bari: Edipuglia, 2007.

Treggiari, Susan. *Roman Marriage: Iusti Coniuges from the Time of Cicero to the Time of Ulpian*. New York: Oxford University Press, 1991.

Tuori, Kaius. *Ancient Roman Lawyers and Modern Legal Ideals: Studies on the Impact of Contemporary Concerns in the Interpretation of Ancient Roman Legal History*. Frankfurt am Main: Klostermann, 2007.

"Augustus, Legislative Power, and the Power of Appearances." *Fundamina* (2014): 938–45.

"Dig. 34,2,33: The Return of the Cross-Dressing Senator." *Arctos* 43 (2009): 191–200.

Empire of Law: Nazi Germany, Exile Scholars and the Battle for the Future of Europe. Cambridge: Cambridge University Press, 2020.

"Greek Tyranny and Roman Emperors During the Severan Period: A Case Study of P. Col. 123 and SEG 17.759." *BICS* 55 (2012): 111–19.

"Hadrian's Perpetual Edict: Ancient Sources and Modern Ideals in the Making of a Historical Tradition." *JLH* 27 (2006): 219–37.

"Legal Pluralism and the Roman Empires." In *Beyond Dogmatics*, edited by John Cairns and Paul du Plessis, 39–52. Edinburgh: Edinburgh University Press, 2007.

The Emperor of Law: The Emergence of Roman Imperial Adjudication. Oxford: Oxford University Press, 2016.

"The Ius Respondendi and the Freedom of Roman Jurisprudence." *RIDA* 51 (2004): 295–338.

"The Myth of Quintus Mucius Scaevola: Founding Father of Legal Science." *Legal History Review* 72 (2004): 243–62.

Turcan, Robert. *Héliogabale et le sacre du soleil*. Paris: Michel, 1985.

Turpin, William. "The Law Codes and Late Roman Law." *RIDA* 32 (1985): 339–53.

Tushnet, Mark. "Critical Legal Studies: A Political History." *Yale Law Journal* 100 (1991): 1515–44.

"Following the Rules Laid Down: A Critique of Interpretivism and Neutral Principles." *Harvard Law Review* 96 (1983): 781–827.

The American Law of Slavery, 1810–1860: Considerations of Humanity and Interest. Princeton: Princeton University Press, 1981.

Tyler, Tom. *Why People Obey the Law.* New Haven: Yale University Press, 1990.

Tziovas, Dēmētrēs, ed. *Re-Imagining the Past: Antiquity and Modern Greek Culture.* Oxford: Oxford University Press, 2014.

Uden, James. *The Invisible Satirist: Juvenal and Second-Century Rome.* New York: Oxford University Press, 2015.

Unger, Roberto Mangabeira. "The Critical Legal Studies Movement." *Harvard Law Review* 96 (1983): 561–675.

Urso, Gianpaolo. "Cassius Dio's Sulla: Exemplum of Cruelty and Republican Dictator." In Lange and Madsen (eds.), *Greek Intellectual*, 13–32. Leiden: Brill, 2016.

Vacca, Letizia. "In tema di bonorum possessio contra tabulas." *BIDR* 80 (1977): 159–93.

Van Voorhis, Julie, and Mark Abbe. *Imperial Colors: The Roman Portrait Busts of Septimius Severus and Julia Domna, Sidney and Lois Eskenazi Museum of Art, Indiana University.* Bloomington: Giles, 2023.

Varner, Eric. *Mutilation and Transformation: Damnatio Memoriae and Roman Imperial Portraiture.* Boston: Brill, 2004.

"Portraits, Plots, and Politics: Damnatio Memoriae and the Images of Imperial Women." *MAAR* 46 (2001): 41–93.

Vernay, Eugène. "Note sur le changement de style dans les constitutions impériales de Dioclétien à Constantin." In *Études d'histoire juridique offertes a Paul Frédéric Girard*, 2: 263–74. Paris: Geuthner, 1913.

Veyne, Paul. *Le pain et le cirque: Sociologie historique d'un pluralisme politique.* Paris: Éditions du Seuil, 1976.

Vidas, Moulie, and Catherine Michael Chin, eds. *Late Ancient Knowing.* Berkeley: University of California Press, 2015.

Vigneron, Roger. "L'antiféministe Loi Voconia et les Schleichwege des Lebens." *Labeo* 29 (1983): 140–53.

Vittinghoff, Friedrich. *Der Staatsfeind in der römischen Kaiserzeit: Untersuchungen zur damnatio memoriae.* Berlin: Junker und Dünnhaupt, 1936.

Volterra, Edoardo. "L'ouvrage de Papirius Iustus Constitutionum Libri XX." In *Symbolae iuridicae et historicae Martino David dedicatae*, edited by Hans Ankum, Robert Feenstra, and Wilhelmus Leemans, 215–23. Leiden: Brill, 1968.

Wacke, Andreas. "Die potentiores in den Rechtsquellen: Einfluss und Abwehr gesellschaftlicher Übermacht in der Rechtspflege der Römer." *ANRW* 2.13 (1980): 562–607.

Wagemann, Arnold. *Deutsche Rechtsvergangenheit als Wegweiser in eine deutsche Zukunft*. Jena: Fischer, 1922.

Waldron, Jeremy. "Stare Decisis and the Rule of Law: A Layered Approach." *Michigan Law Review* 111 (2012): 1–32.

Wallace-Hadrill, Andrew. "Civilis Princeps: Between Citizen and King." *JRS* 72 (1982): 32–48.

"Mutatio Morum: The Idea of a Cultural Revolution." In Habinek and Schiesaro (eds.), *The Roman Cultural Revolution*, 3–22. Cambridge: Cambridge Philological Society, 1997.

Wankerl, Veronika. *Appello ad principem: Urteilsstil und Urteilstechnik in kaiserlichen Berufungsentscheidungen (Augustus bis Caracalla)*. Munich: Beck, 2009.

Waters, Kenneth. "The Second Dynasty of Rome." *Phoenix* 17 (1963): 198–218.

Watson, Alan. *Legal Transplants: An Approach to Comparative Law*. Charlottesville: University Press of Virginia, 1974.

"Review of T. Honoré, 'Emperors and Lawyers.'" *TvR* 50 (1982): 409–14.

The Law of Succession in the Later Roman Republic. Oxford: Clarendon Press, 1971.

The Spirit of Roman Law. Athens; London: University of Georgia Press, 1995.

Watson, Alan, Paul Krueger, and Theodor Mommsen, eds. *The Digest of Justinian*. 4 vols. Philadelphia: University of Pennsylvania Press, 1985.

Weaver, Paul. *Familia Caesaris: A Social Study of the Emperor's Freedmen and Slaves*. Cambridge: Cambridge University Press, 1972.

Weber, Max. *Wirtschaft und Gesellschaft*. Tübingen: J. C. B. Mohr (P. Siebeck), 1922.

Weeda, Leendert. *Horace's Sermones Book 1: Credentials for Maecenas*. Berlin; Warsaw: De Gruyter, 2019.

Welch, Kimberly. *Black Litigants in the Antebellum American South*. Chapel Hill: The University of North Carolina Press, 2018.

Wen, Shanshan. *Communal Dining in the Roman West: Private Munificence towards Cities and Associations in the First Three Centuries AD*. Leiden; Boston: Brill, 2022.

Wenger, Leopold. *Die Quellen des römischen Rechts*. Vienna: Holzhausen, 1953.

"Ein Prozess von Caracalla in Syrien: Zu einer neu bekannt gewordenen Inschrift." *AIPhO* 11 (1951): 469–504.

Westermann, William, and A. Arthur Schiller. *Apokrimata: Decisions of Septimius Severus on Legal Matters*. New York: Columbia University Press, 1954.

Wheatley, Natasha. *The Life and Death of States: Central Europe and the Transformation of Modern Sovereignty*. Princeton: Princeton University Press, 2023.

Whewell, Emily. *Law Across Imperial Borders: British Consuls and Colonial Connections on China's Western Frontiers, 1880–1943*. Manchester: Manchester University Press, 2020.

Whitman, James. *The Legacy of Roman Law in the German Romantic Era: Historical Vision and Legal Change*. Princeton: Princeton University Press, 1990.

Whitmarsh, Tim. *Greek Literature and the Roman Empire. The Politics of Imitation*. Oxford; New York: Oxford University Press, 2001.

Wibier, Matthijs. "Legal Education and Legal Culture in Gaul During the Principate." In *Law in the Roman Provinces*, edited by Kimberley Czajkowski, Benedikt Eckhardt, and Meret Strothmann, 462–85. Oxford: Oxford University Press, 2020.

"Legal Education, Realpolitik, and the Propagation of the Emperor's Justice." In Hekster and Verboven (eds.), *Impact of Justice*, 86–102. Leiden; Boston: Brill, 2019.

"Marcus Antistius Labeo and the Idea of Legal Literature." In Ziogas and Bexley (eds.), *Roman Law and Latin Literature*, 125–44. London: Bloomsbury, 2022.

"Transmitting Legal Knowledge: From Question-and-Answer Format to Handbook in Gaius' Institutes." In *Between Orality and Literacy: Communication and Adaptation in Antiquity*, edited by Ruth Scodel, 356–73. Leiden: Brill, 2014.

Wieacker, Franz. *Römische Rechtsgeschichte: Quellenkunde, Rechtsbildung, Jurisprudenz und Rechtsliteratur*. 2 vols. Munich: Beck, 1988.

"Textkritik und Sachforschung: Positionen in der gegenwärtigen Romanistik." *ZR* 91 (1974): 1–40.

Textstufen klassischer Juristen. Göttingen: Vandenhoeck und Ruprecht, 1960.

"Zur gegenwärtigen Lage der romanistischen Textkritik." In Paradisi (ed.), *La critica del testo*, 1099–1122. Florence: Olschki, 1971.

Wilcken, Ulrich. "Zu den Kaiserreskripten." *Hermes* 55 (1920): 1–42.

"Zur Propositio libellorum." *APF* 9 (1930): 15–23.

Wilkes, John. *Diocletian's Palace, Split: Residence of a Retired Roman Emperor*. Sheffield: Ian Sanders Memorial Committee, 1993.

Willems, Constantin. *Justinian als Ökonom: Entscheidungsgründe und Entscheidungsmuster in den Quinquaginta decisiones*. Cologne: Böhlau Verlag, 2017.

Williams, Craig. *Roman Homosexuality*. Oxford: Oxford University Press, 1999.

Williams, Wynne. "Caracalla and the Authorship of Imperial Edicts and Epistles." *Latomus* 38 (1979): 67–89.

"Caracalla and the Rhetoricians: A Note on the Cognitio de Goharienis." *Latomus* 33 (1974): 663–67.

"The Libellus Procedure and the Severan Papyri." *JRS* 64 (1974): 86–103.

Winterer, Caroline. *The Culture of Classicism: Ancient Greece and Rome in American Intellectual Life, 1780–1910*. Baltimore: Johns Hopkins University Press, 2002.

Witschel, Christian. *Krise, Rezession, Stagnation?: Der Westen des römischen Reiches im 3. Jahrhundert n. Chr.* Frankfurt am Main: Clauss, 1999.

Wood, Susan. "A Too-Successful Damnatio Memoriae: Problems in Third-Century Roman Portraiture." *AJA* 87 (1983): 489–96.

Woodman, Anthony. *Velleius Paterculus: The Caesarian and Augustan Narrative (2.41–93)*. Cambridge; New York: Cambridge University Press, 1983.

Woodman, Anthony, and Ronald Martin. *The Annals of Tacitus: Book 3*. New York: Cambridge University Press, 1996.

Woolf, Greg. *Becoming Roman: The Origins of Provincial Civilization in Gaul*. Cambridge; New York: Cambridge University Press, 1998.

Woudhuysen, George. "Uncovering Constans' Image." In Burgersdijk and Ross (eds.), *Imagining Emperors*, 158–82. Leiden; Boston: Brill, 2018.

Woytek, Bernhard. "Elagabalus and the 'Aedes Dei Invicti Solis Elagabali' in Rome: The Numismatic Evidence." *NC* 179 (2019): 205–24.

Yiftach-Firanko, Uri. "Law in Graeco-Roman Egypt: Hellenization, Fusion, Romanization." In *The Oxford Handbook of Papyrology*, edited by Roger Bagnall, 541–60. Oxford; New York: Oxford University Press, 2009.

Youtie, Herbert, John Winter, Leiv Amundsen, and Orsamus Pearl. *Papyri and Ostraca from Karanis*. Vol. VI. Ann Arbor: The University of Michigan Press, 1944.

Zanker, Paul. *Augustus und die Macht der Bilder*. Munich: Beck, 1987.

Zaremby, Justin. *Legal Realism and American Law*. Bloomsbury, 2013.

Zatloukal, Valerie. "Max Kaser's 'Roman Law as a Community Order' and the 'Crisis of Roman Law' under the Nazi Regime." *Journal on European History of Law* 11 (2020): 16–29.

Zehnacker, Hubert. "Quelques remarques sur Ie revers du nouvel aureus d'Octavien (28 av. J.-C)." *BSFN* 58 (2003): 1–3.

Zetzel, James. *Critics, Compilers and Commentators: An Introduction to Roman Philology, 200 BCE–800 CE*. New York: Oxford University Press, 2018.

Zimmermann, Reinhard. *Roman Law, Contemporary Law, European Law: The Civilian Tradition Today*. Oxford: Oxford University Press, 2001.

Ziogas, Ioannis. *Law and Love in Ovid: Courting Justice in the Age of Augustus*. Oxford: Oxford University Press, 2021.

"Orpheus and the Law: The Story of Myrrha in Ovid's Metamorphoses." *Law in Context* 34 (2016): 24–41.

Ziogas, Ioannis, and Erica Bexley, eds. *Roman Law and Latin Literature*. London: Bloomsbury, 2022.

Zucca, Raimondo. "La Tavola di Esterzili e la controversia finium tra Vanacini e Mariani in Corsica." In *La Tavola di Esterzili: Il conflitto tra pastori e contadini nella Barbaria sarda*, edited by Attilio Mastino, 185–205. Sassari: Gallizzi, 1993.

Zuiderhoek, Arjan. *The Politics of Munificence in the Roman Empire: Citizens, Elites and Benefactors in Asia Minor*. Cambridge; New York: Cambridge University Press, 2009.

Index of Terms

Index of Sources

Studies in Legal History *(continued from page ii)*

Kristin A. Olbertson, *The Dreadful Word: Speech Crime and Polite Gentlemen in Massachusetts, 1690–1776*
Edgardo Pérez Morales, *Unraveling Abolition: Legal Culture and Slave Emancipation in Colombia*
Lyndsay Campbell, *Truth and Privilege: Libel Law in Massachusetts and Nova Scotia, 1820–1840*
Sara M. Butler, *Pain, Penance, and Protest: Peine Forte et Dure in Medieval England*
Michael Lobban, *Imperial Incarceration: Detention without Trial in the Making of British Colonial Africa*
Stefan Jurasinski and Lisi Oliver, *The Laws of Alfred: The* Domboc *and the Making of Anglo-Saxon Law*
Sascha Auerbach, *Armed with Sword and Scales: Law, Culture, and Local Courtrooms in London, 1860–1913*
Alejandro de La Fuente and Ariela J. Gross, *Becoming Free, Becoming Black: Race, Freedom, and the Law in Cuba, Virginia, and Louisiana*
Elizabeth Papp Kamali, *Felony and the Guilty Mind in Medieval England*
Jessica K. Lowe, *Murder in the Shenandoah: Making Law Sovereign in Revolutionary Virginia*
Michael A. Schoeppner, *Moral Contagion: Black Atlantic Sailors, Citizenship, and Diplomacy in Antebellum America*
Sam Erman, *Almost Citizens: Puerto Rico, the U.S. Constitution, and Empire*
Martha S. Jones, *Birthright Citizens: A History of Race and Rights in Antebellum America*
Julia Moses, *The First Modern Risk: Workplace Accidents and the Origins of European Social States*
Cynthia Nicoletti, *Secession on Trial: The Treason Prosecution of Jefferson Davis*
Edward James Kolla, *Sovereignty, International Law, and the French Revolution*
Assaf Likhovski, *Tax Law and Social Norms in Mandatory Palestine and Israel*
Robert W. Gordon, *Taming the Past: Essays on Law and History and History in Law*
Paul Garfinkel, *Criminal Law in Liberal and Fascist Italy*
Michelle A. McKinley, *Fractional Freedoms: Slavery, Intimacy, and Legal Mobilization in Colonial Lima, 1600–1700*

Karen M. Tani, *States of Dependency: Welfare, Rights, and American Governance, 1935–1972*

Stefan Jurasinski, *The Old English Penitentials and Anglo- Saxon Law*

Felice Batlan, *Women and Justice for the Poor: A History of Legal Aid, 1863–1945*

Sophia Z. Lee, *The Workplace Constitution from the New Deal to the New Right*

Mitra Sharafi, *Law and Identity in Colonial South Asia: Parsi Legal Culture, 1772–1947*

Michael A. Livingston, *The Fascists and the Jews of Italy: Mussolini's Race Laws, 1938–1943*

Printed in the United Kingdom by TJ Clays Ltd.